The Multilingual Citizen

ENCOUNTERS

Series Editors: Jan Blommaert, *Tilburg University, The Netherlands*, Ben Rampton, *Kings College London, UK*, Anna De Fina, *Georgetown University, USA*, Sirpa Leppänen, *University of Jyväskylä, Finland* and James Collins, *University at Albany/SUNY, USA*

The Encounters series sets out to explore diversity in language from a theoretical and an applied perspective. So the focus is both on the linguistic encounters, inequalities and struggles that characterise post-modern societies and on the development, within sociocultural linguistics, of theoretical instruments to explain them. The series welcomes work dealing with such topics as heterogeneity, mixing, creolization, bricolage, crossover phenomena, polylingual and polycultural practices. Another high-priority area of study is the investigation of processes through which linguistic resources are negotiated, appropriated and controlled, and the mechanisms leading to the creation and maintenance of sociocultural differences. The series welcomes ethnographically oriented work in which contexts of communication are investigated rather than assumed, as well as research that shows a clear commitment to close analysis of local meaning making processes and the semiotic organisation of texts.

All books in this series are externally peer-reviewed.

Full details of all the books in this series and of all our other publications can be found on http://www.multilingual-matters.com, or by writing to Multilingual Matters, St Nicholas House, 31–34 High Street, Bristol BS1 2AW, UK.

ENCOUNTERS: 11

The Multilingual Citizen

Towards a Politics of Language for Agency and Change

Edited by
Lisa Lim, Christopher Stroud and Lionel Wee

MULTILINGUAL MATTERS
Bristol • Blue Ridge Summit

DOI https://doi.org/10.21832/LIM9658

Library of Congress Cataloging in Publication Data

Names: Lim, Lisa editor. | Stroud, Christopher editor. | Wee, Lionel, 1963- editor.

Title: The Multilingual Citizen: Towards a Politics of Language for Agency and Change/Edited by Lisa Lim, Christopher Stroud and Lionel Wee.

Description: Bristol, UK; Blue Ridge Summit, PA : Multilingual Matters, 2018. | Series: Encounters: 11 | Includes bibliographical references and index.

Identifiers: LCCN 2017044120| ISBN 9781783099641 (pbk : alk. paper) | ISBN 9781783099658 (hbk : alk. paper) | ISBN 9781783099689 (kindle)

Subjects: LCSH: Multilingualism—Social aspects. | Cultural pluralism. | Language policy.

Classification: LCC P115.45 .M53 2018 | DDC 306.44/6—dc23 LC record available at https://lccn.loc.gov/2017044120

British Library Cataloguing in Publication Data

A catalogue entry for this book is available from the British Library.

ISBN-13: 978-1-78309-965-8 (hbk)
ISBN-13: 978-1-78309-964-1 (pbk)

Multilingual Matters

UK: St Nicholas House, 31–34 High Street, Bristol BS1 2AW, UK.
USA: NBN, Blue Ridge Summit, PA, USA.

Website: www.multilingual-matters.com
Twitter: Multi_Ling_Mat
Facebook: https://www.facebook.com/multilingualmatters
Blog: www.channelviewpublications.wordpress.com

The policy of Multilingual Matters/Channel View Publications is to use papers that are natural, renewable and recyclable products, made from wood grown in sustainable forests. In the manufacturing process of our books, and to further support our policy, preference is given to printers that have FSC and PEFC Chain of Custody certification. The FSC and/or PEFC logos will appear on those books where full certification has been granted to the printer concerned.

Typeset by Nova Techset Private Limited, Bengaluru and Chennai, India.
Printed and bound in the UK by the CPI Books Group Ltd.
Printed and bound in the US by Edwards Brothers Malloy, Inc.

Contents

Contributors

Umberto Ansaldo's interests range from language contact, multilingualism and language evolution, to linguistic typology and the study of diversity. He is currently working on a project on linguistic nationalism and language revival. He is the author of *Contact Languages: Ecology and Evolution in Asia* (Cambridge University Press, 2009), and co-author of *Languages in Contact* (with Lisa Lim, Cambridge University Press, 2016). His recent editorial work includes 'Is the Language Faculty Non-Linguistic?' with N.J. Enfield, and 'Languages as Adaptive Systems' with E.O. Aboh, both published in *Frontiers in Psychology*. He is also the founding editor of the journal *Language Ecology* (John Benjamins). He is Professor of Linguistics at the University of Hong Kong.

Paul Bruthiaux has a PhD in Linguistics from the University of Southern California. His work has appeared with Oxford University Press and Multilingual Matters as well as in journals such as *TESOL Quarterly, Applied Linguistics, Written Communication*, and *English Today*. He now works as a freelance language consultant and editor, based in Thailand. He is the co-author (with William L. Gibson) of an annotated translation of French explorer Alfred Raquez's 1899 travelogue entitled *In the Land of Pagodas*, published in 2017 by Nordic Institute of Asian Studies, with *Laotian Pages*, a sequel originally published in 1900, to follow in 2018.

Estêvão Cabral (PhD, Political Science, Lancaster University, UK, 2002) has done research on the political history of East-Timor, on literacy during the years of Resistance to the Indonesian occupation of East-Timor, and on language policy in post-independence East-Timor. In 2004, he conducted post-doctoral fieldwork in East-Timor, with British Academy funding. From 2009 to 2012, he did further research in East-Timor on adult literacy, with a research project at Tilburg University, The Netherlands. He is currently a Research Associate of the Babylon Centre, Tilburg University.

Blasius Agha-ah Chiatoh is Associate Professor of Linguistics at the University of Buea in Cameroon. For many years, he was on the staff of the NACALCO Centre for Applied Linguistics where he served as a field researcher and projects coordinator. Specializing in literacy, Blasius has over the years developed a special bias for language planning, bi-multilingual education and sociolinguistics. He has also been a consultant with the UNESCO Institute for Lifelong Learning. He is currently the chair of the Department of Linguistics. He has published extensively, both nationally and internationally.

Feliciano Chimbutane received his PhD from the University of Birmingham, UK. He is Associate Professor of Educational Sociolinguistics at Universidade Eduardo Mondlane, Mozambique. His research interests include languages and education (planning, policies and practices), with focus on classroom practice and the relationship between classroom discourse, day-to day talk and the wider socio-political order. His publications include *Rethinking Bilingual Education in Postcolonial Contexts* (Multilingual Matters, 2011), *Bilingual Education and Language Policy in the Global South* (co-edited with Jo Shoba, Routledge, 2013), and *Multilinguismo e Multiculturalismo em Moçambique: Em Direcção a uma Coerência entre Discurso e Prática* (co-edited with Perpétua Gonçalves, Alcance Editores).

Ana Deumert is Professor at the University of Cape Town. Her research programme is located within the broad field of African sociolinguistics and has a strong transdisciplinary focus. She has worked on the history of Afrikaans (*The Dynamics of Cape Dutch*, 2004), co-authored *Introducing Sociolinguistics* (with Rajend Mesthrie, Joan Swann and William Leap, Edinburgh University Press, 2009), and the *Dictionary of Sociolinguistics* (with Joan Swann, Rajend Mesthrie and Theresa Lillis, 2004). Her latest book looks at mobile communication from a global perspective (*Sociolinguistics and Mobile Communication*, Edinburgh University Press, 2014). Her current work explores the use of language in political movements.

Kathleen Heugh is a socio-applied linguist with a research focus on multilingual education. She has advised 35 national governments on language policy in Africa, Asia, Eastern Europe, and South America. She led the first national sociolinguistic survey of South Africa, designed the first system-wide multilingual assessment of secondary school students, and has undertaken system-wide and multi-country evaluation research for governments and international development agencies, including UNESCO. She uses multilingual pedagogies in teaching students of English and linguistics at the University of South Australia. Together with Christopher Stroud and Piet van Avermaet, she is Editor of the Bloomsbury Series, Multilingualisms and Diversities in Education.

Rickard Jonsson is a Professor and Director of the section for Child and Youth Studies, Stockholm University, Sweden. His linguistic ethnographic research concerns masculinity, sexuality, ethnicity and language use. Inspired by Judith Butler's theoretical work combined with narrative analysis of talk in interaction, Jonsson investigates the construction of young masculinities in everyday school life. Jonsson has been published in journals such as *Journal of Linguistic Anthropology, Gender and Language* and *Journal of Anthropology and Education*. He is the author of the two monographs *Blatte betyder kompis* and *Värst i klassen* (Ordfront).

Gregory Hankoni Kamwendo is a Professor and Dean of the Faculty of Arts at the University of Zululand in South Africa. His research interests lie in the field of language policy and language planning, and language education. Some of his papers have been published in journals such as *Current Issues in Language Planning; Language Policy; Language Problems and Language Planning; International Journal of the Sociology of Language; Journal of Multilingual and Multicultural Development; Nordic Journal of African Studies; International Review of Education*; and *English Today.*

Caroline Kerfoot is Associate Professor and Director of the Centre for Research on Bilingualism, Stockholm University. Her research focuses on multilingualism, identities, and epistemic justice in schools characterized by high levels of diversity and flux. Her latest book *Entangled Discourses: South-North Orders of Visibility* (Routledge, 2017, with Kenneth Hyltenstam) explores the shifting structures of power and asymmetrical relations between North and South that render some types of knowledges, practices, repertoires, and bodies more legitimate and therefore more visible. She has published in journals such as *Applied Linguistics, Language and Education, Linguistics and Education, International Multilingual Research Journal, TESOL Quarterly.*

Lisa Lim is Associate Professor and Head of the School of English at The University of Hong Kong. Her research centres around multilingualism, language contact, language endangerment, and urban linguistic diversity, with particular interest in the language practices in Singapore, Sri Lanka, and Hong Kong, and the Peranakan community. She is co-author (with Umberto Ansaldo) of *Languages in Contact* (Cambridge University Press, 2016), and founding co-editor of the journal *Language Ecology* (John Benjamins). She serves on the editorial boards of *Language, Culture and Curriculum*, and the Mouton book series 'Dialects of English'. She developed and directs the online resource LinguisticMinorities.hk, and writes a fortnightly column 'Language Matters' for Hong Kong's *South China Morning Post*'s Sunday *Post Magazine* (see http://www.scmp.com/author/lisa-lim).

Marilyn Martin-Jones was the founding Director of the MOSAIC Centre for Research on Multilingualism, University of Birmingham (2007–2010). She is now an Emeritus Professor based at the Centre. Over the last four decades, she has been engaged in critical, ethnographic research into language and literacy practices in different multilingual classrooms and community contexts in the UK. She also has a keen interest in research methodology. Her most recent volume (with Deirdre Martin) is *Researching Multilingualism: Critical and Ethnographic Perspectives* (Routledge, 2017). She is also editor (with Joan Pujolar) of the Routledge book series Critical Studies in Multilingualism.

Stephen May is Professor of Education in Te Puna Wānanga (School of Māori and Indigenous Education) at the University of Auckland. He is an international authority on language rights, language policy, bilingualism and bilingual education and critical multicultural approaches to education. He has published over 100 articles and book chapters, along with numerous books, including, most recently, *The Multilingual Turn* (2014) and *Language and Minority Rights* (2nd edn, 2012). He is Editor-in- Chief of the 10-volume *Encyclopedia of Language and Education* (3rd edn, 2017), His homepage is http://www.education.auckland.ac.nz/uoa/stephen-may

Tommaso M. Milani is Professor of Multilingualism at the University of Gothenburg, and Visiting Professor of Linguistics at the University of the Witwatersrand, Johannesburg. His research interests include language ideological debates, multilingualism, critical discourse analysis, and semiotic landscapes. He has recently edited the book *Language and Masculinities: Performances, Intersections, Dislocations* (Routledge, 2015), and is working on a monograph on the spatial semiotics of affect in South Africa (contracted with John Benjamins). He is the editor of the journals *African Studies* and *Gender and Language*.

Suwilai Premsrirat, PhD (Monash University), is the Founding Director of the Resource Center for Documentation, Revitalization and Maintenance of Endangered Languages and Cultures, Mahidol University, Thailand. She has researched ethnic minority languages since 1975. Her major publications include a five-volume *Dictionary and Thesaurus of the Khmu Language in Thailand, Laos, Vietnam and China* and *Ethnolinguistic Maps of Thailand*. Under her direction, Mahidol University staff have facilitated language revitalization and education programs in 25 minority languages. Since 2006 she has directed the Patani Malay-Thai Bi/Multilingual Education Project in Thailand's violence-plagued Deep South, which received the UNESCO King Sejong Literacy Prize 2016.

Christopher Stroud is Senior Professor in Linguistics and Director of the Centre for Multilingualism and Diversities Research at the University of the Western Cape, and Professor of Transnational Multilingualism at Stockholm University. He has researched and taught in Sweden, Papua New Guinea, Mozambique, Singapore and South Africa, and has published in English, Swedish and Portuguese in journals such as *Language Policy, Journal of Linguistic Anthropology, Journal of Sociolinguistics, Sociolinguistic Studies, Semiotics, International Journal of Bilingualism and Bilingual Education, Journal of Multilingual and Multicultural Development* and *Multilingual Margins*. He is a Fellow of the Academy of Science in South Africa (ASSAf), and co-edits a series for Bloomsbury together with Kathleen Heugh and Piet van Avermaet entitled 'Multilingualisms and Diversities in Education'.

Lionel Wee is Provost's Chair Professor in the Department of English Language and Literature, Faculty of Arts and Social Sciences, at the National University of Singapore. He sits on the editorial boards of the *Journal of Sociolinguistics, Applied Linguistics, English World-Wide, Sociolinguistic Studies* and *Multilingual Margins*. His books include *Language Without Rights* (Oxford University Press, New York, 2011), *The Language of Organizational Styling* (Cambridge University Press, 2015), and *The Singlish Controversy: Language, Culture and Identity in a Globalizing World* (Cambridge University Press, forthcoming).

Preface and Acknowledgements

This collection of papers has been long in the making. Conceived in 2007 – following the workshop 'The Multilingual Citizen: Towards a Politics of Language for Agency and Change', hosted in Cape Town – it is finally seeing the light of day 10 years later. In addition to the delays that are inevitable when working with a numerous and diverse group of contributors around the globe, each with their own commitments – many regularly spending months incommunicado in the field – numerous significant events occurred in the years of the development of the volume, which contributed to its protracted evolution. To name just a few, roughly chronological: one of us had part of our house collapse, resulting in a computer crush and the consequent challenge of safe retrieval of the files of the volume from the drive; one of us relocated, changing continents and jobs; (the same) one of us became pregnant and had a baby; all three of us have held major administrative responsibilities at our respective institutions at some point, with one of us currently in full swing of her School headship; and most recently, one of us has been caught up in the violent, traumatic campus protests over university fees in South Africa. Still, we persevered. Working with this volume, we three editors in particular have regularly met at different venues in the world – Singapore, Hong Kong, South Africa, Mozambique, Sweden and the Netherlands – not only to deliberate on the progress of the volume, but also to enjoy what is now almost two decades of friendship and collegiality. The 10 years have seen us grow strong affective and academic ties built on the promise and aspiration, hope and belief that the book would one day see the light of day. Fortune favours the brave indeed: all contributors, authors and editors alike, are still alive and kicking, and able to reap the delights (and sweet nostalgia) of seeing the volume printed by Multilingual Matters. That we are published now is, more than anything, a testament to our contributors' patience and good faith – not just in us, but, more significantly, in the value of what the volume holds.

We thank all our contributors for keeping the faith – and good humour – and for their invaluable work on rights and citizenship with their respective communities. We also thank the numerous colleagues who provided astute reviews of the various chapters: Bassey Antia, Zannie Bock, Paul Bruthiaux, Suresh Canagarajah, Charlyn Dyers, Kenneth Hyltenstam, Paulo Israel, Karsten Legere, Beatriz Lopez, Tommaso Milani, Donna Patrick, Peter Pluddemann, Mastin Prinsloo, Tan Ying Ying, Ruanni Tupas, Quentin Williams. We are so pleased that Jan Blommaert, who was also at the 2007 workshop, together with the other series editors found our proposal attractive and were glad to include the volume in their Encounters series. We thank them too for their insightful comments on the manuscript in its entirety. At Multilingual Matters we are grateful to Tommi Grover, Kim Eggleton and Anna Roderick for their continued enthusiasm and support, and infinite patience and understanding.

Although much has changed during the 10 years, much remains the same. Because of the time lag between the conception of the papers and their surfacing in this volume, each author was recently asked to reflect on what might have changed since submitting the original manuscript, and to prepare a short retrospective to their chapters sketching this. Not all authors felt the need to append additional notes, but for those who did, the content makes for depressing reading. It is striking how little has improved in the conditions for speakers of smaller languages on the peripheries, who remain as marginalized today as they were 10 years ago, perhaps even more so in an increasingly integrated transnational world. Our hope is that this volume will contribute some substance of interest to future work addressing the constraints and potentials for living multilingually.

Lisa Lim, Christopher Stroud and Lionel Wee
Hong Kong, South Africa and Singapore
June 2017

Introduction

Christopher Stroud

University of the Western Cape and Stockholm University

Preamble

Exactly 10 years prior to the publication of this book, in 2007, a group of us met at a workshop on linguistic citizenship convened at the Two Oceans Aquarium in Cape Town. This was one of a series of three workshops that were held in South Africa and Sweden, and that brought together common threads and activities of two research and development projects that were inaugurated at the initiative of Kathleen Heugh and myself, and in which we participated as the principal researchers. Both projects were funded by the then Swedish Agency for Research Cooperation with Developing Countries (SAREC), the Swedish International Development Cooperation Authority (SIDA) and the National Research Foundation (NRF) South Africa. The collaborative projects under which the workshops fell were:

- *Multilingualism in an Integrated View of Development: Democracy, Human Rights and Citizenship* (a joint UWC–SAREC project in which the University of the Western Cape (UWC) and Stockholm University collaborated).
- *Representations and Practices of Multilingualism in a Transformative South Africa: Language, Identity and Change in a South African Educational Institution* (a joint SIDA–NRF project, in which UWC, the Human Sciences Research Council (HSRC) and Stockholm University collaborated).

The first meeting had taken place two years earlier in February 2005, and had been attended by an eminent list of wise elders in the field of language policy, planning and education from across Africa, Australia, Europe and South-East Asia. The title of that event was 'Workshop on Multilingualism in Development: Education in an Integrated Society'.

The intention with the workshop was to explore the role of multilingual-ism across a range of fields, such as democracy, health and economy, and to discuss how language education (both formal and informal) could contribute to a more integrative treatment of these issues. One of the points of departure for this event was a document written by Kenneth Hyltenstam and myself, originally prepared as a working document for SIDA, entitled 'At the nexus of vulnerability: Multilingualism in development' (now published for the first time as Hyltenstam & Stroud, 2016). Plenary papers addressed the various themes covered in the pre-circulated document; these were presented by: Ayo Bamgbose (Department of Linguistics and African Languages, University of Ibadan, Nigeria) who spoke on 'Multilingualism and democracy'; Paulin Djité (then at the School of Languages and Linguistics, University of Western Sydney, Australia) who presented a paper on 'Multilingualism and economy'; Claire Penn (Department of Speech Pathology and Audiology, University of the Witwatersrand, South Africa), who spoke on 'Multilingualism and health'; and Kathleen Heugh (then at the Human Sciences Research Council, South Africa, today at the University of South Australia in Adelaide), who presented a paper on 'Multilingualism and education'. A number of other participants offered presentations that addressed country-specific issues: Ethiopia (Alem Eshetu, Institute for Language Studies, Addis Ababa University), Mozambique (Feliciano Chimbutane, Faculdade de Letras, Eduardo Mondlane University), Tanzania (Casimir Rubagumya, Department of Foreign Languages and Linguistics, University of Dar es Salaam), South Africa (Peter Plüddemann, PRAESA, University of Cape Town, and Caroline Kerfoot, then Faculty of Education, University of the Western Cape) and Zambia (Kyangubabi Chiika Muyebaa, Ministry of Education). Paul Bruthiaux (then Department of English, Hong Kong Institute of Education, Hong Kong) played a vital and energetic role as discussant to the papers.

The second workshop in the series was held at Stockholm University in 2006 with the title 'Transnational Politics of Language and Development'. The goal for this workshop was an exploration of the idea of multilingualism as a set of politically embedded social practices and ideologies that serves to organize and regulate social life in systematic ways, and that like other forms of social categorization (such as gender or race) are involved in complex, structurations of power. Speakers included Lionel Wee (National University of Singapore), Paul Bruthiaux (then of the National Institute of Education, Singapore), Kathleen Heugh (then of the Human Sciences Research Council, Cape Town), Feliciano Chimbutane, (University of Eduardo Mondlane, Maputo), Matthews

Makgamatha, Human Sciences Research Council, Pretoria) and Caroline Kerfoot (then University of the Western Cape).

Towards Linguistic Citizenship

The third and final workshop in the series makes up the contents of this volume. The papers for 'The Multilingual Citizen: Towards a Politics of Language for Agency and Change'[1] were initially presented at the Two Oceans Aquarium in Cape Town in 2007. The invitation to the participants referred to recent developments in African societies, where civil society and non-state actors more generally (churches, non-government organizations (NGOs), associative networks of economy) were increasingly contributing to processes of democratization and development within and across national borders. New discourses of health, sexuality, economy education and workers' rights – often promoted in part by organizations with a transnational reach – are reconfiguring the relationship between state and civil society, and notions such as re-traditionalization, decentralization and participative democracy are bringing in more complex and layered concepts of citizenship (Benhahib, 2002). Considering the important strategic role of language for equitable and participative access to valuable symbolic and material markets, the overarching question posed for the event was what implications such societal transformations carry for the role of local linguistic resources specifically (in education, politics, health and the economy), and for a politics of language more generally. The invitation to participants noted how one important approach to managing local linguistic resources had been that of linguistic human rights, a notion that was increasingly being seen to be both conceptually and practically problematic (compare Blommaert, 2005; Stroud, 2001; Stroud & Heugh, 2004; Wee, 2005, 2006), although it continued to rally support in many circles (e.g. Grin, 2005; May, 2005).

To a greater degree than the two previous occasions, this workshop came to focus more attention on discussing a blueprint for what might comprise an empowering politics of language for agency and change. We were particularly interested in listening closely to the experiences of our participants from a variety of contexts with respect to the practicalities – and ideologies – of working with vulnerable and disempowered speakers in multilingual contexts, often minority speakers. We had begun developing a notion of *Linguistic Citizenship* that we felt to be more productive in offering a strategic framework for conceptualizing linguistically mediated change than that of linguistic human rights (LHR). Authors such as Blommaert (2005), Stroud (2001), Stroud and Heugh

(2004) and Wee (2005), among others, had suggested that the notion of rights is applicable to language only with difficulty; that rights discourses *de facto* create many of the problems they were originally set to resolve; that rights discourses assume a particular type of political agent, social order and form of governmentality that is non-existent in many societies; that rights policies tend to ignore the many contingent materialities needed for their successful implementation; and that rights discourses construct unequal opportunities for individual and social agency. Many of the issues have to do with the legal and institutional structures that LHR sets up, through which language mediates agency and participation. These are structures (e.g. watch-dog institutions, such as the Pan-South African Language Board, PANSALB) that simultaneously define what may count as a legitimate language, and who can be considered a legitimate speaker (often ruling out non-standard varieties of a language). The structures of LHR also assume a particular type of *politico-lingual subject*, namely a community (group rights) or speaker (individual rights) with adequate economic and symbolic resources with which to engage politically around language issues in Habermasian public spaces (compare Stroud, 2009, for a comprehensive discussion of these points).

Linguistic citizenship refers to cases when speakers exercise agency and participation through the use of language (registers, etc.) or other multimodal means in circumstances that may be orthogonal, alongside, embedded in, or outside of, institutionalized democratic frameworks for transformative purposes. On occasion, this may involve engaging with language through a rights framework, but often – given the constraints noted in the previous paragraph and the narrow focus on language *tout court* rather than what language practices do and mean – linguistic citizenship involves more. It refers to what people do with and around language(s) in order to position themselves agentively, and to craft new, emergent subjectivities of political speakerhood, often outside of those prescribed or legitimated in institutional frameworks of the state. So-called 'service delivery protests' on the streets of South Africa, with their highly multilingual and multimodal articulation in chants, placards, songs – and violence – comprise examples of how forms of semiosis are creatively deployed to create a disruptive space for 'citizen' engagement for those whose voices are habitually silenced. It is also a space where the medley of languages and song, and the temporal and rhythmic unfolding of the march, create new socialities, if only momentarily, that break down or traverse conventional distinctions and socialities based on race, ethnicity or language in an exercise of what Phelan (1995) calls a 'politics of affinity'.

Likewise, Somali refugees in Ugandan camps are also exercising linguistic citizenship when they use the resources – teaching spaces under trees, chalk and boards, etc. – provided by a foreign NGO to teach English literacy for their own purposes of learning to read the Quran (Kathleen Heugh, personal communication, August 2015). They are exercising their agency, and pursuing a goal that is important to *them*, but likely not to the 'keepers' of the programme. They are doing so on the sidelines and margins of the formally structured literacy programme, taking part in 'informal' networks of learning at the same time as they create the conditions for participating in new roles in alternative communities of practice.

In both of these cases, we see how people use a variety of (self-authored) linguistic (and multimodal) practices to sculpt alternative political and ethical, religious and epistemological subjectivities to what is otherwise given. It is the linguistic/multilingual practices in the emergence, negotiation, refusal or engagement with these (often) tenuous and non-authorized subjectivities that is the focus of linguistic citizenship as an area of enquiry. Thus, one way of looking at linguistic citizenship is as an approach to a politics of language and multilingualism departing from a notion of *vulnerability*, understood here as the emergent and sensitive process of *disinhabiting* imposed and linguistically mediated subjectivities.

What this might mean in practice, and the wider implications of entertaining, such a notion as linguistic citizenship, can be illustrated with the following example from an initiative in the use of local indigenous languages at primary school level in a rural educational district in Mozambique.

Vegetables and Language

In a district approximately one hour outside of Maputo, Mozambique, an interesting primary school feeding initiative is underway that exhibits many of the characteristics of linguistic citizenship. Mozambique has long had experimental programmes in mother-tongue-based bilingual education, first under the auspices of United Nations Educational, Scientific and Cultural Organization (UNESCO), and subsequently under the directorship of various NGOs. Although indigenous African languages are recognized and affirmed as a national resource, the affirmation of rights to national languages has been of little consequence for the provision of these languages in the state National System of Education. For the last 15 years, the programmes have carried the status of experimental ventures, still to be fully evaluated, and in recent years, under a new Minister of Education, the national programme has come to a more or less complete standstill.

The disjunct between rights accorded and languages denied underscores how citizenship and rights are not co-temporaneous or identical discourses. Whereas citizenship is contingent, historical and political, rights are depoliticized, ahistorical and universal (Yeatman, 2001). The paradox of rights is that, although they are universal, appeals to them are situated in local space and time and filtered through contingent local political, social and economic structures by which the specifics of each nation-state polity constrain the choice of rights and to what extent that choice is actually provided for. Language practices, as well as thinking on language, are highly situated, historical and contextualized phenomena. It is these local contingencies that – in situations where rights may be recognized or not – frame the real work of (linguistic) citizenship.

Despite the lack of provisions, or rather because of it, a group of teacher educators have taken the unique initiative to insert a mother tongue/bilingual component into an ongoing NGO-initiated programme to stem immediate drop-out and improve pass-rates across the compulsory school system (compare Hyltenstam & Stroud, 1993). The ostensible motivation for this component is to reinforce early literacy.

Language, Subjectivity and Vulnerability

One important feature of this context is that the literacy materials used are worked out and developed on site by teacher educators and linguists in consultation with community members. The consultative production of materials has brought with it an ongoing revision of the 'official' orthographies and lexica of the local languages, as well as methodologies, such as the ordering of graphemes taught, etc., of teaching them. The importance of this event becomes clear when seen through the lens of historical dispossession.

Frantz Fanon, psychiatrist and revolutionary from Martinique, in the first line of his first chapter in *Black Skin, White Masks*, had noted 'the fundamental importance' of language in the (violent) formation of racialized, colonial, subjectivities. He remarks on how 'speaking pidgin means imprisoning the black man and perpetuating a conflictual situation where the white man infects the black man with extremeley toxic bodies' (Fanon, 2008: 17), and says how 'addressing a black man in pidgin means "you stay where you are"' (Fanon, 2008: 17). According to Fanon (2008: 1), for a colonial subject to speak means 'to exist absolutely for the other', bringing home how language was/is very much a part of a powerful system of (racialized) subjugation and production of vulnerabilities.

Critical studies of colonial linguistics are rife with examples of the strategic use of language to define non-metropolitan languages as 'native', 'incomplete', 'inadequate', and their speakers as 'childlike', 'ignorant' and 'uncivilized', labels that effectively invisibilzed and silenced the voices of the colonial subject (Stroud, 2007). These (socio)linguistic processes were a key dimension in the construction and replication of a societal order built up around particular types of *sociality*, such as race, ethnicity, gender (compare Stroud, 2007).

Contemporary vestiges of colonial conceptualizations of language and otherness are found in how ex-colonial languages are indexically organized in relation to indigenous languages. In the Mozambican context, for example, African languages and Portuguese continue to be framed *discursively* as inhabiting distinct temporalities. Indigenous languages are spoken about either as languages of the pristine past or languages in dire need of intellectualization/modernization in order to become viable for future use. They are seldom seen in their present forms as anything but incomplete, and often disregarded as languages able to voice the contemporary concerns of their speakers.

It is here that the engagement of the community in working with the graphemes, sounds and lexicon of the language gains its significance. Modernization and intellectualization of languages are usually the purview of specialist linguists and lexicographers. However, the active involvement of the community shifts the epistemological authority in deciding what languages are and what they may mean, together with the production of materials, to the local collective of stakeholders. This is an empowering tactic in the sense that the voice of the community stakeholders is being put into text and made legitimate.

LHR, as currently conceived, tends towards a privileging of official values and perceptions of what might constitute the language in question, and can only entertain the legitimacy of alternative language practices as part of the 'language' with difficulty. Although authors such as Skutnabb-Kangas (2000) do recognize the legitimacy of non-standard varieties and the difficulty of distinguishing, say, speakers of lectal or perceived substandard varieties of 'standard languages', such as Tsotsitaal, from 'languages' such as Afrikaans, other authors such as Petrovic (2006) and Wee (2005) have pointed to a number of fundamental difficulties in attempting to extend a rights framework to such varieties.

Linguistic citizenship, on the other hand, highlights the importance of practices whereby vulnerable speakers themselves exercise control over their languages for a variety of purposes precisely to avoid the othering that comes with linguistic imposition. It draws attention to the ways in which alternative voices can be inserted into processes and structures that otherwise alienate. When speakers exercise linguistic citizenship, they also forge decolonial subjectivities, built on the foundation of other forms of sociality than identity in terms of ethnicity or race.

Multilingualism as an Ethics of Others

Linguistic citizenship carries an injunction to critically rethink the notion of 'multilingualism'. This is because reformatting vulnerable subjectivities in re-working language also has implications for understanding the politics of how linguistic diversity has been constructed and constrained, and how encounters across difference have been framed linguistically. Despite the majority of postcolonial states at independence replacing structures of colonial patriarchical and paternalistic liberalism with new forms of coexistence, the ideological blueprints of colonial orders across society have remained resiliently in place. Multilingualism, commonly understood as the co-existence and juxtaposition of more than one language, is one such mechanism whereby essential features of colonial social logics are reconfigured in contemporary 'postcolonial' societies. While ostensibly promising a trope for linguistic (and cultural) diversity, multilingualism is best seen, in common with other forms of neoliberal governance, as a response to 'the effects of anti and postcolonial movements in the liberal world'. It does this by 'allowing cultures a space within liberalism without rupturing the core frameworks of figuring experience' (Povinelli, 2011).

LHR is one such mechanism in the construction of disempowering forms of multilingualism, as they have tended to channel discourses on diversity into specific predetermined cultural and linguistic identities (Stroud, 2001; Stroud & Heugh, 2004), often undergirding ethnolinguistic stereotyping in the form of monolingual and uniform identities. These are not necessarily 'socialities' or forms of social engagement in encounters of difference that speakers themselves feel comfortable with, and may very well perpetuate insidious forms of coloniality-modernity. Often, in such cases, rights become a technique of social discipline that orders and regulates citizens into state-accepted social taxonomies, or that strategically disadvantages some groups over others (Stroud, 2009).

Mbembe (2017), echoing Fanon, has argued the need to find other forms of sociality through which to engage others outside of the conventional collectivities based in race, ethncity, etc. Such a suggestion opens up exciting vistas for also rethinking multilingualism as a site for a more ethical engagement with others across difference. Although the area where the Mozambican school is located is fairly homogeneous in terms of what languages speakers identify with, other work across Africa is exploring ways of developing literacies in multiple languages simultaneously, using the resources of all languages in one teaching/learning space (compare Lupke, in press, on language-independent writing in West Africa).

Contingent Materiality

Many of the minority and vulnerable populations that are in need of language/multilingual provisions are also in need of access to health, housing, clean water and a sustainable economy. This is particularly the case in contexts of the South, but easily applies to many migrant contexts in the geopolitical north. Linguistic citizenship emphasizes that language collectivities (affiliations, communities, etc.) are what Nancy Fraser (1995: 85) has called *bivalent collectivities*. This means that neither recognition nor social-economic redress alone is sufficient to alleviate vulnerability, but that *both* recognition of a language and the economic viability of its community of speakers must be attended to.

Circumstances differ for different collectivities. Different linguistic minorities have different histories and hold different positions in networks of political discourses. Universal definitions of social categories, such as 'language minority', may obscure these potential differences (Maher, 2002: 21). As Cowan *et al.* (2001: 11) point out, the '[d]iscourse of rights is neither ethnically unambiguous nor neutral', and, in practice, rights discourses carry widely divergent implications and produce very unequal subjects with different opportunities for agency (compare Stroud, 2009).

In the Mozambican initiative, activities around language have been inserted into an existing school feeding programme designed to alleviate the poor nutrition and everyday hunger of rural children. Food is a problem in the poverty- and drought-stricken communities of rural Mozambique, and the school feeding programme, together with nutritional information, and the vegetable gardens run by volunteers from the communities themselves, are crucial contributions to the health and well-being of the young students. However, school efficiency (which has yet to be fully documented) is importantly a combination of linguistically focused strategies and an economics of food. We see here the intimate connection in this case between the material contingencies of the local situation and the successful/feasible introduction of a set of activities and practices around local languages. No less importantly, this is part of a larger set of community-driven involvement in vegetable gardens, in school clubs, etc., that introduce new structures of sociality and engagement within and across communities.

Linguistically Mediated Futures

Linguistic citizenship entertains a wider conception of how linguistically mediated change is brought about. The consultative community-driven local language activities are ostensibly adapting to and reinforcing the official monoglot Portuguese programme of schooling. In the case of this school, what goes on in the classrooms is children learning to read and write, sitting up straight and learning to be disciplined. For all intents and purposes, the materials are reinforcing the national curriculum. However, with each input from the community, the programme screws are being loosened another notch. The introduction of other voices and agents into the process of teaching/learning shifts its significance slightly. In the everyday iteration of teaching/learning, the signature literally is changed, as lines of power, chains of authority are dispersed and made more rhizomatic. New structures of consultation, production and witness alter the import of 'the school system'.

Linguistic citizenship attends to those occasions where a 'taking hold of language' goes hand in hand with the transforming of sociopolitical structures and institutions. Linguistic citizenship works to change or shift – however minimally, for example in terms of orthography, or in terms of a purpose of an activity – the rules of engagement: it shifts the chain of command of a programme or institution, away from those tasked with authoring or participating in terms of other, more included actors; it works in subtle ways to alter or create a tributary while the programme unfolds, creating a crease in the unfolding, a perturbation, an interruption. The slow build-up of a confederacy of singular actions and events across different scales – from the everyday practices of classroom interaction, to the higher order lobbying of NGOs with officials from the Ministry – contributes to building a momentum that will ultimately lead to a turbulent tip and the introduction of a new normative regime (Stroud, 2015, 2016). Change is taking hold in the cracks and fissures of the system.

Linguistic Citizenship: A Politics Through/of Language for the Present

The two frameworks offer two distinct, but overlapping, construals of the broader semiotic resources and institutional practices required for political engagement around contentious issues of equity and justice of vulnerable populations.

Linguistic citizenship is a semiotically mediated politics of the present. It situates agency and participation in a different mesh of political, administrative and discursive practices to LHR, interrogating how change and transformation are linguistically mediated outside, alongside or on the margins of state structures and institutions that are designed to selectively service or deny language rights to speakers. In contradistinction, the resources that LHR discourses produce are accessible mainly through state-sanctioned institutions that promote practices, such as the description and normalization of (competing) hegemonic standard varieties of language connected to (strategically) essentialist identities.

The contradictions and tensions specific to the politics of LHR revolve around authenticity of group membership and ownership of particular speech practices. This offers minorities a very limited political space and privileges a select set of semiotic practices for how marginalized speakers may express themselves and be heard. Not surprisingly, these aspects of rights discourses disadvantage significant factions of speakers who, for lack of symbolic and human capital, or for contingent material reasons, subsequently lack agency and voice. Linguistic citizenship, on the other hand, engages with the contradictions and tensions arising from the historical imposition of vulnerable subjectivities and the manufacture of multilingual spaces as sites of contention and competition for scarce resources. Instead, it looks to how linguistic practices and forms accompany the emergence of more autonomous senses of self, and how multilingualism may be reconceptualized as spaces for an ethics of (linguistically mediated) engagement across difference. Such a politics of affinity (Phelan, 1995) and broad alliance deconstructs old socialities, such as race and ethnicity, in favour of agency through 'whatever singularities'. In contradistinction to LHR as an *affirmative* politics of multilingualism that takes its rationale from a politics of identity and recognition rooted in a colonial construct of language, linguistic citizenship as a *transformative* politics deconstructs vulnerable identity ascriptions layered into languages and the structural mechanisms of their maintenance. In so doing, it also carries the potential to deconstruct arbitrary divisions between groups in favour of broad coalitions that cut across linguistically based groupings in the interests of a larger, more comprehensive and inclusive strategy. At the same time, linguistic citizenship highlights processes and forms of linguistically mediated structural change that often go unnoticed.

The Volume

This volume is a selection, with section commentaries, of some of the papers delivered at the workshop. Our ambition with the volume, as with the workshop, was to take a step beyond a politics of language framed in terms of LHR towards one firmly anchored in a transformative notion of linguistic citizenship. We were particularly interested in drawing out what implications these two approaches might carry for work on marginalized and vulnerable language communities and speakers. Ideally, we wanted to be able to conceptualize productive perspectives on linguistic citizenship on the basis of well-construed, empirical case studies. We therefore invited authors to discuss this issue with respect to their own work in the areas of multilingualism, marginality and development. We asked for their experiences and reflections from concrete attempts at promoting minority languages – in particular, perhaps, the adequacy of the legal frameworks in place to mediate and enforce linguistic rights. We wanted to know under what conditions, for example community mobilization, rights solutions work, and in what ways they fail. More importantly, are there forms of engagement that are best accounted for in terms of linguistic citizenship? To what extent did civil society organizations raise (and resolve) language issues outside of state structures? For what purposes? And how might a distinction between a public and subaltern sphere impact on questions of power, agency and voice with respect to language?

These were questions that we felt could initiate a productive dialogue on the theme. Not all the themes were dealt with equally, and some themes not at all. However, in general, much of the ground we had hoped to cover has been covered in the chapters of this book. We therefore offer this collection as a set of ongoing conversations on critical topics of importance to a more equitable and ethical engagement with marginalized and vulnerable speakers and their languages.

Note

(1)   Most of the participants at the workshop are represented with chapters and commentaries in this volume. Notable absences are Marcelino Liphola (University of Eduardo Mondlane), Omondi Oketch (Maseno University, Kenya), Casimir Rubagumya (University of Dar es Salam) and Barbara Trudell (Summer Institute of Linguistics).

References

Benhabib, S. (2002) *The Claims of Culture: Equality and Diversity in the Global Era.* Princeton: Princeton University Press.

Blommaert, J. (2005) Situating language rights: English and Swahili in Tanzania revisited. *Journal of Sociolinguistics* 9 (3), 390–417.

Cowan, J.K., Dembour, M. and Wilson, R.A. (2001) Introduction. In J.K. Cowan, M. Dembour and R.A. Wilson (eds) *Culture and Rights: An Anthropological Perspective* (pp. 1–26). Cambridge: Cambridge University Press.

Fanon, F. (2008) *Black Skin, White Masks* (revised edn). New York: Grove Press.

Fraser, N. (1995) From redistribution to recognition? Dilemmas of justice in a post-socialist age. *New Left Review* 212 (July/August), 68–91.

Grin, F. (2005) Linguistic human rights as a source of policy guidelines: A critical assessment. *Journal of Sociolinguistics* 9 (3), 448–460.

Hyltenstam, K. and Stroud, C. (1993) Final report and recommendations from the Evaluation of Teaching Materials for Lower Primary Education in Mozambique (with Kenneth Hyltenstam). II. Language Issues. Stockholm: Gotab AB. (Also in Portuguese, INDE; Eduardo Mondlane Press, 1996, and as Sociology of Education and Culture Reports No 18, Stockholm: LHS Förlag).

Hyltenstam, K. and Stroud, C. (2016) At the nexus of vulnerability: Multilingualism in development. Working Papers in Urban Language & Literacies, Paper 200. King's College London.

Lupke, F. (under review) Escaping the tyranny of writing: West African regimes of writing as a model for multilingual literacy. In K. Juffermans and C. Weth (eds) *The Tyranny of Writing: Ideologies of the Written Word*. London: Bloomsbury.

Maher, K. (2002) Who has the rights to do rights? Citizenship's exclusions in an age of migration. In A. Brysk (ed.) *Globalization and Human Rights* (pp. 19–43). Berkeley: University of California Press.

May, S. (2005) Language rights: Moving the debate forward. *Journal of Sociolinguistics* 9 (3), 319–347.

Mbembe, A. (2017) *Critique of Black Reason*. Columbia: Duke University Press.

Petrovic, J. (2006) Linguistic Human Rights and the (Post)liberal Conundra of Dialect and Language. Paper presented at the meeting of the American Educational Studies Association, Spokane, Washington.

Phelan, S. (1995) The space of justice: Lesbians and democratic politics. In L. Nicholson and S. Seidman (eds) *Social Postmodernism*. Cambridge: Cambridge University Press.

Povinelli, E. (2011) *Economics of Abandonment: Social Belonging and Endurance in Late Liberalism*. Durham and London: Duke University Press.

Skutnabb-Kangas, T. (2000) *Linguistic Genocide in Education – Or Worldwide Diversity and Human Rights*? New Jersey: Lawrence Erlbaum Associates.

Stroud, C. (2001) African mother tongue programs and the politics of language: Linguistic citizenship versus linguistic human rights. *Journal of Multilingual and Multicultural Development* 22 (4), 339–355.

Stroud, C. (2007) Bilingualism: Colonialism, postcolonialism and high modernity. In M. Heller (ed.) *Bilingualism: A Social Approach* (pp. 25–49). New York: Palgrave Press.

Stroud, C. (2009) Towards a postliberal theory of citizenship. In J. Petrovic (ed.) *International Perspectives on Bilingual Education: Policy, Practice and Controversy* (pp. 191–218). New York: Information Age Publishing.

Stroud, C. (2015) Turbulent deflections. In C. Stroud and M. Prinsloo (eds) *Moving Words: Language, Literacy and Mobility* (pp. 206–216). New York/London: Routledge.

Stroud, C. (2016) Turbulent linguistic landscapes and the semiotics of ctizenship. In R. Blackwood, E. Lanza and H. Woldemariam (eds) *Negotiating and Contesting Identities in Linguistic Landscapes*. London/New York: Bloomsbury.

Stroud, C. and Heugh, K. (2004) Linguistic human rights and linguistic citizenship. In D. Patrick and J. Freeland (eds) *Language Rights and Language Survival: A Sociolinguistic Exploration* (pp. 191–218). Manchester: St Jerome.

Wee, L. (2005) Intra-language discrimination and linguistic human rights: The case of Singlish. *Applied Linguistics* 26 (1), 48–69.

Wee, L. (2006) Responding responsibly: Some remarks on Skutnabb-Kangas, Kontra and Phillipson. *Applied Linguistics* 27 (4), 748–743.

Yeatman, A. (2001) Who is the subject of human rights? In D. Meredyth and J. Minson (eds) *Citizenship and Cultural Policy* (pp. 104–119). London: Sage Publications.

Part 1

Language Rights and Linguistic Citizenship

1 Linguistic Citizenship

Christopher Stroud
University of the Western Cape and Stockholm University

The capacity to live with difference is, in my view, the coming
question of the 21st century
Stuart Hall

Introduction

A major challenge of our time is to build a life of equity in a fragmented world of globalized ethical, economic and ecological meltdown. In this context, language takes on singular importance as the foremost means whereby we may engage politically and ethically with others across difference. However, any attempt to address this concern would need to comprise a critical and fundamental rethinking of the idea of 'multilingualism' itself. Contemporary understandings of multilingualism are the nomenclature par excellence of how we have come to conceptualize and regiment our relationship to different others. However, the construct, with its colonial pedigree, continues to engage and contain diversity in ways that reproduce essential features of colonial social logics in contemporary 'postcolonial' societies (compare Stroud & Guisemmo, 2015). Non-metropolitan languages, for example, especially in the African context, are positioned vis-à-vis metropolitan languages (English, French, Portuguese) in a different temporal discourse as languages in the 'becoming' (in need of intellectualization), or languages of times past (in need of revitalization). In both cases, the temporal displacement of speakers of these languages produces a subaltern who is only able to engage linguistically in the present through the words of the metropolitan language. (For an extended argument, see Stroud & Guissemo, 2015.) In other words, there is an important sense in which the crisis of humanity we are experiencing as a crisis of diversity and voice is deeply entwined with a subterranean crisis of a politically fraught notion of language itself. Thus, if we are to engage seriously with the lives of others, an imperative is reconceptualizing language in ways that can promote a *diversity of voice* and contribute to a *mutuality and reciprocity* of engagement across difference.

This chapter offers the notion of *linguistic citizenship* as a blueprint for a conceptual space within which to think differently – politically and ethically – about language and ourselves. In what follows, I provide a short chronological overview in the second section of the idea of linguistic citizenship. I emphasize how acts of linguistic citizenship do not only challenge ideas we hold about language and multilingualism, but also contribute to an agentive and transformative understanding of the idea of citizenship itself. In the third section, I illustrate this argument further with a case study of Kaaps, a stigmatized variety of Afrikaans spoken in the Cape Flats of South Africa. The section offers an analysis of a performance of a Hip Hop Opera called *Afrikaaps*, as well as a documentary on the making of the opera, which shows how a new sense of language emerges simultaneously with a new sense of self, dignity and citizenship.

In the final section of the chapter, I discuss how the idea of linguistic citizenship might contribute to a construal of 'multilingualism' as a *space of vulnerability*. This is a space where speakers meet different others in disruptive and unsettling encounters that *interrupt* the status quo (Pinchevski, 2005), and where senses of self may be juxtaposed and refashioned as part of the deconstruction of dominant voices and more equitable linguistic engagement with others.

Linguistic Citizenship: Early Beginnnings

Linguistic citizenship is fundamentally an invitation to rethink our understanding of language through the lens of citizenship and participatory democracy, at the same time that we rethink understandings of citizenship through the lens of language. The conjuncture of these two terms troubles both our conventional ideas of the 'linguistic' as well as how we think about 'citizenship'.

The concept of linguistic citizenship is a Southern and decolonial concept that arose out of the contradictions surrounding programmes and practices of mother tongue and bilingual education in the 1990s in the context of the geopolitical South. The contradiction lay in the fact that similar investments in language teaching provisions for mother tongue/ bilingual education, such as literacy materials, grammars, orthographies, dictionaries, teacher-training programmes and infrastructure delivery, resulted in very dissimilar outcomes in different contexts. An extensive meta-analysis suggested that a key parameter distinguishing successful from failed programmes was whether, and to what extent, community members found vernacular/local language provisions useful in their everyday management of issues, such as employment, economy and (local/provincial) politics of housing, education and health (Stroud, 2001). Importantly, the longer-term viability of mother tongue/bilingual programmes was dependent on the degree to which the community itself was actively involved in developing and administering the programme, for example, by contributing to the establishment of orthographic conventions or choice of curriculum content (Stroud, 2002). A good example of the importance of participation was a local mother-tongue programme in Ghana developed in conjunction with an HIV prevention programme for youth and adults – also involving an adult literacy programme – by a consortium of stakeholders (including Lufthansa, Nestlé and a German non-government organization (NGO)), the success of which was due to the local community engagement it inspired (Stroud, 2001). The importance of an engaged, committed and agentive community for successful programme outcome was thrown into relief by the relative unsustainability of the then prevailing models of top-down interventions designed in the North, often administered by foreign NGOs and aid organizations. The notion of linguistic citizenship was thus born out of the felt need for a perspective that situated linguistic practices and representations of speakers firmly within their everyday sociopolitical strivings for agency, transformation and participatory citizenship.

At the time, the prevailing political and educational philosophy of language relevant to multilingualism was that of Linguistic Human Rights (LHR). The idea of linguistic citizenship challenged LHR by referencing Nancy Fraser's (1995) distinction between 'affirmative remedies' and 'transformative remedies'. The argument was that LHR was in all essentials an affirmative remedy, an instance of a politics of recognition that, quite contrary to the intentions of its proponents, maintained and reproduced the status quo to the detriment of minority languages and to the disadvantage of their speakers. One reason for this is that LHR discourses are subject to all the exigencies of how power is exercised and structured in a State, with the resulting technologies and tropes of language description reproducing specific political and local construals of language.

Alexandre Jaffe (1999: 28) had earlier noted how 'forms of language activism that reproduce a dominant language ideology also reproduce the structures of domination', replicating in this way a colonial linguistic dynamic in contemporary time. An illustrative case in point is that of the South African Northen AnaNdebele National Organization that lobbied parliament to accord official status to siNdbele in the South African constitution (Stroud & Heugh, 2004). In response, the state agency responsible tasked the speakers of the language themselves to *prove* that siNdebele was *de facto* a distinct language and therefore eligible to be considered for official recognition. This led to the community actively contesting an earlier classification of siNdebele as a 'variety', thus creating a situation of conflict and division both within and between the designated linguistic groups. The siNdebele case illustrates how a linguistics of standardization, officialization and intellectualization reconstructs minority languages in the image of official standard languages; by excluding and reconstructing forms that articulate alternative voices, minority languages come to embody the social ideologies, class differences and standard/non-standard distinctions that led to the oppression of these languages and the hierarchization of their speakers in the first place.

This is just one example of how seemingly expert and technical procedures of linguistic codification mask contested legislation, competing ideologies and social conflict in a community, as well as disguises the selective agency of its workings (Stroud, 2001, 2009; Stroud & Heugh, 2004). Multilingualism seen in a LHR framing appears as one technology among a broad battery of disciplinary and regulatory practices (Comaroff, 1998: 32) deployed by the state in pursuit of its continued reproduction – including the *de facto* marginalization of minority languages.

If LHR remains mainly silent on the issue of how it is imbricated in the replication of existing institutional power structures of particular nation-states, linguistic citizenship seeks instead to lay bare this conspiracy by offering a different approach to language and multilingualism. Linguistic citizenship is a transformative concept (Fraser, 1995). It critically interrogates the historical, sociopolitical and economic determinants of how languages are constructed, at the same time as it pinpoints the linguistic, structural and institutional conditions necessary for change. Linguistic citizenship sees linguistic collectivities as *bivalent*, a notion that refers to the fact that, for language, 'neither socioeconomic maldistribution or cultural misrecognition are an indirect effect of the other, but ... both are primary and co-original' (Fraser, 1995: 85). It is the bivalency of linguistic collectivities that ties the refiguration of language to a deconstruction and reconstitution of social life and its institutions. This is why, when local languages were perceived by their speakers as central to community transformation, in a context where linguistic decisions were managed by the speakers themselves in structures of participatory engagement, the mother tongue/bilingual programmes could boast a successful implementation. It is also the bivalency of linguistic collectivities that allows us to see language and citizenship as two sides of the same coin – citizenship as mediated by forms of language, while

forms of language in turn emerge out of the fluid and shifting entanglements of social engagement (Stroud, 2009: 217).

'Citizenship' in linguistic citizenship

The sense of citizenship referenced here is not the limited notion of
nation-state citizenship that the term usually calls to mind. Isin (2009; see
also Isin & Nielsen, 2008) has argued that 'our dominant figure of citizenship has changed throughout the 20th century' (2009: 368), and that we
need a 'new vocabulary of citizenship' (2009: 368). He notes how in
today's world:

> new actors articulate claims for justice through new sites that involve
> multiple and overlapping scales of rights and obligations (...). The mani-
> fold acts through which new actors as claimants emerge in new sites and
> scales are becoming the new objects of investigation. (Isin, 2009: 370)

Isin introduces the notion of 'acts of citizenship' to refer to those 'deeds
by which actors constitute themselves (and others) as subjects of rights'
(2009: 371), or, alternatively, as those with 'the right to claim rights'. He
argues that 'the manifold acts through which new actors as (rights) claim-
ants emerge in new sites and scales' forces us 'to theorize citizenship as an
institution in flux embedded in current social and political struggles that
constitute it' (Isin, 2009: 368). Today, those who engage in such 'acts of
citizenship' do not necessarily hold the conventional *status* of citizen (as,
in Isin's conception, citizenship is not a status, but an act). Rather, acts of
citizenship are the practices whereby new actors, seeking recognition in the
public space in order to determine a new course of events, shift *the location
of agency and voice*. In this respect, 'acts of citizenship' contribute to
'transformative' remedies in the sense of Nancy Fraser (1995), viz. remedies that attempt to deconstruct and restructure the political economic
status quo and its institutions, and to bring about new social relations.

Isin's emphasis on the fluidity and dynamism of the 'fields of contestation around which certain issues, stakes, interests, etc., assemble' (e.g.
sites, such as gender, sexuality and language), and the 'scopes of applicability (so-called "scales") that are appropriate to these fields' (going
beyond conventional scopes such as state, nation, to include also sub- and
supranational groupings), is borne out by the contemporary multiplication
of 'citizenships', such as *sexual citizenship*, or *intimate citizenship*, and
similar constructions. This is in keeping with the way in which struggles
to extend the meaning of citizenship have historically brought about

different ways of 'knowing' political subjects onto arenas of public and political discourse, with important consequences for key reforms in the social, political, economic or sexual rights of citizens. A *political* notion of citizenship emerged with the vote, and linking citizenship to economic rights and obligations accompanied the rise of trade unions and the development of welfare legislation. In the earlier years of the 20th century in Europe, and in the wake of the women's suffrage movement, the notion of citizenship was extended to also encompass issues of gender, and more recently also race and ethnicity. It is in this sense that 'citizenship' is used in conjunction with 'linguistic' – as an acknowledgement of the deeply entangled dependencies between language and politics, and as a pointer towards how a different construal of language may open up new political scenographies. Attention to complexities and subtleties of language practices (just as with an appreciation for different sexualities) can initiate and sustain state remedies for more encompassing and inclusive forms of citizenship agency and participation.

The 'linguistic' in linguistic citizenship

The other side of the coin is that the diverse and complex configurations of citizenship outside of the conventional understandings of politics usher in alternative construals of language. This point is well illustrated by the recent years' insurgent citizenship (Holsten, 2007) movements: From Occupy movements, such as the Greek *Outraged* or the Spanish *Indiginados*; through movements, such as *Black Lives Matter*; to Fall movements, such as *Rhodes Must Fall*. Each of these groups articulate their protest and claims to agency through a variety of semiotic means (compare for example Stroud, 2016, on the turbulent semiotics of a South African occupy movement). In like manner to the complexities of citizenship, linguistic citizenship recognizes that speakers' expression of agency, voice and participatory citizenship may require the use of a variety of semiotic means ranging over unconventional, non-institutionalized uses of language, to forms of embodied semiotic practice, such as the bearing of tattoos or corporeal use of space. Importantly, in the process of engaging with the social and political issues that affect them deeply – wrestling control from political institutions of the state, putting forward claims for new forms of inclusion or promoting and deliberating on contested stakes and interests – speakers reconfigure language through the creation of new meanings, repurpose genres and transform repertoires by using their language over many modalities (compare Williams & Stroud, 2013, 2015 for an analysis of performance genres, such as stand-up comedy, in this latter regard). In other words, just as the term 'citizenship' points to a fluid space of contestation, so should the term 'linguistic' not be confused with the idea of language as the artefactual product of formal linguistic analysis only. Speakers use a spectrum of expression outside of what is normatively (and narrowly) considered institutionally appropriate language to express agency, voice and desire for inclusiveness and participation. Linguistic citizenship encourages us to critically rethink the notion of 'linguistic' as practices that can be known through a variety of discourses and modalities.

Linguistic citizenship and utopia

An important feature of citizenship as a notion is what Anderson (2008) refers to as its 'utopian surplus'. The contestations played out in 'acts of citizenship' frequently *prefigure* a better world. Fighting for sexual or transracial citizenship is tantamount to anticipating or imagining a world in which harmful categories and systems of othering are deconstructed. The 'utopian' in this case does not refer to the conventional idea of a non-place in a non-time usually associated with the concept, but the condition detailed by Ernst Bloch (1986) that references a better way of living that is *foreshadowed* in the present (and past) but is as yet *unrealized* (compare Anderson, 2008). These foreshadowings may often be experienced as aesthetic or euphoric resonances of subjectively experienced events or states: Linguistic citizenship carries a utopian surplus in this sense. It is about the experiences that people may have of language practices and representations that capture – however fleetingly – a different significance of language to life, and life to language. Thus, the conjuncture of 'citizenship' with 'linguistic' also references an idea of language that has disruptive and interrogative qualities (compare Anderson, 2002, 2008; Bloch, 1986), and that functions as an affordance to point us toward how language and speakers might appear 'otherwise' (compare Povinelli, 2011).

It is this utopian dimension of linguistic citizenship that is illustrated in the next section in the analysis of the performance of the Hip Hop opera Afrikaaps. In the performance, Afrikaans is re-imagined at the same time as the institutional and interactional conditions for this reimagining are refigured.

Afrikaaps

Performance/popular culture is a key site for a politics of the everyday that bears many resemblances to other acts of citizenship where actors seek to constitute themselves as subjects of rights. Speaking of the African context generally, Dolby argues that 'people's everyday engagements with popular culture [...] must be a central component of understanding emergent public spaces and citizenship practices in Africa, present and future' (Dolby, 2006: 34); popular culture is 'a site of struggle, a place for the negotiation of race, gender, nation and other identities and for the play of power' (Dolby, 2006: 33). Simone (2008: 76) talks of popular culture as a 'form of collective endeavor that converts differences of power and legitimacy into forms of which everyone can participate and benefit from, without the outcomes being the product of consensus, conciliation or brokered deals'.

The musical *Afrikaaps* is such a politically significant performance, and it is an excellent example of linguistic citizenship in action. In order to grasp the import of the event of *Afrikaaps* (performance and documentary) for linguistic citizenship, it is necessary to contextualize it in the racialized history of South Africa. Post-apartheid South Africa inherited a complex, shifting and divisive system of racial classification that continues to seep into the minutiae of everyday life of the majority of South Africans. The structural category of race remains a primary mould into which everyday interactions and identities are cast, providing an enduring and familiar trope, a point of certainty amid the messy ambiguities of post-apartheid transformation. Despite the persistence of race as a lived category, *discourses of racialization* – that is, the words and ways through which people construct and navigate race on an everyday basis – are fluid, shifting and entangled, 'a complicated multiplicity of identifications producing, reproducing and transforming identities under changing social and historical circumstances' (Walker, 2005).

Practices and representations of language comprise a particular category of racialization discourse. Afrikaans was one of the two official languages of South Africa up until the transition in 1994, when the new constitution recognized 11 official languages. It is a language born out of early encounters across difference: Slave creole contact between speakers of Early Dutch, Portuguese, French, English, Malay, Tamil and Arabic, with local speakers of Khoi and San languages, forged through colonial language and ideology struggle, and consolidated in the hegemony of apartheid (Giliomee, 2005). This lineage, however, does not figure strongly in mainstream representations of Afrikaans, which remain predominantly resonant with discourses of ethnic/racial purity. Its creole origins notwithstanding, or rather because of this, Afrikaans has been stringently policed with white Afrikaans practices designated as 'pure' Afrikaans or Standard Afrikaans, and offset against particular ideologically loaded named varieties closely tied to coloured identity that were seen as distorted speech (Adhikari, 2005, 2006; Alexander, 2013).

It is in this complex of race and language that *Afrikaaps* gains its significance for understanding the idea of linguistic citizenship. The *vulnerability* of fragmentation, uncertainty and confusion said to accompany the notion of coloured (e.g. Adhikari, 2006) finds rich expression in contestation over the 'stigmatized language of coloured speakers: Kitchen Afrikaans, coloured people's parlance or patois, coloured language, coloured Afrikaans, "Capey" or "Gammat-taal"' (Blignaut, 2014: 2; Small, 1972; for a debate on mainstreaming Afrikaans and the focus on its varieties, see Alexander, 2013; Dyers, 2008: 52; Hendricks, 2012; Hendricks & Dyers, 2016; Prah, 2012). *Afrikaaps* is the more recent articulation of these contests, one that not only dares to question the very ownership of Afrikaans itself, but reveals it to be born out of 'erasure' of other speakers.

The theatre piece *Afrikaaps* is fundamentally about reclaiming ownership and authority over Afrikaans – a powerful tool of white racial hegemony throughout South Africa's history. It offers an alternative narrative about Afrikaans by recuperating lost meanings, and by linking the language and its history to the lives of its speakers long hidden or ignored. The blurb from the 2010 Encounters film festival tells us that:

> On the surface, *Afrikaaps* appears to be a theatre piece within a film, based as it is on the creative processes and performances of the critically acclaimed stage production of the same name. But rather than depending on the drama on stage and the production's prominent characters to carry the narrative, Valley finds revealing moments from the cast's and production crew's personal narratives that transcend what happens on stage. *Afrikaaps*, the film and the stage play, breaks ground by boldly attempting to reclaim Afrikaans – so long considered a language of the oppressor – as a language of liberation.

The Hip Hop opera presents a richly alternative representation and celebration of Afrikaans that simultaneously reveals the historical and contemporary processes of invisibilization, and social and racial disengagement that still go into the making of Standard Afrikaans, encouraging us to imagine a world of racial entanglement, mutual susceptibility and an alternative ethics of encounter.

The documentary on the making of *Afrikaaps* is directed by Dylan Valley. It highlights the temporal unfolding of what came to be known as the Afrikaans language: from its creole beginnings and its Arabic scripture to its latter-day standardization. By drawing on hip-hop, traditional Malay humour and personal narratives, the documentary follows the staging of the Afrikaaps theatre (the participants involved in it), the expert and non-expert definitions of Afrikaans, and the history of Afrikaans

from colonialism into post-apartheid South Africa. The story of the com-
plicated history of Afrikaans is elegantly performed by hip-hop artists
Emile XY?, Jitsvinger, Bliksemstraal, Blaq Pearl and artists Jethro, Kyle
Shepherd, Moenier Parker and Shane Cooper.

We can identify four main themes around which the documentary is
structured: Afrikaans as borne out of the *pain and turbulence* of a colonial power that elided and misrepresented encounters and entanglements
with others; *multivocality*, emphasizing how Afrikaans comprises a multitude of more or less audible voices; *embodiment, aesthetics and performance* as central to the reclaiming and reconstruction of the language
voices; chronotopical speakerhood, where to be a speaker of Afrikaans is
to (re)invoke and echo historical voices and genres. Ultimately, the opera
comes to foreshadow a notion of legitimate speakership tied to the
euphoric sensibility of a new-found dignity.

Turbulence and pain

As mentioned earlier, Afrikaans was born out of encounters of difference in the cackle of contesting voices – the slave-owners, the Khoi inhab-
itants and the various migrant demographics. Rather than ignoring this
turbulence, the documentary structures its representation around this
trope throughout – in the choice of voices it chooses to highlight, in the
personae it casts as commentators and in the themes and contents of the
lyrics it presents. Catherine, the producer, highlights its turbulent history
in her introductory comment:

> The purpose of the show is that we deal with the history of Afrikaans and
> it goes on into the 50s where people are then not only dispossessed of
> their language but they are also dispossessed of their homes and in that
> process their identities are fractured.

Neville Alexander, the iconic Director of the Program for Alternative
Education in South Africa (PRAESA), and, before his death, one of the
country's most influential language activists, remarks explicitly on the
violent roots of Afrikaans:

> As die Kho', die San, en die Slawe veral nie gedwing was om Hollands of
> Nederlands te leer nie of te praat nie, dan sou die taal Afrikaans eintlik
> nie onstaan het nie.

> 'If the Khoi, the San and especially the slaves had not been forced to learn
> Dutch then Afrikaans would not have existed'.

The turbulent history of Afrikaans is hammered home in the documentary through the insertion of old newsreel shots of the demolition of District Six, a coloured area in Cape Town out of which residents were forcefully removed under the apartheid Group Areas Act. The participants in the documentary are laying bare the violence and revoicing to which they have been subjected throughout history – the darker side of a politics of institutionalized linguistic recognition. This historical perspective is cleverly inserted via Afrikaaps into the quotidian reality of contemporary South Africa. Valley recounts, for example, how a cast member was arrested during the production of the theatre piece, stitching this event into the documentary as an illustration of 'racial' unfairness of South African justice.

Multiple voices

The second theme running through the theatre piece is found in the framing of *Afrikaaps* as 'attuned to multitude of identities, subject positions and positions of interest' (Stroud, 2009: 213). This is a core aspect of linguistic citizenship that recognizes citizenship/language as the syncretic outcome of 'a capacity to act *in relation*' (Osborne & Rose, 1999: 758), often on the cusp of normative regimes of language and citizenship.

The multivocality of *Afrikaaps*, simultaneously underscoring the power differentials between voices, is brought out by Moenier, one of the participants in the opera, in the following verse:

(1)
MOENIER:
1. Ek is 'n *number* met 'n storie ou pel
    'I'm a number with a story old pal'
2. Van hoe my mense hulle *feelings* en geheime vertel
    'About how people talk about their feelings and secrets'
3. Ek was gebore daar in *Europe* met 'n ander taal
    'I was born in Europe with a different language'
4. Maar innie Kaap was ek gekap met 'n creole style
    'But in Cape Town I was produced with a creole style'
5. Ek is ook baie gesing met 'n ghoema sang
    'I've been sung a lot with a ghoema song'
6. Ek vat jou hand Zanzibar en Dar Es Salaam
    'I take your hand from Zanzibar to Dar Es Salaam'
7. *Dutch Sailor Boy*
8. Wat sing jy daar?
    'What are you singing?'

9.   Sal jy mind as ek vir jou 'n klein vragie vra
     'Do you mind if I ask you a question'
10. Sing jou *song* gou weer, en dan 'n nogger keer
     'Sing your song again, and then again'
11. Nou kan ek mos al my broese dai *song* leer
     'Now I can teach all my brothers that song'
12. Oor 'n uur of twee sal ons dai *number* ken
     'Over an hour or two we'll know that song'
13. Met 'n *smile* sing ons hom *now and then*
     'We'll sing that song now and then with a smile'

Moenier's thematization offers an account of Afrikaans that not only challenges the taken-for-granted trope of Afrikaans as a 'European' language, but also (albeit indirectly) interrupts ideas of language as something that is abstract and disembodied. In his lyric, Moenier traces the origins of Afrikaans in migration and creole entanglements, with roots stretching from Zanzibar and Dar Es Salaam, with important milestones celebrated in the *ghoema* song. The *ghoema* harks back to the musical culture of the 17th-century Malay slaves, and was a celebration of their being granted freedom in 1834. His words draw attention to how one effect of cycles of disruption, re-formation and juxtaposition is that *no single group of speakers can lay claim to ownership or authenticity* of the language, as successive encounters across difference and layered entanglements of speakers have contributed to the rhizomatic character of Afrikaans today.

At the same time, his words invite us to rethink the relationships of power underlying particular practices and understandings of language(s) – such as who may decide what a language is, or which speakers count as legitimate, a central aspect of linguistic citizenship. Moenier, in line 11 'Now I can teach all brothers that song' and in line 13 'We'll sing that song now and then with a smile', is indicative of how this act of linguistic citizenship opens Afrikaans up for a broader-based engagement, and new-found sense of ownership of a language on behalf of its speakers.

Corporeal entanglements

The third theme of the piece frames the multivocal imaginary of Afrikaans as *entanglements* of circumstances and people. It invites us to imagine Afrikaans as something that gives voice to a diversity of experiences and life-forms in place of Afrikaans as hegemonic monologue.

The following verse from the scene production by Emile XY?, perhaps one of the best known rappers in South Africa, highlights the complexities and extent of entanglements.

(2)
EMILE:
1. Ek is dai dammies player
   'I'm that dominoes player'
2. Kennetjie en als doels
   'Kennetjie and other games'
3. Ek was n ANC supporter
   'I was an ANC supporter'
4. En nou se ek sy Ma se...
   'Now I say they're Mother...'
5. Ek is dai Boesman taal tolke
   'I'm that Bushman language translator'
6. Corner Broker
7. Gooi nee jou tol
   'Throw down your spinning top toy'
8. Want hiesa gaan djy stoeke
   'Cause here you'll have to play'
9. Ek is dai mass murderer
   'I'm that mass murderer'
10. Tyre Burner
11. Minimal wage, sub-economic earner
12. Ek's dai dokter, lawyer, politician
    'I'm that doctor, lawyer, politician'
13. Innie ghetto
    'In the ghetto'
14. Wait a minute
15. Most of them moved out
16. Awe!
    'Cool!'

In the above, Emile performs his lyrics indexing local cultural practices and performances. He rhymes about favourite past-times and games: playing dominoes and little chin (*kennetjie*), the latter a children's game where an opponent hits a short stick with a longer stick in the air to be caught by fielders. In lines 2 and 3, the performer suggests that he was once a supporter of the African National Congress (ANC), but now he chides the party (quite probably due to its inability over the years to deliver on its promises to create a racially just society). He further rhymes that he sees himself as a translator of Bushman language (possibly Khoi or San languages), thereby embodying the historical development of Afrikaaps. And he suggests that when people encounter him, they will expect that he will be able to stylize his language like a Corner Broker (line 6), an informal trader who sells fruit and other affordable products on the corner of streets in the townships of Cape Town, known for their loquacity. But, we note, how he in is Afrikaap's cloak, he is also the mass murderer, the tyre-burning protester and the professional who has fled the ghetto.

There is an embodiment of language and linguistically mediated identities in this skit. These do not manifest as narrow racializations, but rather as a corporeal kaleidoscope of entangled selves. The significance of Emile XY?'s verse lies in his breaking down of identity stereotypes by merging and mixing different personae in the body and voice of the same speaker. He is using Afrikaans to literally mediate an embodiment of diversity (compare Jean Nancy's 'being singular plural' or 'being-with') – ethnic, racial, social class – in contradistinction to how the language is usually represented as located solely in the body of the white, middle-class, 'Afrikaner'.

Chronotopical selves

The embodied representation of Afrikaaps is echoed in the fourth theme running across the theatre piece, the chronotopical self.[1] The wealth of different genres articulated across a range of semiotic, multimodal resources – poetry, Hip Hop, song, dance and speech styles in character sketches – allow the linking of selves across historical time and colonial/postcolonial space. The students interviewed in the documentary configure themselves as present-day embodiments of historical personae, echoing Moernier and Emile XY?'s spatio-temporal reach of entangled bodies and voices (Soudien, 2014). In Figures 1.1 and 1.2, the learners are demonstrating their skill in the age-old genre of Ghoema, a central feature of contemporary Cape coloured dance culture.

In Figure 1.1, the three pupils are dancing to the rhythm of a banjo, with the pupil on the left swinging his arms, the one in the middle slapping his chest and the pupil on the right acting the fool and pulling funny and weird faces. Their performance intimately glues together varieties of Afrikaans, body movement and facial expression into a chronotopical and embodied representation of Afrikaans that reaches back to, and indexes, the historical liberation of the Malay slaves. An interesting take in the documentary, visible in the figure, is that the backdrop to the Afrikaaps dance is the Afrikaans lesson teaching Standard Afrikaans comparatives on the board behind the student. The Standard Afrikaans framing of the fronted, student performance serves to sharpen the sense of physical transgression carried in Afrikaaps.

Figure 1.1 Students performing Ghoema, from *Afrikaaps* documentary

Dance, song, gesticulation, mimicry allow for the insertion of current language practices and their speakers in a multidimensional historical narrative on the origins, continuities and ruptures of language. The dance, gestures and facial expressions also bring an *aesthetic* framing to Afrikaans, a form of reclaiming of an authoritative voice, unconventionally articulated, that offers an appreciation of Afrikaans that goes well beyond standard accounts of what it means to 'know' a language.

Figure 1.2 Ghoema performers, from *Afrikaaps* documentary

The euphoric speaker

In the documentary, knowing a language 'bodily' comes with a euphoric sense of well being. Throughout the documentary, we note an ecstasy of liberation, dignity, autonomy, agency and inclusivity as one voice after the other tells its story of Afrikaans in the documentary, morphing Afrikaans into a vision of *Afrikaaps*. We get a sense of this aesthetic and euphoric experience of Afrikaans in the following excerpt from the opening scene of the documentary in the voices of the school children. After watching the play *Afrikaaps* at the Baxter theatre in Cape Town, three pupils briefly reflect on how it has overturned some of their preconceived ideas of not just the language they speak, but also their sense of self.

(3)
Multiple school pupils:
Pupil 1:   I feel 'Uh!'
              'It was mind blowing'
Pupil 2:   Ek het noot gewiet van my voorvaders
              Praat deur my nie.
              'I never thought that my forefathers speak through me'.
Pupil 3:   Ek gat nie meer soe skaam wees om te praat soes ek praat nie.
              Ek gat nie weer compromise op die taal vir ander mense nie.
              'I will not be shy anymore to speak the way I speak'.
              'I will not compromise anymore on the use of my language because of other people'

From initially expressing strong surprise and revelation, the first two pupils' comments reveal how they see themselves and their forefathers differently through their 'discovery' of Afrikaaps. It is notable here how acts of linguistic citizenship serve to carry cowed bodies and souls into a transformed space, where speaking Afrikaans allows participants to – momentarily, at least – feel and act with dignity.

This sentiment is also echoed in the words of Dylan Valley: For Valley, the making of the Afrikaaps documentary and the theatre production involves a personal journey as well as understanding of the history of his own community (AfricAvenir Windhoek, 2010):

> I think that young South Africans especially will enjoy it, particularly the 'coloured' community as it might reveal parts of their heritage they have never known about. I myself certainly never knew the extent to which the Malays, the Khoi and the San had shaped the language until I started researching this for myself.

Afrikaaps as an act of linguistic citizenship

The documentary scopes how contentious issues in the practice and representation of a local and racially stigmatized version of Afrikaans are at the heart of speakers' search for a politically transformative agency, and its structural and institutional conditions. The participants *collectively* toppled a well-established regime of language that for years has relegated Cape Flats Afrikaans to a 'kitchen jargon', and reconstituted it as something removed from the straitjacket of the artefact of language. Rather than promoting a story of an emerging and focused linguistic standard, and far from fixing the language to a specific time, place or embodied identity, the various characters that personify Kaaps celebrate a broad span of non-standard ways of talking, made up of a wide range of registers (criminal argots, children's rhymes and poetic adoptions of Khoisan languages, playful exercise of clicks), forms of play and musical gigs, dance moves and comic forms and rhythms. We witness a highly chronotopical rendition of the 'language', fluid and scripted for and by the different individual histories, repertoires and biographies.

The processes at work in rethinking Afrikaans are not those of any one social identity or political alignment, but emerge out of a web and multiplicity of relations and histories. Instead of a singular, determinate authenticity with an immaculate and unsoiled pedigree, Afrikaans is represented as heteroglossic and polyphonic, evident in the variety of tropes and genres through which knowledge of Afrikaaps is reclaimed. This is nothing less than an ontological refashioning of what it means to be an Afrikaans speaker through engaging in practices of language that 'interrupt' the linguistic status quo, and that refigure language as a *repertoire* of multiple registers and varieties, linguistic or multimodal/transmodal.

Discussion

I opened this chapter with a concern about the constraints on an ethical engagement with difference posed by conventional understandings of multilingualism. I suggested that we needed to reshape the linguistic ground on which such engagements with others are made, and went on to discuss the idea of linguistic citizenship as an inroad to such a reshaping. I argued that linguistic citizenship points to a construct of language that differs in important ways from the colonial construct we continue to struggle with.

The colonial construct of language was one of the Cartesian knowledge structures that undergirded a global project of subjugation. Grosfoguel (2013) writes about how the development of the human, social and physical sciences went hand in glove with the four genocides of the modern world: The expulsion of the Jews from Spain; the Spanish conquest of the Americas; the Witch burning of the Middle Ages; and the black Atlantic slave trade. One consequence of the genocides was to engineer a violent proliferation of Otherness – a systematic creation of insurmountable difference and division.

Linguistics as a field of knowledge grew out of a colonial project intent on capturing the voices of the colonial subaltern. As a technology for constraining and containing the diversity of others, it scoped constructs of language out of processes of invisibilization of voice, denial of (racial) entanglements and suppression of histories, processes that were more or less violent and trauma laden. Not surprisingly, the imposition generally of alien structures and meanings onto local languages, and the revoicing of local knowledge, produced in the colonial subject a sense of existing 'absolutely for the other' (Fanon, 2008), a Fanonian psychic split characterized by feelings of disconnect from a dignified sense of self and human value. The story of Afrikaans as told in the theatre piece and recounted in the documentary is exactly this story. To speak Afrikaans is to enact the story of the *re-voicing* of the colonial other. Afrikaans is the silencing of histories, and the authoring of different shades of speakerhood on indexical markets of race, ethnicity and social division. Processes of linguistic codification and translation determined what was 'sayable' about and within the language, erasing speakers' local knowledges about Afrikaans in the process. These events comprised, to all intents and purposes, an effective form of *epistemicide* (de Sousa Santos, 2010), that is, the eradication of a body of knowledge through epistemic violence. It is this we have seen in the construct of Afrikaans, and it is this construct of language that underpins an *affirmative* strategic understanding of multilingualism.

A *transformative* construct of languages is visible in the acts of linguistic citizenship that refigure Afrikaans into Afrikaaps. These acts reframe semiotic practices of citizenship away from a totalizing sense of language, building a new sense of language that is radically different, one that is literally staged as an exercise of participatory citizenship that de-links the chains of hegemonic thought about language, its institutions and their history. In contradistinction to a colonial construct of language, the Afrikaaps performances highlight complexity of entanglement, display the rhizomatic roots of Afrikaans, and convey its turbulent and disrupted historical unfoldings. What has been perceived or presupposed as a stable regime of structure and meaning is laid open for contest. The re-voicing of Afrikaans means that authority over and ownership of the language is – momentarily at least – 'shifted' away from the grammarians and lexicographers to the *speaker* of

Afrikaans. Simultaneously, acts of linguistic citizenship such as these not only interrupt and reshape forms of speech and practices of speaking. They also unsettle the existing racialized tensions and power relations bound up in linguistic forms as part of a more general transformative dynamic in contemporary South Africa. Thus, the rethinking of Afrikaans takes place together with an articulation of a utopic and disruptive act of (inclusive) citizenship. Afrikaaps carries with it a new sense of self and future, as well as, importantly, a transformed understanding of the self in the past. The *linguistic reconnect* of self and language through Afrikaaps is something very different to the experience of *alienation* and disempowerment that typified the Fanonian colonial condition of a linguistically induced 'psychic split'. Both the musical itself and the documentary reveal ways of living differently through language, going against the grain. Together with the emergence of 'Afrikaaps', selves are refigured and a new, vocal, political voice that seeks to reclaim ways of speaking deeply entwined with alternative thinking of what it means, and has meant, to be a speaker of Afrikaaps emerges. In this sense, it is an act of linguistic citizenship that is *transformative* in the sense of Nancy Fraser. It is also a utopian act in that the documentary foreshadows through tropes of euphoria what still needs to *become*.

Linguistic citizenship, then, offers a construct of language deeply entwined with, and productive of, a different form of engagement with difference. Instead of 'invisibilization', we find 'appearance' and 'emergence'; alongside 'recognition' or 'affirmation' by others, we find more *agentive* forms of visibility, such as 'spectacle' and 'performance'. And beyond a bloodless understanding of language as a disembodied structure, we see language through the lens of bodies and souls. Interesting is the *euphoria* speakers feel in coming across linguistic moments of unpredictability and surprise (as in the dawning realization of the cast that the young school pupils are accomplished practitioners of Ghoema); or the 'mind-blowing' revelation experienced by the school children that Afrikaaps also foreshadows the potential to live otherwise.

Linguistic citizenship might (wrongly) be construed as a flight of fancy, an imaginative excess, referring as it does to a 'pre-dawning of language and society that is "not-yet-conscious"' (Anderson, 2002: 216) and for which the material and objective conditions of fulfilment may not yet exist. However, it is precisely in this utopic potential that the notion of linguistic citizenship finds its rationale and its full transformative promise. Acts of linguistic citizenship, such as Afrikaaps, illustrate how the euphoric and aesthetic refiguration of language may reshape the ground on which engagements with others are made and simultaneously rejuvenate or transform the chronotopical self. Linguistic citizenship is fundamentally about a different ethics of linguistically mediated alterity, an alternative way of living with and through difference. As an idea of language that has disruptive and interrogative qualities (Anderssson, 2002, 2008; Bloch, 1986) it points us toward how language and speakers might appear 'otherwise' (compare Povinelli, 2011), a pre-requisite for the planning of more equitable futures.

Multilingualism seen through the lens of linguistic citizenship can be understood in like manner as a site that has traditionally worked to order speakers through languages into differential spaces of erasure, surveillance, censorship or recognition (compare Kerfoot & Hyltenstam, 2017, on the notion of 'orders of visibility'). The different temporalities in which African languages are placed vis-à-vis colonial languages such as Portuguese, English or French – with African languages as languages of a glorious past or a yet-to-be intellectualized future as opposed to the ever-present, fully fledged languages of the metropole – determines, and legitimizes, inequality of encounter and power relations in contemporary time in important institutions, such as education, politics, science, etc. (compare Stroud & Guissemo, 2015). As with the case of Afrikaaps, speakers come to relate to their languages and histories (and relate themselves to metropolitan languages and histories) in ways framed by particular circumstances of (post)colonial encounter.

Rethinking 'multilingualism' through the lens of linguistic citizenship would offer some traction in thinking about new, future, orderings of speakers and languages that go beyond or side step the more familiar affirmative politics of recognition with its dangers of colonial replication. Linguistic citizenship seeks to interrupt such colonial regimes of language by building an inclusiveness of voice in ways that repairs and rejuvenates relationships to self and others. Such rethinking would be cognizant of the historical particularities and context dependencies of different *multilingualisms.*

Linguistic citizenship would help bring to prominence the centrality of multivocality and aesthetic, euphoric 'appreciation' of language for how selves come to inhabit speakerhood, with possible implications for a variety of ways of 'knowing language' that linguistics is only just beginning to explore. No less importantly, it could provide a script to help (re)position questions of language in the flesh and blood of their speakers. This could have ramifications across a spectrum of social arenas: From education and language socialization (e.g. the importance of embodied genres in diasporic childrens' language learning; compare Pennycook, 2015), through more nuanced understandings of the reach and nature of 'hate-speech' (challenging the militant liberal claim that 'sticks and stones may break my bones but names can never hurt me'), to acknowledging cosmological genres of ancestor dialogue (e.g. in arbitrating land claims in Australia or on the African continent; Kathleen Heugh, personal communication, 2015).

Linguistic citizenship implies a process of engagement that opens doors for respectful and deconstructive negotiations around language forms and practices, lays the groundwork for a mutuality and susceptibility to alternative forms of being-together-in-difference. This is the 'utopian dynamic' of linguistic citizenship that could help reconstruct multilingual encounters as a moment for the celebration of difference rather than the suppression of voice (in language, speech norms or social identity) (compare Stroud, 2001). In this sense, it could also suggest registers with which to talk about the learning of conventionally designated (other) languages in terms of refashioning senses of self at the same time as alternative ways of relating to the susceptibilities of others are created.

Kulick (nd) in a note on Levinas has underscored how 'to engage in language is to enact and express dimensions of the vulnerability and mutual susceptibility that are constitutive of human existence'. It is such an ethics of alterity that is immanent to linguistic citizenship and that provides the vantage point from which to think critically about multilingualism in novel ways.

Note

(1) For some recent and valuable work on chronotope in sociolinguistics, see Blommaert (2015) and Blommaert and De Fina (2017).

References

Adhikari, M. (2005) *Not White Enough, Not Black Enough: Racial Identity in the South African Coloured Community*. Athens: Ohia University Press.
Adhikari, M. (2006) Hope, fear, shame and frustration: Continuity and change in the expression of coloured identity in white supremacist South Africa, 1910–1994. *Journal of South Africa Studies* 3 (3), 467–487.
AfricAvenir Windhoek (2010) *Afrikaaps*. See http://www.acpfilms.eu/htdocs/uploads/Afrikaaps.pdf (accessed September 2015).
Alexander, N. (2013) *Thoughts on the New South Africa*. Johannesburg: Jacana Press.
Anderson, B. (2002) A principle of hope: Recorded music, listening practices and the immanence of utopia. *Geografiska Annaler* 84B (3–4), 211–227.
Anderson, B. (2008) Affective urbanism and the event of hope. *Space and Culture* 11 (2), 142–159.
Bloch, E. (1986) *The Principle of Hope* (3 vols). Oxford, UK: Blackwell.
Blommaert, J. (2015) Chronotopes, scales and complexity in the study of language in society. *The Annual Review of Anthropology* 44, 105–116.

Blommaert, J. and De Fina, A. (2017) Chronotopic identities: On the timespace organiza-tion of who we are. In A. de Fina and J. Wegner (eds) *Diversity and Superdiversity* (pp. 1–14). Georgetown University Press.

Blignaut, J. (2014) n Ondersoek na die taalgebruik ni *Son* as verteenwoordigend van Kaapse Afrikaans. MA thesis, Stellenbosch University, Stellenbosch.

Comaroff, J.L. (1998) Reflections on the colonial state in South Africa and elsewhere: Factions, fragments, facts and fictions. *Social Identities* 4 (3), 321–361.

De Sousa Santos, B. (2010) *Epistemologies of the South. Justice Against Epistemicide.* London: Taylor and Francis.

Dolby, N. (2006) Popular culture and public space: The possibilities of cultural citizen-ship. *African Studies Review* 49 (3), 31–47.

Dyers, C. (2008) Language shift or maintenance? Factors determining the use of Afrikaans among some township youth in South Africa. *Stellenbosch Papers in Linguistics* 38, 49–72.

Fanon, F. (2008) *Black Skin, White Masks* (revised edition). New York: Grove Press.

Fraser, N. (1995) From redistribution to recognition? Dilemmas of justice in a 'post-socialist' age. *New Left Review* 212, 68–91.

Grosfoguel, R. (2013) The structure of knowledge in Westernized universities: Epistemic racism/sexism and the four genocides of the long 16th century. *Human Architecture: Journal of the Sociology of Self-Knowledge* 11 (1), 73–90.

Giliomee, H. (2005) *The Afrikaners: A Biography.* Tafelberg Publishers.

Hendricks, F. (2012) Iluminating the neglected: A view on Adam Small's literary integra-tion of Kaaps. *Tydskrif vir Letterkunde* 49 (1), 95–114.

Hendricks, F. and Dyers, C. (2016) *Kaaps in Focus.* Blomfontein: Sun Media.

Holston, J. (2007) *Insurgent Citizenship: Disjunction of Democracy and Modernity in Brazil.* Princeton: Princeton University Press.

Isin, E.F. (2009) Citizenship in flux: The figure of the activist citizen. *Subjectivity* 29, 367–388.

Isin, E.F. and Nielsen, G.M. (eds) (2008) *Acts of Citizenship.* London, UK: Palgrave MacMillan.

Jaffe, A. (1999) *Ideologies in Action: Language Politics in Corsica.* New York: Mouton de Gruyter.

Kerfoot, C. and Hyltenstam, K. (2017) *Entangled Discourses: South-North Orders of Visibility.* Ndew York and London: Routledge.

Nancy, J.-L. (2000) *Being Singular Plural.* Stanford: Stanford University Press.

Osborne, T. and Rose, N. (1999) Governing cities: Notes on the spatialisation of virtue. *Environment and Planning, Society and Space* 17, 737–760.

Pennycook, A. (2015) Early literacies and linguistic minorities. In C. Stroud and M. Prinsloo (eds) *Language, Literacy and Diversity. Moving Words* (pp. 206–216). New York and London: Routledge.

Pinchevski, A. (2005) The ethics of interruption: Towards a Levinasian philosophy of communication. *Social Semiotics* 15 (2), 211–234.

Povinelli, E. (2011) *Economies of Abandonment: Social Belonging and Endurance in Late Liberalism.* Durham/London: Duke University Press.

Simone, A.M. (2008) Some reflections on making popular culture in Urban Africa. *African Studies Review* 51, 75–89.

Small, A. (1972) Adam Small in gesprek met Ronnie Belcher. *Gesprekke met Skrywers* 2 (pp. 93–105). Kaapstad, Johannesburg: Tafelberg-Uitgewers.

Stroud, C. (2001) African mother tongue programs and the politics of language: Linguistic Citizenship versus Linguistic Human Rights. *Journal of Multilingual and Multicultural Development* 22 (4), 339–355.

Stroud, C. (2002) *Towards a Policy for Bilingual Education in Developing Countries.* New Education Division Documents, 10. Stockholm: Erlanders Novum AB.

Stroud, C. (2009) A postliberal critique of language rights: Toward a politics of language for a linguistics of contact. In J.E. Petrovic (ed.) *International Perspectives on Bilingual Education: Policy, Practice and Controversy* (pp. 191–218). Charlotte: Information Age Publishing.

Stroud, C. (2016) Turbulent Linguistic Landscapes and the Semiotics of Ctizenship. In Robert Blackwood, E. Lanza and H. Woldemariam (eds) *Negotiating and Contesting Identities in Linguistic Landscapes* (pp. 1–14). London and New York: Bloomsbury.

Stroud, C. and Guisemmo, M. (2015) Linguistic Messianism. *Multilingual Margins: A Journal of Multingualism from the Periphery* 2 (2), 6–19.

Stroud, C. and Heugh, K. (2004) Linguistic human rights and linguistic citizenship. In D. Patrick and J. Freedland (eds) *Language Rights and Language Survival: A Sociolinguistic Exploration* (pp. 191–218). Manchester: St Jerome.

Walker, M. (2005) Race is nowhere and race is everywhere: Narratives from black and white South African university students in post-apartheid South Africa. *British Journal of Sociology of Education* 26 (1), 41–54.

Williams, Q. and Stroud, C. (2013) Multilingualism in transformative spaces: Contact and conviviality. *Language Policy* 12 (4), 396–405.

Williams, Q. and Stroud, C. (2015) Linguistic citizenship: Language and politics in postnational modernities. *Journal of Language and Politics* 14 (3), 406–430.

2 Essentialism and Language Rights

Lionel Wee
National University of Singapore

Introduction

Essentialism assumes that 'the attributes and behaviour[1] of socially defined groups can be determined and explained by reference to cultural and/or biological characteristics believed to be inherent to the group' (Bucholtz, 2003: 400). In some cases, the appeal to essentialism may be *strategic* (Cowan *et al.*, 2001: 10; McElhinny, 1996), in that group members or advocates acting on their behalf are deliberately treating as stable and clearly defined phenomena that (they are aware) are in fact highly fluid, variable or even conflicting. Bucholtz (2003: 401) suggests that strategic essentialism is typically intended as a short-term measure, although 'not all participants who commit themselves to an essentialist position necessarily recognize it as a temporary tactic'. In the field of sociolinguistics, Bucholtz offers gender studies and research on African-American Vernacular English as examples of essentializing efforts being (strategically) undertaken by researchers in order to help gain legitimacy for the otherwise devalued language practices of women and African-Americans.

The process of engaging in research is (arguably) particularly conducive to encouraging and even institutionalizing an attitude of critical scrutiny. Consequently, Bucholtz's suggestion that strategic essentialism, as deployed in research, has a built-in shelf life that mitigates any problems that might arise from a long-term reification and elevation of selected traits or practices and their linkages with particular groups seems plausible enough. The problem is that once we move beyond the boundaries of research, it is not obvious that a clear distinction between strategic and non-strategic essentialism can be maintained, nor is it certain that strategic essentialism can be described as a short-term tactic. This is because the appeal to essentialism tends to intersect with an appeal to cultural rights.

As Cowan *et al.* (2001: 1) observe, 'constituting one historically specific way of conceptualizing the relations of entitlement and obligation, the model of rights is today hegemonic, and imbued with an emancipatory aura'. The combination of essentialism and a rights discourse gives rise to the belief that societies are morally and legally obligated to prohibit discrimination on the basis of cultural differences, the substantive effect of which is to create a sense that social groups possess 'rights-to-difference' (Ford, 2005: 4).[2] Laying claim to cultural rights is therefore intended to (i) allow a group to preserve its distinctiveness (typically construed as a set of associated cultural traits or practices), and (ii) ensure that in the course of such preservation attempts, the group is not unjustly penalized by other, possibly more dominant, groups, understood by their very otherness to possess a different constellation of distinctive traits or practices.

Claims to cultural rights have formed the basis for many of the social categories that inform today's identity politics, including those pertaining to ethnicity, nationality, gender, sexuality and language. In the particular case of language as a cultural right, May (2005: 327) acknowledges that there is an 'essentialist tendency' especially in:

> ... arguments for language ecology (LE), as well as those linguistic human rights (LHR) arguments that are predicated on LE principles. Such arguments assume – in their less sophisticated manifestations, explicitly, and even in their most sophisticated forms, at least implicitly – an almost ineluctable connection between language and (ethnic) identity. This often-unquestioned language/identity link is then used, in turn, to justify any associated 'collective' language rights claims ...

May rightly cautions against moving from the essentialist extreme to the assumption that just because language is not an inevitable feature of identity, it is also unimportant, arguing that 'while language may not be a *determining* feature of ethnic identity, it remains nonetheless a *significant* one in many instances' since 'particular languages clearly *are* for many people an important and constitutive factor of their individual, and at times, collective identities' (May, 2005: 330, italics in original). May's own position is that advocacy of language rights 'does not *necessarily* entail an essentialized, static view of the language-identity link, or a homogenous conception of the wider linguistic group' (May, 2005: 332, italics in original). Drawing on the work of Will Kymlicka (1995), May instead suggests that the key issue is 'one of cultural and linguistic *autonomy* rather than one of retrenchment, isolationism, or stasis' (op cit., italics in original; see also May, 2005: 124). Group members and their advocates, according to

May, are not so much seeking to preserve some past cultural practice, however imagined, as they are trying to maintain their membership in a distinct culture without interference from others.

There are, however, reasons for believing that May is being too optimistic when he suggests that a claim for cultural – in this case, language – rights can simply aim at maintaining a distinct and autonomous identity without any resultant slippage towards essentialism. This is because the discourse of rights itself, quite aside from any cultural practices that may constitute its object, already contains essentializing tendencies. In order for traits/practices to be the kind of thing that a group can claim entitlement of, both the group and the traits/practices, as well as the relationship between the two, have to be ontologically constituted as having a unity and consistency that allows each to be coherently identified. There is therefore significant appeal to erasure (Gal & Irvine, 1995) as heterogeneity internal to the group, variability in the traits/practices and changes in the relations between them, are all downplayed or even ignored so that the nature of the claim can be made to fit the dictates of the discourse of rights. In this way, *contra* May, essentialism does not necessarily mean stasis. Essentialism is able to accommodate change in that some changes to a trait/practice may be viewed as having a relatively superficial effect that does not compromise its authenticity, while other changes may be seen as having a more fundamental effect that does compromise the authenticity of the trait/practice. The point to bear in mind is that there is no objective way to decide which changes are superficial and which are not, since what counts as authentic is itself the outcome of politically negotiated processes of authentication (Bucholtz, 2003: 408), *including* those processes sanctioned by a rights discourse (see, in particular, the discussion of *reinvention* following).

And once enshrined as rights, it is not at all easy for the group to subsequently disavow its essentialized relationship with the relevant traits/practices. This is because the group is not necessarily unanimous in the first place with all of its members agreeing to treat the essentialism as strategic; some members are in fact quite likely to be deeply committed to the essentialist position. Even for those adopting a stance of strategic essentialism, there is always the fear that any public acknowledgement that some degree of distortion/oversimplification was involved in the claims being made could lead to the hard-worn rights being rescinded. Finally, even in situations where rights petitioners have explicitly sought to reassure the general public that their claims are temporary – needed only in order to redress a historical condition of social and economic inequality – actual socio-political developments quickly indicate that such assurances presuppose a degree of social control that is 'illusory', since 'any "temporary" policy whose duration is defined by the goal of achieving something that has never been achieved before, anywhere in the world, could more fittingly be characterized as eternal' (Sowell, 2004: 6–7). The reason is that groups and individuals will quickly act to take advantage of the situation, redesignating themselves (where possible) as members of the 'preferred group', thus changing the original socio-demographics that the rights were intended to redress (Sowell, 2004: 8). Or some members of the group (typically non-elite members and thus those in most need of help) will benefit less than others; this uneven distribution of benefits internal to the group, coupled with the issue of inter-generational transfer – since patterns of distribution are more likely than not to be inherited (Bourdieu, 1984; Bourdieu & Passeron, 1977) – means that there is no clear time period when *all* members of the group can be said to have benefited equally from the rights provision. In these ways, the 'original' situation that a rights-based approach was intended to remedy is never a stable, much less a static, one. And so, whether strategically engineered or otherwise, essentialism in the context of a rights discourse is extremely difficult to dismantle.[3]

The discourse of rights, despite its 'emancipatory aura', is thus neither ethically unambiguous nor neutral (Cowan *et al.*, 2001: 11). It is therefore crucial that, rather than automatically assume that rights are 'a good thing', we analyse them for the kinds of effects they bring about (compare Freeman, 2002: 85). The purpose of this chapter, then, is to explore in detail the intersection between a rights discourse and cultural identity claims, focusing on the particular case of language rights.[4] A rights discourse, I argue, imposes the following three effects.

(i) Selectivity: Since not all the practices associated with a social group are appropriate candidates as the objects of rights, a rights discourse exerts pressure such that only a few selected practices are privileged over others (Ford, 2005: 71).

(ii) Reinvention: In some cases, the pressure to come up with appropriate practices can lead a group to engage in reinvention, such as modifying the practices in ways that fit the demands of a rights discourse. This may include providing the practices with the necessary authentication[5] demanded by rights-conferring authorities, and asserting that these practices unanimously reflect the collective history of the group (Tamir, 1993: 47).

(iii) Neutralization: A rights discourse neutralizes the distinction between strategic and non-strategic essentialism. This means that an essentialist claim (strategic or otherwise), once locked into the rights discourse, has no clear 'exit strategy', making it difficult for such a claim to work as a temporary tactic (Ford, 2005: 68).

Some of these effects undoubtedly exist independently of a rights discourse, but the point I am pursuing here is that these effects are exacerbated by the demands of this discourse, such that the rights tail comes to wag the cultural dog. The result is a situation where 'rights may be *constitutive* of cultures and their associated identities' (Cowan *et al.*, 2001: 11, italics in original; see also Ford, 2005: 73), rather than simply protecting them.

I organize the chapter as follows. In the following section, I provide an overview of critical investigations into rights discourse, focusing in particular on how it encourages essentialism. I then attend specifically to language rights and consider, in turn, the effects of selectivity, reinvention and neutralization, drawing on data from Singapore, South Africa and Sri Lanka, respectively. In my concluding remarks, I visit the liberal ideology that grounds much of today's understanding of rights, and suggest that unlike other cultural practices, language is necessarily illiberal. It should consequently be ruled out as the object of any rights discourse. Instead, language issues in a pluralist society are better approached within a framework of 'deliberative democracy' (Deveaux, 2005), which allows the connections between language and other socio-cultural issues to be foregrounded.

Rights Discourse: The Essentials

Barry (2001: 252ff) points out that there is a tendency to defend a cultural practice on the grounds that 'simply in virtue of forming part of the group's culture, it is essential to its well-being'. The corollary of this is that any change to the nature of the practice, particularly if such change is seen as being imposed from outside the group, can be taken to be a threat to the group's cultural identity. However, by citing a variety of examples of such defenses (the 1835 Maori massacre of the Moriori people: '... these we killed ... It was in accordance with our custom'; the clubbing of seals by Canadian sealers: 'My family has gone sealing for generations ... It's a vital part of our culture'; the killing of whales by the Chukchi: 'the right to hunt whales when it is deemed a traditional part of their culture and diet'), Barry argues that:

> ... if there are sound reasons against doing something, these cannot be trumped by saying – even if it is true – that doing it is a part of your culture. The fact that your (or your ancestors) have been doing something for a long time does nothing in itself to justify your continuing to do it. (Barry, 2001: 258)

Ford (2005) delivers a similar critique in his discussion of *Renee Rogers et al. v. American Airlines, Inc.,* (1981), where the plaintiff was a black woman seeking damages against the airline for prohibiting employees from wearing an all-braided hairstyle. Rogers' assertion was that 'the "corn row" style has been, historically, a fashion and style adopted by Black American women, reflective of cultural, historical essence of the Black women in American society' (quoted in Ford, 2005: 23). Ford, however, points out that:

> What's clear is that the assertion that cornrows are the cultural essence of black women cannot be taken as conclusive evidence that a 'right-to-cornrows' is an unadulterated good thing for black women. Even if we take it on faith that cornrows represent black nationalist pride as against the integrationist and assimilationist coiffure of chemically straightened hair, it's clear that a right to cornrows would be an intervention in a long-standing debate *among* African-Americans about empowerment strategies and norms of identity and identification. More generally, it is by no means clear that an argument that presumes that blacks or black women have a cultural *essence as blacks* or *as black women* is a vehicle of racial empowerment. A right to group difference may be experienced as meddlesome at best and oppressive at worst even by some members of the groups that the rights regime ostensibly benefits. For the black woman who dislikes cornrows and wishes that no one – most of all black women – would wear them, the right not only hinders her and deprives her of allies, but it also adds insult to injury by proclaiming that cornrows are *her* cultural essence as a black woman. (Ford, 2005: 25, italics in original)

Ford further observes that 'if an all-braided style is the cultural essence of black women *by law*', this would imply that non-black women who adopted braids might be seen as '"white Negro" wanna-bes':

> It's likely that a right premised on the immutable link between blacks and braids will discourage white and Asian women from wearing braids by sending the message that the hairstyle 'belongs' to another social group. Although a right to cornrows might seem only to enhance the freedom of potential cornrow wearers, it is arguably better understood as a policy of segregation through which a set of grooming styles are [sic] reserved for a particular group. (Ford, 2005: 26, italics in original)

The observations by Barry and Ford are relevant to the suggestion that groups engage in rights claims only in order to secure cultural and linguistic autonomy without making any claims involving essentialism. Notice, first of all, that the autonomy of the rights-claiming group *vis-à-vis* other groups or society at large is secured on the basis that the cultural practice in question represents the group's collective identity. Thus, the autonomy of the group is privileged over the possibility that individual members within the group may in fact have a different view of said practice, or may even reject its putative role as a representative practice. As a result, there is enormous pressure on the group to present a unified front, which means that dissenting members, rather than voicing a different opinion that might undermine the group's rights claims, may have no choice but to adopt a stance of silence instead (Tamir, 1993: 47). It therefore seems clear that the group's autonomy is being achieved at the expense of that of its individual members.

Second, the idea that autonomy implies freedom from interference by other groups is simply unrealistic. If what is being aimed at is a conception of multiculturalism where different groups co-exist in separate cultural cocoons, then this is simply a weaker version of apartheid (compare Wallerstein, 1991: 73–75; see also Turner, 1993b), as it fails to recognize that in any plural society, some form of social interaction and cross-cultural 'seepage' is inevitable. Even if such cultural separatism is not being aimed at, entrenching practices as rights makes it difficult for groups to dynamically negotiate and accommodate changes to the practices in response to changing social conditions. This is because a rights discourse is usually intended as an attempt to enforce a legal limit on the social and political power of the state or that of a more dominant group, in order that the 'threatened' group can then be free to continue its practices in a maximally unfettered manner (compare Ford, 2005: 68). But rather than being conceptualized as freedom from outside interference, the idea of autonomy is better recognized as the ability to reciprocally negotiate, at a variety of levels (individual, intra-group and inter-group), about how much change to any kind of practice is acceptable, tolerable or even desirable. Unfortunately, the often hard-fought and adversarial conditions under which rights are gained tend not to encourage this kind of reciprocal engagement (Turner, 1993a: 175–176).

The combination of privileging group autonomy over that of its individual members with the understanding of autonomy as freedom from meddling by non-members leads to the idea that rights can be used to curb interference from without, and so allow the rights-claiming group to freely express its cultural identity. This points clearly to an assumption of essentialism. It treats the group's identity as *sui generis*, pre-existing, intrinsic, thus privileging it above and beyond the diverse lived experiences of its members. It enshrines the practice as one that genuinely reflects the group's identity only insofar as the integrity of the practice is maintained. That is, the practice is perceived to reflect the group's 'intrinsic' autonomy rather than undesirable influences 'from without', for only in this way can it be seen as helping the group maintain its distinctiveness.

A rights discourse therefore does not simply reflect or protect an existing cultural practice. It transforms the practice by institutionalizing it as being especially important, and in this way, elevates the selected practice over other practices that might also be said to be just as relevant to the group's identity. As a consequence, the rights discourse comes to play a constitutive role in the culture of the group, since it helps to mark some practices as being more significant than others, more worthy of group attention and support. A rights discourse thus encourages essentialism by insisting that particularly strong reasons be given for according the selected practice the status of a right. And the strongest possible reason that can be given is that the practice embodies an essential property of the group.

Having looked at how a rights discourse encourages essentialism, I now explore its various effects on claims involving language rights, beginning with selectivity.

Selectivity

Selectivity is built into the notion of rights because it is not the case that anything can or should be accorded the status of a right. To allow this would be to trivialize the idea of a right. As Waldron puts it:

> ... the language of rights is used to refer to any demand that an individual interest should be protected or promoted ... and *accorded decisive moral importance*. (Waldron, 1993: 32, italics added)

Although selectivity is clearly a separate issue from standardization, Milroy's (2001) discussion of the ideology of a standard is still relevant here. As he observes, once a particular variety has been chosen as the standard, other varieties, by implication, are non-standard and consequently, less prestigious. 'In this conceptualization, the dialects become, as it were, satellites that have orbits at various distances around a central body – the standard' (Milroy, 2001: 534). Similarly, selectivity manifests itself as the selection of a particular linguistic code of sufficient importance to represent a group's cultural identity, with the consequence that other varieties – whether intentionally or not – are diminished in stature, or even denigrated. Speakers who insist on using the non-selected codes may be judged less sophisticated, less respectable or even unpatriotic. It may also be the case that clinging to these non-selected codes prevents the speakers from participating in status domains of influence, such as those of politics or education.

Consider, as an example, the case of Sri Lanka, where the ethnic conflict between the minority Tamils and the majority Sinhalese revolves around language issues, framed variously as 'mother tongue versus English' and 'Tamil versus Sinhala' (Canagarajah, 2005: 419–420, 424). In 1990, after years of increasingly hostile anti-Tamil policies by the Sinhala government, the militant Liberation Tigers of Tamil Eelam (LTTE) managed to set up a regime that was intended to be autonomous. According to Canagarajah:

> ... the regime insisted on Tamil Only and Pure Tamil in certain extreme terms when they established their *de facto* state in 1990. This policy also served to prove themselves more Tamil than the middle-class politicians ... they found support for the argument that it is only in creating a separate state of homogeneous Tamil community that the mother tongue could be empowered. ... Their own monolingual/monocultural ideology has always been claimed by the LTTE as evidence that they were more faithful to the Tamil cause. (Canagarajah, 2005: 424–425)

The insistence on only Tamil has proven more effective *vis-à-vis* Sinhala than English, since there is a desire for Tamil–English multilingualism among many ordinary Tamils, who associate English with socioeconomic mobility and liberal values (Canagarajah, 2005: 438). Despite this, the LTTE cannot be seen to support such multilingualism since 'the reason they won the leadership in the struggle for Tamil rights ... is because they could come up with a more populist and radical slogan ... to give up their language policy is political death' (Canagarajah, 2005: 441). The result is an emphasis on 'pure' Tamil and the concomitant marginalization of those Tamils for whom code-mixing might actually constitute a normalized language practice. In other words, the selectivity of Tamil in its purest form helps legitimize the denigration of other codes that may be mixed or hybridized varieties, and that are considered illegitimate precisely because of their perceived linguistic purity. As a consequence, speakers for whom such hybridized creoles (Blommaert *et al.*, 2005) are in fact naturalized ways of speaking may end up being penalized. Thus, in the LTTE-governed regime of Jaffna with its emphasis on pure Tamil, warnings are given that the use of English is 'damaging traditional Tamil culture and hindering the nationalist struggle' (Canagarajah, 2005: 425). Petitions or applications to the police, the courts and village councils are likely to be rejected if these are made in mixed Tamil.

Such penalization can in fact be gleaned from the following example (from Canagarajah, 2005: 426), where a Tamil woman applying for a travel permit is observed to have unwittingly used an English borrowing (*wedding*) in what is otherwise supposed to be an exchange conducted in pure Tamil.

Officer: *appa koLumpukku een pooriinkaL?*
            'So why are you traveling to Colombo?'
Woman: *makaLinTai* wedding-*ikku pooren*
            'I am going for my daughter's "wedding"'.
Officer: *enna? unkaLukku tamiL teriyaataa?* England-*ilai iruntaa vantaniinkal?*
            'What? Don't you know Tamil? Have you come here from "England"?'
Officer: *enkai pooriinkaL?*
            'Where are you going?'
Woman: *cari, cari, kaLiyaaNa viiTTukku pooren, makan*
            'Okay, okay, I am going to a wedding, son'.

The woman's use of *wedding* immediately leads to a rebuke from the government officer and 'although *it takes some time for her to realize her blunder,* she corrects herself as her petition can easily be turned down for such mistakes' (Canagarajah, 2005: 426, italics added).

Reinvention

Whether one wishes to speak non-judgmentally of 'nationalist imaginings' (Anderson, 1991) or adopt a more evaluative stance on their truth/falsity (Hobsbawm, 1990; see May, 2001: 68), it has been widely recognized that the formulation of language policies is inevitably influenced by ideologies of various sorts (Fishman, 1973: 31–32; Spolsky, 2004). The issue at hand, however, is not simply that 'imaginings' occur, perhaps necessarily, whenever a group of people attempts to construct a shared identity and sense of destiny. It is that a rights-based approach forces such imaginings to take on starkly defined contours so as to satisfy the demands of legality, which I refer to here as reinvention. Since claims to rights tend to take place in the context of 'competitive struggles' between groups (Turner, 1993a: 175–176), such claims may be challenged, and this creates a 'need to make a *clear case* to counterbalance an opposing one' (Clifford,

1988: 321, italics added). However, as Ford points out, a legal demand for clarity conflicts with the flux and variability of actual lived cultural practices:

> The legalism of difference discourse encourages, and rights-to-difference require, formal conceptions of social identity that easily can be asserted in courts. Courts and judges will most likely protect cultural styles that can be easily framed in terms of fixed categories, bright-line rules and quasi-scientific evidence. Courts will want experts to testify as to the content of the group culture, they will want lists of specific and concrete manifestations of the culture. Judges are likely to want the culture to be fixed and knowable and will want the protected behavior to be reflexive so as to distinguish culture from merely deviant behavior.
>
> ...The blame lies with the very project of trying to define group differences with sufficient formality as to produce a list of traits at all. (Ford, 2005: 71)

Likewise, as Clifford tells us in his discussion of the Mashpee's 1976 claim for tribal status in Cape Cod, legal understandings of culture contain a 'bias toward wholeness, continuity and growth' (Clifford, 1988: 338; see also Cobo, 1987). This is despite the fact that:

> Groups negotiating their identity in contexts of domination and exchange persist, patch themselves together in ways different from a living organism. A community, unlike a body, can lose a central 'organ' and not die. All the critical elements of identity are in specific conditions replaceable: language, land, blood, leadership, religion. Recognized, viable tribes exist in which any one or even most of these elements are missing, replaced, or largely transformed. ...
>
> Metaphors of continuity and 'survival' do not account for complex historical processes of appropriation, compromise, subversion, masking, invention and revival. ...
>
> The related institutions of culture and tribe are historical inventions, tendentious and changing. They do not designate stable realities that exist aboriginally 'prior to' the colonial clash of societies and powerful representations. (Clifford, 1988: 338–339)

These problems are illustrated in the dilemma faced by speakers of Northern siNdebele in South Africa (Stroud, 2001). Although both Northern and Southern siNdebele coexisted as part of the Nguni group, only speakers of the latter had their language officially recognized under apartheid because they had accepted the offer of a homeland. This was the situation that was inherited by the new South African Government in 1994, so that Northern siNdebele speakers still found themselves excluded from any discussion of language rights. This led the Northern AmaNdebele National Organization (NANO) to lobby the government and the Pan South African Language Board (PANSALB) to have their language officially recognized. However, the call was rejected because, as one PANSALB executive explained (quoted in Stroud, 2001: 349, italics in original), 'we could not promote their case until we had clarity on whether Northern SiNdebele was a *separate language* from Southern SiNdebele'. As in Singapore's Speak Mandarin Campaign (discussed previously), where each dialect was not seen as a language, Northern siNdebele was considered a dialectal variant of Southern siNdebele, and until proven otherwise, could not be considered sufficiently important to warrant the status of a right.

As a result, Northern siNdebele speakers have to accommodate a rights discourse that 'views language as an essentially unproblematic construct – an identifiable ontological entity' (Stroud, 2001: 348). As Stroud describes it:

> NANO found itself in the position of having to argue that Northern SiNdebele was a language, which meant a grassroots investment in developing orthography, grammar and glossaries for school. The organization also developed grassroots strategies to demand the use of SiNdebele as a medium of instruction in primary education … In other words, the community have actively contested the original official classification of its language as a variant of a larger cluster of Ndebele languages. …
>
> The Northern SiNdebele case shows that marginal groups need to seize power over the discourses and representations of language that define them … . (Stroud, 2001: 349)

While Stroud does not himself emphasize this point, it seems clear that the activities involved in constructing an orthographic system for the language, in providing a grammar and glossaries, and in ensuring that the language can be used as a medium of instruction, all will lead to transformations in the language itself[6] (Cooper, 1989: 33; Wee, 2005). The language will necessarily undergo functional elaboration, codification and graphization (see also Blommaert, 2001: 137), since any language that is used as a medium of education or has its lexicon reflected in glossaries will have to undergo some degree of standardization, where there is pressure towards the elimination of otherwise informally tolerated linguistic variation (Milroy & Milroy, 1999). Furthermore, the pressure to present

Northern siNdebele as a language that is *equal to* but *distinct from*
Southern siNdebele will undoubtedly also encourage various linguistic
innovations that serve just this particular purpose of marking a different
group identity (compare Bucholtz & Hall, 2004: 385; King, 1994; Pullum,
1999: 44).

This kind of reinvention in and of itself is neither necessarily good nor
bad. The point that is worth noting, though, is this. The reinvention that
the Northern siNdebele speakers are engaged in here is a direct response
to the dictates of a rights discourse, which assumes that (i) only a language
(as opposed to a dialect) is worthy of being granted rights status, and (ii)
there exist clear and unambiguous criteria for the language–dialect distinction. Community resources are thus pooled specifically in order to
satisfy these assumptions.

Neutralization

With selectivity and reinvention, there is arguably a much greater
degree of agency available to rights petitioners since they can make
decisions – however constrained – regarding which language should be the
object of a right, and what kinds of efforts ought to go into making a case
for such a right. In contrast, neutralization draws attention to the limits
of agency, since despite any intention to restrict the tenure of a right, once
enshrined as such, the right becomes extremely difficult to dismantle. This
indicates another difference – a sequential one – between selectivity and
reinvention, on the one hand, and neutralization, on the other. The first
two precede the granting of a rights status, whereas the third is concerned
with what happens after this has been granted.

Returning now to the language conflict in Sri Lanka, when in 1956, a
new government under Solomon Bandaranaike was elected, this was on
the platform that Sinhala would serve as the official language of Sri Lanka.
Crucially, we should note that Bandaranaike's own commitment to the
Sinhalese cause was 'strategic'. According to Sowell:

> Like so many militant group leaders in other countries, Bandaranaike
> himself was not at all representative of those in whose name he spoke
> stridently. He was an Oxford-educated, Christian, Sinhalese aristocrat
> (his godfather was the British colonial governor), who grew up speaking
> English and unable to speak Sinhala. But, like some other Sinhalese poli-
> ticians of his time, Bandaranaike became Buddhist, Sinhala-speaking and
> an extremist on language, religion, and Sinhalese culture. His own goals
> were neither religious nor ideological. He wanted to be prime minister –
> and he succeeded. (Sowell, 2004: 85)

Thus, Bandaranaike's adoption of an extremist position on Sinhalese language and culture was purely driven by his desire to become prime minister. Once this goal had been achieved, he then set about trying to moderate his own anti-Tamil policies, 'but this only set off howls of protest from other Sinhalese demagogues with political ambitions of their own, including a future president, J.R. Jayawardene' (Sowell, 2004: 86). Bandaranaike was however quite intent on mitigating some of his extremist measures, and tried to put into place an accord with the Tamils. Tragically, this led to his assassination in 1959 by a Sinhalese Buddhist extremist who felt that this amounted to a betrayal of the Sinhalese cause (Sowell, 2004: 87).

If we compare Bandaranaike's stance with that of the LTTE (see previous), we see evidence from both sides of the civil conflict of how essentialist positions (Sinhala only, Tamil only) are adopted by political and military leaders in order to gain popular support in the struggle for rights on behalf of the Sinhalese and Tamil communities, respectively. Furthermore, proponents of these different positions are each victims of their own successes in that they are unable to moderate their respective platforms without the risk of losing their power base, since any such moderation would be vulnerable to the charge that it jeopardizes the very right that it is supposed to champion. In this way, once an essentialist position is intertwined with the discourse of rights, it then takes on a life of its own regardless of whether it was intended strategically or not. The reasons for this are fairly obvious. Neither groups and their members nor their cultural practices are ontologically fixed and homogenous entities, though a rights discourse treats them as such. But precisely by doing so, a rights discourse ignores the dynamic struggle for goods, services and privileges that results when a particular linguistic practice is given the status of a right.

For example, Bandaranaike's 'Sinhala only' policy gained popular support because it was seen as a response to a situation where Tamils were disproportionately represented in the upper echelons of Sri Lankan society. This policy therefore provided the rationale behind the implementation of preferences and quotas that limited the Tamils' education and employment prospects, and included allowing Sinhalese applicants to meet lower standards for university admission than their Tamil counterparts (Sowell, 2004: 86). The link between language and socio-economic privileges, predictably, meant that any attempt to loosen the connection would lead to protests from the Sinhalese. And of course, there is always the issue of different cohorts internal to the group. Not all Sinhalese benefit from the 'Sinhala only' policy in exactly the same manner or at the same time. Thus, while some may later on be willing to moderate the policy, others will still feel that they have not sufficiently been compensated to justify the policy's weakening or dismantling. Likewise, the declining socio-economic prospects for the Tamils triggered, in response, a strong pro-Tamil reaction. By the same token, there was an attempt by the LTTE to create, within its own autonomous regime, a connection between the Tamil language and socio-economic privileges. Again, predictably, any weakening of this connection becomes extremely difficult to achieve since it could lead to accusations from different cohorts within the Tamil community that the LTTE are losing their commitment to the very ideals that legitimized their ascendancy to political power.

The reason, therefore, why a rights discourse neutralizes the distinction between strategic and non-strategic essentialism is that groups and their members are not 'inert blocks of wood to be moved here and there according to someone else's grand design' (Sowell, 2004: 7–8). A rights discourse has the unfortunate effect of freezing group relations and privileges, while in reality, socio-cultural differences and inequalities are constituted by *ongoing and ever-changing processes* of struggle, as individuals *qua individuals* as well as *qua group members* strategically utilize available resources to maintain, enhance or transform their various life-chances.

Conclusion

We have seen that a rights discourse encourages essentialism by imposing sharp and rigid boundaries on cultural practices that are fundamentally at odds with their more fluid and dynamic nature. In short, a rights-based approach confines and restricts 'behavior, expression and identity to precisely the degree to which it protects them' (Ford, 2005: 90).

In the case of language practices, the notion of language rights is particularly problematic because, perhaps more so than other cultural practices, language is 'irreducibly dialectic in nature', 'an unstable mutual interaction of meaningful sign forms, contextualized to situations of interested human use and mediated by the fact of cultural ideology' (Silverstein, 1985: 220). Other cultural practices are by comparison relatively stable. For example, a prohibition against the consumption of pork or the wearing of a turban or cornrows, are practices that are fairly easy to distribute in a homogenous manner across all the relevant members of a group (notwithstanding the question of individual preferences). These practices involve a high degree of agency in that individual actors make conscious decisions about whether or not they wish to observe group restrictions concerning diet, dress or hairstyle. Consequently, changes in how these practices are observed are more easily detected, and are thus more amenable to discussions and debates regarding their acceptability both to the group itself and to the wider society. These practices therefore can constitute fairly clear boundaries that distinguish members from non-members. In contrast, language practices are extremely variable since control over lexicogrammatical resources and how these are used is highly dependent on the gender, status and age of individual members (Spolsky, 2004: 9), as well as the kinds of activities they engage in (Levinson, 1992). This means that language is never distributed uniformly across even what might be considered the same cultural group (since there will certainly be internal socio-cultural distinctions along the lines of gender, age, status, etc. and acceptable associated activities). And unless interaction between members and non-members is completely eliminated, some form of linguistic exchange – perhaps starting with code switching and resulting in fused lects (Auer, 1999)[7] – is also inevitable. Also, such exchanges can have subtle effects on speakers' communicative resources, effects that the speakers themselves may not be aware of nor consciously be able to control.[8] All of this makes it even more critical to appreciate that, among the different kinds of cultural practices, language is particularly unsuitable for enshrinement within a rights discourse.

Such a conclusion does not deny the critical role language plays in influencing the distribution of socio-cultural and economic resources (Heller & Martin-Jones, 2001: 2, 419). But what it does suggest is that treating language as a right tends to obscure the changing interests and needs of different individuals and groups, unduly favouring normative or identity-based claims (Deveaux, 2005: 343). This suggests that instead of a rights-based approach to language, it would be more feasible to aim for an approach that emphasizes 'strategies of negotiation and compromise' (Deveaux, 2005: 344), allowing speakers to draw attention to the ways in which social trajectories and cultural aspirations may be significantly influenced by a variety of language codes. Such an approach can be gleaned in the notion of linguistic citizenship (Stroud, 2001: 353, italics in original; also Stroud & Heugh, 2004) which 'denotes the situation where speakers themselves exercise control over their language, deciding *what* languages are, and what they may *mean*, and where language issues ... are discursively tied to a range of social issues – policy issues and questions of equity'.

In his elaboration of linguistic citizenship, Stroud (this volume) outlines an anti-essentialist stance, shifting focus away from 'groups' and 'people' (prominently emphasized by the linguistic human rights approach) to the transformative potential of collective actions and 'sociating' relationships, and in so doing, emphasizing the importance of 'voice'.[9] The grassroots level at which different collectivities begin to articulate and challenge hegemonic conceptions of the language, identity and institutional privilege nexus reminds us that relationships that exist between groups, as well as the practices that serve to materialize these relationships, are not always fluid. In this regard, the anti-essentialism of linguistic citizenship is not a celebration of unencumbered agency. Rather, it serves as a call to better understand how the co-constitutive nature of the relationship between language and social structure can open up or close down opportunities for democratic participation. A linguistic citizenship perspective thus valuably raises the question of how community members can find or create a platform from which their voices become heard. In this way, linguistic citizenship serves to confront the complexity involved in resource redistribution and status recognition while still recognizing the problematic status of what counts as a language. Citizenship has historically been an avenue by which a host of different issues (from economic rights to gender to sexuality) are thrown up for public discussion, and broadening the concept to issues of language, Stroud (2001: 347) suggests, can provide a platform for foregrounding 'the enormous political potential residing in the formulation of alternative and complex representations of identity and language that is waiting to be harnessed'. Linguistic citizenship is therefore concerned with debating '*the representations, practices and ideologies* of language and society that circumscribe communities of speakers in their everyday associational networks, or "sites of mediation"' (Stroud, 2001: 350, italics in original).

The need to open up spaces for such debates has been underscored by Deveaux (2005: 347, italics in original), who adopts the framework of deliberative democracy (Bonham, 1998; Dryzek, 2000), where:

> ... what is aimed at is a more *transparent* political process in which cultural group members can present some of their concerns about particular practices and arrangements, and these concerns and interests – and the normative justifications that may or may not attach – are then subject to critical scrutiny and evaluation in democratic processes of deliberation and negotiation. Political deliberations about the contested practices should aim to provide an accurate description of the *lived form* of contested cultural practices (for this is often precisely what is in dispute) as well as some account of what the concrete, practical interests of diverse participants are, and finally, should aim to generate negotiated political compromises.

An approach along the lines of linguistic citizenship and deliberative democracy[10] has the merit of allowing not just changing conceptions of languages, but is also better able to accommodate the fact that 'languages are inherently hybrid, grammars are emergent and communication is fluid' (Canagarajah, 2007: 233). In this regard, it is worth noting Deveaux's (2005: 351) suggestion that any deliberation ought to be bound by a principle of revizability (compare the earlier discussion of neutralization), which stresses that decisions that have been reached can always be revisited at a later point in time.

While the general idea of cultural rights remains a controversial one, the specific idea of language rights is especially problematic because the changing nature of language in its various social contexts is fundamentally at odds with the essentializing proclivities of a rights discourse, as demonstrated in the discussion on selectivity, reinvention and neutralization. Furthermore, unlike other cultural practices, language is particularly illiberal, since in *any* social activity some choice of code must be made, thus simultaneously privileging some groups of speakers and marginalizing others. This means that rather than treating language as a practice that can or should be enshrined as a right, it should instead be consistently treated as the target of debates and discussions that highlight its dynamic connections with the distribution of non-linguistic goods.

Retrospective

One of the concerns in my work on language rights has been to emphasize how much the discourse of language rights relies on the drawing of sharp boundaries, including boundaries demarcating named languages as unproblematically delimitable systems, and boundaries demarcating communities of speakers who are positioned as holders of rights regarding their traditionally affiliated languages. And as I have tried to show in my contribution to this volume (see Wee, 2011, for further discussion), such boundary marking is in no small part attributable to the fact that a rights-based discourse contains essentializing tendencies.

In recent years, interestingly, the momentum in much of current sociolinguistic and applied linguistic scholarship has been towards giving even more emphasis to the implications and problems associated with boundary marking, calling for a greater appreciation of the need to come to grips with what Weber and Horner (2012: 117) refer to as the 'fluid multilingual realities of today's world'. This is a multilingual fluidity that has been variously characterized as translanguaging (García, 2009), polylanguaging (Jørgensen, 2008), metrolingualism (Pennycook

& Otsuji, 2015), transidiomaticy (Jacquemet, 2005) and translingual practices (Canagarajah, 2013a, 2013b). This proliferation of terms is one indicator of the increased awareness of fluid language use, as scholars attempt to provide analyses of how resources from linguistic systems – otherwise conventionally demarcated by language names –are merged in ways that point to speakers' 'transformative capacity to mesh their resources for creative new forms and meanings' (Canagarajah, 2013a: 1–2).

The analytical focus of much of this work has been primarily on the domains of education and workplace communication, leaving unaddressed the implications of fluid multilingualism for the notion of language rights. In these works, it has been argued that such fluidity across language boundaries represents sociolinguistically natural behaviour, so that when speakers (whether at school or the workplace) are actually forced or obligated to stick only to the linguistic resources conventionally located within the boundaries of named languages, this is in fact an artificial constraint on their communicative practices.

In comparison with such domain-specific analyses, however, the broader and more general implications for language rights remain relatively unexplored. But if such multilingual fluidity is indeed sociolinguistically natural, then it becomes a highly relevant question to ask what kind of purpose might be served by the notion of language rights, especially if what this notion does is to impose artificial constraints on communication. And my argument in this chapter, of course, has been precisely that the languages rights discourse does make such impositions.

A not unexpected answer to the question might be that, in the face of fluid multilinguality, language rights provide speakers from ethnic minority communities with the necessary recourse to ensure the survival and continuity of their languages and cultures. But such a viewpoint brings us right back to problematic essentialist assumptions, since it is via change and adaptation that languages and cultures 'survive'.

Moreover, in the context of recent arguments about the need to be more cognizant of implications of superdiversity (Blommaert & Backus, 2013; Vertovec, 2007), it has become even more urgent than ever before that we ask how societal spaces can be linguistically managed into the ways that address the conditions of urban diversity and socioeconomic inequality (Hogan-Brun, 2012: 145). Superdiversity points to the exponential increase in situations where interactants from (dramatically) different social, cultural and linguistic backgrounds have to live, work and play together in relative harmony. Socioeconomic inequality requires linguistic adaptation on the part of all speakers, be they from minority or dominant cultures. Fostering conviviality and social cohesion under such circumstances requires a willingness to accept, and even treat as banal, boundary crossing rather than over-emphasizing boundary maintenance. The entrenchment of boundaries is thus not conducive to the development of adaptation, social cohesion or tolerance under conditions of superdiversity. Instead, what is necessary for a 'politics of togetherness' (Amin, 2012: 79) is an attitude that considers boundary crossing to not only be a matter of course, but something that might even be a desirable consequence of diversity; and more importantly, an attitude that adopts a knowingly reflexive outlook towards the fact that even as boundaries (linguistic and otherwise) are crossed or continue to be drawn and redrawn, they are fundamentally 'fictive' in nature (Slater & Ritzer, 2001: 266).

I would therefore suggest that phenomena, such as fluid multilingualism and superdiversity, only strengthen the arguments against essentialism and language rights rather than inviting us to reconsider entertaining them. At the same time, I am aware that a common response to the rapid pace of social changes and increase in diversity is to return to essentialist thinking (Wee, 2010). That is, essentialism is often difficult to displace precisely because there is a need for assurance or stability in how we navigate the social world, and the more complex the world becomes, the greater this need. Essentialism – in spite of, or perhaps because of, its discriminatory nature –provides for the user an uncomplicated if simpleminded guide as to the nature of the social world: how it is (or appears to be) and how it ought to be (or not to be). This, however, provides us with an understanding of why essentialism persists; it does not give us a reason to accept it.

In this regard, a more sophisticated alternative to language rights is linguistic citizenship. The sophistication of linguistic citizenship arises from its clear recognition of the fact that language use is inextricably tied to change and resemioticization. As Stroud explains:

> A notion of linguistic citizenship is thus attuned to the implications of multitude of identities, subject positions, and positions of interest that suggest reframing semiotic practices of citizenship away from a totalizing sense of language and toward such notions as *fracturedness, hybridity, partiality,* and *perspective.* Rather than the idea of language, central to linguistic citizenship are the notions of genre and multilingual repertoires. (Stroud, 2009: 209, italics in original)

It is this shift away from 'a totalizing sense of language and toward … fracturedness, hybridity, partiality and perspective' that more than ever before needs to be cultivated as societies become increasingly complex and diverse. And it is my conclusion that the adoption of a language rights discourse unfortunately shifts us instead in the wrong direction.

Notes

(1) Bucholtz's reference to 'attributes and behaviour' reflects a distinction between the kinds of qualities that a group may be said to possess and the activities that it engages in. In this paper, I use the terms *traits* and *practices* to make a similar distinction, but as a matter of expository convenience, where the distinction is not critical, I use *practices* as a cover term.

(2) Fraser (1997: 2) makes the same point when she notes that a criterial feature of the 'post-socialist condition' has been a shift in the nature of political claims from a concern with social equality to a concern with group difference (see also Taylor, 1994).

(3) May (2001: 117–118, following Kymblicka, 1995) proposes three kinds of rights: Self-government rights for national minorities, which include the possibility of secession; polyethnic rights for ethnic minority groups to protect cultural and linguistic differences; and special-representation rights for groups disadvantaged by prevailing political processes that limit their chances of effective representation. Self-government and polyethnic rights are intended to be permanent, while special-representation rights are temporary and no longer apply 'once the oppression and/or disadvantage has been limited'. The problem is that rights petitioners may want recognition of (their) rights without necessarily buying into the sub-distinctions and associated time frames. This is further complicated by the fact that the three kinds of rights are not mutually exclusive (May, 2001: 118). For example, an ethnic minority group that is economically disadvantaged may qualify for polyethnic as well as special-representation rights. But once economically successful (assuming the operational criteria for economic success are not themselves contested), the group (according to May) no longer qualifies for special-representation. However, convincing the group to give up this right is an altogether different matter.

(4) I am therefore not necessarily arguing against cultural rights *tout court*. Though I do have doubts about the feasibility of cultural rights in general, I am concerned in the present chapter specifically with language rights.

(5) Bucholtz and Hall (2004: 385) point out that authentication often involves 'the rewriting of linguistic and cultural history'. I am specifically concerned in this chapter with the kinds of rewriting demanded by a rights discourse.

(6) Spolsky (2004: 11) makes the same point when he observes that corpus planning activities and status planning activities are not easily separable from each other.

(7) Auer (1999) suggests that there is a unidirectional continuum from code switching to language mixing to fused lects. This progression is contingent in the sense that it is not necessary for the move from one end of the continuum to continue all the way to the other. The main difference, as Auer (1999: 321) points out, is between code switching and language mixing, on the one hand, and fused lects, on the other. The difference lies in the possibility of alternation. With code switching and language mixing, speakers still have the option of deciding whether or not to juxtapose elements from different varieties. With fused lects, speakers no longer have such an option; the drawing together of elements from erstwhile different varieties has stabilized to the point where it constitutes a grammatical obligation or constraint.

(8) Speakers who code switch are not always aware that they are doing so (Blom & Gumperz, 1972). A good example comes from Papua New Guinea (Kulick, 1992; Spolsky, 2004: 5), where adult speakers were unaware that their patterns of language use were slowly changing from monolingual Taiap towards code-switching between Taiap and the Tok Pisin brought back by younger men returning from work in distant plantations. Requiring speakers to constantly monitor their speech for violations of 'purity' (as in the Sri Lanka example discussed above) only impedes communicative fluency, which depends significantly on the use of routinized and formulaic expressions (Nattinger & DeCarrico, 1992; Wray, 2002).
(9) I thank an anonymous reviewer for highlighting this point.
(10) For further discussion of language issues in the context of deliberative democracy, see Wee (2010).

References

Amin, A. (2012) *Land of Strangers*. Cambridge: Polity Press.

Anderson, B. (1991) *Imagined Communities: Reflections On the Origins and Spread of Nationalism*. London: Verso.

Auer, P. (1999) From codeswitching via language mixing to fused lects: Toward a dynamic typology of bilingual speech. *International Journal of Bilingualism* 3, 309–332.

Barry, B. (2001) *Culture and Equality: An Egalitarian Critique of Multiculturalism*. Cambridge, MA: Harvard University Press.

Blom, J.-P. and Gumperz, J.J. (1972) Social meaning in linguistic structures: Code-switching in Norway. In J.J. Gumperz and D. Hymes (eds) *Directions in Sociolinguistics* (pp. 407–434). New York: Holt, Rinehart and Wilson.

Blommaert, J. (2001) The Asmara Declaration as a sociolinguistic problem: Reflections on scholarship and linguistic rights. *Journal of Sociolinguistics* 5 (1), 131–142.

Blommaert, J. and Backus, A. (2013) Superdiverse repertoires and the individual. In I. de Saint-Georges and J.-J. Weber (eds) *Multilingualism and Modality: Current Challenges for Educational Studies* (pp. 11–32). New York, NY: Springer.

Blommaert, J., Collins, J. and Slembrouck, S. (2005) Spaces of multilingualism. *Language & Communication* 25, 197–216.

Bonham, J. (1998) The coming of age of deliberative democracy. *Journal of Political Philosophy* 6 (4), 400–425.

Bourdieu, P. (1984) *Distinction: A Social Critique of the Judgment of Taste*. Cambridge, MA: Harvard University Press.

Bourdieu, P. and Passeron, J.-C. (1977) *Reproduction in Education, Society and Culture*. London: SAGE Publishing.

Bucholtz, M. (2003) Sociolinguistic nostalgia and the authentication of identity. *Journal of Sociolinguistics* 7, 398–416.

Bucholtz, M. and Hall, K. (2004) Language and identity. In A. Duranti (ed.) *The Blackwell Companion to Linguistic Anthropology* (pp. 369–394). Oxford: Blackwell.

Canagarajah, S. (2005) Dilemmas in planning English/vernacular relations in post-colonial communities. *Journal of Sociolinguistics* 9 (3), 418–447.

Canagarajah, S. (2007) After disinvention: Possibilities for communication, community and competence. In S. Makoni and A. Pennycook (eds) *Disinventing and Reconstituting Languages* (pp. 233–239). Clevedon: Multilingual Matters.

Canagarajah, S. (ed.) (2013a) *Literacy as Translingual Practice*. New York: Routledge.
Canagarajah, S. (2013b) Literacy and mobility: Toward pedagogies of traveling texts. Talk delivered at the Department of English Language and Literature, National University of Singapore, 21 August 2013.
Clifford, J. (1988) *The Predicament of Culture: Twentieth-Century Ethnography, Literature and Art*. Cambridge, MA: Harvard University Press.
Cobo, J.M. (1987) *Study of the Problem of Discrimination Against Indigenous Populations, Vol. 5*. UN doc.E/Cn.4/Sub. 2/1986-7/Add.4.
Cooper, R.L. (1989) *Language Planning and Social Change*. Cambridge: Cambridge University Press.
Cowan, J.K., Dembour, M.-B. and Wilson, R.A. (2001) Introduction. In J.K. Cowan, M.-B. Dembour and R.A. Wilson (eds) *Culture and Rights: An Anthropological Perspective* (pp. 1–26). Cambridge: Cambridge University Press.
Deveaux, M. (2005) A deliberative approach to conflicts of culture. In A. Eisenberg and J. Spinner-Halev (eds) *Minorities within Minorities: Equality, Rights and Diversity* (pp. 340–362). Cambridge: Cambridge University Press.
Dryzek, J.S. (2000) Discursive democracy vs. liberal constitutionalism. In M. Saward (ed.) *Democratic Innovation* (pp. 78–89). London: Routledge.
Fishman, J. (1973) Language modernization and planning in comparison with other types of national modernization and planning. *Language in Society* 2, 23–43.
Ford, R.T. (2005) *Racial Culture: A Critique*. Princeton: Princeton University Press.
Fraser, N. (1997) *Justice Interruptus: Critical Reflections on the 'Postsocialist' Condition*. London: Routledge.
Freeman, M. (2002) *Human Rights: An Interdisciplinary Approach, Key Concepts*. Cambridge: Polity Press.
Gal, S. and Irvine, J.T. (1995) The boundaries of languages and disciplines: How ideologies construct difference. *Social Research* 62 (4), 967–1001.
Garcia, O. (2009) *Bilingual Education in the 21st Century: A Global Perspective*. Oxford, UK: Wiley.
Heller, M. and Martin-Jones, M. (2001) *Voices of Authority: Education and Linguistic Difference*. Westport, Connecticut and London: Ablex Publishing.
Hobsbawm, E. (1990) *Nations and Nationalism Since 1780*. Cambridge: Cambridge University Press.
Hogan-Brun, G. (2012) Editorial: Language planning in urban spaces. *Current Issues in Language Planning* 13 (3), 145–147.
Jacquemet, M. (2005) Transidiomatic practices: Language and power in the age of globalization. *Language and Communication* 25, 257–277.
Jørgensen, J.N. (2008) Polylingual languaging around and among children and adolescents. *International Journal of Multilingualism* 5 (3), 161–176.
King, C.R. (1994) *One Language, Two Scripts: The Hindi Movement in Nineteenth-Century North India*. New Delhi: Oxford University Press.
Kulick, D. (1992) *Language Shift and Cultural Reproduction: Socialization, Self and Syncretism in a Papua New Guinean Village*. Cambridge: Cambridge University Press.
Kymlicka, W. (1995) *Multicultural Citizenship: A Liberal Theory of Minority Rights*. Oxford: Clarendon Press.
Levinson, S. (1992) Activity types and language. In P. Drew and J. Heritage (eds) *Talk at Work: Interaction in Institutional Settings* (pp. 66–100). Cambridge: Cambridge University Press. Originally published in *Linguistics* 17, 356–399.

May, S. (2001) *Language and Minority Rights: Ethnicity, Nationalism, and the Politics of Language*. London: Longman.

May, S. (2005) Language rights: Moving the debate forward. *Journal of Sociolinguistics* 9 (3), 319–347.

McElhinny, B. (1996) Strategic essentialism in sociolinguistics of gender. In N. Warner, J. Ahlers, L. Bilmes, M. Oliver, S. Wertheim and M. Chen (eds) *Gender and Belief Systems: Proceedings of the Fourth Berkeley Women and Language Conference* (pp. 469–480). Berkeley, CA: Berkeley Women and Language Group.

Milroy, J. (2001) Language ideologies and the consequences of standardization. *Journal of Sociolinguistics* 5 (4), 530–555.

Milroy, J. and Milroy, L. (1999) *Authority in Language* (3rd edn). London: Routledge.

Nattinger, J.R. and DeCarrico, J.S. (1992) *Lexical Phrases and Language Teaching*. Oxford: Oxford University Press.

Pennycook, A. and Otsuji, E. (2015) *Metrolingualism: Language and the City*. New York: Routledge.

Pullum, G. (1999) African American vernacular English is not standard English with mistakes. In R. Wheeler (ed.) *The Workings of Language: From Prescriptions to Perspectives* (pp. 39–58). London: Praeger.

Rogers, R. *et al.* v. Am. Airlines Inc. (1981) United States District Court for the Southern District of New York, 527 F. Supp. 229, 232.

Ryan, A. (1993) Liberalism. In R.E. Goodin and P. Pettit (eds) *A Companion to Contemporary Political Philosophy* (pp. 291–311). Oxford: Blackwell.

Silverstein, M. (1985) Language and the culture of gender. In E. Mertz and R. Parmentier (eds) *Semiotic Mediation* (pp. 219–259). New York: Academic Press.

Slater, D. and Ritzer, G. (2001) Interview with Ulrich Beck. *Journal of Consumer Culture* 1 (2), 261–277.

Sowell, T. (2004) *Affirmative Action around the World: An Empirical Study*. New Haven: Yale University Press.

Spolsky, B. (2004) *Language Policy*. Cambridge: Cambridge University Press.

Stroud, C. (2001) African mother-tongue programmes and the politics of language: Linguistic citizenship versus linguistic human rights. *Journal of Multilingual and Multicultural Development* 22 (4), 339–355.

Stroud, C. (2009) Towards a postliberal theory of citizenship. In J.E. Petrovic (ed.) *International Perspectives on Bilingual Education: Policy, Practice and Controversy* (pp. 191–218). New York: Information Age Publishing.

Stroud, C. and Heugh, K. (2004) Language rights and linguistic citizenship. In J. Freeland and D. Patrick (eds) *Language Rights and Language Survival: Sociolinguistic and Sociocultural Perspectives* (pp. 191–218). Manchester: St. Jerome Publishing.

Tamir, Y. (1993) *Liberal Nationalism*. Princeton: Princeton University Press.

Taylor, C. (1994) The politics of recognition. In A. Gutmann (ed.) *Multiculturalism* (pp. 25–74). Prince, NJ: Princeton University Press.

Turner, B. (1993a) Outline of a theory of human rights. *Sociology* 27, 485–512.

Turner, T. (1993b) Anthropology and multiculturalism: What is anthropology that multiculturalists should be mindful of? *Cultural Anthropology* 8 (4), 411–429.

Vertovec, S. (2007) Super-diversity and its implications. *Ethnic and Racial Studies* 30 (6), 1024–1054.

Waldron, J. (1993) Rights. In R.E. Goodin and P. Pettit (eds) *A Companion to Contemporary Political Philosophy* (pp. 575–585). Oxford: Blackwell.

Wallerstein, I. (1991) *Geopolitics and Geoculture: Essays on the Changing World System.* Cambridge: Cambridge University Press.

Weber, J.-J. and Horner, K. (2012) *Introducing Multilingualism: A Social Approach.* London: Routledge.

Wee, L. (2005) Intra-language discrimination and Linguistic Human Rights: The case of Singlish. *Applied Linguistics* 26 (1), 48–69.

Wee, L. (2010) *Language Without Rights.* Oxford: Oxford University Press.

Wee, L. (2011) *Language Without Rights.* Oxford: Oxford University Press.

Wray, A. (2002) *Formulaic Language and the Lexicon.* Cambridge: Cambridge University Press.

3 Commentary – Unanswered Questions: Addressing the Inequalities of Majoritarian Language Policies

Stephen May
University of Auckland

In his visceral and poignant critique of the 'savage inequalities' underpinning education in the United States, the American social commentator Jonathan Kozol (1991) makes a particularly telling observation, which I paraphrase here: The wealthy are always the first to deny to others the privileges that they themselves enjoy. I begin with this observation because it encapsulates, for me, the key concern with critical sociolinguistics' recent deconstruction of standardized languages in favour of the far more complex linguistic repertoires of multilingual speakers (with which I largely agree; see May, 2014) and the almost de rigueur dismissal, on that basis, of language rights (LR) for minoritized speakers (with which I do not; see May, 2012a). Both Stroud's and Wee's thoughtful and elegantly argued contributions reflect this prevailing dual consensus, and in my response to them I aim to disentangle, and problematize, the conjunction upon which it is predicated.

My principal point of disagreement with both contributions is in relation to their *unevenness*. To clarify, this is not a criticism of the quality of Stroud's and Wee's scholarship – which remains, as always, exemplary – but rather their *point of focus*. I will argue here that the ongoing deconstruction and dismissal of minority LR, for all its intellectual merits, has nonetheless specific and deleterious sociopolitical and educational consequences. Most notably, it reinforces or entrenches majoritarian language ideologies and related policy, both of which go largely unremarked and unexamined – an endorsement of the status quo ante, in effect. Relatedly, the dismissal of LR for minoritized language speakers leads, ironically, to the further entrenchment and reinforcement of the linguistic inequalities experienced by minoritized speakers, particularly in relation to their differential access to, and interactions in, the public or civic realm of nation-states, as well as in relation to their wider social and educational mobility. It seems to me that this is much like examining and critiquing the already poor and marginalized, along with the often highly negative effects of poverty, while ignoring, or at least understating, the social determinants that structure (though do not always determine) the everyday lives and experiences of impoverished peoples. Given the emancipatory concerns that so clearly underpin Stroud's and Wee's critical sociolinguistic accounts, particularly in their advocacy of linguistic citizenship (LC), this is a significant problem. In effect, the dismissal of LR ends up as a *post hoc* validation of existing linguistic 'hierarchies of prestige' (Liddicoat, 2013), something which, I will also argue, is not resolved or remediated by LC or the notion of deliberative democracy (DD) upon which it is based. Let me explain why. In what follows, I will, for reasons of space, focus primarily on Wee's arguments, drawing connections with Stroud's arguments where I can.

Beating the Minority Strawman

Since Frederik Barth's (1969) influential anthropological critique of ethnicity and related forms of social identity, a social constructionist consensus has emerged over the last 40 or so years that is quick to dispense with any claims to collective identities, along with a related rejection of the apparent fixity of such identities; equating both directly, as Wee does, with the politics of essentialism. This broad social constructionist position on identity – disavowing group identities as inherently determinist – is predicated on the plurality, complexity, fluidity and porosity of individual ones, a position akin to the wider promotion of hybridity, to which I will return shortly. It is perhaps best encapsulated by Rogers Brubaker's (2002) dismissive discussion of the problem of 'groupism'. Along with Barry (2001), Brubaker is particularly dismissive of the role of minority elites, who are seen to mobilize ethnicity (and, relatedly, language(s)) instrumentally to particular (self-interested) political ends. In so doing, these collective identities are often (re)constructed in arbitrary and artificial ways, leading to the process of 'reinvention' that Wee highlights. Both Wee's and Stroud's discussion of the artificial distinction between Southern and Northern siNdebele – with Northern siNdebele moving from a dialect of Southern siNdebele to a separate language, via a LR discourse – is a clear example of this retrospective process of linguistic reconstruction/reinvention.

But the siNdebele example also highlights the two key problems with this social constructionist consensus, which both Stroud and Wee uncritically and unreflexively endorse. The first is its disproportionate focus on minority group identities as the strawmen of ethnic/linguistic determinism. After all, *all* identities are socially constructed and, to some extent at least, fictive, even – and, perhaps, especially – majoritarian ones. National identities are a prime example here, given their historical recency, their construction, almost always *post hoc*, from the politics of nationalism, and their attendant, often deliberate, fabrications of historical memory: 'the rewriting of linguistic and cultural history' that Wee, citing Bucholtz and Hall (2004), highlights (see May, 2012a: Chapter 2 for an extended discussion). As the 19th-century French historian Ernest Renan has observed, for example, 'forgetting, I would even go so far as to say historical error, is a crucial factor in the creation of a nation' (1990: 11). And, of course, national identities, and the linguistic regimes that they impose on their citizens, are also highly selective, prescriptive, and exclusionary in relation to individuals, particularly those for whom the 'national' language is not their dominant language variety.

Which brings me to the second problem: The tacit acceptance of – and related failure to critique – the wider sociohistorical and sociopolitical context that often necessitates the political mobilization of linguistic minorities in the first place. Returning to the example of siNdebele, though this does indeed comprise elements of reconstruction/reinvention, it is no less so than the earlier construction/positioning of Northern siNdebele as a dialect – the result of impositional majoritarian forms of identity and related policies of linguistic hierarchies of prestige (à la Liddicoat), highlighted earlier. Indeed, the nation-state system is replete with examples of the artificial construction of 'national' languages and the related (re)positioning of minoritized language varieties as 'mere' patois or dialects, along with the negative social and educational consequences that ensue for their speakers.

Meanwhile, the role of elites in mobilizing collective identities for political ends is equally evident in majoritarian movements as it is in minority ones – one only has to think of the conception of the US promulgated by the current Trump presidency to see this trend encapsulated. Wee's discussion of Sri Lanka does capture this majoritarian/minoritarian duality to some extent (along with the sociohistorical and sociopolitical dynamics that result in changes from one to the other). But it also begs the question: If language discrimination against the Lankan Tamils (which was, in turn, linked to their wider political and economic exclusion) was a major catalyst of the longstanding civil war, why can't an LR approach that recognizes public multilingualism remediate this – *at least to some extent*? Indeed, this is precisely what seems to have occurred since the defeat of the Liberation Tigers of Tamil Eelam (LTTE) in 2009. The Sri Lankan government went on to establish the Lessons Learned and Reconciliation Commission in 2011. As a result of the Commission's recommendations, Sri Lanka is currently moving towards a formal trilingual state in Sinhala, Tamil, and English, with a particular focus on fostering greater bi/multilingualism in key public language domains (Herath, 2015).

One final point on the disproportionate focus on minorities in these accounts: The presumption, most evident in Wee's analysis, that the *validity* of a minority cultural, linguistic and/or political movement requires unanimity of support, and uniformity of intent, is never likewise applied (nor should it be) to majoritarian political movements or the (inevitably multifarious, and often fissured) communities they represent. This includes the right to dissent/dissensus and the related right of individuals to enter and exit such movements over time, as one might expect.[1] In short, heterogeneity, dissonance, and fluidity are features of *all* social groups and related movements. So why are these features only pathologized in relation to minority movements and their cultural, linguistic, and political aims? Moreover, it is not without considerable irony that to construct minority movements in this way necessarily entails both a totalizing and reductionist 'groupist' analysis, something that both Wee and Stroud purportedly aim to avoid.

Individualism, Agency and the Fetishization of Difference

And this brings me to the related issue of linguistic hybridity as the seemingly necessary counterpoint or counterbalance to the politics of linguistic determinism – a trope valorized and, at times, fetishized in recent critical sociolinguistic accounts that focus on individual multilingual repertoires (see e.g. Blommaert, 2010, 2013; Pennycook, 2010; Pennycook & Otsuji, 2015). As stated earlier, I do not demur substantively from these analyses (see May, 2014) – indeed, they are long overdue. However, I do want to problematize the presumption – also evident in Stroud's and Wee's accounts – that 'transgressive' translanguaging, and the related demolishing of language boundaries, is, by definition, both agentic and emancipatory, a trope of hybridity theory more broadly. This over-emphasizes the influence/impact of individual agency and under-emphasizes, or even simply ignores, the ongoing impact of structural constraints, particularly on the already most (linguistically) marginalized.

My key concern here, as Peter McLaren (1997) has argued of the academic championing of hybridity more broadly, is its 'flattening of difference' – that it presumes, in effect, that all choices are equally available, in this instance, to all multilingual interlocutors. But this is simply not the case since structural constraints often delimit choice(s) and do so differently for individuals, dependent on the social groupings within which they might be situated. Class, ethnic, and gender stratification, and related advantage/disadvantage, objective constraints, and historical determinations inevitably structure identity choices. Failing to address these differential factors puts me in mind of the sociologist Craig Calhoun's acerbic critique of cosmopolitanism – the championing of new global identities over so-called local and national identities – when he observes that it 'obscures the issues of inequality that make [such] identities accessible mainly to elites and make being a comfortable citizen of the world contingent on having the right passports, credit cards, and cultural credentials' (Calhoun, 2007: 286). By framing cosmopolitanism appeals to humanity in individualistic terms, he continues, 'they are apt to privilege those with the most capacity to get what they want by individual action' (Calhoun, 2007: 295).

A similar criticism applies to Stroud's and Wee's advocacy of LC, a form of DD, as the alternative to a LR framework. For a start, both LC and DD presume the relative equality of participants in democratic conversations, along with (as above) unfettered individual agency. Wee argues, drawing on Stroud's (2001: 353) summary of LC, for example, that it 'denotes the situation where speakers themselves exercise control over their language, deciding *what* languages are, and what they may *mean*, and where language issues … are discursively tied to a range of social issues – policy issues and questions of equity'.

While laudatory, this once again fails to account for the wider sociohistorical and sociopolitical conditions that inevitably precede/prefigure (and often confine) these choices. This is not to diminish the importance of agency and voice. Rather, it raises the question of the extent to which such agency and voice can actually achieve substantive change without simultaneously acknowledging and addressing systemic conditions and constraints. And, of course, even when it appears to do so – as Stroud's example of Afrikaaps highlights – there is, ironically, an implicit acknowledgement that the latter necessarily takes both *collective* effort and engagement over time to have any chance of doing so. What's more, such action requires a carving out of autonomous linguistic space (in this instance, from Afrikaans) and yet autonomy, particularly in Wee's account, is constructed as non-dialogic and inward looking, by definition.

To the contrary, autonomy, as many LR advocates argue, is a necessary precondition for a more *even* and *reciprocal* engagement with majoritarian linguistic groups, rather than the unidirectional (majority – minority) one that still so predominates worldwide, as the example of Afrikaaps rightly highlights.

Pathologizing Standardized Language Varieties

Finally, I want to problematize the pathologizing of standardized language varieties that is also a feature of both Stroud's and Wee's accounts. The argument here is that because oral multilingual repertoires are far more complex, fluid, and dynamic than any standardized language variety would allow, the latter can only be seen as yet another artificial linguistic construction and, thus, best avoided. In so doing, Stroud and Wee take particular aim at so-called mother tongue education programmes, arguing that these simply reinforce existing linguistic inventions, and hierarchies, rather than dismantling them. Makoni (2012) makes a very similar argument in relation to his dismissal of indigenous mother tongue education programmes in Africa as merely a vestigial feature of colonization and a further denial of indigenous emancipation rather than its validation. But, as I responded to Makoni at the time (May, 2012b), and it is a response that applies equally to Stroud's and Wee's accounts, this misses a key point: Access to standardized language varieties is pivotal to educational and wider social mobility, all the more important for those who are already linguistically (and educationally) marginalized. Thus, the question becomes which standardized language varieties best serve this purpose? In dismissing indigenous language education programmes, for example, and returning to the issue of the wider deleterious consequences of these arguments, indigenous peoples are once again denied access to any of their *proximal* language varieties in the education of their children. Instead, the *de facto* context of majoritarian language varieties as the only languages of instruction is simply reinforced. This, of course, also entrenches the ongoing colonization and cultural and linguistic (as well as social and political) disenfranchisement of indigenous peoples.

And this is why, for all the potential limitations of LR (and I have acknowledged them widely; see May, 2005, 2012a), I think Stroud and Wee are too hasty in dismissing them *tout court*. Indeed, the recognition of individual (private) multilingualism – again, a welcome development in itself – is not *necessarily* antipathetic to a concomitant recognition of public (communal) multilingualism, despite the inevitable attenuation of the complexities of actual multilingual use, in so doing (Busch, 2012;

May, 2017). Language diversity on the ground will always deconstruct standardized conceptions of languages, to be sure. But this should not, *ipso facto*, preclude the possibility of the public recognition of, and support for, minority languages that LR affords and that LC, for all its potential merits, has yet to prove it can achieve as effectively.

Note

(1) I do not have space to address further the issue of the 'right to exit' with which Wee and other sceptical commentators of minority movements are so concerned. However, I have discussed at length elsewhere how the distinction between 'external protections' and 'internal restrictions', outlined by the political philospher Will Kymlicka (1995, 2001), can remediate the charges of coercion and (potential) illiberality levelled at such movements (see May, 2012a: Chapter 3).

References

Barry, B. (2001) *Culture and Equality: An Egalitarian Critique of Multiculturalism.* Cambridge MA: Harvard University Press.

Barth, F. (1969) *Ethnic Groups and Boundaries.* Boston, MA: Little, Brown and Co.

Blommaert, J. (2010) *The Sociolinguistics of Globalization.* New York, NY: Cambridge University Press.

Blommaert, J. (2013) *Ethnography, Superdiversity and Linguistic Landscapes.* Bristol: Multilingual Matters.

Brubaker, R. (2002) Ethnicity without groups. *Archives Européènes de Sociologie* 53 (2), 163–189.

Bucholtz, M. and Hall, K. (2004) Language and identity. In A. Duranti (ed.) *A Companion to Linguistic Anthropology* (pp. 369–394). Malden, MA: Blackwell.

Busch, B. (2012) The linguistic repertoire revisited. *Applied Linguistics* 33 (5), 503–533.

Calhoun, C. (2007) Social solidarity as a problem for cosmopolitan democracy. In S. Benhabib, I. Shapiro and D. Petranovic (eds) *Identities, Affiliations, and Allegiances* (pp. 285–302). Cambridge: Cambridge University Press.

Herath, S. (2015) Language policy, ethnic tensions and linguistic rights in post war Sri Lanka. *Language Policy* 14 (3), 245–261.

Kozol, J. (1991) *Savage Inequalities.* New York, NY: Harper Perennial.

Kymlicka, W. (1995) *Multicultural Citizenship: A Liberal Theory of Minority Rights.* Oxford: Clarendon Press.

Kymlicka, W. (2001) *Politics in the Vernacular: Nationalism, Multiculturalism, and Citizenship.* Oxford: Oxford University Press.

Liddicoat A. (2013) *Language-in-Education Policies: The Discursive Construction of IIntercultural Relations.* Bristol: Multilingual Matters.

Makoni, S. (2012) Language and human rights discourses: Lessons from the African experience. *Journal of Multicultural Discourses* 7 (1), 1–20.

May, S. (2005) Language rights: Moving the debate forward. *Journal of Sociolinguistics* 9 (3), 319–347.

May, S. (2012a) *Language and Minority Rights: Ethnicity, Nationalism and the Politics of Language* (2nd edn). New York: Routledge.

May, S. (2012b) Contesting hegemonic and monolithic constructions of language rights 'discourse'. *Journal of Multicultural Discourses* 7 (1), 21–27.

May, S. (ed.) (2014) *The Multilingual Turn: Implications for SLA, TESOL and Bilingual Education.* New York, NY: Routledge.

May, S. (2017) National and ethnic minorities: Language rights and recognition. In S. Canagarajah (ed.) *Routledge Handbook of Migration and Language* (pp. 149–168). New York, NY: Routledge.

McLaren, P. (1997) *Revolutionary Multiculturalism: Pedagogies of Dissent for the New Millennium.* Boulder, CO: Westview Press.

Pennycook, A. (2010) *Language as a Local Practice.* New York, NY: Routledge.

Pennycook, A. and Otsuji, E. (2015) *Metrolingualism: Language and the City.* New York, NY: Routledge.

Renan, E. [1882] (1990) What is a nation? In H. Bhabha (ed.) *Nation and Narration* (pp. 8–22). London: Routledge.

Stroud, C. (2001) African mother tongue programs and the politics of language: Linguistic citizenship versus linguistic human rights. *Journal of Multilingual and Multicultural Development* 22 (4), 339–355.

Part 2

Educating for Linguistic Citizenship

4 Affirming Linguistic Rights, Fostering Linguistic Citizenship: A Cameroonian Perspective

Blasius A. Chiatoh
University of Buea

Introduction

Language plays a central role in the conceptualization and practice of the theories of democracy and citizenship, and policies that do not acknowledge minority languages invariably also impose the status of irrelevance and silence on their speakers. Those that suffer most from this situation are members of marginalized communities, that is, speakers of non-official mother tongues (Stroud, 2009: 191). In such settings, language planning, instead of strengthening the citizenship of the population, rather becomes an instrument of disenfranchisement and disempowerment. Through non-recognition and exemption of languages from mainstream communication, language policy application reinforces the vulnerability of their respective populations. Processes of educational empowerment operate solely in foreign official languages and socio-economic and political opportunities in the wider community are made available only in these languages. Speakers of non-official languages (generally reserved for the home and other personal/communal domains) are thus subjected to automatic exclusion. This deliberate choice of foreign official language policy practically lends legality to the deprivation of the agency and participation of these speakers and communities. From the perspective of public perception, its sustained application in the educational system and other domains clearly constitutes tacit formalization and normalization of marginality based on language.

In Cameroon, linguistic diversity and the question of linguistic identity, national belonging and citizenship are a living reality. Despite its numerous indigenous languages, the country operates an exclusive foreign official language policy based on English (for Anglophones) and French (for Francophones) for indigenous people. Also, notwithstanding constitutional recognition of the importance of promoting national languages as an aspect of national cultures, English and French enjoy the exclusive right of presence in education and all official spheres with national languages practically relegated to the background. Through this policy, applied since reunification (in 1961), the country has opted for systematic redefinition and reconstruction of its national cultural identity and consequently, the redefinition of its citizens' identities, sense of belonging and voice. In this chapter, I examine language planning and policy in Cameroon from the perspective of affirmation and promotion. I argue that in linguistically diverse environments, promotion of minority languages and respect for their speakers is best attained through a grassroots-based approach, that is, an approach that seeks to articulate a form of linguistic citizenship. I briefly discuss the role of government and other actors, such as non-government organizations (NGOs) in creating the conditions for such an approach.

Background Information

Multilingualism is commonly acknowledged as a norm in Africa (Makoni & Trudell, 2009; Wolff, 1999). An outstanding feature of this multilingualism is inequality observed in the sizes and status of languages in the nation. While in some countries, all indigenous languages are treated simply as minority languages, thus depriving them of official status, in others, some of the languages, by virtue of their numerical strength, are recognized as dominant languages and so assigned official status. Quite often, though, the important dividing line is drawn between dominant foreign official languages and minority-dominated indigenous languages, even if sometimes, foreign official languages are actually spoken only by a small minority of the overall national population on a daily basis. In Cameroon, despite the fact that three of the approximately 250 languages, namely Pidgin, Beti-fang and Fulfulde, are spoken by fairly large numbers of speakers, they have not been recognized as majority languages. This perception has promoted government officials and even some linguists to conclude that a national official language (NOL) for Cameroon is unnecessary – a position that Nanfah (2006) rightly dubs as 'a policy of resignation'. For this category of Cameroonians, English and French should be the only official languages because there is no national language that is representative enough to serve official functions. In reality, though, it must be noted that a large majority of the country's languages are spoken by fewer than 100,000 people, as seen in Table 4.1, from Rosendal (2008: 17).

Given the complexity of the situation and the ambition of language planning to provide the best or optimal, most efficient and most valuable alternative solutions to solving language problems (Rubin & Jernudd, 1971), making appropriate choices of languages for use in specific domains becomes highly problematic. The colonial legacy left behind does not make matters any easier. In Cameroon, addressing the question of multilingualism from the perspective of language planning models necessitates making distinctions at three levels. First, we must choose between the two foreign languages (English and French) as to which of them should play which functions in official communication. Although seemingly easy, this is no easy matter to handle because, despite constitutional provisions for the equality in status of both languages, French practically enjoys *de facto* supremacy over English by virtue of the large size of its speakers. Evidence of the seriousness of the matter comes from the fact that Cameroon is quite often referred to simply as a Francophone country. And on the ground, there is much concrete evidence to support this, especially when one considers the country's linguistic preferences with respect to official documents and in vital domains, such as governance, economy, education, mass media, and military training and command. Over the years, this linguistic inequality has led to tacit discrimination and marginalization of Anglophones, with the result being the development of strong anti-francophone sentiments among the latter. The inability to bring about balanced recognition of the two official languages has contributed to fuelling demands for a return to the pre-reunification arrangement that should

Table 4.1 Number of national languages in Cameroon and number of speakers

Group	Number of speakers	Number of languages
1	<1000	38
2	1000–10,000	117
3	10,000–100,000	97
4	100,000–700,000	16
5	No number given	11
Total		279

culminate in the acquisition of independence and autonomy for Anglophones (Chiatoh, 2006: 146).

Second, there is the need to differentiate between the foreign official and national languages as to which of them should be assigned privileged status in official communication. Since 1961, with the reunification of English and French Cameroons, the solution to this problem has been the adoption of a foreign official language policy and the *ipso facto* relegation to the background of national languages. But, as hinted earlier, this solution has proven to be counter-productive. Neither official language speakers nor national language users appear satisfied with the alien identities that the present official language policy imposes on citizens.

Third, there is the question of choosing from among Cameroon's many languages, which should become the NOL(s). The problem here is the fear of the domination of one or more national languages over others, particularly the very extreme minority ones. It appears that most citizens support neutral languages, thus their preference for English and French. There are those who are of the opinion that no matter which national language(s) is chosen, this choice will be far more appropriate than relying entirely on foreign languages. Proponents of this view hold that languages, such as Pidgin, Beti-fang and Fulfulde, enjoy wide enough use to be raised to the status of official languages. In fact, they are used in at least three regions (provinces), and are also widely spoken across the national boundary. Opponents of this view fear the eventual domination of these languages over the rest of the languages. Their fears are buttressed by endemic political ethnicization and tribalization orchestrated by successive administrations.

With this reality, linguistic and cultural diversity is equated with linguistic complexity and so viewed as a problem rather than a resource (Ruiz, 1984) in national development planning. Public and private authorities find a perfect comfort zone in foreign languages, which, piecemeal, become the ideal mediums of official communication. In this way, issues of identification and democratic participation are forfeited fairly quickly with the adoption of a foreign official language policy for native populations. However, what the policy creates is inherent exclusion based on language. This foreign official language policy has created unimaginable levels of inequalities with respect to power, opportunity and rights distribution. The mastery of foreign languages constitutes the gateway to opportunity, while national languages represent different forms of deprivation and rejection. Clearly, the policy is one that promotes counter-values, and, as such, is basically responsible for inequalities and the lack of the spirit of belonging among citizens, frustration and other ills that plague our society. This situation surely accounts for the inability of people in this country to engage in democratic participation. We see, then, clearly how the parameters of national language planning models constrain the terms in which remedies can be sought and choices of language made.

The challenges faced by national language planning models are aggravated by the mobility, fluidity and 'linguistic fall-out' of modernity, and the inability of the planning models to cope with such fluidity. For example, we have today a new generation of children in urban centres, who although bilingual in the foreign official language or languages (here used in contrast to the much-desired NOLs) and possibly an urban lingua franca, are growing up with no indigenous mother tongue, that is, they have only English or French as their first language (Chiatoh, 2012: 6; Tadadjeu, 1998: 3). These children come either from families where parents do not share a common language, or those who share a common language but, because of the perceived prestige of the foreign official language, discourage the use of an indigenous language at home. Quite often, these are very highly educated parents, but occasionally too we have averagely educated parents who, for the same reasons, are unfavourable toward an indigenous language as the home language. Even among families that use a national language at home, there is still a growing number of children who look down on their national language (Bitjaa Kody, 2001: 100–124). Even if the last situation pertains only to a tiny minority of the national population, and so constitutes an exception rather than a rule, it does, all the same, represent a potentially dangerous twist in the life of the nation. In fact, even if there are no indications that the exception will some day become the rule (Tadadjeu, 1998: 4), it is abnormal for a country to remain indifferent to such a phenomenon. In a survey conducted in 2010 among incoming students in the Department of Linguistics at the University of Buea, 32 out of 160 students (19.9%) had only a foreign language as their mother tongue. This is certainly not a negligible percentage.

In other words, the complex, dynamic and shifting multilingual repertoires of Cameroonians undermine the search for easy solutions in models of national language planning. Instead of enhancing peaceful coexistence between and among cultures, language planning models in such an ambivalent situation only prepares – even 'populates' – the stage for identity conflicts that often culminate in incredible levels of frustration. In fact, since reunification in 1961, the implementation of the English–French bilingual policy has resulted in systematic polarization of the country. First, its implicit preference for French and the reduction of English to a minority second-class language has led to serious divisions and frictions between Anglophones and Francophones. In addition, the total exclusion of national languages from official communication domains particularly in education has created an additional dimension of polarization with the national versus foreign official language dichotomy. Here, we have what Rubagumya (2007: 7) dubs 'three-tier citizenship'. In Rubagumya's view, in terms of language repertoire, it is possible to distinguish three types of citizens, viz. global citizens, local citizens and semi-citizens. According to him, global citizens are those who have access to English and, in the Tanzanian case, Kiswahili. They are global citizens because of their ability to communicate with the outside world and their access to internal jobs, thanks to their mastery of English. Local citizens on the other hand are those who have access to Kiswahili and to one or more ethnic languages. They can participate in many socio-economic and political events transacted in Kiswahili. As for semi-citizens, they have access neither to English nor to Kiswahili. These are citizens who can only function in domains where an ethnic community language is in use. The three-tier theorization fits squarely into the Cameroonian situation, except that in the place of Kiswahili, we may have one or the other of three languages of wider communication (LWC), namely, Pidgin, Beti-fang and Fulfulde, as highlighted earlier on. There is thus a major problem of meeting the challenge of mainstreaming identities in a society that is linguistically polarized in more ways than one. With the entrenched discrimination and marginalization that this entails, there is a deep-rooted feeling of inferiority and exclusion among speakers of less privileged languages, especially given that no single Cameroonian language enjoys official status at the present moment. Furthermore, whatever solution is chosen, the risk is that the way language issues are formulated in national language planning models and the limited range of remedies sought will continue to trouble the exercise of voice and participation of many speakers of so-called minority languages, even while they impose or create differentially valued hierarchical identities.

Conceptualizing Linguistic Diversity

Given the above, the way forward would appear to be an approach with some form of official recognition of linguistic diversity and multilingualism. Thinking about diversity of a resource provides a starting point for rethinking how democratic participation and voice may be enhanced through language policy or activism. For example, the Sapir-Whorf hypothesis postulates that the structure of a language determines the way in which speakers of the language perceive the world (Wardhaugh, 2002: 220). A weaker version of this hypothesis is that the structure of language does not determine the world-view, but still remains extremely influential in predisposing the speakers of a language toward adopting a particular world-view. In line with this view, Jiang observes that:

> It is commonly accepted that language is a part of culture, and that it plays a very important role in it. Some social scientists consider that without language, culture would not be possible. Language simultaneously reflects culture, and is influenced and shaped by it. In the broadest sense, it is also the symbolic representation of a people, since it comprises their historical and cultural backgrounds. (Jiang, 2000: 328)

From a philosophical perspective, Jiang holds that language and culture makes a living organism with language being the flesh and culture the blood. In this connection, without culture, language would be dead and without language, culture would have no shape. Also well documented is the fact that human society is essentially multilingual in nature (Starkey, 2002: 9), and therefore potentially rich in different 'world views'. Without necessarily subscribing to the somewhat 'essentialist' assumptions underlying these organic formulations of language and culture, we are nevertheless able to acknowledge that linguistically mediated *perspective* and *voice* are essential dimensions of deliberative democracies, systems of governance where citizens deliberate on the best way forward on political matters. Stroud reminds us:

> Language, from the perspective of Linguistic Citizenship, is both the means and the target for democratic 'effort', and multilingualism is both a facilitative and constraining factor in the exercise of democratic citizenship and voice. In particular, it takes linguistic diversity and difference as a prime means (rather than a problem) for material realization of democracy. It recognizes the manifold sites and the many linguistic practices through which citizenship is managed, attempting to account for the way both local and transnational solidarities are built across categorical identities through interpersonal negotiation in multi-scaled spaces (fluid political identities, broad alliances, and so forth). (Stroud, 2009: 208–209)

If diversity is a prerequisite for a truly participative and deliberative democracy, it follows that *not* acknowledging diversity is tantamount to denying voice and participation of difference. Proper appreciation of national linguistic resources thus critically determines the manner of perception and mobilization for (deliberative) democratic participation, which, in turn, influences the cultivation of democratic citizenship. If linguistic diversity is understood as the presence of more than one language in society, then the exploitation of this diversity in creating real opportunities for 'voice' becomes a major priority. Insights into these issues necessitate profound understanding of the interrelationships between the concepts of linguistic rights and participatory citizenship within the perspective of national development.

Thus, if language is a crucial variable in national development, this is essentially because of its role in providing the resources for the articulation of voice and the exercise of participatory citizenship within (and across) specific territorial boundaries. Since languages necessarily have speakers or users, processes of citizenship cultivation unquestionably call for adequate recognition and strengthening of the voices of different language speakers. Put differently, it is hard to imagine that citizens who are deprived of their daily modes of communication can freely belong, enjoy full rights and privileges and be truly dutiful towards the nation. In complex linguistic environments, this implies paying serious attention to the language factor in the definition and harnessing of citizenship for democratic practice. Starkey contends:

> Language is one of the most important social and cultural markers of identity and the international community in its essence is multilingual. Although relations between language and communities can be a source of tension within and between nations, the achievement of equality in multilingual communities is a demonstration of the possibility of success of democracy and may be considered exemplary of the very essence of democracy. (Starkey, 2002: 9)

What Starkey is saying here is that democratic activity becomes a legitimate practice and the concrete expression of rights and citizenship within the nation. The modern nation should uphold democratic citizenship, here understood as active citizenship, in all efforts geared towards broadening the scope of participation, in linguistically diverse contexts. Full active participation also entails tolerance and accommodation of differences, particularly linguistic and cultural differences, as the foundation for recognition and respect of linguistic rights of citizens on grounds of mainstream and minority language identification. Starkey warns:

> Issues of language, identities and participation are common to policies for the teaching of and learning both of languages and of democratic citizenship. Central to both is an awareness of and concern for human rights as a legal and ethical basis for citizenship and for education. (Starkey, 2002: 9)

In respect of the above, recognition and respect of linguistic human rights and democratic citizenship is crucially linked to the status and use of languages (Skutnabb-Kangas & Phillipson, 1995). With respect to the role of multilingualism in providing access to voice and agency, we must determine whether or not citizens enjoy the rights and opportunities to fully belong and to what extent they are capable, in their exercise of these rights, of influencing the processes of socio-economic and political evolution.

Accordingly, marginalization and voice deprivation are, by and large, essentially linguistic issues, since they constitute the basis of violation or affirmation of a true participatory citizenship.

However, citizenship becomes quite debatable especially in situations where linguistic diversity becomes a handy tool for the perpetuation of exclusion and marginalization. This is the case, as we have seen, for citizens in multilingual environments characterized by extreme minority languages, since the distinction between majority and minority linguistic statuses in itself already constitutes the basis for inequalities between different language speakers. Power and rights distribution tends to follow the direction of mainstream languages so that minority groups are subject to *de facto* exemption in the national development effort. In the light of the above, hegemonic policies, because they militate in favour of the unchallenged monopolistic presence of foreign languages in multilingual spaces, basically constitute the sources of imbalanced distribution of rights, opportunities and obligations, and so are fundamentally undemocratic. How, for instance, can people whose visibility and voice have been neutralized be expected to constitute the nexus for the achievement of national unity? The result is that today, honesty compels us to admit that, despite the dismissal of national languages, the achievement of peace and unity is more of an illusion than a reality. In fact, the foreign official language policy constitutes the very foundation on which exclusion and deprivations are exacted. Certainly, such exactions, because they perpetually deepen the wounds of discrimination and separation, can never guarantee peace and unity. People are discriminated against because they speak either English or a dispreferred indigenous language. Even more important is the fact that schools serve as sites for the construction of exclusive foreign identities and values.

This means that language policies that constrain participation in democratic processes of citizens, who have as their most effective mode of communication a national language, are basically anti-citizenship, and so highly questionable. In other words, since the users of foreign languages in minority settings always constitute a small fraction of the overall national population, it is clearly doubtful that a process that is essentially intolerant to non-foreign languages can ever be said to be truly democratic. Arguably, in minority contexts, language planning is a perfect enterprise for managing linguistic diversity and promoting democratic practice through careful management of differences as the platform for dismantling inequalities and enabling citizens to find their voices in matters of public policy. It requires a re-examination of existing policies, indeed, a determination of the degree to which these policies facilitate and guarantee the promotion of equality, membership acceptance and balanced rights, privileges and obligations. This is the basis for mutual recognition and acceptance, indeed, the foundation for the construction of social cohesion. However, the national foreign language policy is actually the outcome of a particular language planning model (based in a nation-state paradigm) that provides particular affordances and constraints for what 'remedies' are possible. This model in turn is based on the (colonial) premise that the best way to ensure unity is to silence alternative voices (as Stroud notes in the introduction of this volume).

There is thus the need for revision and reformulation of language policies and practices with emphasis on linguistically mediated voice and agency for an active participatory citizenship in the enterprise of national development. It means adopting policies that fundamentally break the tradition of imposed invisibility and silence of minority groups through the rejection of their linguistic wealth (Stroud, 2009).

Language Revitalization and the Survival of Linguistic Citizenship

Given the inadequacy of an exclusive foreign language planning model, it is clear that, for any policy to fully cater for the issue of participatory citizenship in minority language settings, it must have as its starting point the minority languages of the communities, since it is these languages that give them their identities and confer on them legitimate rights of voice. Thus, we have argued for the importance of enhancing linguistic diversity. The multilinguality of voice has also been discussed, and its importance for democratic deliberation and the sharing of perspective noted. Therefore, as a process that is committed to developing and upgrading the status and functions of hitherto unwritten languages, language planning ought to be essentially concerned with capturing 'voice'. In the same vein, language endangerment and loss are crucially linked to the endangerment of linguistic and citizenship rights, in fact, even birth-rights as McCarty opines:

> ... language loss and revitalization are human rights issues. Through our mother tongue, we come to know, represent, name, and act upon the world. Humans do not naturally or easily relinquish this birthright. (McCarty, 2003: 2)

If language loss is essentially a human rights issue in the sense that it orchestrates the forsaking of unique minority identities, then language revitalization is empowerment of these rights. In this way, revitalization of language can be seen as a semiotic resource for the (re)construction of agency and self-representation, an economic resource and site of political and economic struggle (Lim & Ansaldo, 2007: 7), rather than blowing new life into 'a language' only. In short, revitalization is the only hope for survival of identities and the maintenance of diversity (Abbi, 2004: 9). In Cameroon, government attitude towards language revitalization has been one of laissez-faire and laissez-aller, so much so that revitalization activities have been undertaken mainly by NGOs, and to some extent by individual researchers. There needs to be a more concerted effort at all levels to ensure that language planning, of which revitalization is a vital component, is focused on mechanisms for ensuring respect and promotion of 'alternative voices'.

This position does not in any way suggest the sufficiency of indigenous languages for participatory citizenship. Far from it; any such suggestion would be too limited and inappropriate in the sense that it is neither realistic nor desirable for anyone in a situation of linguistic diversity to claim the right to a single identity and use of just one language. Rather, as Stroud (2001) points out, affiliative and broad networks are the order of the day in multilingual societies – as situations demand. In light of this, a most acceptable alternative language planning model of linguistic citizenship is one that empowers minority language speakers to re-appropriate their linguistic rights as a starting point towards fostering active citizenship. The model should recognize and tolerate linguistic differences among individuals and communities within the nation. But even this is not sufficient from the point of view of linguistic citizenship.

Ways Forward

Over the past several decades, it has become clear that countries that function principally through foreign official languages suffer an enormous democratic deficit. With progress in applied linguistic research, coupled with growing national consciousness on the matter and global pressures, most governments now recognize another alternative to the foreign official language model, that is, the mother tongue-based bilingual approach – an approach that recognizes the mother tongues or first languages of learners as indispensable resources in the learning of another or other languages. In some situations, this self-realization has been accompanied by public and private input into the language planning enterprise. Regrettably, though, the recognition of alternative planning seems to mean different things to different countries with different historical backgrounds, especially with regard to colonial history. In former British colonies, government attitude towards national languages is largely positive. This can probably be explained by the fact that the British operated an Indirect Rule policy that encouraged the use of local languages in schools (Mba & Chiatoh, 2000: 1–21; Todd, 1983: 162–171). Generally speaking, these countries have made significant progress towards democratization. With respect to French former colonies, the attitude has, until recently, been quite hostile, except perhaps, with predominantly Muslim countries in West and North Africa. The situation is even worse in the so-called Communauté Economique et Monétaire de l'Afrique Centrale (CEMAC) zone, otherwise known in English as the Central African Economic and Monetary Union, which visibly still holds the vestiges of colonization. In this part of the continent, we have some of the highest levels of mental colonization and cultural erosion. Evidently, it is in these countries that we find the least commitment towards positive democratic evolution and respect for human rights. With language policies and practices that are essentially dismissive of national languages, these countries are certainly not the best environments for the promotion of citizenship based on linguistic diversity, democratic practices and legitimate cultural identity construction. In this connection, Stroud cautions:

> Linguistic citizenship refers predominantly to a view on language and politics that recognizes the manifold challenges posed by late modern contexts of migration and multilingualism for democracy and voice and takes as a central point of departure the desirability of constructing agency and maintaining voice across media, modalities, and context. (Stroud, 2009: 208)

Stroud's contention clearly enlightens us on the necessity to recognize the important interrelationship between linguistic citizenship and politics, which must acknowledge not only the need to accommodate and promote linguistic citizenship, but also to admit the many challenges that migration and democracy exact on voice. As such, no matter how linguistically complex the context of application may be, democratic citizenship discourses must pay special attention to the role of language in defining the identity of a nation. In situations of linguistic diversity, a 'rights-based' approach to participatory citizenship implies empowerment of people and communities on the basis of language and educational choices. Democratic citizenship thus acknowledges the relationship between citizenship and freedom of participation in democratic activity. This, in my opinion, should involve the following considerations.

(1) Free choice and equality of opportunity with respect to language and education.
(2) Sensitiveness to and respect for all issues of individual and collective identification, belonging and full participation.
(3) Official recognition and promotion of minority linguistic resources as the primary ingredients of broad-based identification and active participation.
(4) Recognition and facilitation of language policy and planning as an integral part of the processes of democratization and development.

What we should emphasize here is the need for any such anti-hegemonic language planning to carefully consider the place of schooling in designing language policies and citizenship promotion. Even if in most cases schools have failed to ensure the promotion of citizenship ideals, they nevertheless remain the most appropriate sites for such promotion. This argument is very well captured by Winstead as follows:

> Schools, in the form of educational instruments of state, have historically taken on the role as purveyors of citizenship ideals, however, they and their state sponsors have been remiss in providing for 'additive' inclusion and participation of these potentials. (Winstead, 2007: 335)

The situation Winstead deplores here is quintessentially African. Although African schools have arrogated upon themselves the responsibility of providing citizenship education, they have proven unable to ensure active citizenship through full integration and sustained use of the languages of minority groups. It follows, therefore, that there must be a corresponding process of revitalization of dispossessed minority languages. These languages should be systematically led to regain and ensure maintenance of their viability and vitality within multilingual market spaces.

What this implies is that current language planning initiatives in Cameroon should be perceived as central processes in the reaffirmation and the fostering of linguistic citizenship.

In fact, the educational system – the ideal site for the cultivation of a culture of democratic citizenship – rather than affirming and empowering citizens for active participation, instead lays the groundwork for intolerance and non-accommodation of difference. Expectedly, the consequence of such policies and practices can only be systematic exclusion and marginalization of minority groups.

An (educational) politics of language rooted in the mother tongue is thought to provide the ideal framework for multilingual identities that enable citizens to enjoy rights and privileges and so become more dutiful to societal demands. Such approaches often build on the recognition that in multilingual settings, our mother tongue is a key component of our personal, social and cultural identity (Krumm, 2004: 64). In other words, in such societies, monolingual identities are insufficient in conferring on citizens their rights, privileges and obligations. Rootedness in an indigenous mother tongue and the mental and behaviour patterns connected with this language, instead of serving as the grounds for intolerance and foreignness (Krumm, 2004: 67), actually constitute the foundation for mutual acceptance and tolerance. People, who have learnt to value their own identities, are not only more successful in learning about the values of others, but are also successful admitters and accommodators of differences that such learning entails. Practical experience points to the tendency for people to be more tolerant towards known people and values than unknown ones. The same should happen to the learning of languages and learning through languages. In promoting linguistic citizenship in linguistically diverse environments, therefore, we must bear in mind the necessity for the recognition of multiple identities and opportunities as the cornerstone of active citizenship.

In the next section, I review an attempt to develop an affirmative politics on the basis of educational language rights pointing out some of the shortcomings. In particular, I note that the model is built on the idea of recognizing the different *identities* thought to be layered into different languages. I note also that such a model is not *transformative* in the sense of linguistic citizenship in that it does not break with the idea of linguistically mediated identity as a founding principle. I then move on to discussing how such a model could take a step closer to a transformative design by introducing more languages and thus emphasizing multilingualism and affiliative links between speakers of different languages, and by shifting the process of educational language planning away from a top-down mode (reliant on traditional notions of planning such as identity) towards a more participatory and grass-roots approach.

Language Planning and Citizenship: A Cameroonian Perspective

From the preceding discussion, it is evident that in multilingual societies, exclusive foreign language policies directly infringe on the rights and citizenship of those who, on a daily basis, operate, for the most part, using national languages. For these individuals and communities, language development implies the (re)affirmation of threatened and/or lost minority voice. Over the past three decades, the need has arisen to reframe discourses on language, cultural identity and rights-based education as an alternative to the foreign official language approach. The question has and continues to revolve around potential challenges involved in promoting sustained learning in essentially minority tongues. Despite general agreement on the insufficiencies of an exclusive foreign language policy consensus is yet to be achieved on the need for, and practicalities of, national language promotion. In fact, even within linguistic circles, there is no common agreement on the best possible model. In this section, I present the model that has been experimented since 1981 and highlight proposals for restoring a multilingual culture.

The model experimented and proposed for Cameroon recognizes the inevitability of multilingualism and multicultural practices in public spaces. Known as *bilinguisme identitaire* or the identity bilingualism model (Tadadjeu, 1998), this model acknowledges, a priori, the centrality of indigenous mother tongues in the definition of the identities and rights of citizens. It recognizes the mother tongue as the expression of the child's natural identity, indeed, their cultural identity card (ID) that reflects their uniqueness and so should unarguably serve as the basis of their rights recognition and promotion. It acknowledges the pertinence and indispensability of national languages in balancing the bilingual equation. In the classroom, the first language of instruction is an indigenous mother tongue, to which is added the first official language (OL1), which the child discovers progressively. It is opposed to the official language bilingualism model, which acknowledges only the promotion of English and French. With this new orientation, it is no longer proper to make reference to bilingualism in Cameroon without qualifying it as either 'identity' or 'official language'. Conceived within the framework of the Operational Research Program for Language Education in Cameroon (PROPELCA), the model seeks to demonstrate, among other things, that the choice of language policy has serious implications on the manner in which citizens are integrated into decision-making processes and that the current policy, owing to its hegemonic nature, is inappropriate for the country. However, this model, though positive towards national language identity, has its own limits. First, it recommends an early-exit approach to mother tongue education, where the use of national languages as mediums of instruction ends in the third grade, thereby, giving way for official languages for the rest of the cycle as observed in Table 4.2. This is contrary to the findings of a great deal of empirical research (e.g. Collier & Thomas, 2004) that find seven years of mother tongue instruction to be the more optimal alternative.

In the identity bilingual model, we see that in Grades one and two, the mother tongue serves as the medium of instruction, the most appropriate way of ensuring identity and rights promotion, but very quickly gives way to the official language. Besides, we observe that while in Grade One, the time allocation for the L1 is 75%, while that for OL1 in Grade Seven is 85%. This is an indication that the role of the OL1 is much more important than that of the L1. An important clarification here is that unlike in 1981, when the primary cycle consisted of seven years, today it is limited to just six years. Theoretically, this means the disappearance of the 15% of the time allowed for L1 learning and so the need for revision of the time allocations. The situation is further compounded by the fact that since 2000, foreign official language bilingualism is being reinforced with the compulsory teaching of the second foreign official language (OL2), that is, French for Anglophones and English for Francophones. Even if its implementation is not yet effective, this clearly points to un-preparedness, on the part of educational authorities, to endorse bilingual education based on the mother tongues of learners (MLE) planning and citizenship enforcement model for the country. MLE enhances learning, boosts self-confidence in the pride of learners and their prospects for remaining longer in the school system, etc. and provides environmental conditions that strengthen the use and further development of local, indigenous, heritage and regional languages in written texts (Heugh & Skutnabb-Kangas, 2010: 317–318).

Table 4.2 Experimented and PROPELCA time distribution (Tadadjeu, 1995)

	Mother tongue (MT)	First official language 1 (OL1)
Grade One	75%	25%
Grade Two	60%	40%
Grade Three	40%	60%
Grade Four to Seven	15%	85%

At the secondary level, the model follows an extended trilingualism approach in which the child acquires in addition to their mother tongue, the first and second official languages and then a second national language (language of cultural opening) of their choice. This language of cultural opening permits the child to broaden their cultural experience and so facilitates their integration into the national community. Another vital dimension of the model is its application in non-formal (adult) literacy learning. Here, the primary framework for cultivating a sense of cultural identity and linguistic citizenship is the family. If this is the case, then the families and communities that own the languages should be empowered to use these languages in their written forms. Like the formal model, the adult literacy model needs to be bilingual, that is, involving the L1 and the OL1. In this way, while the L1 confers on the adult learner their cultural identity, the OL1 enables them to gain access into the world of information in the OL1.

However, perhaps the kernel of the problem is the emphasis on 'identity'. This, with its essentialist overtones, in itself is problematic for linguistic citizenship (compare also Wee, this volume) and the question is to what extent the strength of the model resides here – if any at all. In one sense, the discourse of identity associated with the model is a consequence of the situation in Cameroon and of the discourse of the times, where identity is meant to capture the authentic, traditional, as opposed to the imposed foreign (English and French), and the consequent need to qualify 'bilingual' in this framework. A model that departs in some way from a narrow focus on identity model is one that introduces more than two languages, the outlines of which I present in the next section.

A More Extended Perspective of the Application of the Identity Bilingual Model: From Affirmation to Transformation

As Stroud (2001: 346) observes, linguistic citizenship 'is a more theoretically grounded and adequate conceptualization of the problems confronting a politics of language than [...] the notion of linguistic human rights' in that it points towards the democratic potential of moving beyond identity and the need for modes of language planning that go beyond models that take identity as a founding concept.

Given that 'identity bilingualism' is a community language approach, and considering the limits of its current conceptualization, there is a strong need for further reflections on the model. In the paragraphs that follow, I propose a revised and more extended version of application of the model. As indicated above, the early exit nature of the approach suggests its inability in properly addressing linguistic citizenship issues in education. What is required is a model that ensures greater citizenship empowerment through reinforced linguistic integration that acknowledges the co-existence of more than one national and the foreign official languages in education and in day-to-day communication. In this model, the point of departure is bilingualism that gradually becomes trilingualism from the third grade with the introduction of a regional (provincial) language. In this new orientation, we propose equal time allocations of 50% for the LI and OL1 as indicated in Table 4.3.

Equal allocation for the L1 and OL1 here does not insinuate equal mastery of the two languages, but rather indicates the determination to provide maximal input required by the learners to become trilinguals. The allocation gives rooms for continuous reinforcement of the L1 skills even as the learners are exposed to the OL1. A critically important aspect of this new orientation is its recognition of regional languages (RLs) and NOLs. At the primary level, the mother tongue (L1/L1) and the first foreign official language (OL1) are co-mediums of instruction. In fact, the OL1 is taught along more or less the same lines as it is taught today. In addition to this bilingual immersion, there is a NOL that is taught as a subject (orally) in the third year and in writing as from the fourth year. At the secondary level, all the languages except the L1, the OL1 and the NOL are taught as subjects on the timetable. The regional language facilitates social and linguistic integration into the regional community in an upward enriching process towards a more solid national linguistic identity and linguistic citizenship. At the national level, the model recognizes the place of NOLs, to be selected from among the most widely spoken languages of the country, such as Pidgin, Beti-fang and Fulfulde. Perhaps, it is important to mention that Pidgin is by far the most widely spoken language in Cameroon with about two million speakers (Lewis, 2009). Given that these languages, like English and French, constitute a great threat to the local languages, it shall be important that in addition to learning them, the children should also learn their local languages or the languages of the

Table 4.3 PROPELCA time distribution

	Mother tongue (MT/L1)	First official language (OL1)
Grade One	50%	50%
Grade Two	50%	50%
Grade Three	50%	50%
Grade Four to Seven	50%	50%

local environment/receiving communities for rural-urban immigrants. Where the NOL is the national and/or regional language, the populations concerned will be encouraged to learn another NOL of their choice. The NOLs and foreign official languages will henceforth be the languages of science and technology in higher education. Given the weaknesses of Cameroon's present language policy, successful promotion of this model will demand the adoption of a policy that favours official investment in key components of the model, such as teacher training, textbook production and curriculum development.

As Table 4.4 indicates, the dual medium approach will be applied at the primary and secondary levels with the possibility of additional languages being taught as disciplines on the timetable. More specifically, at the primary level, learning will take place in the L1 and OL1 with the RL and NOL1 taught as subjects. At the secondary level, learning will be conducted in the OL1 and NOL1, while the L1, RL and OL2 will be taught as subjects. At the tertiary level, instruction will be carried out in OL1 and NOL1 with the possibility of specialization in the NOL1. Eventually, these two could serve as languages of science, information and technology. The major benefit of the model proposed here is that it caters for linguistic rights and citizenship of even the smallest linguistic groups and thus reduces the incidence of their domination and marginalization.

However, the most important aspect of the model from the perspective of linguistic citizenship is its bottom-up–top-down approach (Alexander,

Table 4.4 Proposed educational language options

Level	Language	Function	Status
Primary	MT/L1	Medium	Compulsory
	OL1	Medium	Compulsory
	RL	Subject	Compulsory
Secondary	OL1	Medium	Compulsory
	NOL 1	Medium	Compulsory
	MT/L1	Subject	Compulsory
	RL	Subject	Compulsory
	OL2	Subject	Compulsory
Tertiary	NOL1	Subject + Subject	Compulsory
	OL1	Medium + Subject	Compulsory
	OL2	Subject	Compulsory
	NOL2	Subject	Compulsory

1992): it places local communities at the centre of language planning activity. This is critical to the whole endeavour, given that the linguistic rights of minority communities can only best be taken care of by the communities themselves. The achievement of the identity bilingualism goal permits the families and communities concerned to play their complementary roles as promoters of their children's learning. In line with the new law on decentralization, which empowers local councils to promote national languages and literacy, the communities become permanent partners in designing language policy and ensuring their application. It is this model that, over the years, has been proposed for adoption by government (Tadadjeu & Chiatoh, 2005: 131). Regrettably, its acceptance is taking rather too long to become reality.

Of course, we must admit the impossibility of achieving this objective in the absence of NGOs, which have over the past several decades, revealed themselves as the most reliable and thus irreplaceable agents of linguistic rights protection through minority language development (Mba & Chiatoh, 2000: 9). At the centre of this activity will be language committees or academies that serve as local community technical organs for the development and promotion of minority languages. It is the managing body responsible for conception and execution, initiation and guiding of the production and popularization of the use of literature, and organizing the training of personnel for child and adult education (Chiatoh, 2011; Sadembouo, 1996: 277). In this community-based process, alternatively referred to as local ownership (Tadadjeu et al., 2001: 2–30) and community response (Chiatoh, 2005), government, through its institutions, plays a purely supervisory, regulatory and financial resource provision role. It assumes the function of guarantor of policy implementation. It is this process that linguistic citizenship can provide alternative insights into.

Conclusion

In this chapter, I have presented language planning as a process of planned restoration of (voice) and the fostering of citizenship. Restoring voice and fostering citizenship have been treated as inextricably interwoven language promotion processes. In a context where linguistic rights have suffered violations for very long decades owing to the exclusion of the indigenous languages of the citizens in important oral and written domains, affirming these rights can only be possible through reclaiming the place of these languages in public spaces, particularly in education. These languages should become the basis of individual and collective identification and access to vital information in the nation. Considering that much of the voice reclamation and linguistic affirmation work has been carried out solely by private bodies, it would be necessary that government undertakes to sustainably support the process. However, there are major hindrances in realizing this. A major requirement in this direction is the adoption of an alternative language policy capable of ensuring the accommodation of these languages as well as other languages of national and international import in the educational system and in other relevant domains. It shall thus be of great importance if the government initiates actions that favour official investment in the promotion of local indigenous languages as an integral component of citizenship cultivation in Cameroon. As such, exclusive promotion of foreign official languages in education should henceforth be regarded as inadequate in the achievement of a viable Cameroonian linguistic citizenship in this era of globalization marked by minority language endangerment.

Linguistic citizenship thus involves acknowledgement of linguistic diversity and of minority language empowerment, not as completely different and distinct, but as the starting point of a broader and more inclusive material and symbolic representation. In fact, we need to formulate a politics of language that is sufficiently attuned to the sociolinguistics of language contact and issues of power and identity in developing contexts (Stroud, 2003: 19–20). This is especially so because in Cameroon, minority languages are highly threatened with extinction owing to the growing dominance of foreign languages in official domains. Minority recognition here is a significant step towards mainstreaming individuals and communities, thereby maximizing their visibility and voices in socio-political and economic spaces. It is the admission that in multilingual settings, the ideal identities and citizenships are those that respect the multiplicity of languages and values.

In this light, linguistic citizenship is both a source and finality of affirmative and positive transformative action.

References

Abbi, A. (2004) Vanishing diversities and submerging identities: The Indian case. *Dialogue on Language Diversity, Sustainability and Peace* (pp. 1–10). Barcelona, 20–23 May 2004.

Alexander, N. (1992) Language planning from below. In R.K. Herbert (ed.) *Language and Society in Africa: The Theory and Practice of Sociolinguistics* (pp. 143–150). Wits: Witwatersrand University Press.

Bitjaa Kody, Z.D. (2001) Attitudes Linguistiques à Yaoundé AJAL N° 2 (pp. 100–124).

Chiatoh, B.A. (2005) Assessing community response to literacy in a multilingual context: The case of Cameroon. Unpublished PhD dissertation, University of Yaounde.

Chiatoh, B.A. (2006) Language, cultural identity and the national question in Cameroon. In P. Mbangwana, M. Kizitus and M. Tenno (eds) *Language, Literature and Identity* (pp. 144–152). Cullivier Verlag Gottingen.

Chiatoh, B.A. (2011) Towards the development of a functional Bafaw literacy programme. In E. Chia, V. Tanda and N. Ayu'nwi (eds) *The Bafaw Language (Bantu A10)*. Bamenda: Langaa RPCIG.

Chiatoh, B.A. (2012) Language and the Cameroonian classroom: Theory, practice and prospects. Unpublished ms.

Collier, V.P. and Thomas, W.B. (2004) The astounding effectiveness of dual language education for all. *NABE Journal of Research and Practice* 2 (1), 1–20.

Errington, J. (2004) Getting language rights, shifting linguistic traditions. *Collegium Antropologicum* 28 (Suppl. 1), 43–48.

Heugh, K. and Skutnabb-Kangas, T. (2010) Multilingual education works when 'peripheries' take the centre stage. In K. Heugh and T. Skutnabb-Kangas (eds) *Multilingual Education Works: From the Periphery to the Centre* (pp. 316–342). New Delhi: Orient Black Private Limited.

Jiang, W. (2000) The relationship between culture and language. *ELT Journal* 54 (4), 328–334.

Krumm, H.-J. (2004) Heterogeneity: Multilingualism and democracy. *Utbilding and Demokrati* 13 (3), 61–77.

Lewis, P.M. (2009) *Ethnologue: Languages of the World,* 16th ed. Dallas, Texas: SIL.

Lim, L. and Ansaldo, U. (2007) Identity alignment in the multilingual space: The Malays of Sri Lanka. In E. Achimbe (ed.) *Linguistic Identity in Multilingual Postcolonial Spaces* (218–243). Cambridge: Cambridge Scholars Press.

Makoni, S. and Trudell, B. (2009) African perspectives on linguistic diversity: Implications for language policy in education. In J.A. Kleifgen and G.C. Bond (eds) *New Perspectives on Language and Education* (pp. 32–47). Bristol: Multilingual Matters.

Mba, G and Chiatoh, B.A. (2000) Current trends and perspectives for mother tongue education in Cameroon. *AJAL* 1, 1–21.

McCarty, T.L. (2003) Revitalizing indigenous languages in homogenizing times. *Comparative Education* 39 (2), 147–163.

Nanfah, G. (2006) Exoglossic language policy and national unity in Africa: The Cameroon model. In P. Mbangwana, K. Mpoche and T. Mbu (eds) *Language, Literature and Identity* (pp. 129–143). Gottingen: Cuvillier Verla g.

Pashby, K. (2008) Demands on and of citizenship and schooling: 'Belonging' and 'diversity' in the global imperative. *Brock Education* 17, 1–21.

Rosendal, T. (2008) *Multilingual Cameroon: Policy, Practice, Problems and Solutions.* Gothenburg Africana Informal Series, N° 7. Department of Oriental and African languages, University of Gothenburg.

Rubagumya, C.M. (2007) A three-tier citizenship: Can the state in Tanzania guarantee linguistic human rights? EdQual Working Paper N° 5.

Rubin, J. and Jernudd, B.H. (eds) (1971) *Can Languages be Planned?* Honolulu: University of Hawai'i, East-West Centre.

Ruiz, R. (1984) Orientations in language planning. *Journal of the National Association for Bilingual Education* 8, 15–34.

Sadembouo, E. (1996) Starting a language committee (Lecture notes.) An introduction to literacy principles, methods and materials. Yaounde: SIL.

Skutnabb-Kangas, T. and Phillipson, R. (eds) (1995) *Linguistic Human Rights: Overcoming Linguistic Discrimination.* Berlin/New York: Mouton de Gruyter.

Starkey, H. (2002) *Democratic Citizenship, Languages, Diversity and Human Rights.* Guide for the Development of Language Education Policies in Europe: From Linguistic Diversity to Plurilingual Education. Strasbourg: Council of Europe.

Stroud, C. (2001) African mother-tongue programmes and the politics of language: Linguistic citizenship versus linguistic human rights. *Journal of Multilingual and Multicultural Development* 22 (4), 331–356.

Stroud, C. (2003) Retheorising a politics of language for development and education. In K. Fraurud and K. Hiltenstam (eds) *Multilingualism in Global and Local Perspectives* (pp. 17–29). Stockholm: Centre for Research on Bilingualism.

Stroud, C. (2009) A postliberal critique of language rights: Towards a politics of language for a linguistics of contact. In J. Petrovic (ed.) *International Perspectives on Bilingual Education: Policy, Practice and Controversy* (pp. 191–218). Information Age Publishing.

Tadadjeu, M. (1995) National Languages Education Program in Cameroon, Yaounde: PROPELCA Team.

Tadadjeu, M. (1998) Bilinguisme Identitaire et Apprentissage d'une Troisième Langue: Le Cas du Cameroun. Université de Yaoundé 1 et Centre ANACLAC de Linguistique Appliqué.

Tadadjeu, M. and Chiatoh, B.A. (2005) Mother tongue-focused bilingual education in Cameroon. In N. Alexander (ed.) *Mother-Tongue-Based Bilingual Education in Southern Africa: The Dynamics of Implementation.* Project for the Study of Alternative Education in South Africa (PRAESA), University of Cape Town.

Tadadjeu, M. Mba, G. and Chiatoh, A.B. (2001) The process of local ownership of multilingual education in Cameroon. *AJAL* 2, 2–30.

Todd, L. (1983) Language options for education in a multilingual society: Cameroon. In C. Kennedy (ed.) *Language Planning and Language Education* (pp. 160–171). London: George Allen & Unwin.

Wardaugh, R. (2002) *An Introduction to Sociolinguistics.* London: Blackwell Publishers.

Winstead, L. (2007) Starting with children in schools: The social inclusion of immigrant children via an alternative dual language program. In A. Ross (ed.) *Citizenship Education in Society* (pp. 355–362). London: CiCe.

Wolff, E.H. (1999) Multilingualism, modernisation, and mother tongue: Promoting democracy through indigenous languages. *Social Dynamics: A Journal of African Studies* 25 (1), 31–50.

5 Education and Citizenship in Mozambique: Colonial and Postcolonial Perspectives

Feliciano Chimbutane
Universidade Eduardo Mondlane, Mozambique

Introduction

Citizenship in Mozambique is best appreciated when framed against the historical and sociopolitical trajectory of the country. This is because citizenship has historically been shaped by the Portuguese colonial discourse, the struggle for liberation, the construction of a socialist state and the current process of democratic transformation of the country. This broad context substantiates the view that citizenship is by its very nature contingent, historical and political (Yeatman, 2001). In all stages mentioned above, language and education emerged as key elements in the construction and exercise of citizenship in Mozambique. The language and education policies adopted all through those years came to be ideological platforms for sustaining colonial and postcolonial regimes – they have always been intimately linked to the kind of citizen and the kind of society envisaged. The linkage between education and citizenship foregrounds the role of educational institutions in assigning value to linguistic and non-linguistic resources as well as in regulating access to them (compare Martin-Jones, 2007; Stroud, 2003). It is based on this role of education in determining and legitimating political power and economic opportunity that studies in Tollefson (2002) suggest that language policies in education play a key role in organizing social and political systems.

This chapter focuses on the interface of politics of language, education and citizenship. Special attention is devoted to the role of education and language ideologies in the definition and forging of the ideal citizen in the sociopolitical periods mentioned above. The argument is that in both colonial and postcolonial eras the construction and experience of citizenship in Mozambique has, among other things, been inextricably bound up with political efforts towards the management of multilingualism and multiculturalism, that is, the management of diversity. Compared with the early periods of independence, it can be argued that though still timid there has now been a shift from homogenizing political discourses to those that celebrate diversity and difference. I use the framework of linguistic citizenship (Stroud, 2001, 2009; Stroud & Heugh, 2004) to analyse this shift in language policies, discourses and practices.

In this chapter I have three major sections. I start with a critical analysis of language policies, educational goals and citizenship in colonial and early years of independence in Mozambique. In this section, I show how in both periods Portuguese was officially constructed as the language of identity. In a subsequent section I highlight the shift in language politics in Mozambique – from monolingual discourses around Portuguese to discourses on multilingualism and diversity. I take bilingual education as an example of new spaces being opened in Mozambique for community participation and agency, that is, spaces for exercising alternative forms of linguistic citizenship. I end the chapter with remarks highlighting the key points presented and discussed in the study.

Monolingual Discourses and Politics: The Essentialist Link Between Portuguese and Citizenship

As in other postcolonial countries, the same language ideology and policy that prevailed during colonial rule and during the liberation struggle were maintained at independence in Mozambique. Though with different justifications, Portuguese enjoyed the status of official language, and African languages remained likened to lower functions. Whereas the status of Portuguese in the colonial era, including in education, was linked with the alleged civilization and nationalization mission of Portugal, Frelimo's decision to maintain Portuguese as the official language during the liberation struggle and after independence was allegedly to ensure national unity. That is, despite differences in terms of political-ideological orientations, in both cases the marginalization of African languages was supposedly to ensure the materialization of the State's project of a harmonious society built around the Portuguese language.

Language, education and citizenship in colonial Mozambique

As with other colonial powers, Lisbon also adopted different approaches to citizenship in different historical periods in Mozambique.

However, there were two distinct periods that seem to have foregrounded the core characteristics of the citizen envisaged by the Portuguese. These periods were mainly moulded by the type of education provider and the purpose of education offered at the time. The first period was when the education of the natives was almost entirely left in the hands of missionaries and the aim was allegedly to 'civilize' the local 'primitives' by imparting to them the word of God as well as Portuguese values and practices. The second period was when education became a prerogative of the State, and was chiefly geared towards the preparation of local elites to serve the economic, cultural and political interests of Portugal. In both cases, Portugal envisaged a docile and subservient citizen, that is, a loyal citizen who identified himself with the ideals of the Portuguese citizenship. However, this ideology in education had the side effect of producing a pool of nationalists who would later lead civic actions and the fight against the colonial masters.

Education for civilization, nationalization and discrimination

In the early stages of Portuguese colonialism, the education of the natives was entirely provided for by missionaries, especially Roman Catholic missionaries. Indeed, in his historical analysis of colonial education, Belchior (1965) points out that education was at the hands of missionaries from the so-called period of discovery (15th century) to the proclamation of the Organic Status of the Portuguese Catholic Missions of Africa and Timor in 1926.

The main objective of education in these early stages of colonialism was allegedly to civilize the natives. This would later include the so-called *nacionalização* or nacionalization of the natives. Nationalization was part of the assimilationist ideology. The main goal of this ideology was the 'integration (of the natives) within the Portuguese nationality through language, education and Christianity' (Cruz e Silva, 2001: 66). In other words, the goal was to ensure that the natives assumed 'Portuguese citizenship'. As Buendía Gómez (1999) points out, the role of the Catholic missions in this assimilationist programme shows how the Catholic Church played a key role in the ideological foundation of the Portuguese colonization of African territories.

The counterbalance to this assimilationist policy of Portugal was attempted by the Protestant churches, which were more liberal and against the nationalization goal set by Lisbon (see Buendía Gómez, 1999; Cruz e Silva, 2001). The Protestants' goal was to 'de-nationalize' (*desnacionalizar*) as it were or even 'to undo the Portuguese' (*desaportuguesar*) in the natives, mainly through the promotion of local languages and cultures.

This challenge to the State's assimilationist policy led the Portuguese administration to establish legislative measures to control the activities of Protestant churches (see Belchior, 1965; Cruz e Silva, 2001).

The role of Protestant churches in promoting African languages and in helping liberate the minds of the locals merits a few comments here. As Stroud (2007) notes, unlike the Catholic Church, which for a long period of time was against the translation of religious materials into local languages, the Protestants 'saw written, *standardized* local languages as instruments of modernization' (Stroud, 2007: 32) and the best way of evangelizing local peoples. The use of African languages as media of instruction and for religious functions had the side effect of contributing to the maintenance of these languages (Skutnabb-Kangas, 2008) as well as giving them a 'social and symbolic value as languages of potential political agency' (Stroud, 2007: 32). As a matter of fact, the anti-assimilationist education perspective pursued by the Protestants helped the youth to become aware of the value of their ancestral cultures as well as nurtured in them the sense of belonging. This explains why many of the first anti-colonial nationalists came from Protestant churches (see Cruz e Silva, 2001). Eduardo Mondlane, regarded as the founder of Frelimo, is such an example.

The establishment of the *Estado Novo* or Corporate State (1926–1974) and the associated *de jure* collaboration between the Portuguese State and the Catholic Church in an educational and ideological mission started a new era of colonial education provision. A discriminatory education system was then established. This system encompassed two types of education: Official education (*ensino oficial*), designed for children of colonial settlers and *assimilados* (Portuguese citizens), and a rudimentary education (*ensino rudimentar*) for the natives, namely those positioned as non-citizens, and run by missionaries (Cruz e Silva, 2001; Errante, 1998; Mazula, 1995). The justification for this discriminatory system of education is clearly expressed in the following statement by Mário Malheiros, the then Director of Public Education in Portugal:

> Taking into account that primitive peoples can only slowly be civilized and considering that the populations of the colonies consist of civilized and primitive individuals, two types of primary education have been institutionalized in the Portuguese colonies: one for Europeans and *assimilados* and the other for the primitives. (Almeida, 1979: 221, quoted in Buendía Gómez, 1999: 59)

This racist statement mirrors the then European ethnocentric philosophy, which regarded the natives, derogatively called *cafres* (kaffirs), as retarded just because they did not speak Portuguese and did not lead their lives according to European cultural standards.

The natives could, however, become *assimilados* and qualify for Portuguese citizenship if they met the requirements set by the *Portaria* (Edict) 317 of 9 January 1917. The *assimilados* were black Africans and *mulatos* (mulattoes) assumed to have acquired the Portuguese language and associated cultural values and practices. Proficiency in Portuguese was one of the *sine qua non* 'legal' conditions for the local Africans to rise to the status of *assimilado*, that is, the status that could allow them to move from the condition of objects/subjects to that of second-class citizens. The *assimilados* were, therefore, a tiny minority of privileged locals who were ranked lower than the white Europeans and higher than the large majority of the indigenous population.

While official education was aimed at preparing an educated elite that could best serve the colonial interests of the State, the aim of rudimentary education was to equip the natives with rudimentary knowledge and moral values. This differentiation in terms of objectives shows how, compared with official education, rudimentary education was less ambitious in terms of the type of citizen envisaged: the graduate from rudimentary education should only have enough skills and knowledge to ensure his/her employability and 'proper' behaviour in society. This included being docile and subservient to colonial authority. This analysis is substantiated by the following statement made by Cardeal Cerejeira in 1960: 'we are trying to reach the natives widely and in depth in order to teach them how to read and count, not to make doctors out of them' (quoted in Mondlane, 1975: 59). This statement may indicate that the Portuguese State was aware of the fact that providing quality education to the colonized would be a source of social and political participation and an eventual path towards contestation of colonial power.

Colonial education ideology as a two-pronged stick

The context described above substantiates the view of colonial education, especially its mission of forming a local elite, as a two-pronged stick (Rassool, 2007): on the one hand, it responded to the need of a local educated elite to serve the purposes of colonial administration of the occupied territories, but, on the other hand, it prepared a pool of citizens who were able to better understand and challenge colonial exploitation and oppression. It is no wonder that the first liberation movements in Mozambique and in other former Portuguese colonies were formed by this class of citizens and their descendants (see Cruz e Silva, 2001; Mateus, 1999). That is, despite their privileged socioeconomic position when compared with that of ordinary indigenous peoples, these educated natives started to challenge their masters openly, contesting exploitation and oppression. They eventually mobilized their marginalized fellow-countrymen to follow suit. This can be regarded as a confirmation of the predictions and fears of colonial powers. For example, according to Rassool (2007), by educating the locals exclusively through the medium of African languages, among other things, the Germans intended to avoid the emergence of an educated elite in European languages, who could place themselves on the same footing as the colonizers and threaten colonial rule. In relation to Mozambique, Cruz e Silva (2001) also notes that by offering poor quality education to the natives, Portugal wanted to prevent the 'growth of an educated elite which would compete with the white population and ascend to political positions against the regime' (Cruz e Silva, 2001: 69) That is, by offering poor quality education to the natives, the Germans and the Portuguese wanted to prevent the educated colonized from gaining political consciousness and questioning colonial administration.

However, social injustices and the independence of other African countries in the 1960s fuelled the emergence of anti-colonial, nationalist groups in Mozambique and in other Portuguese colonies in Africa (see Cruz e Silva, 2001; Mateus, 1999). Three anti-colonial groups formed the *Frente de Libertação de Moçambique* (Mozambican Liberation Front, hereafter Frelimo) in Tanzania in 1962. The fact that the leaders of these groups where part of the few Africans who were meant to be good 'Portuguese citizens' substantiates the view that colonial education ideology was a two-pronged stick.

The profile of the ideal militant constructed, and the ideology of unity followed by Frelimo during the liberation struggle against the Portuguese colonial domination, deserve a brief comment here as they influenced key political decisions taken immediately after independence. Given the ethnolinguistic diversity of the members of the organization, Frelimo declared Portuguese as the official language of communication within the movement and also the language of administration of the areas then liberated from the colonial rule. As Katupha (1994) points out, Portuguese was symbolically conceived as the enemy's weapon in the hands of Frelimo (see also the statement by Graça Machel in the next subsection). In contrast, African languages only served as vehicles for 'emotional expression of nationalism, expressed in nationalist dances and songs' (Katupha, 1994: 91). Within this ideological setup, the militants should fight against any kind of division or differentiation within the army as well as combat all forms of exploitation. As will become apparent in the next subsection, these ideological perspectives guided the early stages of independent Mozambique.

Independence, socialist revolution and the formation of Homem Novo

When the Peoples' Republic of Mozambique was proclaimed in 1975, Frelimo established a one-party socialist state and adopted a Marxist–Leninist orientation. At the international level, Mozambique joined the Socialist block and steered the creation of an anti-imperialist regional coalition of *Estados da Linha da Frente* (Frontline States). As I show later in this subsection, the educational ideology adopted in the early years of independence and the ideal citizen envisaged by the State were consistent with this political orientation.

From the language point of view, the Frelimo government declared the former colonial language (Portuguese) as *the* official language of the country. In contrast, no official status was granted to African languages. That is, the same language ideology that prevailed during the colonial rule and during the liberation struggle was maintained at independence, though with a different justification. As stated in the introduction to this section, whereas the hegemony of the Portuguese language in colonial rule was consistent with the civilization and nationalization goals of Lisbon, the Frelimo government decision to maintain Portuguese as the official language was allegedly to ensure national unity, a political-ideological project that included the bid to eradicate tribal, ethnic and regional differences. This postcolonial language ideology is substantiated in the quote from Fernando Ganhão, the then Rector of Universidade Eduardo Mondlane and one of the most influential Frelimo thinkers at the time:

> The decision to opt for Portuguese as the official language of the People's Republic of Mozambique was a well pondered and carefully examined political decision, aimed at achieving one objective: the preservation of national unity and the integrity of the territory. (Ganhão, 1979: 2)

As hinted at earlier on, this decision was a follow-up to the vision pursued during the struggle for independence, when Frelimo adopted Portuguese as the unifying language for fighting the enemy (Katupha, 1994). This connection to the past is spelled out in the following statement by the then Minister of Education and Culture, Graça Machel:

> The need to fight the oppressor called for an intransigent combat against tribalism and regionalism. It was this necessity of unity that forced the only common language upon us – the language which had been used to oppress could assume a new dimension. (Machel, 1979: 6)

In other words, during both the anti-colonial struggle and after indepen-dence, Frelimo constructed the view that Portuguese, the language of the former enemy, should be adopted and used 'in the service of social change' (Ricento, 2006: 4). In contrast, multilingualism had been conceptualized as the seed source of tribalism and regionalism, which should be com-bated vigorously (see also a retrospective critical analysis by Honwana, 2015). This ideological positioning was epitomized by the declaration of Portuguese as the language of national unity (*língua da unidade nacio-nal*). This explains why the use of local African languages in formal domains and functions was not tolerated until recently, including in schools. As a consequence, these languages lacked political support, they remained neglected and those speakers who did not additionally possess Portuguese proficiency remained marginalized and disempowered, as Portuguese maintained its role as the *sine qua non* symbolic instrument for meaningful socioeconomic and political citizenship. Moreover, because mobilization around ethnolinguistic values was ideologically sus-picious, speakers of African languages were also denied the exercise of linguistic citizenship. This may broadly explain the absence or scarcity of civil society-based initiatives and structures for the promotion and devel-opment of African languages.

The homogenizing language ideology discussed above was consistent with a wider political project of a nation-state founded on egalitarian and revolutionary principles. Under this ideology, 'equality meant sameness and the annihilation of difference' (McEwan, 2005: 183). Frelimo assumed that in order to build a harmonious socialist society, all citizens should be treated the same way and differences of all sorts should be overridden. Within this ideological setup, there was a vested interest in marking a historical discontinuity between the 'tribal' past and the 'national-revolutionary' present, as happened in other then socialist-oriented African countries, such as Angola and Tanzania (see Blommaert, 2014' in relation to Tanzania[1]).

Within this national project of a homogeneous and egalitarian society, the school was symbolically regarded as the forge of the *homem novo*, literally 'new man' (Machel, 1975). Based on a Marxist ideological frame-work, *homem novo* was defined as a citizen free of obscurantism, super-stition and bourgeois mentality, one who assumed the values of socialism (República Popular de Moçambique, 1983). What this implied was, among others, a call for a discrediting of the capitalist worldview and abandonment of all traditional beliefs and practices thought to be in con-flict with 'scientific' wisdom. These included beliefs in crafting, in tradi-tional medicine, in the power of ancestral forces and in God. In fact, with the exception of the call not to believe in God, these culturally based 'undesirable' attributes remind us of those that the model of citizen envisaged by the colonial civilizing mission attempted to expurgate – in both cases, the abandonment of traditional values and practices was a key feature of a 'good' citizen.

The formation of the *new man* led to the development of Portuguese language syllabus and materials around political and social themes, such as the national liberation struggle, national heroes, women's emancipation, proletarian solidarity, life in community, etc. To put it simply, Portuguese language classes became an arena for the promotion of socialist values and patriotic awareness among Mozambican children, rather than language lessons per se.

Readiness to perform State-defined missions was another socialist value worth being considered here. As in Sparta, the *new man* had no control over his own educational and/or professional aspirations and trajectories, but the State. For example, it was the State who defined which school, programme or profession one should be in. After graduating, one could not individually search for employment, but had to wait for a non-negotiable placement by State authorities, including placement in the army. State-centred decisions such as these had at least two types of consequences for citizenship, the effects of which can still be felt nowadays. On the one hand, they contributed to the forging of disempowered citizens, ones lacking individual autonomy and who could not act without the State's guidance or intervention. On the other hand, since these measures were taken as a denial of individual freedom of choice, they prompted dissatisfaction and resistance to State authority, especially from the youth. For example, groups of young students resisted their compulsory placement in teacher training programmes, a measure that the State had taken in response to the massive shortage of teachers after the sudden departure of most of the few trained teachers at independence.

The prominence ascribed to education in the socialist project explains why during the civil war (1976–1992) *Resistência Nacional Moçambicana* (Mozambican National Resistance, hereafter Renamo) had the destruction of schools and killing of teachers as part of their main targets – these were perceived as the sources for the dissemination of the socialist state ideology and preparation of future Marxists. In other words, destroying the school meant destroying the forge of *homem novo*.

In summary, the language ideologies followed in both colonial times and the immediate years after independence attempted to isolate and suppress African languages (and their speakers) and to give prominence and acknowledgement to Portuguese. These ideologies foreground an essentialist link between language and identity, hence the construction of Portuguese as the legitimate unifying language of the Portuguese empire, in colonial times, or of the Mozambican nation-state, after independence. As acknowledged throughout this section, although the status of *assimilado* citizenship and post-independent citizenship are structurally and ideologically very different notions, they are both based on the perceived role of Portuguese as a key instrument for realizing the blueprint of the State.

Multilingual Discourses and Politics: Spaces for Linguistic Citizenship

The framework of linguistic citizenship (Stroud, 2001, 2009; Stroud & Heugh, 2004) offers sensitizing lenses for analysing language ideologies, discourses and practices attested in Mozambique from the 1990s. Within this framework, linguistic citizenship 'refers predominantly to a view on language and politics that recognizes the manifold challenges posed by late modern contexts of migration and multilingualism for democracy and voice and that takes as a central point of departure the desirability of constructing agency and maintaining voice across media, modalities and context' (Stroud, 2009: 208). Among other things, the notion of linguistic citizenship and the underpinning view of language, as a political construct 'tied to material and symbolic wealth' (Stroud, 2001: 351), suggest that political recognition of low status languages should go hand in hand with dispensations that enable economic visibility to the concerned linguistic communities.

Democratic transformation and voice: Unity in difference

The year 1990 marks one of the memorable turning points in Mozambican history: the Frelimo government started peace talks with Renamo and introduced a new Constitution (República de Moçambique, 1990) which, for the very first time, set the ground for a multi-party political system and a market-oriented economy. The talks between Frelimo and Renamo culminated in the Rome Peace Agreement of October 1992. This agreement brought the conflict, which lasted for 16 years, to an end.

The 1990 Constitution also marked the turning point in the State's discourse and politics about the relationship between Portuguese and African languages, opened up a new era in terms of the relationship between the

State and the civil society and set the stage for an emerging civil society below the State. For the first time in Mozambican history, it is enshrined in the Constitution that the State promotes the development and increased use of African languages[2] in public life, including in education (compare República de Moçambique, 1990, Article 5). Despite the change in structure, the spirit of the 1990 Constitution was maintained in the revised version now in force. In its Article 9, the new text of the Constitution reads as follows:

> Article 9: The state values the national languages as a cultural and educational heritage and promotes their development and increased use as vehicles of our identity. (República de Moçambique, 2004: 7, Chapter I)

In addition to Article 9 of the Constitution, the use of African languages in education is backed by Article 4 of decree 6/92 on the National Education System, which states that:

> Under the framework defined within the current decree, the National Education System must value and develop the national languages, promoting their gradual introduction in the education of the citizens. (República de Moçambique, 1992:104)

This multilingual and multicultural ethos has been further reinforced by successive legal provisions, such as the Country's Cultural Policy adopted in 1997 (República de Moçambique, 1997). In that document, the government of Mozambique restated its commitment to promoting cultural development and its role in creating the conditions for respect for cultural diversity, including religious and ethnolinguistic differences. In relation to the local African languages, the document reads as follows:

> National languages are important assets as they are the main repositories and vehicles of national traditions, the communication instruments for the overwhelming majority of Mozambicans and *key elements for the involvement of citizens in social, economic and political life.* (República de Moçambique, 1997: 122, my highlighting)

Among other things, this statement foregrounds the State's recognition of the role of African languages as key instruments for the exercise of linguistic citizenship for the majority of the population. This shift 'illustrates the way that the politics of recognition stresses the existence and legitimacy of incommensurable – or at least distinct – domains of culture, values, and mores' (Rose, 2001: 7). As Stroud (2007) suggests, the shift witnessed in the 1990s was, in part, influenced by Renamo's accommodation of tradition and local languages in their ideological view of rights and sociopolitical participation. Anticipating the post-war multiparty competition, Frelimo had to embrace the ideals of multilingualism, multiculturalism and 'retraditionalization' of administration and governance to (re)conquer the hearts and minds of an important segment of the population that had been lost as a result of unpopular revolutionary measures, including those envisaging the eradication of tribes and traditional forms of authority.

Despite the fact that neither of the above legal provisions is binding, they can be regarded as evidence of the decline of homogenizing and assimilationist language policy discourses in Mozambique. Among other things, the new discourses and legal provisions on language open spaces for the promotion and upgrading of African languages and associated cultural practices as well as for the exercise of linguistic citizenship. For example, this openness has lent legitimacy to both intellectuals and ordinary citizens to debate language issues and to shape new forms of multilingual and multicultural provision in education. The introduction of bilingual education in Mozambique in 2003 is a remarkable consequence of the current openness of 'ideological and implementational spaces' (Hornberger, 2002) in the country. As Chimbutane (2011) has noted, the introduction of bilingual education has reopened the debate over language and multilingualism, with some actors arguing for the perpetuation of the hegemonic status of Portuguese and others arguing for the promotion of African languages and/or for the complementary use of these competing languages as media of education and development. Chimbutane shows how citizens who had lived in neighbouring countries where African languages have long been officially used in education, economy and governance, such as South Africa and Zimbabwe, tend to be more favourable to mother tongue-based bilingual education and to multilingualism than those who had never been exposed to such language policy experiences. Another example of the ideological and implementational shift has to do with the important role ascribed to African languages in the locally based policy of governance currently pursued by the ruling government. Following the failure of highly centralized, top-down systems of governance both internally and internationally (see Rose, 2001), Frelimo has defined the district as the centre of national development. The aim of this district-based development strategy is the decentralization of government functions down to the district level. In this context, non-governmental organizations (NGOs) and development partners are sponsoring and/or carrying out capacity-building initiatives aiming at improving local government's democratic procedures, as well as preparing civil society groups to effectively participate in local governance. The rationale behind these initiatives is that the local government is a privileged arena for deepening democracy and constructing participatory citizenship, as is also understood in the South African political context (see McEwan, 2005). This development strategy is opening spaces for the official use of African languages for local governance and citizen participation in decision-making. For example, for the first time in independent Mozambique, the government institutionalized the position of interpreter (African languages–Portuguese–African languages) in the public sector, which can be taken as the State's recognition of the role of African languages for community participation in local socioeconomic development and governance. These interpreters have been mediating the communication between individuals/grassroots groups and meso- and top-level representatives of the State. In this sense, it can be said that African languages are starting to officially compete with Portuguese as *de facto* languages of governance and citizen participation at least at the local level.

The shift analysed in this subsection indicates that, at least in discourse, the ability to speak the Portuguese language is no longer officially assumed to be the *sine qua non* condition for legitimate participation in social, economic and political life in Mozambique. That is, other forms of citizenship tend to be recognized, including in formal discourse.

Bilingual education: A space for community participation and agency

The introduction of bilingual education in Mozambique opened up an arena for some form of community participation and agency in language-in-education decision-making. This section provides illustrative examples of the way communities are starting to influence decisions on language matters in the education sector, an example of exercise of linguistic citizenship.

The bilingual education programme has been included in the Mozambican educational system since 2003. In this programme, in addition to Portuguese, a local language has also been used as a medium of instruction. Sixteen local African languages have been selected as languages of instruction in the first 3 years of schooling, a role which is taken up by Portuguese at Grade 4. According to Instituto Nacional do Desenvolvimento da Educação (INDE) (2008), there were 14 bilingual schools in 2003, 23 in 2004, and 81 in 2008. Estimates indicated that the number of schools had increased to about 200 in 2010, 400 in 2011, and 551 in 2015.

The analysis of the process that led to the selection of the 16 languages of instruction seems to indicate that this was essentially a political decision heavily influenced by civil society pressures. Indeed, taking into account such factors as the poor development of local African languages, the limited in-country expertise in language development and bilingual education provision, as well as financial constraints of different sorts, the initial proposals advanced by experts in public *fora* were that the programme should have started with about five to seven local African languages as media of instruction, and progressively extend this role to other languages as human capacity was built and once corpus planning for the initial languages had been consolidated and expanded to new languages (compare Instituto Nacional do Desenvolvimento da Educação/Ministério da Educação, 2001). However, as successive proposals were publicly discussed, some language groups felt excluded and lobbied the government to include their language(s) in the set of local languages chosen for education. As a consequence, the number of languages proposed increased throughout the different stages of the public debate and, certainly for the sake of national harmony, instead of excluding, the decision-makers opted for integrating as many languages as possible in the system. This led to the eventual increase in the number of languages selected from the initial five to seven to 16 languages.

Despite the technical oddness of the decision to include as many local African languages as possible in education, it can be taken as evidence of the work of linguistic citizenship: in a democratic context where political power is ascribed via the ballot box, the ruling government has been 'forced' to opt for the more inclusive decisions. This represents a turning point in Mozambican history since, in contrast to the past, communities are now taking part in decision-making processes concerning planning and implementation of education programmes.

Bilingual education in Mozambique is facing implementational constraints of different sorts (see Chimbutane, 2011; Chimbutane & Benson, 2012; Instituto Nacional do Desenvolvimento da Educação, 2008, among others). However, it has proved to be contributing to the transformation of rural schools from being islands detached from the communities they serve, to settings where school/academic and local knowledge meet and cross-fertilize (Chimbutane, 2011). Local teachers, parents and other community members are involved in the development of local African languages and education materials in these languages. In addition to co-operating in the transfer of local knowledge to schools, parents and other community members are also overseeing and influencing the form of the language and content that schools are passing onto their children (Chimbutane, 2011).

In contrast to ordinary models of education, the development of African languages and school materials in these languages is not a process in which experts or central level institutions orchestrate and impose forms of language to local teachers and communities. Rather, it is a joint enterprise. For example, faced with the need for technical terms in African languages, teachers have turned to experienced community members to learn specialized terms that they have then adapted to their teaching needs. Conversely, communities are also learning technical terms and new genres in their own languages from teachers and pupils. For example, teachers are contributing to the dissemination of the standardized orthographies of local African languages used in schools into the communities, especially in the religious field. Pupils are teaching their parents technical terms that they had never thought existed or were possible in their native languages. In turn, parents are also serving as intellectual resources for their children, as they help them with their homework. In this context, teachers now view parents as valid intellectual partners in the education of the pupils.

Although meso-level practitioners, such as the linguists involved in bilingual education, have more technical expertise than local level practitioners (e.g. the development of standardized orthographies), they either do not speak the languages they are required to work with or, when they speak them, they usually do not have full command of them. In this context, these experts are 'forced' to negotiate with the locals, who are usually more proficient in their languages, in order to find joint solutions to the complex challenges encountered in bilingual education, including that of improving the orthographies, coining technical terms and developing teaching and learning materials in those languages. This is what can be called symmetrical collaboration among social networks for the purpose of enhancing teaching and learning experiences (Moll, 1992; Moll *et al.*, 1992). That is, mainly thanks to the use of shared languages, the traditional top-down school-community relationships are being eroded and less elitist forms of co-operation are being built. As has been widely recognized, grassroots participation has the advantage of building local ownership of bilingual education programmes, one of the conditions recurrently associated with the effectiveness and sustainability of this form of education, including in Africa (e.g. Alidou, 2004; Bamgbose, 1999; Stroud, 2001; Tadadjeu & Chiatoh, 2005).

The collaboration between speakers and language experts in status and corpus planning of African languages illustrates the enactment of linguistic citizenship, taken as 'the situation where speakers themselves exercise control over their language, deciding *what* languages are, and what they may *mean*, and where language issues (especially in educational sites) are discursively tied to a range of social issues – policy issues and questions of equity' (Stroud, 2001: 353). Moreover, this collaboration and cross-fertilization also substantiates the view of linguistic citizenship as a 'process of engagement that opens doors for respectful and deconstructive negotiations around language forms and practices' (Stroud, this volume).

The transformative processes described above are lending visibility to African languages in local communities and in society at large, which may lead to their reconstruction, not only as symbols of identity and belonging, but also as resources that can lead to political participation and socio-economic rewards in both formal and informal markets (Chimbutane, 2011). However, the vagueness of the language policy adopted in Mozambique may have negative consequences on long-term educational provision in African languages, as has happened elsewhere in Africa. As a matter of fact, in the absence of policy explicitness, lack of top-level corpus planning initiatives and efforts aimed at developing local languages for education and considering that the current legislative provisions are not binding, there is no means of holding decision-makers and policy-makers accountable. For example, despite the increasing demand for bilingual education in rural Mozambique, central education authorities have been reluctant to expand the programme to new schools and areas. This reluctance has led some local level education authorities and NGOs to provide bilingual education without always obtaining official permission from central decision-makers (Instituto Nacional do Desenvolvimento da Educação, 2008), as they should do under the current top-down system of education management in the country. It was based on this kind of evidence that Chimbutane and Benson (2012) noted that the top's failure to create adequate conditions for implementing bilingual education seems to have provided opportunities for local communities and educators to become true owners of the process. This can be considered a remarkable result, especially considering that 'unlike other postcolonial contexts where top-down processes have been resisted out of misunderstanding or suspicion that learners would be prevented from learning a dominant language, Mozambique's "accidental" bottom-up involvement appears to be a strength of the implementational process' (Chimbutane & Benson, 2012: 11).

Nevertheless, as mentioned, despite the improvements in terms of promotion of African languages and associated cultural values, Portuguese language proficiency is still the *sine qua non* prerequisite for effective political, social and economic mobility in Mozambique. The lack of this resource still prevents citizens from (i) expressing themselves in meso- and top-level decision-making arenas, including in the Parliament, (ii) defending themselves fairly in courts, (iii) doing business with financial institutions, (iv) acquiring new skills and knowledge when this language is the medium of communication, and (v) getting prestigious and well-paid jobs (Gonçalves & Chimbutane, 2015). In a nutshell, as in the colonial era, the lack of Portuguese language proficiency, which is often associated with lack of academic qualifications, is still a constraint to the exercise of what is commonly perceived as the ideal citizenship in Mozambique. This has led some citizens to question the usefulness of learning through African languages in the official domain of school, meaning that for them these could in some way be 'the wrong sort(s) of capital' (Blackledge, 2001). This substantiates the view of linguistic communities as typically bivalent collectivities in the sense that '*both* recognition of a language and the economic visibility of its community of speakers need to be attended to in order to bring about productive use of a language' (Stroud & Heugh, 2004: 199). That is, it is not enough to formally recognize a language if the speakers of that language do not enjoy economic visibility in a given society. This is an issue that needs to be addressed, including by the State, if discourses on multilingualism are to be effectively transformed into legitimate practices of linguistic citizenship. The notion of linguistic citizenship is appropriate to address this issue as it intimately links 'questions of language to sociopolitical discourses of justice, rights and equity' (Stroud, 2001: 351).

Closing Remarks

Taking a historical and sociopolitical perspective, I have shown how citizenship in Mozambique has been linked with language ideologies and educational goals set in different periods of the history of the country. In both colonial and postcolonial Mozambique, the construct of citizenship has been intimately linked with political efforts towards the management of multilingualism and multiculturalism. The assimilationist goal of the Portuguese colonial education aimed at a loyal and acculturated citizen, one who could serve the interests of the colonial state. I showed how the *assimilados*, the privileged local citizens, not only served the colonial power, but also played a crucial role in the destabilization and eventual destruction of the Portuguese empire.

Two major stages characterized the type of citizen envisaged by Frelimo in independent Mozambique. In the early stages, Frelimo aimed at forging a *new man*, a patriotic socialist citizen, free from traditional beliefs and practices and jointly liable with the oppressed peoples around the world.

Based on homogenizing and egalitarian principles, Portuguese was defined as the language of national unity. In contrast, African languages and local traditions remained marginalized as in the colonial period.

I used the lenses of the framework of linguistic citizenship to analyse language politics and practices in Mozambique from the 1990s. I showed how from there on Frelimo has embraced some form of liberal socioeconomic and political perspectives, which changed the relationship between the State and the citizens. As a result, citizens organized themselves in political and civic groups, starting to cooperate but also challenge State decisions. In this democratic era, Frelimo started to construct the view that unity was still possible in diversity. In this context, African languages and associated cultural practices started to make their ways into official domains, especially in education and local governance. This ideological move confirms the definition of post-socialist contexts as being characterized by the 'shift in the grammar of political claims-making from claims of social equality to claims of group difference' (Cowan et al., 2001: 2, quoting Fraser, 1997).

In the current context of democratic transformation of the country, individual citizens and civil society groups are using all opportunities and means at their disposal to have their voices heard by the government. In spite of improvements in terms of democratic participation, the lack of Portuguese language proficiency associated with high levels of illiteracy and lack of experience in participatory democracy still prevent the majority of the population from enjoying full citizenship in Mozambique. To put it differently, participation in the public life of society is still a prerogative of a very few, mainly those who possess Portuguese proficiency and academic qualifications. The majority of citizens can only participate in decision-making processes at the local level.

Bilingual education seems to be setting the ground for future participation of historically marginalized groups in formal decision-making domains. The official use of African languages for education and for local governance is so far enabling local communities to participate in educational, administrative and political decision-making processes relevant to their lives. This substantiates the theoretical point of the linguistic citizenship framework that societies can have and should recognize different forms of participatory engagement at different levels and through different languages and not just through the official language, as it is the case of Portuguese in Mozambique. The hope is that this use of African languages in schools will be, in fact, a step towards their institutionalization as legitimate languages of full and equal citizenship. Meanwhile, these citizens who rely exclusively on African languages for substantive socioeconomic and political participation are still 'disempowered' in the sense that they are often confined to the local-level decision-making and cannot engage with the State directly (McEwan, 2005), but through mediators.

Given the above environment, one can conclude that despite improvements from the 1990s, democratic and inclusive citizenship in Mozambique could still be enhanced if African languages are accorded official status and the voices of their speakers are legitimately heard not only at the grassroots level, but also at high-level decision-making spheres, including in the Parliament. Bilingual education seems to be giving us a hope as the small space so far open to African languages through this form of education is already leading to dynamic processes of citizenship's claims and appropriation. However, even in this arena, the adoption of early-exit transitional models of bilingual education, the government's reluctance to expand the programme countrywide (despite the demand) and the lack of an explicit and de jure language policy in Mozambique may lead one to question whether there is, in fact, a top-level agenda to empower African languages and their speakers or the use of these languages in early stages of primary education is just a conduit aiming at scaffolding the acquisition of Portuguese and assimilation of cultural resources associated with this language.

I also assume that although language policies and legislation on language are not sufficient conditions to guarantee the empowerment of African languages and their speakers. However, I can still argue that they are essential to legitimate language practices that can contribute to change societal attitudes towards those languages and lend visibility to their speakers. Positive attitudes towards low status languages and supporting language ideologies are key in promoting such languages and their speakers. In the case of Mozambique, openness in official discourse and favourable legislation on language diversity enable citizens to legitimately explore new forms of participatory engagement around African languages as it is happening in bilingual schools and local government arenas. In a liberal era where States are assumed to play a facilitating role rather than a tutelary role (see Rose, 2001), citizens are expected to organize themselves in order to promote low status languages and develop alternative forms of linguistic citizenship. The civil society pressures that led the Mozambican government to extend the number of African languages in bilingual education – from five to seven to 16 – indicate that organized citizens can use their capacity and power to lobby and even 'force' the State to develop participatory structures around African languages at all levels of governance and create the necessary dispensations to enable socioeconomic and political visibility to speakers of these languages.

Notes

(1) In fact, the Mozambican revolutionary model of national unity is parallel to the *Ujamaa* political-ideological model of development in Tanzania, although they differ in terms of the languages chosen to mediate them. Whereas Mozambique opted for the former colonial language, Tanzania adopted Swahili, an endogenous language, to articulate the socialist revolution. The similarities between the two countries are not incidental: Tanzania hosted and trained Frelimo freedom fighters during the liberation struggle and, in some way, mentored the post-independence socialist government.

(2) African languages spoken in Mozambique are officially referred to as 'national languages', irrespective of their geographic coverage or number of speakers.

References

Alidou, H. (2004) Medium of instruction in post-colonial Africa. In J.W. Tollefson and A.B.M. Tsui (eds) *Medium of Instruction Policies: Which Agenda? Whose Agenda?* (pp. 195–214). London: Lawrence Erlbaum.

Bamgbose, A. (1999) African language development and language planning. *Social Dynamics* 25 (1), 13–30.

Belchior, M.D. (1965) Evolução política do ensino em Moçambique. In *Moçambique: Curso de Extensão Universitária* (pp. 635–674). Lisboa: Instituto Superior de Ciências Sociais e Política Ultramarina.

Blackledge, A. (2001) The wrong sort of capital? Bangladeshi women and their children's schooling in Birmingham, UK. *International Journal of Bilingualism* 5 (3), 345–369.

Blommaert, J. (2014) *State Ideology and Language in Tanzania* (2nd edn). Edinburgh University Press. Retrieved from http://www.jstor.org/stable/10.3366/j.ctt14brzit (accessed June 10, 2017).

Buendia Gómez, M. (1999) *Educação Moçambicana – História de um Processo: 1962–1984*. Maputo: Livraria Universitária.

Chimbutane, F. (2011) *Rethinking Bilingual Education in Postcolonial Contexts*. Bristol: Multilingual Matters.

Chimbutane, F. and Benson, C. (2012) Expanded spaces for Mozambican languages in primary education: Where bottom-up meets top-down. *International Multilingual Research Journal* 6 (1), 1–14.

Cowan, J.K., Dembour, M-B. and Wilson, R.A. (2001) Introduction. In J.K. Cowan, M-B. Dembour and R.A. Wilson (eds) *Culture and Rights: Anthropological Perspectives* (pp. 1–26). Cambridge: CUP.

Cruz e Silva, T. (2001) *Protestant Churches and the Formation of Political Consciousness in Southern Mozambique (1930–1974)*. Basel, Switzerland: P. Schlettwein Publishing.

Errante, A. (1998) Education and national personae in Portugal's colonial and postcolonial transition. *Comparative Education Review* 42 (3), 267–308.

Ganhão, F. dos R. (1979) O papel da língua portuguesa em Moçambique. Delivered at *1° Seminário Nacional sobre o Ensino da Língua Portuguesa*, October 1979. Ministry of Education and Culture, Maputo.

Gonçalves, P. and Chimbutane, F. (eds) (2015) *Multilinguismo e Multiculturalism em Moçambique: Em Direcção a uma Coerência entre Discurso e Prática*. Maputo: Alcance.

Honwana, L.B. (2015) A rica nossa cultura. In P. Gonçalves and F. Chimbutane (eds) *Multilinguismo e Multiculturalism em Moçambique: Em Direcção a uma Coerência entre Discurso e Prática*. Maputo: Alcance.

Hornberger, N.H. (2002) Multilingual language policies and the continua of biliteracy: An ecological approach. *Language Policy* 1, 27–51.

Instituto Nacional do Desenvolvimento da Educação (2008) Balanço do ensino bilingue em Moçambique. Report presented at *I Seminário Nacional de Balanço da Implementação do Ensino Bilingue em Moçambique*, 4–5 December 2008. Maputo, Mozambique.

Instituto Nacional do Desenvolvimento da Educação/Ministério da Educação (2001) *Programa do Ensino Básico: 1º Ciclo*. Maputo: Instituto Nacional do Desenvolvimento da Educação/Ministério da Educação.

Katupha, J.M. (1994) The language situation and language use in Mozambique. In R. Fardon and G. Furniss (eds) *African Languages, Development and the State* (pp. 89–96). London: Routledge.

Machel, G. (1979) Discurso de abertura. Delivered at *1º Seminário Nacional sobre o Ensino da Língua Portuguesa*, October 1979. Ministry of Education and Culture, Maputo.

Machel, S.M. (1975) Discurso de abertura do Comité Central da FRELIMO em Inhambane. In J. Reis and A.P. Muiuane (eds) *Datas e Documentos Históricos da FRELIMO* (pp. 431–448). Maputo: Imprensa Nacional.

Martin-Jones, M. (2007) Bilingualism, education and the regulation of access to language resources. In M. Heller (ed.) *Bilingualism: A Social Approach* (pp. 161–182). London: Palgrave.

Mateus, D.C. (1999) *A Luta pela Independência: Formação das Elites Fundadoras da FRELIMO, MPLA e PAIGC*. Mira-Sintra, Portugal: Editorial Inquérito.

Mazula, B. (1995) *Educação, Cultura e Ideologia em Moçambique: 1975–1985*. Maputo: Fundo Bibliográfico da Língua Portuguesa/Edições Afrontamento.

McEwan, C. (2005) Gendered citizenship in South Africa: Rights and beyond. In A. Gouws (ed.) *(Un)thinking Citizenship: Feminist Debates in Contemporary South Africa* (pp. 177–197). Aldershot/Hants, UK: Ashgate Publishing Company.

Moll, L.C. (1992) Bilingual classroom studies and community analysis: Some recent trends. *Educational Researcher* 21 (2), 20–24.

Moll, L.C., Amanti, C., Neff, D. and González, N. (1992) Funds of knowledge for teaching: Using a qualitative approach to connect homes and classrooms. *Theory into Practice* 31 (2), 132–141.

Mondlane, E. (1975) *Lutar por Moçambique*. Lisboa: Sá da Costa.

Rassool, N. (2007) *Global Issues in Language, Education and Development: Perspectives from Postcolonial Countries*. Clevedon: Multilingual Matters.

República de Moçambique (1990) Constituição da República. *Boletim da República*, I Série, No. 44, 22 de Dezembro. Maputo: Imprensa Nacional de Moçambique.

República de Moçambique (1992) Sistema Nacional de Educação. *Boletim da República*, I Série, No. 12, 23 de Março. Maputo: Imprensa Nacional.

República de Moçambique (1997) Política cultural e estratégias de sua implementação. *Boletim da República*, I Série, No. 23, 10 de Junho. Maputo: Imprensa Nacional.

República de Moçambique (2004) *Constituição da República (actualizada)*. Maputo: Imprensa Nacional de Moçambique.

República Popular de Moçambique (1983) Sistema Nacional de Educação. *Boletim da República*, I Série, No. 19, 6 de Maio. Maputo: Imprensa Nacional de Moçambique.

Ricento, T. (ed.) (2006) *An Introduction to Language Policy: Theory and Method.* Oxford: Blackwell.

Rose, N. (2001) Community, citizenship and the third way. In D. Meredyth and J. Minson (eds) *Citizenship and Cultural Policy* (pp. 1–17). London: SAGE Publishing.

Skutnabb-Kangas, T. (2008) Human rights and language policy in education. In S. May and N.H. Hornberger (eds) *Encyclopedia of Language and Education, 2nd edition, Vol. 1: Language Policy and Political Issues in Education* (pp. 107–119). New York: Springer.

Stroud, C. (2001) African mother-tongue programmes and the politics of language: Linguistic citizenship versus linguistic human rights. *Journal of Multilingual and Multicultural Development* 22 (4), 339–355.

Stroud, C. (2003) Postmodernist perspective on local languages: African mother-tongue education in times of globalisation. *International Journal of Bilingual Education and Bilingualism* 6 (1), 17–35.

Stroud, C. (2007) Bilingualism: Colonialism and postcolonialism. In M. Heller (ed.) *Bilingualism: A Social Approach* (pp. 107–119). London: Palgrave.

Stroud, C. (2009) Towards a postliberal critique of language rights: Towards a politics of language for a linguistics of contact. In J. Petrovic (ed.) *International Perspectives on Bilingual Education: Policy, Practice and Controversy* (pp. 191–218). New York: Information Age Publishing.

Stroud, C. and Heugh, K. (2004) Language rights and linguistic citizenship. In J. Freeland and D. Patrick (eds) *Language Rights and Language Survival: Sociolinguistic and Sociocultural Perspectives* (pp. 191–218). Manchester: St Jerome Publishing.

Tadadjeu, M. and Chiatoh, B.A. (2005) Mother tongue-focused bilingual education in Cameroon. In N. Alexander (ed.) *Mother Tongue-based Bilingual Education in Southern Africa: The Dynamics of Implementation* (pp. 123–136). Cape Town: PRAESA.

Tollefson, J.W. (ed.) (2002) *Language Policies in Education: Critical Issues.* London: Lawrence Erlbaum Associates.

Yeatman, A. (2001) Who is subject of human rights? In D. Meredyth and J. Minson (eds) *Citizenship and Cultural Policy* (pp. 104–119). London: SAGE Publishing.

6 Paths to Multilingualism? Reflections on Developments in Language-in-Education Policy and Practice in East-Timor[1]

Estêvão Cabral and Marilyn Martin-Jones[2]
Tilburg University, The Netherlands; University of Birmingham, UK

Introduction

This chapter presents our reflections on developments in language-in-education policy and practice in East-Timor in the years since Independence in 2002. We focus on two policy developments. (1) The creation and implementation of the national language-in-education policy, involving the use of the two official languages, Portuguese and Tetum.[3] This policy has been implemented, in a phased manner, in all state schools since 2002. (2) Recent policy moves towards the introduction of a mother-tongue-based, multilingual education programme (MTB-MLE), involving the use of a wider range of languages, including languages that are spoken in different regions of this multilingual nation, that is, the languages that are described as 'national languages' in the Constitution. This second policy move has been made, on a relatively small scale, since 2008, and the MTB-MLE programme is still being piloted.

Both policies provide pathways to multilingualism through schooling, albeit in different ways. They entail different combinations of language resources and different curricular arrangements. They are also underpinned by different discourses, which circulate on different scales – local, national and global. We have been prompted to write this chapter because the recent calls for the development of a MTB-MLE programme in

East-Timor and the launch of a pilot project have given rise to intense language ideological debates. There is therefore a pressing need for reflection on the nature and significance of these two educational pathways to multilingualism and the discourses associated with them need to be unpacked. There is also a need to build a sense of what is happening locally, as different educational pathways are being developed and consolidated. Attention needs to shift to the pedagogic and communicative practices that are emerging in local schools and classrooms. The notion of 'linguistic citizenship' proposed by Stroud (2001, 2009) and Stroud and Heugh (2004) offers some useful pointers as to how researchers and educationalists might redirect their gaze. Local teachers are already engaging in small, local acts of linguistic citizenship as they interpret and appropriate language-in-education policies in ways that are fine-tuned to local social and linguistic conditions. We argue that there is much to be learned from close study of such situated, classroom-based practices about the limits and potential of particular educational pathways to multilingualism.

We begin our chapter by presenting a brief sketch of the sociolinguistic landscape of East-Timor. Then, bearing in mind Blommaert's (1999: 6) argument about the need to take account of the historicity of sociolinguistic data relating to language ideologies and language practices, we provide a historical account of the changes that took place in the social and symbolic significance of Tetum and Portuguese from 1975 to Independence. In the two following sections, we consider the two post-Independence developments in language-in-education policy mentioned above. We look at the multi-layered policy processes involved in the creation of these two educational paths to multilingualism and we unpack some of the policy discourses that are associated with them. In the final section, we turn to the notion of linguistic citizenship and we reflect on how this can guide efforts to build an understanding of the significance of the communicative and pedagogical practices emerging 'on the ground', in local schools and classrooms, and we consider the role of sociolinguistic and ethnographic research in throwing light on this key dimension of policy implementation.

The Sociolinguistic Landscape of East-Timor

The 'languages' of East-Timor

Estimates vary as to the total number of 'languages' that are spoken within the national boundaries of East-Timor (Bowden & Hayek, 2007; Hull, 1998). According to Hayek (2000), the estimates range from 15–20. It depends on whether local varieties get classified as 'languages' or

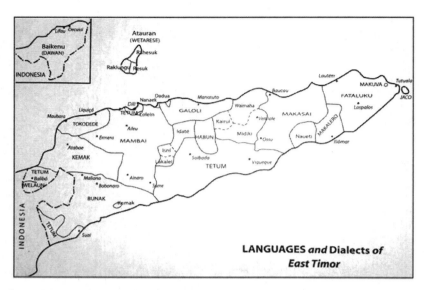

Figure 6.1 Distribution of the language varieties spoken in East-Timor
(Source: Hull, 1993)

'dialects' and on how language names are assigned. Tetum is spoken most widely. According to the 2004 National Census (Direcção Nacional de Estatística, 2006: 80), 86% of the population indicated an ability to speak Tetum, while only 25% claimed it as their first language. This clearly reflects its role as a language of wider communication and as a second language for many East-Timorese.

The National Census of 2004 also showed that a number of other language varieties are spoken by a substantial proportion of the population covered by the census. Figure 6.1 shows the distribution of these other language varieties across the country. This is one of several linguistic maps available. A note of caution is necessary here though, since existing maps vary in the way in which they record the names of different language varieties and differentiate between them. (For an extended and informative discussion of the language data from the 2004 National Census, see Taylor-Leech, 2009, 2011.)

Languages introduced to East-Timor

In addition to the languages spoken locally, a number of European and Asian languages became part of the social, political and economic fabric of life in East-Timor, at different points in its history. Portuguese was imposed as a colonial language from 1516 to 1975. Chinese language varieties (e.g. Hakka) also came to be spoken in the urban areas of East-Timor during this period, as commercial networks and trade developed with Asia. The Indonesian language was then imposed on the population after the invasion of the territory by the military government in Indonesia and during the 24 years of occupation that followed, from 1975 to 1999. And, lastly, English came to be used in urban areas after the arrival of UN peace-keeping troops in 1999. It was used during the UN administration of the territory from 1999 to 2002 (Appleby, 2010), and it continues to be used, on occasion, as a working language in some governmental and institutional contexts, as the work of international aid agencies expands.

The Changing Social and Symbolic Significance of Tetum and Portuguese

The Indonesian occupation and the East-Timorese resistance

The massive social upheavals brought about by the Indonesian invasion and occupation led to the rapid spread of Tetum. Many civilians moved to urban areas like Dili, the capital city, to seek greater security. Tetum thus became a key language of communication in these areas. In addition, with the increase in the student population under the Indonesian occupation, Tetum became the shared vernacular of an increasingly diverse student body.

Another increasingly significant social space for the use of Tetum was the Catholic Church. There was a steady growth in the size of Catholic congregations during the Indonesian occupation, especially after the Church began to play a role in supporting the East-Timorese Resistance (Cabral, 2002; Smythe, 2004). The Church became an important institutional base for the use and cultivation of Tetum, including literacy in Tetum.

In an earlier article (Cabral & Martin-Jones, 2008), we charted the multiple ways in which Tetum and Portuguese were used, in tandem, during the years of East-Timorese Resistance to the Indonesian occupation. We documented the ways in which different kinds of texts were used and produced by those involved in the Resistance, as they worked on different fronts – military, clandestine and diplomatic. Tetum was the main language for communication on the military and clandestine fronts, while Portuguese was reserved for diplomacy and for the internal political affairs of the Resistance. We also noted that these uses of Portuguese transformed the symbolic value of the language, from that of a code associated with the Portuguese colonial order, to that of an emblem of opposition to Indonesian, the language of the occupying power. We argued that this redefinition of Portuguese resembled the ideological process described in South Africa by Pierce (1990: 18): the redefinition of English in opposition to Afrikaans as a 'People's English'.

In this chapter, we argue that the politics and everyday language and literacy practices of the years of the Resistance laid the foundations for the decision-making about constitutional provisions for different languages in the nation-to-be and in the state educational system. We show how consensus was built, prior to independence, with regard to the adoption of Portuguese and Tetum as co-official languages. This period of debate and consensus-building tends to be overlooked in the current literature on language policy in East-Timor, and we feel that it is important to make this more visible since it helps to explain the depth of commitment among different groups in civil society to the national language-in-education policy put in place on Independence. This policy was not a decision that was made in haste on the eve of Independence in 2002. It was the outcome of extended debate, involving wide participation across different political groupings and the different generations involved in the Resistance.

From resistance to preparation for independence: Building a discursive consensus

By the early 1990s, the leadership of the East-Timorese Resistance was already preparing the ground for Independence. By this time, a national Resistance front had been formed. The front grew in size and significance over the remaining years of the struggle, including not only political parties, but also groups from civil society and from within the Catholic church. It was reconstituted in 1998, as Conselho Nacional da Resistência (CNRT – National Council for Timorese Resistance) (Cabral, 2002; Niner, 2001). The front provided a key forum for discussion of the status of different languages within the Constitution of the nation-to-be. These discussions took place over an extended period. There was wide participation, and a broad consensus emerged. A first draft of the Constitution was discussed at a meeting in Portugal in March 1994, which was organized by FRETILIN[4] (one of two political parties at the time). The FRETILIN position on the co-official status of Tetum and Portuguese was stated in this first draft. This position on Tetum and Portuguese was then endorsed in March 1998, at the first meeting of the CNRT.[5]

The UN administration, a nation-in-waiting and the final debates about the Constitution

From 1999 to 2002, the UN Transitional Administration in East-Timor (UNTAET) provided a framework for more detailed preparations for nation building. In March 2001, the newly elected Constituent Assembly set up a committee to review the terms of the Constitution. The debates about provision for languages were taken forward by this committee, including the question of possible roles for English and Indonesian. The final text of the Constitution regarding the status of different languages in East-Timor were as follows.

- Portuguese and Tetum were adopted as co-official languages.
- Tetum was also defined as a national language.
- In addition, all other language varieties in East-Timor were also defined as national languages and were to be protected and valued by the state.
- English and Indonesian were given the status of working languages.

On Independence in May 2002, the terms of the Constitution regarding language became the main reference for language-in-education policy-making.

The New Nation and the Implementation of Language-in-Education Policy

Changing the language of teaching and learning (LoTL)

In the period immediately after the restoration of Independence in 2002, the main focus was on the replacement of Indonesian by Portuguese as the main language of teaching and learning (LoTL) in the schools. This was a staggered process, starting with the new cohort of students entering school and gradually phasing out the use of Indonesian, year by year. The implementation of this initial language-in-education policy was supported through the establishment of bilateral cooperation programmes, primarily with Portugal and, later, with Brazil (Nicolai, 2004). In 2003, the Ministry of Education[6] addressed the task of designing and implementing a new curriculum for primary education (Ministry of Education, Culture, Youth & Sport, 2004a). This task was undertaken with considerable donor assistance and bilateral cooperation. It was primarily funded by UNICEF. Educationalists from a university in Portugal were involved in developing the new curriculum framework (Shah, 2012).

Moves towards bilingual teaching and learning: Portuguese and Tetum as LoTLs

The new framework (Ministry of Education, Culture, Youth & Sport, 2004b) was introduced in September 2005, starting with Grades 1 and 2. There was renewed emphasis on the use of Portuguese as an LoTL, but there was also consideration of the status of Tetum in primary education and of its role in learning, especially in the early grades. The framework stated the principle that 'Portuguese and Tetum are the languages of instruction' (Ministry of Education, Culture, Youth & Sport, 2004b: 8), and one of the curriculum objectives was declared to be 'the development of two languages at the same time in a process of mutual enrichment' (Ministry of Education, Culture, Youth & Sport, 2004b: 9).

Also seen, in 2004, was the formal adoption of a new standardized orthography for Tetum in a governmental decree. The new orthography had been prepared by the National Institute of Linguistics (*Instituto Nacional de Linguística*, 2004). The decree was issued on 14 April 2004. As Taylor-Leech (2009) points out, this 'Language Decree' actually did more than require adherence to the new Tetum orthography. It also confirmed the fact that Tetum and Portuguese were co-official languages.

The elections of 2007 brought in a new coalition government. The new government made a number of moves that were significant for language-in-education policy: first, in April 2008, the Ministry published explicit guidance on the use of Portuguese and Tetum in teaching and learning within the first cycle of primary education (i.e. from Grade 1 to Grade 4). The proportion of time to be devoted, from 2008 onwards, to the use of Tetum and the use of Portuguese at each grade level was stipulated as follows, reflecting a transitional bilingual education model (Ministry of Education, 2008a).

Grade 1:	Tetum 70%	Portuguese 30%
Grade 2:	Tetum 50%	Portuguese 50%
Grade 3:	Tetum 30%	Portuguese 70%
Grade 4:	Tetum 0%	Portuguese 100%

Second, there were new moves towards broader educational policy development and curriculum reform. New legislation regarding basic education was introduced (the Education System Framework Law – Law 14/2008). This was voted into law on 29 October 2008. This law formally established a system of nine years of free and compulsory basic education. Three years of secondary education were then to follow on from the nine years of basic education.

Particularly noteworthy, within the terms of the Education System Framework Law, were the references to language. Three out of 10 objectives for basic education related to language. These objectives were stated as follows (Ministry of Education, 2008b: 8).

- Ensure mastery of Portuguese and Tetum languages (Article 12d).
- Enable the learning of a first foreign language (Article 12e).
- Develop the knowledge and appreciation for the core values of national identity, national and official languages, East-Timorese history and culture, within a perspective of universal humanism and solidarity and cooperation among peoples (Article 12g).

Constraints on policy implementation

The implementation of the primary curriculum and the development of bilingual education, involving both Portuguese and Tetum as LoTLs, proved to be a major challenge. Initially, there was a shortage of teachers, owing to the departure of many teachers who had taught through the medium of Indonesian (UNESCO, 2008). Knowledge of Portuguese was unevenly distributed among those who remained. A World Bank report (2004: 47) noted that only 6% of teachers indicated with confidence that they were fluent in Portuguese. New teachers, with a working knowledge of Portuguese, were recruited from 2002, but significant numbers of them did not have the appropriate training for work at primary or secondary level (Quinn, 2007; Taylor-Leech, 2011).

From the outset, in-service teacher education relating to the teaching of the Portuguese language and to the use of Portuguese across the curriculum has been widely available. This in-service education includes language courses and courses related to the teaching of different areas of the curriculum through the medium of Portuguese. Support for this teacher education has come from a number of different donors, including Portugal, Brazil, UNICEF and some international non-government organizations (NGOs). However, according to Shah (2011: 76), there have been concerns regarding the 'lack of coordination between training providers' and about the fact that 'training was unevenly provisioned across the country'.

In contrast, there has been relatively little in-service support for teachers regarding the teaching of Tetum or the use of Tetum across the curriculum. Most teachers speak Tetum, but few have had experience of writing it in styles and genres associated with formal education. Teachers have also needed an orientation to the new orthography, but there have been few resources available for this. The only providers have been the relatively small and hard-pressed National Institute of Linguistics and one local NGO called Timor Aid. Quinn (2011) refers to an orientation session run by Timor Aid in 2005.

Textbooks and teaching materials in Portuguese have been in reasonably good supply, owing to the bilateral cooperation with Portugal and Brazil. In contrast, there is a paucity of teaching materials in Tetum, though, as we write this chapter, Timor Aid is preparing to distribute high-quality storybooks in Tetum to all schools in East-Timor.[7] As far as we are aware, there are no bilingual materials available.

Diverse discourses about Portuguese and Tetum

Despite the difficulties involved in policy implementation faced by teachers and despite the uncertainties created by the shifts in policy regarding the in-class use of Tetum and Portuguese, research conducted with teachers in local schools (Da Costa Cabral, 2015; Quinn, 2011) suggests that there is still broad support for the use of both Portuguese and Tetum as LoTLs in the early years of schooling. For example, Quinn (2011) showed that, in 2005/6, teachers remained committed to the national language policy goals and stood by the terms of the Constitution. One teacher participating in Quinn's study was quoted as saying: 'according to the Constitution, Portuguese is now the official language with Tetum, so I teach and use both of them' (Quinn, 2011: 231). Referring to her students' existing knowledge of Tetum and Portuguese, another teacher said: 'Tetum is also an official language and it is a language which they are used to speaking. Personally, the two are important and not only choosing Portuguese' (Quinn, 2011: 231). A third teacher talked about the significant challenges that she faced but showed a commitment to the existing policy, saying: 'it is difficult but let's try to make this thing go forward' (Quinn, 2011: 232).

However, different views about the goals of using Tetum, as well as Portuguese, are still being articulated, along with different ideologies of language and different discourses about the value of Tetum. As Da Costa Cabral (2015) has recently demonstrated, some Ministry officials, parliamentarians and academics interpret the policy as advocating that the two languages should have equal weighting in the classroom, depending on the language capabilities of the teacher. Others see the use of Tetum as a transitional phase, with the ultimate goal being to move towards the sole use of Portuguese as the LoTL. Yet others view Tetum as an auxiliary language to be used alongside Portuguese, in some areas of the curriculum. This view has also surfaced in official curriculum documents, such as:

> Since Tetum is at a preliminary stage of development, the implementation of Portuguese will have precedence, and Tetum may be used as a pedagogic aide in the teaching of disciplines related to the environment, social sciences, history and geography. (Ministry of Education, Culture, Youth & Sport, 2004b: 11)

What we see expressed here is a particular ideology of language, one which evaluates particular languages as not having sufficient 'languageness' (Blommaert, 2006) to be used as LoTLs across the curriculum. Inevitably, views such as these, and the prevailing ambivalence about the status of Tetum in East-Timor, are leading to a hierachization of language values across different educational institutions in East-Timor.

East-Timorese politicians have also contributed to this hierachization through statements about the status of Portuguese and other Timorese languages. For example, in May 2012, a new President, Taur Matan Ruak, took office, a decade after Independence. During his inauguration speech (held at the Portuguese school in Dili), he reaffirmed the role of Portuguese as an official language and as an emblem of national identity. He spoke of the process of drafting the terms of the Constitution of 2002 in the following words: 'Let there be no doubt. The option we chose related to politics, strategy and identity. Portuguese is here to stay' (Timor Hau Nian Doben, 2012, our translation). Later in the same speech, the President made reference to the other languages spoken in East-Timor – languages such as Tetum that are widely spoken in urban settings. He described them as being 'less complex' in grammar and lexis than Portuguese and argued that this made the teaching of Portuguese more challenging. He did however conclude by saying that language teaching methods should take account of the fact that Portuguese is not a 'mother tongue' for most East-Timorese.

Portuguese on wider linguistic and educational markets

Two further developments, one on a national scale and one on a global scale, are also contributing to a hierarchization of language values. First, as in other postcolonial contexts, there is a growing private educational sector in East-Timor. The two most prestigious schools, in Dili, the capital city, use only Portuguese as the LoTL and they follow the National Curriculum in Portugal. There are also a number of Catholic schools that use only Portuguese or both Portuguese and Tetum. Portuguese clearly has growing value on the national educational market and is seen as a resource that is tied to social mobility.

Second, in recent years, there have been increasing moves towards the promotion and commodification of Portuguese as a global language (Oliveira, 2014). Underpinning these moves has been the strengthening of political relations between the leaders of countries where Portuguese is an official language – the so-called Community of Portuguese-Speaking Countries (*Communidade dos Países de Lingua Portuguesa*, CPLP). East-Timor is one of the nation-states within this political bloc. The new commitment to the global diffusion of Portuguese is clearly linked to political and mercantile interests in an increasingly multipolar world. Higher educational opportunities are also being opened up in Brazil and Portugal, as part of these globalist initiatives, for those educated around the world through the medium of Portuguese (Signorini, 2015).

In the light of the promotion of this new 'Portuguese-speaking world' and in the light of the growth of Portuguese-medium private education in East-Timor, new discourses about Portuguese are likely to be emerging and competing with the discourse about the role of both Tetum *and* Portuguese in nation-building – a discourse that has its roots in the years of the Resistance to the Indonesian occupation.

The Introduction of a MTB-MLE Programme

This policy development had very different origins from the one we have just discussed. The MTB-MLE policy proposals arose from the concerns of organizations with a global reach – UN agencies, such as UNESCO and UNICEF, and NGOs working internationally – concerns such as social inclusion in basic education and child-centred pedagogy. Among these organizations, the use of children's first language or 'mother tongue' is widely seen as a means of promoting inclusion and *Education for All*.

Initial policy moves

The first traces of a new discourse about 'mother tongues' appeared in the draft of the National Strategic Plan (NESP), in the section about 'social inclusion policy'. The 'mother tongues' being referred to here were, of course, those designated as 'national languages' in the Constitution.

The lessons and outcomes of various local initiatives and of international studies in basic education have demonstrated the superiority of the use of a learner's mother tongue or first language in improving educational outcomes and promoting Education for All. Decisions about language of instruction, particularly in the early primary years, directly impact upon the accessibility, relevance and quality of learning. The Ministry will promote a national debate to define the basis for a national language-in-education policy to be included as a component of the social inclusion policy. (Ministry of Education, 2008b: 69)

Up to this point, the term 'mother tongue' had not been used in discussions of language-in-education policy in East-Timor. Moreover, this was the first time that the idea of using languages other than Tetum or Portuguese in education had been put forward.

Initial proposals for policy change were aired at a conference that was held in Dili in April 2008. It was jointly convened by the Ministry of Education, UNESCO, UNICEF and Care International and addressed the following theme: *Helping children learn: An international conference on bilingual education in Timor-Leste* (Ministry of Education, 2008a)[8]. In addition to East-Timorese stakeholders (teachers, government officials, academics, representatives of local NGOs and speakers of national languages), participants included a number of representatives of 'international agencies for the promotion of mother-tongue based multilingual education' (MTB-MLE) (Taylor-Leech, 2011: 9).

In 2009 and 2010, the Ministry took the idea of introducing MTB-MLE further, under the auspices of a National Education Commission (NEC). This Commission, which included East-Timorese with different institutional affiliations, served as an advisory body to the Ministry and was chaired by Kirsty Sword Gusmão, the wife of the Prime Minister at the time. She also played the role of UNESCO's goodwill ambassador in East-Timor. The NEC was charged with the task of initiating a process that would lead to the drafting of new policy guidelines on language use in primary schools by the end of 2010, taking into account pre-primary education (for children aged 4 and 5) and the nine years of basic education. In April 2010, the NEC set up a Language-in-Education Working Group, which included Ministry of Education staff, civil servants, curriculum specialists, church and youth representatives, parliamentarians and members of local and international NGOs (Ministry of Education, 2011). Several international consultants and specialists in language-in-education policy and practice were approached with a view to advising the Working Group and assisting in the preparation of a new set of policy guidelines. Following two international missions in 2010, draft policy guidelines on MTB-MLE were prepared.

The new policy guidelines on MTB-MLE were released by the Ministry of Education on 21 February 2011 (Taylor-Leech, 2011, 2013). This date was chosen since it has been established by the United Nations as International Mother Tongue Day. As shown in Table 6.1, the new element in the guidelines was that children's 'mother tongue' or 'first language' (L1) should be used as 'a medium of instruction' during the two years of pre-primary education and that initial literacy instruction in Grade 1 should also be in this language. In Grades 2 and 3, it was proposed that there should be bilingual education, with Tetum being taught as a subject and used as 'a medium of instruction', alongside the L1. Portuguese would then be introduced in Grade 4, with Tetum, in a new pattern of bilingual education. At Grade 4, it was also recommended that the children's L1 should continue to be taught as a subject in the curriculum, as Portuguese/Tetum bilingual education was being developed. After Grade 4, the proposal was that both Portuguese and Tetum should be employed as LoTLs for all remaining years of schooling. It was also recommended that English should be introduced as a compulsory foreign language in Grade 7 (the first year of pre-secondary education) and that Indonesian should be made available as an elective subject in Grade 10, at the beginning of secondary education.

In regions where students speak Tetum as an L1 (e.g. in urban areas), it was proposed that Tetum should be used as a medium of instruction from the pre-primary level onwards.

Since 2013, this MTB-MLE programme has been running on a pilot basis in three regions. Four demonstration schools have been identified in each region. The three regions selected are Oé-Cusse (an enclave in West Timor), Lautém and Manatuto. The national languages most widely

Table 6.1 Model of mother tongue-based multilingual education proposed for East-Timor. Adapted from the policy document produced by the National Education Commission of the Ministry of Education (2011)

Language	Pre-Primary	Primary Education – Grades							Pre-Secondary	Secondary
		1	2	3	4	5	6	7–9		10–12
L1	MoI	MoI	MoI	MoI	Subj	Subj	Subj	Subj		Subj
Tetum			MoI	MoI	MoI	MoI	MoI	MoI		MoI
Portuguese					MoI	MoI	MoI	MoI		MoI
English								Subj		Subj
Indonesian										Subj

L1 = first language; MoI = medium of instruction; Subj = taught as a subject in the curriculum.

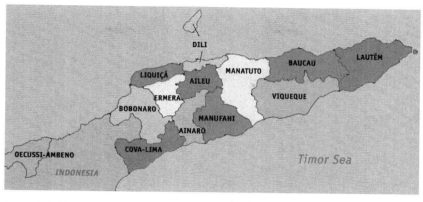

Figure 6.2 The 13 regions of East-Timor (Source: Wikipedia)

spoken in these regions are Baikenu (Oé-cusse), Fataluku (Lautém) and Galolen (Manatuto). These regions are shown in the map in Figure 6.2.

A national debate

Reactions to the new policy guidelines were mixed. A number of local NGOs and student groups held press conferences in which they set out their objections to this policy initiative. The debate then widened, as individuals and groups supporting the MTB-MLE model responded to the objections. These responses were, for the most part, made online or in the East-Timorese, Australian or Portuguese media. One group that was particularly active in responding to objections was called the Network for the Promotion of Multilingual Education (REPETE 13; our translation of the Portuguese title). Details of this debate – the social actors involved, the arguments and counter-arguments – are provided in Cabral (2013). The level of concern generated among different groups in civil society prompted a call for a parliamentary debate on the topic. This took place on 8 February 2012. The Prime Minister, Xanana Gusmão, also issued a press release on 10 February 2012, explaining his position on the issues (Pereira, 2012). As we write this chapter, the pilot project is still underway, but the MTB-MLE programme has yet to be approved by the Parliament.

Unpacking the discourses on either side of the debate

Since the introduction of the pilot version of the MTB-MLE programme, and the ensuing debate, new inter-linked discourses about language-in-education policy have surfaced. Here, we will attempt to explore the linkages between them and to show how they have underpinned different positions in the debate. We focus on three salient discourses: a discourse about 'mother tongues' and 'mother-tongue-based education'; a discourse about linguistic and cultural rights; and a discourse about language and about multilingual education.

Discourse about 'mother tongues' and 'mother-tongue-based education'

UNESCO was, of course, the first UN agency to introduce the idea of 'mother-tongue-based education', as part of a broader child-centred approach. The term 'mother tongue' was employed in the following, much-cited UNESCO statement (UNESCO, 1953, cited in García, 2009: 14): 'Pupils should begin their schooling through the medium of the mother tongue, because they understand it best and because to begin their school life in the mother tongue will make the break between home and school as small as possible'. During the latter half of the 20th century, this principle guided numerous efforts to establish bilingual education programmes in different postcolonial contexts, and in some minority language contexts. However, as Muehlmann and Duchêne (2007: 101) have observed: 'While institutions such as the UN have gained a new visibility in a world increasingly fascinated with international flows, the discourses produced at the UN have remained largely static'.

There has been a recalibration of UNESCO discourses regarding the language of teaching and learning, but the principle of 'mother-tongue-based education' has been retained. For example, in a UNESCO position paper on *Education in a Multilingual World* published in 2003, the organization sets out its 'approach to language and education in the twenty first century' (UNESCO, 2003: 30), in the terms shown below.

(1) UNESCO supports *mother tongue instruction* as a means of improving educational quality by building on the knowledge and experience of the learners and teachers.
(2) UNESCO supports *bilingual* and/or *multilingual education* at all levels of education as a means of promoting both social and gender equality and as a key element of linguistically diverse societies.
(3) UNESCO supports language as an essential component of *intercultural education* in order to encourage understanding between different population groups and ensure respect for fundamental rights.

In point (2) above, we see the original principle of 'mother tongue' use in early primary schooling being linked to a new discourse about the potential of bilingual or multilingual education as a way of addressing social inequality and promoting social inclusion in multilingual contexts. These concerns relate to Millennium Development Goals, such as achieving universal primary education and *Education for All* by 2015. In point (3), we see that the discourse about the use of 'mother tongues' in education is intertwined with a wider UN-based discourse about universal linguistic and cultural rights.

In the recent debate about the MTB-MLE programme in East-Timor, these discourses about 'mother tongues' and about 'multilingual education programmes' were particularly prominent in the arguments put forward by those supporting the programme. Thus, for example, we saw echoes of UNESCO discourses about child-centred education in the Prime Minister's statement to Parliament on 8 February 2012 and in his press release. He focused on the need to cater for children who do not speak Tetum or Portuguese at home, to provide them with access to the school curriculum and to enable them to learn to read and write without having to learn a second language at the same time. He also linked the MTB-MLE programme to the National Education Strategy Framework for 2011–2015. In this way, he situated it within the broad timetable for the achievement of *Education for All* and the Millenium Goals.

Discourse about linguistic and cultural rights

Like the discourse about 'mother tongues', the discourse about 'language rights' and 'language survival' has a long pedigree. As Freeland and Patrick (2004) have pointed out, it is rooted in two movements: (i) a movement known as the Linguistic Human Rights (LHR) movement, which has been led by language activists, educational practitioners and academics who are concerned with the education of children from indigenous groups and other minoritized groups and with the discrimination they face in receiving all of their education through a dominant language; (ii) a movement led primarily by linguists who are concerned about the ongoing decrease in the number of languages spoken in the world. Within this second movement, the arguments about language rights are couched in ecological terms, with reference to the need to preserve cultural diversity. This discourse about 'language rights' and 'language survival' has now been disseminated on a global scale, through particular activist and academic networks (e.g. the NGOs Terralingua and Linguapax) that are linked to UNESCO and through other international organizations, such as the Summer Institute of Linguistics.

In recent years, there has been increasing critique of the LHR movement and the endangered language movement (e.g. Blommaert, 2001; Duchêne & Heller, 2007; Freeland & Patrick, 2004). We will not attempt to survey the problems arising from these political and intellectual movements here. Instead, we will touch on those issues that have particular relevance to the debate about the introduction of the MTB-MLE programme in East-Timor.

One of the arguments that was fielded by REPETE 13, in support of the MTB-MLE project and in response to the critics, made explicit reference, as follows, to 'the rights of the child': 'The right to education in one's mother tongue is a fundamental right enshrined in the Convention on the Rights of the Child (Article 29c)' (REPETE13, 2012). However, in such statements, linguistic and cultural rights are represented as universal and ahistorical, as principles to be observed across all social and political conditions. Therein lies a paradox. As Stroud (2009: 196) puts it, 'the paradox of rights is that, although they are universal, appeals to them are situated in local space and time and filtered through contingent local political, social and economic structures'. Because of the role of the nation-state in distributing scarce cultural and material resources, there are also dangers stemming from the adoption of rights-based discourses. As Stroud (2009: 195) puts it, 'rights discourses encourage groups of speakers to work actively to differentiate themselves from others by claiming unique linkages of language and identity as a way of gaining political leverage in the competition for scarce resources'.

During the East-Timorese debate about the MTB-MLE programme, opponents expressed concern about the prospect of creating divisions between linguistic groups and fostering *suco*-ism (sucos being the smallest administrative units in East-Timor). General concerns were also voiced about the nation splintering into different regionally based groups claiming one particular language variety as the 'emblem' of their unique identity.

Discourses about 'language' and about 'multilingual education'

Recent critical, genealogical accounts of the work of linguists and missionaries during the colonial era (e.g. Errington, 2008; Makoni & Pennycook, 2007; Stroud, 1999, 2007) have drawn our attention to the way in which 'languages', in diverse settings in Africa, Asia and Latin America, were constructed, in essentialist terms, as discrete entities and 'countable institutions' (Makoni & Pennycook, 2007: 2) through the processes of classification, naming and codification. These processes were accompanied by the study of the geographical distribution of speakers of 'distinct languages', through linguistic survey work and the production of linguistic atlases. However, the mapping of the distribution of 'languages' across the regions of a country obscures the complex, multilingual realities on the ground.

Current language maps in East-Timor appear to demonstrate that just one language predominates, region by region, whereas, in reality, the situation is more complex, heterogenous and fluid. Although one 'language' might predominate in one region in terms of sheer numbers of speakers, other 'languages' may also be spoken in some families, villages or urban neighbourhoods. Multilingualism is embedded in the daily lives of individuals and households in each region. The blending of language varieties is a characteristic feature of day-to-day conversations. This is due to a range of social and demographic factors, such as contemporary marriage patterns, increased mobility owing to education, work or commercial activities and access to mobile phone technology, the internet and local radio stations. In addition, as indicated earlier, Tetum is widely spoken as a lingua franca in most regions and in the urban areas.

In the recent debate about the MTB-MLE initiative, critics of the programme raised the question of the impact on smaller linguistic groupings within each region if a 'language' spoken by a group that is numerically dominant is selected for use as the LoTL in the early years. They also voiced concern about the possible creation of new local linguistic hierarchies and new bases for discrimination.

The MTB-MLE programme model assumes that children enter the programme with just one first language (L1). This is clearly not consistent with the multilingual realities we have described above. The model is also based on the idea of 'language separation', across different years of the programme and across different subjects in the curriculum. This is a discourse that has been widely challenged in recent writing on bilingual and multilingual education (Blackledge & Creese, 2014; García, 2009; Lin, 2012; Weber, 2014). Drawing on extended observation and research in multilingual classrooms in Hong Kong, and on extended engagement with educational practitioners (teachers, school heads and teacher educators), Lin (2012: 186) calls for a shift toward the construction of 'multilingual challenge zones'. These are classrooms where 'the curriculum is amplified, not simplified: teachers use "message redundancy" (the key ideas are presented in many different ways, including visuals, multimodalities and multiple linguistic resources)'.

Developing language-in-education policies in a global age: The particular challenge for East-Timor

As we have shown above, the formulation of the policy guidelines for the MTB-MLE programme and the arguments fielded in support of the programme were underpinned by particular discourses about language, about 'mother tongues', about multilingual education, social inclusion and linguistic and cultural rights. We have unpacked some of these discourses and thrown some light on their problematic nature.

In addition, we have endeavoured to show that, in these post-2008 policy moves towards the MTB-MLE model, it is possible to discern the discursive impact of 'partnership' between supranational agencies, such as UNESCO, and the East-Timorese government in the governance of education. Because nation-states like East-Timor have become increasingly positioned as 'partners' with various supranational organizations and donors, in the globalized world of the 21st century, the discourses of such organizations are becoming ever more deeply embedded in policy-making on a national scale.

As a consequence of the introduction of the MTB-MLE programme in East-Timor, the original discourse about nation-building, which led to the commitment to Tetum and Portuguese bilingualism for all (within the state education system), now jostles for place with other discourses about multilingual citizenship in a more complex discursive order. As we showed earlier, the original discourse emerged out of extended debates among East-Timorese over almost two decades. It is a discourse that is shared across different social groups within civil society. The new MTB-MLE discourses have been introduced relatively recently and in a largely top-down manner, with globalized institutions exercising considerable influence. There have now been attempts at consultation with civil society groups, but the arguments in favour of 'mother-tongue-based provision' have not always been made with sufficient clarity and depth.

Linguistic Citizenship from Below

What gets overlooked in contemporary debates about national language-in-education policy or about models of bilingual or multilingual education is what actually happens 'on the ground', in particular schools and classrooms, as policies and programmes are interpreted or appropriated (or reinvented). As Ramanathan (2005: 89) reminds us, drawing on her ethnographic research in different educational settings in Gujarat, India, we need to 'go beyond thinking of language policies as entities that "happen to" humans'. We also need to 'view policies as hybrid entities that draw their force and movement from the lives of real people and their motivations' (Ramanathan, 2005) Parents, local communities, teachers and school heads are, ultimately, those who contribute most directly to the making and (re)fashioning of language policies and the workings of language education programmes.

What this suggests is that more attention should be given to local initiative and local participation in bringing about and consolidating changes in language-in-education policy and practice. As Stroud and Heugh (2004) have argued, this means that we need to adopt a different view of language, education and citizenship and different ways of conceptualizing linguistic and cultural rights. Citing Janoski (1998), they distinguish between four different kinds of rights: legal, political, social (e.g. rights related to access to education) and participation rights. They also note that in a liberal discourse about rights, such as that manifested in the LHR movement, the focus is primarily on legal and political rights. Furthermore, as they rightly observe, 'the effects of globalization and the spread of the western liberal paradigm in conjunction with development aid and capitalism, have given heaviest weight to a liberal interpretation of rights' (Stroud & Heugh, 2004: 192). Instead, what is needed is more attention to social and participatory rights, alongside a top-down granting and safe-guarding of legal and political rights. With regard to language-in-education issues, this would allow for more agency and choice on the part of local stakeholders, in what has come to be known as active 'linguistic citizenship' (Stroud, 2001, 2009; Stroud & Heugh, 2004).

Given the complex discursive pressures on the governance of language-in-education in East-Timor, within the postcolonial and globalizing conditions that we have described in this chapter, the idea of a shift of focus to the local (implicit in the notion of linguistic citizenship) is appealing. It enables us to address pressing questions, such as: How can we build an understanding of what is already happening in local schools and classrooms, within different kinds of educational pathways? How might opportunities be created for local voices to be heard in policy-making? What role might research be able to play? Canagarajah (2005: 197) also argues that we need to turn our gaze to the local. He says: 'Like good ethnographers, we should first observe the practices that are developing in local situations'. In addition, he reminds us that, in postcolonial contexts, ethnography can provide a window on some of the fluidity and overlap in communicative practices that have been obscured historically by the imposition of models of language and of language education from the global north.

This is surely the way forward. Local educational practitioners and teachers play a key role in policy-making 'on the ground', interpreting and appropriating (or reinventing) policy 'on paper' within the daily rounds of school and classroom life. They make things work multilingually and multimodally in ways that are locally meaningful, taking account of the linguistic repertoires and knowledge resources of their students. These are locally situated practices – local acts of linguistic citizenship – that need to be more fully acknowledged and understood. As we noted earlier, research of a sociolinguistic and ethnographic nature is a means of foregrounding local, situated practices such as these, while at the same time, building a broader understanding of how local policy-making processes are shaped by wider social, institutional and discursive conditions.

In addition to opening a window on local practices of policy appropriation, such research can also open up spaces for dialogue with educational practitioners about the limits and potential of particular multilingual and multimodal ways of working in the classroom and about the creation of new, localized pathways to multilingualism. Classroom-based ethnography is well suited to the goal of fostering researcher–practitioner dialogue and collaboration because it involves extensive engagement with research participants over the span of a research project. As Pennycook (2001: 8) has suggested, critical research of this kind can also be oriented to contributing to change in local settings (e.g. through local contributions to in-service teacher education), and to the broader educational process of defining and working towards 'preferred futures'.

Retrospective: January 2016

Since we wrote our chapter for this volume, there has been relatively little change in the terms of the debate about language-in-education policy in East-Timor, and about the two educational paths to multilingualism that we have described. The discourses underpinning the arguments in favour of the recent Mother Tongue-Based, Multilingual Education (MTB-MLE) Project remain the same, and so do those that underpin the arguments in support of the national language-in-education policy, which was introduced in 2002 and which is now explicitly based around the use of both Tetum and Portuguese, as languages of teaching and learning (LoTLs). Diverging views about these two paths to multilingualism are still widely expressed across civil society, among parliamentarians, and even within the Ministry of Education.

While the policy debates continue, we need to build a fuller understanding of the actual ways in which language-in-education policy processes are unfolding, at the local level, in East-Timor, and we need to know more about the ways in which policy prescriptions 'on paper', and different policy discourses, are being interpreted and appropriated by local educational practitioners and teachers. As we have seen from recent research in the ethnography of language policy (Johnson, 2009; McCarty, 2011), language policy processes are complex and multi-layered. For example, Johnson (2009: 141) has argued that language policy implementation needs to be reconceptualized as 'a tripartite set of processes – creation, interpretation and appropriation', involving different social actors, on different scales: local, national and global.

The national language-in-education policy

As we have shown in our chapter, the national language-in-education policy was created by the Ministry of Education, through bilateral cooperation and through donor assistance, and was eventually launched, on Independence, in 2002. Since then is has been interpreted and appropriated by local school heads and teachers, within the daily routines of school and classroom life, in different regions of the country. Teachers, in particular, have been playing a key role in the 'making' of the policy on the ground, drawing on different textual and material resources and taking account of the linguistic repertoires and knowledge resources of their students. As we noted in our chapter, these are locally situated practices, which we could call 'local acts of linguistic citizenship'. They are practices that need to be more fully acknowledged, documented and understood. Local classroom practices are unlikely to be uniform across the national education system, so there is an urgent need for multi-sited research, in different regions of the country.

Building on the tradition of the ethnography of language policy, research of an ethnographic and discourse analytic nature has recently been carried out with teachers in a Dili primary school (Da Costa Cabral, 2015). Through extended classroom observation, over four months of fieldwork, through detailed analysis of multilingual classroom interaction around textbooks in Portuguese and through interviews with teachers and educational practitioners, this researcher provided revealing insights into the ways in which the teachers mediated textbook content for their students. The teachers moved, in subtle and nuanced ways, between Portuguese and Tetum, making conceptual links between the world of the textbook and the local life worlds of the students. The fine-grained discourse analytic dimension of this study was made possible by the fact that the researcher was familiar with both Portuguese and Tetum.

The research by Da Costa Cabral (2015) was carried out in Dili, where most students speak Tetum, so the bilingual pedagogic strategies being developed by the teachers were consistent with the national language-in-education policy for all schools. However, this Dili-based study now needs to be followed up by further detailed ethnographic and discourse analytic research in other regions of East-Timor, where the linguistic repertoires and knowledge resources of students, and their teachers, are different. Such research would give us a window on the specific ways in which teachers and learners, in different regions, are navigating the national language-in-education policy as part of the routine, multilingual interactional life of local schools. It would also enable us to understand how local language resources are blended with Tetum and Portuguese, in ways that are locally meaningful.

The MTB-MLE project

In our chapter, we also traced the policy moves that led to the launch of the MTB-MLE project. Following the drafting of the policy guidelines by international advisors in 2010, and the design of the 'additive' model of multilingual education (Table 6.1), two years (2011–2013) were set aside for planning and for preparation of the pilot phase. The pilot began in 2013 in three regions – Oé-Cusse, Lautém and Manatuto – with four demonstration schools opting in to the pilot in each region. A strategic evaluation of the pilot was carried out in April 2014 by four Australian researchers (Caffery et al., 2014). However, formal approval of the MTB-MLE project by the Parliament and by the Council of Ministers is still awaited.

Concerted efforts continue to be made to engage in communication and advocacy by the individuals, groups and institutions that originally proposed and designed the project. The project is presented in a range of ways: via talks in public fora and at academic conferences (e.g. De Jesus Soares, 2015) and via digital media (e.g. Facebook and YouTube). For example, a video was posted on both these media in December 2015. It was recorded in one of the schools taking part in the pilot in Lautém. The video was presented trilingually: some of the class takes place in Fataluku and some in Tetum, there is ongoing commentary in spoken and written Portuguese, and Tetum and Portuguese appear in the written title of the video, with Tetum appearing first (Aprende ho ha'u-nia Lian Inan/ Aprender com a minha Lingua Materna, 2015; 'Learning with my Mother Tongue', our translation). A recent statement by the UNESCO office in Bangkok makes explicit reference to these attempts to promote the pilot project and give it greater visibility. It also details the work being devoted to the development of orthographies for the local languages involved (Baikenu, Fataluku and Galolen), and to the preparation of teaching materials (UNESCO Bangkok, 2015: 3).

The strategic evaluation of the MTB-MLE pilot was commissioned by the TLNCU (Timor-Leste National Commission for UNESCO) and took account of the ongoing tracking of the pilot (via a baseline and a midline report) by CARE International, a NGO providing support for the project. During their brief 12-day visit to East-Timor, the Australian team made classroom observations in two of the regions where the pilot was based – in Lautem (two schools) and in Manatuto (one school). They observed five pre-primary classes (including the one that appears in the MTB-MLE video) and one Grade 1 class. They also visited schools that were not involved in the MTB-MLE pilot and made brief classroom observations. In addition, they carried out interviews with key stakeholders and assessed teacher-training materials.

The team set out to address four questions: 'How well are the principles of the MTB-MLE policy working, as evidenced by the pilot? What are its benefits? Where can it be modified and improved? How can it be scaled up in Timor-Leste?' (Caffery et al., 2014: II). From the formulation of these questions and from the overall content of the report, it is clear that the work undertaken did not involve any reflection on or interrogation of the discourses underpinning the MTB-MLE project, for example the discourses about 'mother tongues' and 'mother-tongue-based education' long associated with UNESCO; and the discourses about the organization of multilingual education around a 'language separation' approach and an 'additive' model. On a first reading of the report, we assumed that the authors had been constrained by the fact that the evaluation had been commissioned by the TLNCU. We were therefore surprised to see that these discourses surfaced again in the article published in Language Policy, by three of the four original authors of the report (Caffery et al., 2016).

The strategic evaluation report is, however, of interest because it represents a first attempt to conduct independent observations of the local practices unfolding around the MTB-MLE pilot. It has also produced the first soundings of the views of different stakeholders, at the local and national level. It gives an informative account of the positive features of the MTB-MTB project and it is candid about some of the challenges it faces.[9] These positive features and challenges are framed as 'key lessons', which are accompanied by recommendations.

Many of the positive features (reported as 'benefits') of the MTB-MLE pilot actually have considerable relevance for general provision for early years education in East-Timor, whether it is organized as part of the MTB-MLE project or within the mainstream education system. The positive features have been developed and sustained with external financial and technical support and with considerable investment in teacher education. The features identified through the classroom observations include: the use of high-quality teaching materials (e.g. big books, readers and storytelling materials, with illustrations 'reflecting East Timorese realities' (Caffery et al., 2014: 28); the presence of a teaching assistant in each class; the scheduling of in-service teacher education sessions in the regional sites as well as in Dili and some evidence of interactive pedagogy. Another positive feature identified through interviews with stakeholders was the local interest generated and parental involvement in the MTB-MLE pilot. One of the strengths of the report is that it calls for cross-fertilization of ideas between the MTB-MLE project and the mainstream 'path to multilingualism'. Mention is, for example, made of possible collaboration around the development of the early years curriculum for Tetum.

Despite the constraints imposed by short-term consultancy work, the strategic evaluation report does provide useful pointers for future research in schools where the MTB-MLE pilot is based. Some of the challenges to the MTB-MLE project that are mentioned in the report merit closer investigation: Why, for example, did one school withdraw from the pilot? Why do the staff in the Grade 1 class 'still follow the requirements of the mainstream curriculum, even when it goes against the principles of MTB-MLE' (Caffery et al., 2014: 36)?

There is clearly a pressing need for classroom-based research of an ethnographic and discourse analytic nature in some of the schools and classrooms involved in the MTB-MLE pilot. The authors of the report represent – rather unconvincingly – the brief school and classroom observations that they undertook over 12 days as 'School ethnographies' (Caffery et al., 2014: 7). This point is further reinforced in the article published by three of the original authors (Caffery et al., 2016: 7–8). However, some of the fleeting insights from their classroom observations now need to be complemented by ethnographic fieldwork of a much longer duration, by commitment to extended engagement with educational practitioners and teachers and by close analysis of multilingual classroom talk and multimodality. This research also needs to be grounded in multilingual and reflexive research practice of the kind that has been developed by researchers such as Creese et al. (2017). It is in this way, that we are likely to be able to build a deeper understanding of the ways in which local educational practitioners are interpreting and appropriating (or reimagining) the 'principles' of the MTB-MLE model. We will also be able to provide a fuller account of the practices of teaching and learning unfolding in these classes, showing more precisely how teachers are drawing on the language and communicative resources available to them, as they mediate texts with and for their students, in ways that are locally meaningful.

Notes

(1) *East-Timor* is the English version of the name of this nation-state in South East Asia. It is also customary to use the Portuguese name, *Timor-Leste,* or the Tetum name, *Timor-Lorosae,* since these are the two official languages.
(2) The authors would like to acknowledge the advice and assistance of Ildegrada da Costa Cabral, Alan Silvio Ribeiro Carneiro, Danielle Boon and Kerry Taylor-Leech while writing this chapter.
(3) Our spelling of *Tetum* follows that advocated by the National Institute of Linguistics in East-Timor for all writing in English.
(4) FRETILIN stands for Frente Revolucionária do Timor-Leste Independente (Revolutionary Front for an Independent East-Timor).
(5) Estêvão Cabral participated in both of these meetings.
(6) The name of the Ministry of Education changed a number of times from 2002 onwards, as its functions and the scope of its work changed. It was originally the Ministry of Education, Culture, Youth and Sport (MECYS). In 2005, it became the Ministry of Education and Culture (MEC). And, in 2008, it was renamed the Ministry of Education. However, culture remains one dimension of the overall work of the Ministry.
(7) Personal communication with a member of staff at Timor Aid, who provided copies of some of the books (December 2014).
(8) This is an English translation of the original conference theme. The original theme was worded bilingually, in Tetum and Portuguese, as follows: 'Fo tulun atu labarik sira aprende/Ajudando as crianças a aprender'.
(9) The Strategic Evaluation of the MTB-MLE pilot has clearly benefitted from the participation of one researcher, Dr Taylor-Leech, who has been a close observer of and an informed commentator on language policy developments in East-Timor for close to a decade.

References

Appleby, R. (2010) *ELT, Gender and International Development.* Bristol: Multilingual Matters.
Aprende ho ha'u-nia Lian Inan Aprender com a minha Língua Materna/Learning with my Mother Tongue (2015) https://www.youtube.com/watch?v=OV3K0BKme3I (accessed December 16, 2015).
Blackledge, A. and Creese, A. (eds) (2014) *Heteroglossia as Practice and Pedagogy.* New York: Springer.
Blommaert, J. (1999) The debate is open. In J. Blommaert (ed.) *Language Ideological Debates* (pp. 1–38). Berlin: Mouton de Gruyter.
Blommaert, J. (2001) The Asmara Declaration as a sociolinguistic problem: Reflections on scholarship and linguistic rights. *Journal of Sociolinguistics* 5 (1), 131–155.

Blommaert, J. (2006) Language policy and national identity. In T. Ricento (ed.) *An Introduction to Language Policy: Theory and Method*. Oxford: Blackwell.

Bowden, J. and Hayek, J. (2007) Not just Tetum: Language development and the case of Waima'a. In M. Leach and D. Kingsbury (ed.) *East-Timor: Beyond Independence* (pp. 263–274). Clayton, Victoria: Monash Asia Press.

Cabral, E. (2002) FRETILIN and the struggle for independence in East-Timor, 1974–2002: An examination of the constraints and opportunities for a non-state nationalist movement in the late twentieth century. PhD thesis, Lancaster University, UK.

Cabral, E. (2013) The development of language policy in a global age: The case of East-Timor. In J. Arthur Shoba and F. Chimbutane (eds) *Bilingual Education and Language Policy in the Global South* (pp. 83–103). Abingdon, Oxon: Routledge.

Cabral, E. and Martin-Jones, M. (2008) Writing the resistance: Literacy in East-Timor 1975–1999. *International Journal of Bilingual Education and Bilingualism* 11 (2), 149–169.

Caffery, J., Coronado, G., Hodge, B. and Taylor-Leech, K. (2014) The Timor-Leste Mother Tongue Based Multilingual Education Pilot Project: A strategic evaluation. Available at: www.canberra.edu.au/researchrepository (accessed December 16, 2015).

Caffery, J., Coronado, G. and Hodge, B. (2016) Multilingual language policy and mother tongue education in Timor-Leste: A multi-scalar approach. *Language Policy* 15 (4), 561–580.

Canagarajah, S. (2005) Accommodating tensions in language-in-education policies: An afterword. In A.M.Y. Lin and P.W. Martin (eds) *Decolonization, Globalization: Language-in-Education Policy and Practice* (pp. 194–201). Clevedon: Multilingual Matters.

Creese, A., Blackledge, B., Bhatt, A., Jonsson, C., Juffermans, K., Li, J., Martin, P., Muhonen, A. and Takhi, J. K. (2017) Researching bilingual and multilingual education multilingually: A linguistic ethnography. In W.E. Wright, S. Boun and O. García (eds) *Handbook of Bilingual & Multilingual Education* (pp. 127–144). Malden, MA and Oxford, UK: Wiley/Blackwell.

Da Costa Cabral, I. (2015) Multilingual talk, classroom textbooks and language values: A linguistic ethnographic study in Timor-Leste. PhD thesis, University of Birmingham, UK.

De Jesus Soares, F. (2015) Mother Tongue-Based Multilingual Education (MTB-MLE) Pilot Program – A Step towards Providing Quality Education in Timor-Leste. Paper presented at the 5th Timor-Leste Studies Association Research Conference, 'Timor-Leste: The Local, the Regional and the Global', UNTL, 9–10 July 2015.

Direcção Nacional de Estatística (2006) *National Priority Tables: Census of Population and Housing 2004*. Dili: Republica Democratica de Timor-Leste (RDTL), Direcção Nacional de Estatística and United Nations Population Fund (UNFPA).

Duchêne, A. and Heller, M. (eds) (2007) *Discourses of Endangerment: Interest and Ideology in the Defence of Languages*. London/New York: Continuum.

Errington, J. (2008) *Linguistics in a Colonial World*. Oxford: Blackwell.

Freeland, J. and Patrick, D. (eds) (2004) *Language Rights and Language Survival*. Manchester: St Jerome Publishing.

García, O. (2009) *Bilingual Education in the 21st Century*. Oxford: Wiley-Blackwell.

Hayek, J. (2000) Language planning and the sociolinguistic environment in East-Timor: Colonial practice and changing language ecologies. *Current Issues in Language Planning* 1 (3), 400–414.

Hull, G. (1993) *Mau Kolia Tetun: A Course in Tetun-Praça*. Sydney: Australian Catholic Relief and the Australian Catholic Social Justice Council.

Hull, G. (1998) The languages of Timor 1772–1997. *Studies in East-Timorese Languages and Cultures* 1, 1–38.

Instituto Nacional de Linguística (2004) *The Standard Orthography of the Tetum Language: 115 Years in the Making*. Dili: Instituto Nacional de Linguística.

Janoski, T. (1998) *Citizenship and Civil Society: A Framework of Rights and Obligations in Liberal, Traditional and Social Democratic Regimes*. Cambridge: Cambridge University Press.

Johnson, D.C. (2009) Ethnography of language policy. *Language Policy* 8 (2), 139–159.

Lin, A.M.Y. (2012) Multilingual and multimodal resources in genre-based pedagogical approaches to L2 English content classrooms. In C. Leung and B. Street (eds) *English: A Changing Medium for Education* (pp. 79–103). Bristol: Multilingual Matters.

Makoni, S. and Pennycook, A. (eds) (2007) *Disinventing and Reconstituting Languages*. Clevedon: Multilingual Matters.

McCarty, T. (ed.) (2011) *Ethnography of Language Policy*. New York: Routledge.

Ministry of Education, Culture, Youth and Sport (2004a) *Primary Curriculum Implementation Plan: Timor-Leste 2004–2009*. Dili: MECYS, RDTL.

Ministry of Education, Culture, Youth and Sport (2004b) *Education Policy 2004–2009*. Dili: MECYS, RDTL.

Ministry of Education (2008a) *Helping Children Learn: An International Conference on Bilingual Education in Timor-Leste*. (UNICEF, UNESCO and Care International.) Dili: MoE, RDTL.

Ministry of Education (2008b) *Education System Framework Law 14/2008 (Government of Timor-Leste)*. Dili: MoE, RDTL. See www.scribd.com/Structure-Ministry-Education-English/d/35236407 (accessed 9 March 2012).

Ministry of Education (2011) *Mother Tongue-Based Multilingual Education for Timor-Leste: National Policy* (Komisaun Nasional Edukasaun-National Education Commission). Dili: MoE, RDTL.

Muehlmann, S. and Duchêne, A. (2007) Beyond the nation-state: International agencies as new sites of discourse on bilingualism. In M. Heller (ed.) *Bilingualism: A Social Approach* (pp. 96–110). Basingstoke, Hampshire: Palgrave Macmillan.

Nicolai, S. (2004) *Learning Independence: Education in Emergency and Transition in Timor-Leste since 1999*. Paris: International Institute for Educational Planning.

Niner, S. (2001) A long journey of Resistance: The origins and struggle of CNRT. In R. Tanter, M. Selden and S.R. Shalom (eds) *Bitter Flowers, Sweet Flowers: East-Timor, Indonesia and the World Community* (pp. 15–29). Oxford: Rowman and Littlefield.

Oliveira, G.M. (2014) An amplified Atlantic: Portuguese in the linguistic policies of the 21st century. In L. Moita Lopes (ed.) *Global Portuguese: Language Ideologies in Late Modernity*. Abingdon, Oxon: Routledge.

Pennycook, A. (2001) *Critical Applied Linguistics*. Mahwah, NJ: Lawrence Erlbaum.

Pereira, A. (Secretary of State for the Council of Ministers and Official Spokesperson for the Government of Timor-Leste) (2012) Media release: Prime Minister explains Government's policy on Mother Tongue in Parliament, 10 February 2012. See www.timor-leste.gov.tl (accessed 4 March 2012).

Pierce, B.N. (1990) The author responds. *TESOL Quarterly* 24 (1), 105–112.

Quinn, M. (2007) The challenge of realising language and literacy goals in East-Timorese schools. In D. Kingsbury and M. Leach (eds) *East-Timor: Beyond Independence* (pp. 251–262). Melbourne: Monash University Press.

Quinn, M. (2011) The Languages of Schooling in Timor-Leste: Patterns and Influences on Practice. Unpublished PhD Thesis, University of Melbourne.

Ramanathan, V. (2005) Rethinking language planning and policy from the ground up: Refashioning institutional realities and human lives. *Current Issues in Language Planning* 6 (2), 89–101.

REPETE 13 (The Timor-Leste Network for the Promotion of Multilingual Education) (2012) REPETE 13 responds to Rede Feto/FONGTIL on the implementation of the MTB-MLE pilot program, 25 January 2012. See east-timor@lists.rise-up.net (accessed 26 January 2012).

Shah. R. (2011) It takes two (or more) to tango: Partnerships within the education sector in Timor-Leste. *International Education Journal: Comparative Perspectives* 10 (2), 71–85.

Shah, R. (2012) Goodbye conflict, hello development? Curriculum reform in Timor-Leste. *International Journal of Educational Development* 32, 31–38.

Signorini, I. (2015) Portuguese, politics, policy and globalization. In L. Moita Lopes (ed.) *Global Portuguese: Language Ideologies in Late Modernity*. Abingdon, Oxon: Routledge.

Smythe, P. (2004) '*The Heaviest Blow*': *Responses within the Catholic Church to the East-Timor Issue*. New Brunswick (USA) and London: Transaction Publishers.

Stroud, C. (1999) Portuguese as ideology and politics in Mozambique: Semiotic (re)constructions of a postcolony. In J. Blommaert (ed.) *Language Ideological Debates* (pp. 343–380). Berlin: Mouton de Gruyter.

Stroud, C. (2001) African mother-tongue programmes and the politics of language: Linguistic citizenship versus linguistic human rights. *Journal of Multilingual and Multicultural Development* 22 (4), 339–355.

Stroud, C. (2007) Bilingualism: Colonialism and postcolonialism. In M. Heller (ed.) *Bilingualism: A Social Approach* (pp. 25–49). Basingstoke: Palgrave.

Stroud, C. (2009) A post-liberal critique of language rights: Toward a politics of language for a linguistics of contact. In J.E. Petrovic (ed.) *International Perspectives on Bilingual Education: Policy, Practice and Controversy* (pp. 191–217). Charlotte, NC: Information Age Publishing.

Stroud, C. and Heugh, K. (2004) Language rights and linguistic citizenship. In J. Freeland and D. Patrick (eds) *Language Rights and Language Survival* (pp. 191–218). Manchester: St Jerome Publishing.

Taylor-Leech, K. (2009) The language situation in Timor-Leste. *Current Issues in Language Planning* 10 (1), 1–68.

Taylor-Leech, K. (2011) Timor-Leste: Sustaining and maintaining the national languages in education. *Current Issues in Language Planning* 12 (2), 289–308.

Taylor-Leech, K. (2013) Finding space for non-dominant languages in education: Language policy and medium of instruction in Timor-Leste 2000–2010. *Current Issues in Language Planning* 14 (1), 109–120.

Timor Hau Nian Doben (2012) Timor Hau Nian Doben. See http://timorhauniandoben.blogspot.com.au/2012/05/jornalistas.portugueses.deturpam.html (accessed 28 May 2012).

UNESCO (2003) *Education in a Multilingual World: Position Paper*. Paris: UNESCO.

UNESCO (2008) *The State of Education in the Asia-Pacific Region*. Bangkok: UNESCO.

UNESCO Bangkok (2015) Multilingual Education. See www.unescobkk.org/timor-leste (accessed December 16, 2015).

Weber, J.J. (2014) *Flexible Multilingual Education: Putting Children's Needs First.* Bristol: Multilingual Matters.

World Bank (2004) *Timor-Leste: Education since Independence: From Reconstruction to Sustainable Improvement* (Report No, 29784-TP). Washington, D.C: Human Development Sector Unit East Asia and Pacific Region.

7 Language Rights and Thainess: Community-based Bilingual Education is the Key

Suwilai Premsrirat* and Paul Bruthiaux**
*Mahidol University; **Language Consultant

The Language Ecology of Thailand[1]

Thailand is situated at the heart of Southeast Asia and is one of the most complex areas as regards languages and ethnicities in the subregion. The 70 languages of Thailand belong to five language families: Austroasiatic (22), Austronesian (3), Tai (24), Sino-Tibetan (19), and Hmong-Mian (2) (Premsrirat et al., 2004). These languages are hierarchically interrelated within Thai society, with standard Thai, the official and national language, occupying the highest position. Immediately below Thai in the hierarchy are its major regional variants: Kam Muang (Northern Thai), Lao Isan (Northeastern Thai), Pak Tai (Southern Thai), and Thai Klang (Central Thai), each acting as the lingua franca of local communities. Lower still are a number of ethnic minority languages, several of which are at risk of extinction (on which more below). Ethnic minority speakers are therefore bilingual or multilingual and live in a diglossic environment. They speak their ethnic language at home with family, neighbours, and members of their ethnic group. They speak the regional variant of the national language or the national language itself in social domains where the situation demands it or when the people they are speaking to do not understand their ethnic language. In schools and government offices, on formal occasions, and in the media, only standard Thai is used.

In recent decades, increasing globalization in the economy, culture, and communication has led to major shifts in this language ecology, a process that has been exacerbated in Thailand by nationalism, especially as regards the national language and education policies that promote its exclusive use as the medium of instruction in schools. As better job prospects require the use of the national language, the younger generation does not see the value of multilingualism and even harbours negative attitudes toward ethnic languages, which have become stigmatized. As a result, this generation is becoming increasingly monolingual in standard Thai, even among members of ethnic minorities.

At present, at least 15 ethnic languages are considered severely endangered in Thailand. They are small-enclave languages surrounded by larger language groups, and are scattered over various parts of the country. Nine of these languages belong to the Austroasiatic family and are indigenous to mainland Southeast Asia. These are: Chong, Kasong, Sammre, Chung, So (Thavung), Nyah Kur, Lavua, Maniq, and Mlabri. Three belong to the Sino-Tibetan family: Gong, Mpi, and Bisu. Two are Austronesian (Urak Lawoi and Moken/Moklen), and one is Tai (Saek). Among these, Kasong, Sammre, and Chung have no realistic hope of surviving the death of the last few elderly speakers, and they are being documented as extensively as possible. Meanwhile, languages with more speakers, including Northern Khmer, Mon, and Patani Malay, are declining, and even regional variants of Thai, such as Kam Muang (Northern Thai), Pak Tai (Southern Thai), and Lao Isan (Northeastern Thai), are not safe and are showing signs of contraction, especially in the areas of vocabulary and grammar. Only standard Thai is safe.

This loss of languages means the loss of knowledge systems, local wisdom, world views, history, and means of communicating and promoting cultural or ethnic identity at the local level. When language loss occurs among an ethnic minority, the cultural identity of its members is threatened. Language loss leads to a loss of self-confidence, self-esteem, and life-long security. Many students fail in school and thus have no realistic prospects of higher education or good jobs. These students are often considered by outsiders to be slow-witted and destined not to succeed in the modern world. However, some groups are strongly resisting the process of Thainization promoted by the central government, in particular the Patani Malay-speaking people of Thailand's deep south (on which more later). In these communities, many fear that education is being used as a means to destroy their cultural identity, and they reject the exclusive use of standard Thai as the medium of instruction along with the often locally irrelevant content of compulsory public education.

Language Decline and International Responses

Language decline is a widespread issue as a blend of globalization and nationalism contributes to the forced assimilation of diverse linguistic and cultural identities into the dominant culture in many countries world-wide. In response, there is widespread concern among scholars and international organizations over the loss of linguistic and cultural diversity as well as a growing recognition of the role played by both in the quality of education for ethnic minorities. As Wurm notes:

> Every language reflects a unique world view and culture mirroring the manner in which a speech community has resolved its problems in dealing with the world and has formulated its thinking, its system of philosophy, and its understanding of the world around it. With the death of the language, an irreplaceable unit in our knowledge and understanding of human thought and world view has been lost forever. (Wurm, 1991: 17)

Along similar lines, Hinton and Hale argue that:

> ... the loss of languages is part of the loss of whole cultures and knowledge systems, including philosophical systems, oral literacy and musical traditions, environmental knowledge systems, medical knowledge, and important cultural practices and artistic skills. The world stands to lose an important part of the sum of human knowledge whenever a language stops being used. Just as the human species is putting itself in danger through the destruction of species diversity, so might we be in danger from the destruction of the diversity of knowledge systems. (Hinton & Hale, 2001: 5)

Through consecutive campaigns, the United Nations (UN) has responded by calling for the protection and preservation of linguistic and cultural diversity with a view to raising awareness of this issue. For its part, the Universal Declaration on Cultural Diversity (UNESCO, 2001) touches upon the importance of languages in promoting cultural diversity. Specifically, the Action Plan for the implementation of the Declaration defines the role languages should play in the field of education, including respect for the mother tongue, linguistic diversity at all levels of education, and the promotion of multilingualism from an early age. Other examples include UNESCO's (2011) declaration designating 21 February as International Mother Language Day, and the UN's (2008) declaration of 2008 as International Year of Languages, which was accompanied by a list of language-related projects, conferences, publications, and internet forums dealing with such issues as language education, endangered languages, intercultural dialogue, indigenous knowledge, and the language needs of disabled persons. In his 2008 speech announcing the Declaration,

UN Secretary General Ban Ki-moon called for immediate steps to protect and promote endangered languages, and ensure their preservation for future generation, stressing that:

> The loss of these languages would not only weaken the world's culture diversity, but also our collective knowledge as a human race.

In the area of basic education, UNESCO (2001) has long conducted a worldwide campaign in support of the Education for All (EFA) initiative. Working in tandem with the United Nations' Millennium Development Goals and their successor document the Sustainable Development Goals (United Nations, 2015), this has the potential to provide ethnic minorities with the benefits of mother-tongue education. This is in accord with the United Nations' (2007) Declaration on the Rights of Indigenous Peoples, which states that:

> Indigenous peoples have the right to revitalize, use, develop, and transmit to future generations their histories, languages, oral traditions, philosophies, writing systems and literatures.

The Declaration therefore mandates that:

> States shall, in conjunction with indigenous peoples, take effective measures in order for indigenous individuals, particularly children, including those living outside their communities, to have access, when possible, to an education in their own culture and provided in their own language.

UNESCO, UNICEF (United Nations International Children's Emergency Fund), and SEAMEO (Southeast Asian Ministers of Education Organization) also play active roles in promoting mother-tongue education for ethnic minority students around the world or regionally in order to help them succeed in school and be included in the larger society while maintaining their heritage language and culture.

Efforts to Reverse the Situation by Grassroots Communities in Thailand

In what follows, we present two programmes for language revitalization in two distinct minority communities. The perspective we take here, framed in a discourse of linguistic citizenship, is one that sees revitalization as fundamentally a question of community members finding, or creating, a platform from which to launch claims to audibility, visibility, and ethical engagement with the sociopolitical and economic realities under which disempowered minorities live. The concept of linguistic citizenship allows for the recognition of 'the political potential residing in the formulation of alternative and complex representations of identity and language' (Stroud, 2001: 347). The nub of the issue revolves around how hitherto inaudible voices can achieve engagement on national arenas, which is very much a question of how an ethnic minority can preserve its language and cultural identity and be (in this case) Thai at the same time. In response to this issue and to counteract language loss, various forms of language revitalization programmes are being conducted by grassroots communities in Thailand, including the following (Premsrirat, 2007a, 2007b):

- The *tua muang* (traditional northern Thai script) is being taught as a subject in some schools in Northern Thailand. The *tua mon* (Mon script) and Mon literature are being taught in Buddhist monasteries and schools in Mon communities in Bangkok and some provinces in central Thailand.

- Community-based research on language revitalization programmes is being conducted by 24 ethnolinguistic communities in cooperation with university departments working on orthography development and literature production. Those who wish to have their language taught as a school subject work on curriculum development, the production of learning materials, and teacher training. Examples include the Chong, Nyah Kur, and So (Thavung) revitalization programmes. Some groups, including the Chong, the Lavua, and the Gong, are working through community learning centres on language and culture revitalization for the community at large.

- Mother-tongue bilingual education has been adopted in the formal education system for some large language groups in border areas, where populations are facing not only language decline but also chronic academic underachievement. Examples of such programmes, which use the ethnic language as the medium of instruction for thinking, listening, speaking, reading, and writing, include Patani Malay-Thai, Northern Khmer-Thai, and Lavua-Thai.

Community-based language revitalization programmes are also being conducted within the formal school system by small and endangered ethnolinguistic groups, including the Chong, the Nyah Kur, and the So (Thavung). Meanwhile, mother-tongue bilingual education programmes are operating within the formal school system for the benefit of large ethnolinguistic groups in border areas, including Mon, Khmer, Hmong, Pwo Karen, and Patani Malay communities.

This chapter focuses on two community-based education programmes: the Chong language revitalization programme, and the Patani Malay-Thai mother-tongue bilingual education programme. Linguistic citizenship addresses 'the very real materiality of language in minority politics by attending to the fact that linguistic minorities suffer from both structural and valuational discrimination' (Stroud, 2001: 351). This implies the importance of working with language in relation to a wider set of socio-political issues. Therefore, the presentation of the two programmes provides detailed information on the involvement of the community, the challenges met by community members, as well as their response to these challenges, the process of collaborative work, and the success of these efforts in relation to the wider set of sociopolitical contingencies that have imposed minority status on these languages and their speakers.

The Chong Language Revitalization Programme[2]

Chong is an indigenous language spoken in Chanthaburi Province, close to the Thailand–Cambodia border. To date, about 2000 Chong speakers remain. The language belongs to the Austroasiatic language family (Pearic branch). There has been a rapid decrease in the number of Chong speakers over the last 20 years. Hardly any Chong community members below the age of 30 speak Chong, and Thai is their first and only language. Even older community members use Chong in certain situations only. It is classified as being at Stage 7 on Fishman's (1991) Graded Intergenerational Disruption Scale (GIDS), the stage immediately preceding the final stage of endangerment that precedes extinction.

One of the features that make this programme articulate with the idea of linguistic citizenship is that it was initiated by the community itself, whose members perceived that their language was dying and that this was having wider societal implications. They had an express desire to see their language taught to their children at school. They also realized that their language could be written and taught to outsiders, as well as to the younger generation. As a result of this growing awareness, they sought help from Mahidol University. The programme thus began as a cooperative effort bringing together Chong elders, who were aware of the decline of their ethnic language and culture among the young, and linguists from Mahidol University, with whom they had good relations following earlier linguistic fieldwork in the Chong-speaking area, in which Chong speakers were invited to join Field Methods in Linguistics classes so that they themselves would be able to bring their expert knowledge of the language and its practice to the programme.

The pilot project began in 2002, backed by strong community involvement, motivation, and commitment. In this respect, the programme had one of the essential ingredients noted by Stroud (2001, 2002) for a successful outcome (compare also Chimbutane, this volume). The project secured financial support from the Thailand Research Fund (TRF) to conduct community-based research with a view to solving the problem of language shift and to work on a language revitalization programme. The project also received technical as well as moral and psychological support from the Institute of Language and Culture for Rural Development at Mahidol University, as well as from a network of linguists and education experts.

Since the Chong had expressed a strong desire to have their language taught to their children in school, language documentation and language development were needed so that the language could be used in education and therefore as a tool for language revitalization. As part of the school-based language revitalization process, a writing system for Chong was developed, and reading materials were produced. The Chong language is now being taught as a subject (known as Local Studies) to students in three primary schools in the area. The programme covers orthography development, literature and teaching materials development and production, and curriculum development. The project has also led to the development of a Chong Community Learning Centre for the community at large. This recalls the multi-stakeholder and broad and intergenerational engagement typical of successful programmes in developing language provisions for societal purposes that go beyond a narrow purpose of revitalization and documentation (compare Kerfoot, this volume; Ansaldo & Lim, this volume). Furthermore, this has been an endeavour that cuts across ethnolinguistic groups, as groups facing similar challenges, including the Nyah Kur and the So (Thavung), have used the Chong project as a model and are adapting it for their own purposes. This resembles the politics of broad alliances noted by Stroud (2001) for the Weyeyi in Botswana, a group whose members also link language and sociopolitical demands in ways that benefit other minority groups across the board.

Orthography

Since Chong was an unwritten language, a writing system needed to be developed. This was to become a tool for recording the Chong language along with local knowledge and for teaching the younger generation. Orthography development was based on linguistic research into

Chong phonology, which consists of 21 consonants and nine short vowels, each with a corresponding long version. Though Chong is not tonal, it has special phonological features called register complexes, which result from the combination of different modes of vibrating the vocal folds: (1) clear (or modal) voicing; (2) tense (or creaky) voicing; (3) lax (or breathy) voicing; and (4) two modes combined (lax and tense).

Chong orthography is based on the Thai script because most potential users have a basic knowledge of the Thai writing system as a result of the compulsory education they received, and this knowledge is transferable to Chong literacy. A Thai-based script for Chong is also convenient in terms of pedagogy and dissemination because the Thai script can be easily produced on computer keyboards. An additional advantage of a Thai-based orthography is that it is more acceptable to the central Thai authorities than other scripts would be.

In addition to these linguistic principles, Chong orthography development also considered acceptance by the Chong community, which was involved in the development of the script from the very beginning. Before the orthography began to be officially used in schools and publications, it was tested for its practicality and acceptability among the Chong community.

Today, Chong speakers are proud of the orthography now used to represent their ethnic language – because it was developed with their active participation. Moreover, this Thai-based orthography represents their dual identity as members of a unique ethnic community who are also citizens of Thailand.

Literature production

A vibrant minority language literature is essential for language revitalization and minority language education. As part of the Chong revitalization programme, writers' workshops were organized to train native Chong speakers in how to write stories, produce handmade books, and evaluate reading levels within the community. Good writers, storytellers, and artists were identified, and writers were encouraged to write as many stories, folktales, or modern narratives as possible. Young artists were put in charge of drawing pictures for the stories. Seen through the lens of linguistic citizenship, this multimodal and intergenerational activity as sociality allowed for a tapping into voice, resemiotizing and retextualizing traditional authenticities, and voices to contemporary conditions – a reclaiming of voices and a making visible of what had earlier been erased. To date, Chong people have produced a number of stories for pleasure reading as well as teaching purposes.

Curriculum development

The main target group of the Chong revitalization programme is the younger generation within the Chong community. Before the project began, hardly any young people used Chong in their daily communication, and even the elderly did not speak the language in many social situations. It was therefore difficult for parents to speak Chong to their children. About 50 years ago, Chong parents were advised to stop speaking Chong to their children as a way to improve their education in Thai schools. Today, Chong people are aware that one of the best ways to encourage children to learn and speak Chong is to teach the language in school. However, Chong has to be taught as a second language because the children do not speak Chong at home, and Chong as a first language has thus been lost by the younger generation.

The community actively participated in the curriculum development process, preparing all instructional materials and volunteering to be trained as Chong teachers. The Chong language curriculum was designed with the objective of enabling the students to speak, read, and write Chong in an enjoyable atmosphere, gaining an appreciation of their language, and becoming proud of playing a part in the revitalization of their cultural heritage, identity strengthening driven by community concerns, using art and multimodal forms, emphasizing aesthetics (through literature), and giving community members full license to drive and own the project, while bringing into play affect and emotion as well as enjoyment as essential dimensions of building a language (compare the situation for Afrikaaps, Stroud, this volume).

Teaching Chong as a school subject

Teaching Chong in schools is a dream that has come true for the Chong people. As explained above, Chong is now taught in one primary school in the Chong area as part of a subject known as Local Studies, and volunteer teachers are selected from Chong speakers who have authentic Chong pronunciation, are dedicated to the project, and are acceptable to the community. The volunteers are then trained to teach the Chong language.

An initial evaluation (Chaiyaphong et al., 2007) showed satisfactory results. The students are acquiring a knowledge of Chong. They can read, write, and speak to a degree. They enjoy learning Chong. Their parents are happy, the teachers are proud of themselves and their students, and the school principal and staff are positive about the experience. This was demonstrated by a request by the school principal to extend the teaching of Chong to another group of students in a higher grade and to provide occasional Chong language and culture classes for students in other grades in the same school. As a result, a number of Chong parents transferred their children to this school. Moreover, other schools in the area have requested Chong language learning for their students. Although Chong is still taught as a school subject in Chanthaburi Province, the programme serves a model for other ethnic groups facing similar challenges. This programme, as well as the way it has been taken up by other groups, underscores the important role of education as a key institution in the transformation of the status quo (compare Chiatoh, this volume; Chimbutane, this volume). The transformative potential of language education is also illustrated in the following example.

Mother-Tongue Bilingual Education[3]

Apart from the small-enclave ethnic minorities that are losing their language and local wisdom, even large indigenous groups in border areas, including the Patani Malay-speaking people in Thailand's deep south, are facing a similar challenge, though in a more complex situation.

Patani Malay is spoken by 83% of people in the four southernmost provinces of Thailand (Songkhla, Pattani,[4] Yala and Narathiwat).[5] In addition to the social injustices that have long afflicted this part of the country, the ongoing violence and political unrest also stem from language identity issues. Malay identity, as reflected by the Malay language, which is used in daily life, is not officially recognized by the central government. Compulsory public education, which is delivered exclusively in Thai, results in poor attendance and low achievement among Patani Malay-speaking students, who gain few working skills and thus have limited prospects for higher education or employment.

One of the key motivations in terms of linguistic citizenship for working with Patani Malay was to put language at the centre of larger societal framing, by using the local ethnic minority language in education as a way to promote development, peace, and prosperity.[6] Many feared that education was being used to destroy the local language along with the local ethnic and religious identity and that language was being used in the invisibilization of speakers as part of a larger assemblage of dis-agentive practices. Among practices that have historically contributed to the marginalization or invisibilization of Patani Malay speakers is script choice. The Jawi script, which is based on the Arabic script, is commonly used in the region for writing, but is based on Central Malay (an ancient form of written Malay close to Standard Malay), which is related to but different from Patani Malay. While speakers use Central Malay in religious contexts, in which they are expected to memorize texts, this is not suitable as a medium of instruction for children who speak Patani Malay as their mother tongue.

On the other hand, efforts to promote the Thai script for writing Patani Malay have proved controversial. Opponents believe that such efforts could make the teaching and writing of the Jawi script redundant, while those in favour believe that the Jawi script is inadequate for writing Patani Malay, and that Jawi should continue to be taught in religious schools, while only the Thai script should be used in secular schools. In the future, the bilingual programme will consider incorporating the Jawi script into the curriculum in the higher grades of primary education.

A mother-tongue-based bilingual education programme was therefore designed by Mahidol University in three selected Patani Malay communities in Pattani, Yala, and Narathiwat provinces in 2007. Its goal was to help Patani Malay-speaking students retain their Malay identity at the local level while achieving a Thai identity at the national level. It sought to do this by developing the cognitive skills of the learners along with their ability to use Thai as a language of learning in the later years of their primary education.

The project adheres to the following principles of curriculum design: (1) academic development based on Ministry of Education standards, coupled with the community's values and goals; (2) language development in a step-by-step process, starting with the mother tongue (Patani Malay), and gradually bridging to the national language (Thai), while developing the four skills of listening, speaking, reading, and writing in both languages; and (3) sociocultural development that helps students preserve their local cultural identity while developing a national Thai identity.

The Patani Malay-Thai bilingual education programme is a nine-year participatory action research programme conducted jointly by Mahidol University linguists and a Patani Malay-speaking research team. It covers eight school grades, from kindergarten to Grade 6, with 1 year of preparation. The programme supports Patani Malay-speaking children in speaking, listening, reading, and writing in both Patani Malay and Thai, thereby capitalizing on the multilingual resources of these speakers in an educational context.

Patani Malay is used as the medium of instruction from kindergarten to the early grades so that children can gain the necessary skills in all four skills in the mother tongue before bridging to Thai. Thai is then used along with Patani Malay from Grade 1 to Grade 6 of compulsory education. The aim is for children to have established a strong foundation on which to develop their learning skills in other subjects and in their life-long learning.

In these respects, the programme has the expected design characteristics of a good transitional mother-tongue-based bilingual programme that attempts to infuse these languages into the educational system as comprehensively as possible. However, there are also a number of characteristics that set the programme apart from many others, and that have to do with how the activities and daily running of the project are rooted and find resonance in a wide variety of community stakeholders.

One such activity was the establishment of a local research team composed of native speakers, local teachers, and educators from various fields, school administrators, linguists, Islamic community members, village scholars, and young coordinators. This allowed insights into the variegated uses and perceptions of Patani Malay as the most popular language among respondents and the language speakers are most confident using. This wide buy-in also facilitated the use of a language survey to gather information needed for programme planning.

The strong community rootedness of the programme, with its many stakeholders, facilitated awareness-raising about the benefits of mother-tongue bilingual education, mobilizing partners for programme activities, including a local research team consisting of academics and village scholars, and covering four experimental schools. Academics, government officials, the media, and members of the public have offered encouragement and support, agreeing that this type of education will meet the needs of local people and assist with national reconciliation and public security for the whole country – an urgent task given that the conflict has led directly to the death over 6543 people since it flared up again in 2004 (Deep South Watch Report, 2016).

In terms of the specific details of building the programme out of the community, the local research team has been actively involved in developing the written language, a curriculum, lesson plans, teaching materials, songs, and graded reading materials about local stories and local culture and knowledge in both Patani Malay and Thai. This has involved the following.

(1) Developing a writing system for Patani Malay using the Thai script, building on academic as well as native-speaker acceptance and technical feasibility. The resulting Patani Malay orthography helps children transfer to Thai as the main medium of instruction in later grades of primary education.

(2) Developing a curriculum based on national standards but incorporating Patani Malay knowledge and experience into learning materials and activities, using Patani Malay in the early grades and Thai in the later grades as languages of instruction.

(3) Developing teaching materials and graded reading materials in Patani Malay as well as materials supporting students' transfer to Thai.

(4) Recruiting and training bilingual education human resources, including teachers, writers, local culture experts, and workshop organizers to further consolidate the already strong community participation in the programme, with teachers of Patani Malay receiving detailed training covering planning lessons, teaching, and managing bilingual classrooms;

(5) Child-friendly second language acquisition (SLA) methods, including total physical response (TPR) being used to introduce Patani Malay-speaking children to Thai, starting in the last two months of kindergarten 1. The TPR approach allows children to focus on hearing and responding to Thai without being forced to speak Thai at first, thus using other senses and building up an embodied knowledge of language.

An important part of putting this programme in place has been to bring the knowledge and experience gained through this grassroots-driven and -managed venture into a framework of evidence-based policy formulation government institutions find acceptable. This has involved:

(1) Evaluating learners in the four experimental schools and comparing their performance with those of students in mainstream schools;

(2) Building cooperation and networks among governmental and non-governmental funding agencies and technical assistance organizations, as well as influential individuals in society and the media;

(3) Developing and establishing a supportive national language policy.

Creating a sense of security

The project has earned the trust and confidence of local communities, whose members value the efforts made to preserve their language and culture and respect their Malay identity. They see this as a move toward lasting reconciliation and understanding. Ultimately, they feel more secure in their ethnicity and more confident in the education system. The programme thus has an importantly ethical dimension in the way it has built a Patani Malay education on the basis of respect, empathy, and recognition of the problems facing the community, acknowledging the value of the speakers' own resources in working toward solutions (compare Stroud, this volume).

The first group of children in this pilot project completed two years of kindergarten and is now in Grade 3. All of those involved hope that the children will receive a sound education and that they will become proud and productive members of both the Patani Malay community and Thailand. As Tuanyoh Nisani, a kindergarten teacher in Banprachan School (Pattani Province) puts it:

> In addition to being proud of their native language, children have learned to live with others who speak different languages. The same level of language understanding will result in an understanding of all issues. ... An unequal level of language understanding causes mutual dissatisfaction. Thai and Malay people should be able to communicate effectively since we live in the same country.

A comparison of the test scores of Grade 1 learners in pilot Patani Malay bilingual classes with those of learners belonging to a control group found that the students in the pilot classes scored higher (72.14% on average) than those belonging to the comparison group (41.91%) (Sintana *et al.*, 2010). Furthermore, it was observed that the learners in the pilot classes were happier, more talkative, and more creative. They enjoyed going to school, and loved reading and writing. The teachers were happy, and the parents were proud of their children.

Two major factors that contributed to these positive results were local community engagement and a cooperative relationship between the schools and the community members, who worked to ensure that the projects were planned and implemented effectively. Multiple stakeholders, such as local scholars and artists, religious leaders, school administrators, teachers, parents, academics, and other education officials, took part in intensive workshops given by Mahidol University to enable them to develop a curriculum and teaching materials that were culturally appropriate to the existing knowledge of the learners and still met the standards set by the Ministry of Education, thus ensuring that local initiatives met institutional requirements.[7] The curriculum emphasizes meaning and understanding as well as accuracy and higher thinking skills, which will enable the learners to know, understand, and analyse as well as being creative in all types of learning activities.

Throughout the process, community members and stakeholders were actively involved, not only in the development of an orthography, instructional materials, an appropriate teaching methodology, curriculum design, and lesson plans, but also – and most importantly – in providing technical, financial, and psychological support. The future success of the programme relies on the continued support and good faith of all participants. Crucially, the project lays the foundation for significant improvement in the prospects of all children in the south of Thailand.

In many respects, what appears on the surface to be an affirmative project of recognizing and working with language education has some extensive transformative characteristics. These are to be found not least in how volatile and conflict-ridden ethnic divisions have been partially deconstructed and defused thanks to the programme.

Language Rights and Thainess

Threatened languages are commonly those of socially or politically marginalized groups, often ethnic minorities. However, given that these groups enjoy equality of status (at least nominally), there is no reason to expect that they will readily give up their language. In such cases, language shift occurs in a context of forced assimilation, in which current language in education policy does not support – or even prohibits – the use of ethnic languages in schools. This gradually prises students away from their ethnic language and forces them to use the official language only.

In Thailand, both the Chong revitalization programme and the Patani Malay-Thai bilingual education project highlight the determination of ethnic minorities to preserve their heritage language and to use it in education. This is in line with a growing awareness that the linguistic and cultural rights of minorities demand the attention of governments and policy makers, who have a responsibility to preserve and protect diversity and cultural heritage from abuse or extinction. Efforts to reverse language decline and preserve language-related identities present grassroots communities with opportunities to exercise their language rights (Krauss, 1993; May, 2001; Romaine, 2008). However, as we have seen here as well as in many other situations across the world, rights need to be fought for through acts of linguistic citizenship (Stroud, 2001). Exercising linguistic citizenship carries in itself a number of benefits. One such benefit is how acts of linguistic citizenship imply a concurrent ethical framing and sociopolitical concientization. This is because what are seemingly language rights issues are often merely aspects of more extensive sociopolitical conflicts.

In nations that actively respect linguistic human rights, legal frameworks have been established to protect multilingualism. Once language rights have been formally recognized, there is a greater chance that consensus will be reached on ways of ensuring social justice, especially as regards ethnic minorities. This includes the right of minority group members to an education in their own language as well as to access to that language alongside the national language as well as international languages. In principle, language rights should thus serve as an instrument for ensuring that all citizens are entitled to identify with their mother tongue, orally and in writing, and can have this identification accepted and respected by others. In addition to education for minority students in their mother tongue, this also requires the use of the mother tongue in official situations and the assurance that personal citizens whose mother tongue is not an official language of their country of residence can become bilingual (or multilingual if they have more than one mother tongue) in their mother tongue and the official language.

However, in practice, as Stroud (2009) and others (e.g. Wee, this volume) have argued, rights are seldom the panacea for minority groups they are envisaged to be. Part of the reason for this is that what is represented as conflicts around language rights is often deeply embedded in – and symptomatic of – larger issues of power. Furthermore, rights frameworks tend to work well with powerful and resource-rich groups, while they are less accessible to the poor and marginalized (Stroud, 2009). In contrast, linguistic citizenship recognizes the agency and voice of community members in addressing the underlying issues of sociopolitical disempowerment, among other ways by wrestling control of language from conditions of marginalization.

It is evident that indigenous minority groups in Thailand, including the Chong and Patani Malay, wish to retain their ethnic identity while being recognized as Thai citizens. However, this has not been fully endorsed by the authorities, and this lack of recognition perpetuates conflicting perceptions of language and cultural needs as well as lingering fears among minorities. As Jehusen Jeubong, a respected former teacher-supervisor and religious leader in Thailand's deep south, puts it:

> The locals fear that they will lose their language, whereas the authorities fear that Patani Malay-speaking children will not have a good command of Thai. The locals want their children to have a good command of both Patani Malay and Thai, whereas the authority only want them to have a good command of Thai.

This degree of reluctance among some segments of the population is linked to nationalism, and in particular to the issue of Thainess.[8] The concept of Thainess was developed and defined by influential Thai intellectuals, and has been periodically adjusted to a changing society since the

1950s. Its main purpose has been to support and maintain a centralized political regime and a hierarchical social structure. This ideology has had a profound influence on Thai society and culture. In its original formulation, the concept of Thainess is based on three key elements: nation, religion, and monarchy. Central to this ideology is the Thai language, which is seen as key to unifying Thai citizens into one nation, with Buddhism as the religion of the majority and under the universal patronage of the monarch. To be a Thai is not only to have Thai nationality, but also – and crucially – to have a Thai identity, speak Thai, act like a Thai, and behave as a 'good' Thai should, that is, assume one's socioeconomic status according to Thai values. This is the way through which one may be fully accepted by society, and enjoy added opportunities to climb the social ladder to some extent. For members of ethnic minorities, Thainess – or being Thai – should consist of being able to communicate in Thai, enjoying equal rights, and having a sense of belonging to the Thai nation as a Thai citizen. In practice, many members of ethnic minorities feel that they are in effect denied the enjoyment of this status and that they receive few – if any – benefits from Thainess.

In theory, one positive aspect of Thainess is that it should enable all Thai citizens to move up the social hierarchy and be accepted as they do this. A key factor in this process is possession of the Thai language, which, for ethnic minorities, is meant to be acquired through its use in schools, and in particular through the elaboration of a common curriculum to be used throughout the country. For ethnic minorities, a crucial factor entirely bypassed by the ideology of Thainess, is the possibility that it may be possible or even desirable to be happy and proud to be Thai at the national level, while preferring to maintain an ethnic identity at the local level. A direct result of this omission is that, although the promotion of Thainess has been generally successful as regards its primary purpose of nation building, it has greatly contributed to the loss of language diversity, and thereby contributed to cultural conflict among the large language groups in border regions, and, in the case of the Patani Malay of southern Thailand in particular, to ongoing interethnic strife.

However, with strife comes potential solutions, and, as we have seen, there are now concerted efforts by grassroots communities to reverse this situation. For the Patani Malay people of southern Thailand, a region where language identity is both a social and a political issue arising from the fact that it reflects the population's Malay roots, bilingual education is a tool that can allow this ethnic minority to live within Thai society with full dignity. It offers equal status and the ability to communicate in Thai as well as in the mother tongue, a significant step toward true equality of opportunities through education. Projects such as the Chong revitalization programme and the Patani Malay-Thai bilingual education programme – of which each community is the owner and in which it is actively involved through the language development process – constitute effective tools for community participation and empowerment, and are therefore examples of linguistic citizenship in action. Key to success is the ability to mobilize factors in ensuring sustainability, including technical support from an academic institution, external as well as internal financial support, psychological support from all stakeholders, institutional support from government agencies, both local or central, and the public at large, and statutory support.

With the technical support of the range of stakeholders described above, progress is being made in revitalizing and maintaining minority languages and cultural identities in various ways, including through education. Important methods used to this end include: (i) teaching the ethnic language as a school subject, covering not only Chong, as discussed above, but also Nyah Kur, Thavung, and other severely endangered minority languages; and (ii) the provision of mother-tongue bilingual education to larger language groups, including not only Patani Malay, but also Mon and Northern Khmer.

In sum, if the Thai nation is to cope with the complexities of an evolving society, the traditional view of what is good for the nation and its citizens and of the civic virtues required of all Thais should be broadened. This view should incorporate multilingualism and multiculturalism as fundamental components, and promote currently undervalued cultural diversity. To this end, minority ethnolinguistic groups should be offered their own space within Thai society so that they can be empowered to live a dignified life with security, justice, and equal opportunities.

A key requirement of Thainess is that all Thai citizens understand, speak, and write the Thai language to a high standard. For members of ethnic minorities, an additional requirement is that they be allowed to learn and function at the local level in their ethnic language. To achieve this delicate balance between the national and the local, a different type of education is required. This is precisely what efforts by grassroots communities such as the Chong language revitalization programme and the Patani Malay-Thai mother-tongue bilingual education programme aim to achieve.

Conclusion

Despite attempts to ensure freedom of expression and protection from discrimination as fundamental human rights, and despite an implicit recognition of the intimate connection between language and forms of cultural expression, current national language policy in Thailand remains radically out of step with the realities of multilingualism in the country. In particular, a revision of the language in education policy is essential. The policy mandating the exclusive use of the Thai language in public education should be reconsidered. Instead, mother-tongue bilingual education should be promoted with the active participation of the communities concerned, that is, based in linguistic citizenship. More broadly, the recognition and promotion of cultural and linguistic diversity should be at the heart of a multilingual and multicultural policy, the aim of which should be to encourage a sustainably multicultural society, and support a truly multilingual population through the use of ethnic languages in public life, education, and the media. This will not only go a long way toward meeting the legitimate needs of marginalized minorities in Thailand, but also open up opportunities to tap the wealth of accumulated wisdom embodied within such unique cultures and linguistic histories. Moreover, it will provide sustainable public benefits not only in economic terms but also in terms of security, especially in the deeply troubled far south of the country. The recognition and mutual respect that will derive from truly interconnected and synergized communities will bring together Thais from all walks of life and facilitate national reconciliation while improving overall well-being. The notion of Thainess, so effectively infused into the Thai psyche over more than half a century, has undoubtedly been a cornerstone of nation building and the creation of a national identity. However, while it has succeeded in justifying and facilitating a centralized administration, it continues to validate traditional prejudices and social inequalities.

Today, a dynamic and changing society, such as Thailand, demands a contemporary approach to interpreting and managing complex sociocultural issues so that it meets the hopes and expectations of all Thais, as well as universal standards in terms of rights and opportunities. Clearly, the wealth of wisdom carried by the country's ethnic languages should play a key role in this process.

Retrospective: August 2015, June 2017

Despite the strong promotion of the Thainess ideology by the elite and the authorities, it is clear that over the past decade, there has been a great deal more discussion than before about Thailand as a multicultural society and about linguistic and cultural diversity, basic human rights, language rights, and indigenous rights. One example can be seen in the work of the Resource Centre for Documentation, Revitalization, and Maintenance of Endangered Languages and Cultures, Mahidol University, which was established in 2004 to preserve and revive languages in crisis or on the verge of extinction by documenting and revitalizing these languages and training community activists to collect local knowledge and locally produce vernacular literature. Although these have been challenging times in terms of funding and understanding by the public, in recent years, interest in minority languages has grown steadily not only among the ethnolinguistic groups in question, but also among academics as well as the general public. This success and enthusiastic support can be seen in the number of visitors (local and overseas) and the ethnolinguistic groups that have undertaken a revitalization programme using the Mahidol Revitalization Model, which focuses on putting community members at the heart of revitalization efforts through their involvement at every step of the revitalization process – that is, linguistic citizenship. These include orthography development, the creation of a local vernacular literature, the collection of local knowledge, and teaching the local language to the next generation of speakers. The Revitalization Model has now been implemented with the cooperation of 26 language groups according to the distinct needs of each community language. For example, the Patani Malay-Thai mother-tongue-based bilingual education programme, an initiative consisting of participatory research conducted in Thailand's Deep South, though quite unfamiliar to education officials, has been a considerable achievement and an overwhelming success that has encouraged us all to continue with the work and to build on its accomplishments. This programme has addressed long-standing issues of language identity and educational underachievement. As a result, it has been expanded to 15 additional government schools. At the same time, mother-tongue-based bilingual education has also become institutionalized as part of teacher education at Yala Ratchabhat University in Yala Province. A similar approach has also been used with some of the hill tribes in the north of the country, the Mon in the west, and the Khmer in the northeast by non-government organizations (NGOs) as well as academics from the Ministry of Education.

The current draft of the National Language Policy of Thailand initiated and directed by the Royal Society of Thailand strongly supports ethnic languages by specifically devoting one of its six policy pillars to regional languages and ethnic minority languages. Apart from protection and preservation, the use of ethnic languages in the public sphere as well as in education is being actively promoted, as is mother-tongue-based bilingual and multilingual education. Significantly, the mother tongue is recognized as the foundation for teaching and learning additional languages, including Thai, the official and national language, as well as international languages such as English. Hearing-impaired learners are also given the opportunity to learn Thai Sign Language as their mother tongue before learning to read and write Thai, and of course those who have Thai as their mother tongue must learn Thai thoroughly before learning English. According to the public forum organized by the Royal Institute of Thailand in various regions of the country, 90% of those surveyed support this policy. In addition, manuals for Thai-based writing systems for ethnic languages developed by various language groups have been published by the Royal Society of Thailand, including Patani Malay, Northern Khmer, Chong, Nyahkur, and Lavua.

Further evidence of the growing recognition of language diversity comes from the Department of Cultural Promotion's and the Ministry of Culture's joint initiative aiming to register indigenous languages as an Intangible National Cultural Heritage.

The Educational Reform and Human Resources Development undertaken by the current military government has introduced a draft proposal for multicultural education for students in Thailand's Deep South, in all border provinces around the country, and among the hill tribes of the Northern and Western highlands. Furthermore, various forms of mother-tongue education and mother-tongue-based multilingual education have been proposed as an innovation despite the continuing strong promotion of Thainess. If this proposal is accepted and implemented, it will constitute a highly positive step toward Thainess being redefined to embrace language rights in Thailand.

Although many support such educational innovations and wish to see progress in terms of rights, many in the upper levels of the administrative hierarchy may be unwilling or unable to conceptualize the potential of such efforts. This is a perennial problem despite political and strong community support. Often, it is this lack of vision that constrains capacity building and saps the will to deal with challenges on the part of government structures despite obvious enthusiasm for the promotion of language rights among the more enlightened among Thai citizens. However, we remain confident that the desirability of promoting language rights throughout the country will become apparent to growing numbers of Thai people.

These years after the 2014 military coup in Thailand, the political and security situation remains unsettled, and hopes for a quick return to democratic civilian government are fading. Uncertainty has quashed expectations of a dynamic reset to development and progress in many aspects of Thai society, and has left countless plans and initiatives unrealized and at risk of stalling. Among these are proposals for educational reforms concerning cultural diversity and multicultural education, for which the current National Language Policy draft is scheduled for consideration by the government.

In light of the successful completion of the Patani-Thai bilingual education project and its international recognition following its being awarded the UNESCO King Sejong Literacy Prize in 2016, it would be highly regrettable if such vital refinements and innovations in education in Thailand as mother-tongue-based multilingual education (MTB-MLE) should suffer from political inertia. We sincerely hope that this will not be the case and wish for a positive response from the government to forward-thinking ideas about placing multicultural approaches to education at the heart of policy.

Thailand cannot continue to rely on civic virtues and the disciplining hand of its military overseers to guide and unite it through the 21st century. What is needed is high regard for and appreciation of diversity. This includes enlightened attitudes toward the merits of groups and identities that do not necessarily conform to mainstream norms, as well as tools for harnessing the inherent potential of each individual, along with values that promote pride and justice for all Thais as asserts their fundamental right to be truly respected.

Notes

(1) For full details, see Premsrirat (2006a, 2007a, 2007b) and Premsrirat *et al.* (2004).
(2) This description is adapted from Premsrirat (2006b, 2007a, 2007b).
(3) This description is based on Premsrirat (2008, 2009).
(4) Note that the spelling of *Patani* reflects local, that is Patani Malay, pronunciation. Elsewhere in Thailand, the standard transliteration from Thai to the Latin script is *Pattani*, which parallels Thai spelling and syllabic structure: ปัตตานี [pàt.tā:.nī:].
(5) Note that the dialect of Malay spoken in Satun Province to the west of the Patani Malay-speaking sub-region is different from Patani Malay.
(6) This is a new idea that some in Thailand find hard to accept because there are few examples of such programmes in the country.
(7) Despite the support provided by the programme, the benefits of teaching Patani Malay within the formal education system are not yet fully understood by some educational authorities. Even though higher-level government officials generally accept bilingual education, some have no confidence in the use of the mother tongue as a medium of instruction through to the higher grades.
(8) For discussions of the tension between language and ethnicity on the one hand, and national identity on the other, in the Thai context, see Smalley (1994) and Premsrirat (2011).

References

Chaiyaphong, S., Phanphaj, P. and Srisombat, S. (2007) Rai-ngan chabab sombuun rueng kanphattana laksuut kansorn phasaa Chong pen raiwicha thongthin duey kan mee suen ruem khong chumchon tambon Khlongphluu amphue Khichakut changwat Canthaburi [Final report on Chong language curriculum development for the teaching of Local Studies as a school subject with community participation, Khlong Phluu and Ta-Khian Thong Subdistricts, Khitchakut District, Chanthaburi Province]. Unpublished manuscript. Submitted to the Thailand Research Fund (TRF).

Deep South Watch Report (2016) *Than kho mun DSID: Kan wikhro khomun hetkan khwam mai sa-ngop nai phuenthi changwat chaidaen phaktai nai rop pi 2558* [DSID database: The analysis of the unrest situation data in the Southern border provinces in 2013]. See http://www.deepsouthwatch.org/node/7942 (accessed June 2017).

Fishman, J.A. (1991) *Reversing Language Shift*. Clevedon: Multilingual Matters.

Hinton, L. and Hale, K. (2001) *The Green Book of Language Revitalization in Practice*. San Diego, CA: Academic Press.

Krauss, M. (1993) The world's languages in crisis. *Language* 68 (1), 4–10.

May, S. (2001) *Language and Minority Rights*. Harlow: Pearson Education.

Premsrirat, S. (2006a) Thailand: The language situation. In K. Brown (ed.) *Encyclopedia of Language and Linguistics* (2nd edn) (pp. 642–644). Oxford: Elsevier.

Premsrirat, S. (2006b) Language development and language revitalization in Thailand: The case of the Chong Revitalization Program. Salaya, Thailand: Institute of Language and Culture for Rural Development, Mahidol University.

Premsrirat, S. (2007a) Endangered languages of Thailand. *International Journal of the Sociology of Language* 186, 75–93.

Premsrirat, S. (2007b) Revitalizing ethnic minority languages. *Sangsaeng Magazine* 18, 8–11.

Premsrirat, S. (2008) Language for national reconciliation: Southern Thailand. *Enabling Education Network Magazine (EENET)* 12. See http://www.eenet.org.uk/resources/eenet_newsletter/news12/page12.php (accessed October 2017).

Premsrirat, S. (2009) Bilingual education for national reconciliation in Southern Thailand: A role for Patani Malay and Thai. Paper presented at the SEAMEO Project on Mother Tongue as Bridge Language of Instruction in Southeast Asian Countries: Policy, Strategies, and Advocacy, February 2009, Bangkok.

Premsrirat, S. (2011) Redefining Thainess: Preserving diversity, promoting unity. Paper presented at the 11th International Conference on Thai Studies, July 2011. Bangkok.

Premsrirat, S., Choosri, I. and Suwankasses, S. (2004) *Ethnolinguistic Mapping of Thailand*. Salaya, Thailand: Institute of Language and Culture for Rural Development, Mahidol University.

Romaine, S. (2008) Language rights, human development, and linguistic diversity in a globalizing world. In P. van Sterkenburg (ed.) *Unity and Diversity of Languages* (pp. 85–96). Amsterdam: John Benjamins.

Sintana, S. Lambensa, P. and Je-ni, Y. (2010) Raingan rueng kanpramern phonsamrit kanrian kansorn baeb thawi phasaa phasaa Thai lae phasaa Malayuthin nai rongrian si changwat chaidaen phaktai prathet Thai [Report on an assessment of the bilingual teaching and learning program using Thai and Melayu dialects in schools in the four southern border provinces of Thailand]. Unpublished manuscript. Institute for Southern Border Area Research and Development, Yala Rajabhat University.

Smalley, W.A. (1994) *Linguistic Diversity and National Unity: Language Ecology in Thailand*. Chicago, IL: University of Chicago Press.

Stroud, C. (2001) African mother-tongue programs and the politics of language: Linguistic citizenship versus linguistic human rights. *Journal of Multilingual and Multicultural Development* 22 (4), 339–355.

Stroud, C. (2002). *Towards a Policy for Bilingual Education in Developing Countries*. New Education Division Documents 10. Stockholm: Erlanders Novum AB.

Stroud, C. (2009) A postliberal critique of language rights: Toward a politics of language for a linguistics of contact. In J.E. Petrovic (ed.) *International Perspectives on Bilingual Education: Policy, Practice and Controversy* (pp. 191–218). Charlotte, NC: Information Age Publishing.

UNESCO (2001) Universal Declaration on Cultural Diversity. See http://portal.unesco.org/en (accessed October 2017).

UNESCO (2011) International Mother Language Day. See http://www.unescobkk.org/education/multilingual-education/international-mother-language-day (accessed October 2017).

United Nations (2007) Declaration of the Rights of Indigenous Peoples. See www.un.org/esa/socdev/unpfii/documents/DRIPS_en.pdf (accessed October 2017).

United Nations (2008) International Year of Languages. See http://www.un.org/en/events/iyl. (accessed October 2017).

United Nations (2015) Sustainable Development Goals. See http://www.un.org/sustainabledevelopment/sustainable-development-goals (accessed October 2017).

Wurm, S.A. (1991) Language death and disappearance: Causes and circumstances. In R.H. Robins and E.M. Uhlenbeck (eds) *Endangered Languages* (pp. 1–18). Oxford: Berg Publishers.

8 Commentary – Linguistic Citizenship: Who Decides Whose Languages, Ideologies and Vocabulary Matter?

Kathleen Heugh
University of Adelaide

Introduction

Linguistic citizenship is discussed in this volume in relation to education in four southern countries, each of which has its own particular history of internal conflict, occupation and ongoing political tensions and debates. The tensions coalesce along predictable lines of dissonance between local language practices, needs, perspectives and ideologies on the one hand, and those held and mediated through the ideologies and instruments of state policy on the other hand. A further tier of complexity, that of external debates and ideologies of language, is one that intersects with debates that have been largely conceptualized or influenced by those circulating in the global north, is introduced in two of the chapters.

Below I attempt to pull out a few of the threads that weave through each of the four chapters that address issues of linguistic citizenship in education. Before I begin, I think it worthwhile noting that we owe a debt to two West African scholars, Ayo Bamgbose (1987) and Beban Chumbow (1987), for our understanding of how in contexts of considerable linguistic diversity, language planning has greater productive traction for local communities when articulated at the local level, than appears possible via top-down policy measures. Three decades later, the centralized administrations of many southern countries remain woefully unwilling and/or underprepared for productive engagement with diversity (e.g. Bamgbose, 2014;

Chumbow, 2013). To a greater or lesser extent, we see this unfolding in the four chapters that discuss language education policy and planning in relation to linguistic citizenship in this volume.

The first two of these are contextualized in Africa. Chiatoh discusses linguistic citizenship in relation to community-based language development in Cameroon, while Chimbutane discusses the intersection of political ideology and language through the struggle for, and during, post-liberation Mozambique. Two chapters focus on Southeast Asia. Premsrirat and Bruthiaux discuss localized language development in Thailand, the only country in Southeast Asia to have escaped European colonization. Nevertheless, it is a country in which extreme asymmetries of power are evident, demarcated along lines of ethnicity and language. Cabral and Martin-Jones situate their discussion of language debates in East Timor, a country that has experienced successive periods of colonization, several hundreds of years of Portuguese occupation, followed by a relatively short-lived Indonesian occupation (1975–1999). Cabral and Martin-Jones draw attention to the politics of language in East Timor as these surface in two or three apparently different discourses involving multiple stakeholders within the fledgling post-conflict and liberated country. The internal discourses in East Timor appear to have become entangled with other, potentially competing discourses that circulate within an influential missionary linguistics' agency, the Summer Institute of Linguists (SIL), and global UN affiliate bodies, UNESCO and UNICEF.

The domestic debates in all four chapters include contested notions of the status and use of local, national and official languages, as well as of different understandings of the ideologies and practices of bilingual and multilingual education. Each of these is enmeshed also with debates that circulate in neighbouring countries and regions, as well as those that circulate in the global north (see also several discussions of north–south entanglements in Kerfoot & Hyltenstam, 2017). Whatever these debates and however they travel, at the heart of the matter is the extent to which ordinary people, most especially people whose communities, are marginalized, are able to voice their point of view, express agency and thus use their linguistic expertise to participate as citizens at local, regional and national levels. Individual and community linguistic expertise and agency, whether in collaboration with or resistance to decision-making at various levels of policy-making, public service, economic enterprise, education and health, is the substance of linguistic citizenship.

Linguistic citizenship is thus the individual claim and exercise of the right of citizens to voice, to be heard, and to act upon whichever dimension of a person's linguistic repertoire as may be useful in circumstance or purpose. Agency rests with the individual and the community where responsibilities for communal well-being are co-owned (e.g. Heugh, 2017; Watson, 2014).

For linguists, this is an opportunity:

> Linguistic Citizenship is an invitation to rethink our understanding of language through the lens of citizenship at the same time that we rethink understandings of citizenship through the lens of language (Stroud, this volume).[1]

Most obviously, the discussion of linguistic citizenship in these chapters intersects with local and international debates of language rights (or linguistic human rights); and also with notions of mother tongue, bilingual and multilingual education, and mother-tongue-based multilingual education. I address the issue of language rights first, and the issue of terminological and semantic differences second.

Rights and Asymmetries, Citizenship and Agency

Asymmetrical power relations between the state and external agencies on the one hand and marginalized communities and individuals on the other hand have been recognized as rendering discourses of language rights that are either ineffective or used to amplify asymmetries (e.g. Ruiz, 1984; Stroud, 2001; Stroud & Heugh, 2004). In either case, they have not served to offer meaningful opportunities for empowerment of communities in Africa, or perhaps even beyond Africa. This was particularly obvious, for example, during South Africa's apartheid years where the former National Party government used language rights to effect unequal socio-economic and political division along lines of ethnolinguistic separation from 1948 to 1994 (Heugh, 1995, 1999). On the other hand, where marginalized communities exercise their agency to assert and claim their rights to use their languages in key domains, such as in education, we find acts of participatory citizenship at the local, marginalized community level. We see this in three of the settings in this section – Cameroon, Mozambique and Thailand – where bottom-up initiatives and the opportunities leverage local participation, voice and agency. We also see this in the case of citizens who are comfortable using either Tetum[2] or Portuguese in East Timor. In each of these settings, the state is or has been either antithetical towards or shown little interest in the dynamics of diversity and citizenship for people and communities on the margins and/or those who speak minority languages. In three of the case studies here, Cameroon, Mozambique and Thailand, we see collaborations of multiple stakeholders in which individual and community-driven leverage repositions marginal community languages in relation to mainstream state language policies in education. In regard to community participation in collaboration with linguists and other stakeholders, Premsrirat and Bruthiaux illustrate the development of Chong and Patani Malay-Thai for use alongside the official Thai language in education. This is in a context in which disparities or asymmetries are among the most extreme in the world, and conflict between ethnolinguistic communities may become issues of serious conflict. Chiatoh demonstrates this in relation to very many community-based language committees in marginal and borderland contexts of Cameroon. However, these remain largely at the community level in non-formal education, since at the state-level, official French (mostly) – English bilingual policy continues to ignore not only lesser used Cameroonian languages, but also the three widely used languages, Pidgin, Beti-fang and Fulfulde. Chiatoh points out that successive governments have amplified and fanned ethnolinguistic division and anomie, which then becomes a convenient foil to the use of Cameroonian languages as either national languages or languages in education. The losers of course are individual citizens and communities of people who inhabit the peripheries and borders, and although Chiatoh does not discuss this, these are also likely to be the people who would lose their habitats subsequent to government contracts for logging of up to 80% of Cameroonian forests (Cerutti *et al.*, 2013). For Chiatoh, linguistic citizenship arises within individuals and marginal communities themselves. This is not something promised, as is often the case with constitutional and other legislative provisions for language rights, for the simple reason that it is not in the interests of many governments to solidify language rights in practice. Linguistic citizenship in Cameroon is thus evident where community members engage in reciprocal partnership with generative activities that advance linguistic and cultural acts of citizenship. In no way does this remove the responsibility of the state for such matters, rather, the argument points towards an articulation and assertion of interests from actors on the fringe that insist on space to engage and to resist. Local non-government organisations (NGOs) that work with collaborative and reciprocal intent are able to strengthen the conditions for agency, so that collaborative exchanges of expertise and knowledge among linguists and local actors contribute towards ownership, participation and citizenship. Community-based initiatives in Cameroon have benefitted from local engagements and co-operation, and they have also benefitted from the participation of the SIL missionary organization that works in highly diverse and southern parts of the world for both evangelical purposes and to promote literacy in local languages. However, the relationship between the local and external agents is ambiguous (Anchimbe, 2013) and it is not clear to what extent SIL introduces language education concepts and programmes that may ultimately serve or disserve local communities (see also discussion of East Timor below).

While the asymmetry of relationships between the state and civil society remains acute in Cameroon and Thailand, Chimbutane demonstrates that in Mozambique, subsequent to several periods of post-colonial regimes of governance, civil society, especially over the last decade, has exerted pressure on government. The lasting imprint of Portuguese administration on the socio-political history and linguistic diversity of Mozambique illustrates successive policies that have promoted Portuguese for reasons of national unity, the ideology that ascribes linguistic diversity to socio-political division, and to more recent iterations that exhibit more favourable stances towards the promotion of local (African) languages in education. Since 2003, a limited but growing number of languages has been included in early transition (local language to Portuguese) in school education. The Mozambican government, albeit hesitantly, is taking on board the concept of linguistic diversity, and has attempted to grapple with the possibility that diversity does not have to equate with disunity. The challenges to which Chimbutane draws attention include an inadequate preparedness for multilingual provision in education, the shortcomings of which risk scuppering multilingual education in the medium to long term. On the other hand, Chimbutane and Benson (2012) suggest that this shortcoming may provide opportunities for local participation and interventions that strengthen the position of local languages alongside Portuguese over the medium to longer term. Nevertheless, Chimbutane, like Chiatoh, and Premsrirat and Bruthiaux, insists that ultimate responsibility for adequate and appropriate education remains with the state. This includes mechanisms that serve to strengthen the participatory presence of endogenous languages in public as well as civil settings. In the Mozambican case, civil society has in the meantime exerted pressure upon government to extend bilingual education involving from its initial commitment to between five and seven, to 16 Mozambican languages alongside Portuguese from 2015.

Language rights in each of Thailand, Cameroon and Mozambique is not so much the state dispensing of rights and thereby retaining or amplifying asymmetrical relationships, but of individuals and communities reducing the asymmetry by 'speaking back', insisting and acting on voice, whether from outside or from within formal education. This does not mean that the state sheds responsibility or that all responsibility is handed over to less powerful communities. Rather, it is that linguistic citizenship involves assertive engagement at the community level in order to negotiate and insist on some degree of reciprocity from the state. In the case of Cameroon, it has not been possible to achieve reciprocity from the state, and thus an alternative, community-led, system has taken root (see also Chiatoh, 2014). In the case of Thailand, ironically, never having been colonized by Europe, this country has not experienced post-colonial liberation, and thus here, the inequities may be more entrenched for minority communities in the south and north of the country than they are in post-colonies. The implication for education is that where communities participate in language education developments, these may lead to promising developments rooted in local communities as we see in Cameroon, Mozambique and Thailand. This is because communities are invested in these developments and investment may return increasing returns over time.

There are other examples where we see, even at the village level in post-conflict Uganda (Sentumbwe & Heugh, 2014) and environmentally ravaged Ethiopia (Heugh, 2014), that vulnerable communities exercise agency to participate in local educational development that includes local languages. In the Ugandan case, the emphasis has been on bringing children back into schools after 30 years of insurgencies and terror. In so doing, parents and grandparents have come into the schools and set up complementary village adult literacy and numeracy programmes. These have led to community-led non-formal early childcare and education, and also the establishment of village saving schemes that lead on to an emergent ecology of micro-enterprises. In remote Ethiopia, this has led to a growing of local expertise in various aspects of language development, including the establishment of small printing and publishing businesses, as well as the collaborative development and resourcing of community centres. In both the Ugandan and Ethiopian cases, communities at the extreme perimeters of their countries know all too well the pointlessness of awaiting state dispersal of resources connected to a language rights agenda.

There is nevertheless risk where the asymmetry of power between marginal communities and the state is particularly acute, as it is in Thailand, Cameroon and possibly also in East Timor. It is in these contexts that external agencies, such as international NGOs and bodies associated with UNESCO and UNICEF, however well-meaning, may bring pressures to bear that unintentionally silence local voice and agency.

Charitable, philanthropic and missionary agencies often bring with them pre-formulated or pre-packaged views of language, and language and literacy education programmes that have been developed in external contexts that may not suit local contexts. Because of the asymmetries of power, external resources and expertise are vertically arranged and indexed above local expertise and knowledge. Cabral and Martin-Jones draw our attention to potential consequences of this in the case of East Timor, where post-liberation language education policy, Tetum–Portuguese bilingual education, has been challenged by pressure groups favouring a trilingual policy for students in schools. 'Mother-tongue-based multilingual education' (MTB-MLE) involving local language, Tetum and Portuguese is currently being trialled in East Timor, apparently with mixed results, and concern on the part of Cabral and Martin-Jones is that this may intersect with externally driven agendas that disregard the particular multilingual ecology of East Timor. The adoption of the concept of MTB-MLE in the discourses of language education policy and practice in East Timor offers ethnographers an interesting dilemma that can be analysed at a number of levels.

The first question that needs to be asked is whether or not the official bilingual Tetum–Portuguese education policy has the theoretical, pedagogical and functional capability of reducing and eliminating inequities between marginal communities and those closer to the urban centres of power. This question ties in with a second, that relates to whether or not a Tetum–Portuguese policy synchronizes with or facilitates community-level participatory citizenship in the remote and rural peripheries. Cabral and Martin-Jones also ponder these questions. On the other hand, does an externally introduced language policy agenda, such as MTB-MLE facilitate community-level participation if it is driven by assumptions and templates arrived at prior to reaching marginal communities in East Timor? Where the asymmetries are stark, as they are in East Timor, there is a risk that such programmes may replicate ill-fitting ones that hark back to colonial times, unless they are appropriated, indigenized and managed by East Timorese communities. There is an obvious oddity in the use of MTB-MLE in East Timor, and this has to do with the use of the English variant of the term 'mother tongue' as opposed to the Portuguese *língua materna*. It is perhaps the adoption of an English term in a context in which Portuguese and Tetum co-exist as languages of wider communication that signals a conceptual mismatch between the pedagogy and policy and the contextual setting into which is has been brought.

Mother Tongue, MTB-MLE and Competing Southern and Northern Ideologies of Multilingualism

The issue raised by Cabral and Martin-Jones above, and implicit also in the chapters authored by Chiatoh, Chimbutane, and Premsrirat and Bruthiaux, relates to terminology and conceptual positioning of multilingualism in education. This is serious and deserves careful consideration at a number of levels. The term 'mother tongue' itself has been critiqued first in northern-oriented literature and also by African scholars who have recast northern-framed critiques (see for example critiques in Ansaldo, 2010; Makoni & Pennycook, 2007). It is also problematized here by Cabral and Martin-Jones in their questioning of MTB-MLE in East Timor.

In this section, I try to address some of the vexatious issues relating to claims and counter-claims over the semantics of terminology that is used in relation to people who make use of multilingual repertoires. I do this in the context of recognizing linguistic citizenship and asking the question, 'Who decides who can use which term to mean what, exactly?' If we use the lens of linguistic citizenship, then surely it is the communities themselves who decide. If northern-oriented scholars assume to tell people in southern contexts how they ought to understand and use concepts, then surely they engage in hegemonic practices, and thus serve to deny or invisibilize southern voice?

Southern scholars have for some time discussed the linguistic diversity in the global south (96% of the world's languages, Lewis *et al.*, 2016) as involving both multilingualism and 'multilinguality' (e.g. Agnihotri, 2014). Even though recent mobilities of people change the linguistic dynamics of the global north, the south continues to experience the complexities of linguistic diversity on scales and dimensions not yet experienced in the global north (e.g. Heugh, 2015; Kusch, [1970] 2010). Accompanying a growing interest in multilingualism in northern contexts has been a recognition that contemporary northern views of bilingual education have evolved subsequent to the Canadian immersion and other dual language immersion programmes in the second half of the 20th century. However, it has now become clear that these programmes have not taken into account the ways in which people living in linguistically diverse communities develop their languages, thus they are cast as deficient (e.g. García, 2009; Heller, 2007). A second line of argument from northern perspectives is that the concept of 'mother tongue', in frequent use in southern contexts, is problematic or lacks authenticity. Cabral and Martin-Jones, in this volume, for example point out that the term is believed to have been popularized in northern contexts subsequent to a report on the use of local languages in education in African countries, *The Use of Vernacular Languages in Education* (UNESCO, 1953). It needs to be noted, however, that UNESCO actually made use of several terms depending upon context, including: vernacular, local language, language of the immediate community, regional language, national language, *langue maternelle*, and *lingua materna*. In South Africa, the term *moedertaal* ('mother language') was used during the apartheid years. The terminological use of 'tongue' is curious. It appears only in an English translation of related terms used in other languages that might more accurately have been translated as 'mother language'. The northern critique of the term surfaces variously, as part of a perspective considers the term reductionist or essentialist, potentially sexist and discriminatory towards men, and in all probability introduced by missionaries (e.g. Makoni, 2003). The most serious claim is that the term therefore is thus reductionist and inauthentic. Aware of this and earlier controversies about the usage of this term during apartheid, and aware also of the lack of empirical data to support the more recent claims, I have made ongoing effort over a period of 30 years to find evidence that supports the view that the concept of a mother language or mother tongue lacks community authenticity or relevance. This has included questionnaires in surveys during fieldwork in rural contexts of Ethiopia, Uganda and South Africa. It includes conversations with colleagues, mostly in parts of Southern Africa and India, and during fieldwork conducted in numerous countries, most especially in rural and remote settings. The survey data and anecdotal evidence that I have collected does not coincide either with northern-held critiques of the term, nor with those that appear to be based on anecdotal evidence in Makoni (2003) or Makoni and Pennycook (2007). Instead, I find ethnographic accounts that shed light on the longue durée of the concept and its societal relevance. For example, my colleague of 30 years, Pamela Maseko points out that:

> I do not recognize the voice of my grandmother in narratives that position rural women as subservient or in subaltern relationships with men. I do not recognize the missionary narratives of isiXhosa-speaking women. I remember that my grandfather was expected to consult with and negotiate with my grandmother about every important family decision. He had to wait for my grandmother's decision before he could convey a decision to other men in the family or in the community (Maseko, personal communication, 2015; see also Maseko, 2016).

Maseko's recollections of her grandmother and other rural women in a rural community of the Eastern Cape are that women, particularly mothers and grandmothers, historically held considerable power. Women made the decisions about their children's education, behaviours and expectations. Men were expected to and did consult women about every important decision that needed to be made regarding immediate and extended family business and politics. Daughters-in-law, particularly were expected to adhere to language regimes of respect, *hlonipha*, insisted upon by their mothers-in-law. Maseko's archival research has uncovered literary works of AmaXhosa writers of the 19th and early 20th centuries, including that of a woman writer, Nontsizi Mgqwetho, writing between 1920 and 1929. Mgqwetho's texts dispel the notion of 'women as voiceless' (Maseko, 2016). Writing some time later than Mgqwetho, Titilayo Ufomata demonstrates the power of women's voices in West Africa where women's ownership of local languages and the languages of the marketplaces thoroughly undermine apparent regimes of men's supremacy (Ufomata, 1998). Similarly, Ousseina Aliou demonstrates the voice and agency of Muslim women in Africa, also using local languages to exert agency in ways that are not recognized in western or northern narratives of women, particularly Muslim women in Africa (Alidou, 2005). The concept of mother language in African contexts is part of the ecology of language practices that include practices of power and women's agency.

A common trope in western/northern feminism is the need (a) to cast women in Africa as voiceless, and (b) to speak on behalf of women of Africa (Alidou, 2005; Heugh, 2011). Such tropes of course serve only to deny African women's expression of voice. In this context, the dismissal of the validity of the concept of mother language is another variant of this. The concept behind the term 'mother language' pre-dates colonial and missionary interference. It carries semantic significance of women's power and agency, quite different from those ascribed to it by many who critique its use from the outside. What remains problematic to the 21st century ear is the visceral use of 'tongue' in the English translation 'mother tongue'. The concept, however, is one that carries symbolic weight and pre-dates colonial or missionary interference.

Ajit Mohanty has on several occasions discussed with me that the term conceptualized as 'mother language' has a long history also in India, certainly one that predates the establishment of any of the UN agencies in the mid-20th century (Mohanty, 2010, 2012, personal communication). I have asked various community-based informants in Orissa, Rajasthan and Madya Pradesh whether or not the concept or term is regarded as pejorative, or diminishing of anyone's language practices in these settings. Again, I have yet to find an informant who agrees with this position, except where people wish to disguise or hide their linguistic affiliations. In the absence of empirical data advanced to support the supposed frailty or inappropriacy of concepts, such as mother language in southern settings, I argue that it is important to exercise caution and respect for the views of people who themselves may make use of such terms. In so doing, it is important to recognize that vocabulary and terminology undergo changes that do not translate easily from one context or set of language practices to another. We need to be able to separate northern ideologies of language from socio-political contexts in which southern practices differ in substantial ways, and that result in different ideologies. It may also be necessary to separate what have become pejorative connotations with the English term 'tongue' from the concept that appears more frequently, and perhaps as less visceral in other languages, that is, as in 'mother language'. It needs to be noted that the concept of a mother language does not in any way deny horizontal practices of multilingual people in most southern settings. Rather, multilingualism and multilinguality involve repertoires that include both vertical and horizontal dimensions of language practices (e.g. Heugh, 2015).

I now return to the term mother-tongue-based multilingual education (MTB-MLE). As the term suggests, it emerges from a setting in which English, rather than French, Portuguese or Spanish, has been a former colonial language. In fact, it originated in South Africa among colleagues with whom I worked closely in the pre- and post-apartheid years.

It is astonishing to note how this term has been picked up, and how rapidly it has travelled outside of Africa over the last decade. Its history is not well known, and there are local level political debates about its validity and advisability in the South African context, and even among those who were intimately connected with its formulation.[3] The point here is that, owing to the circulation of debates in Africa in relation to the use of African languages in education, the terminological use of MTB-MLE was taken from South African debates to the African Academy of Languages (ACALAN), an affiliate organization of the African Union from about 2002 onwards. A large 25-country study of mother-tongue and bilingual education in sub-Saharan Africa under the auspices of the Association for the Development of Education in Africa (ADEA), UNESCO and the German development agency, Gesellschaft für Technische Zusammenarbeit (GTZ), brought evidence of the poor longitudinal effects of weak and early transition from local to international language models of education in Africa (Heugh, 2006, in Alidou et al., 2006). The

Report, presented to the Ministers of Education in Africa in Libreville in 2006, was followed by each of the Ministers of Education from the 25 countries represented at the Libreville meeting agreeing to implement stronger bilingual or multilingual programmes based on the mother tongue across their state systems. This has resulted in wide-ranging changes and approaches within UNESCO and related bodies, and it has resulted in a number of high-profile UNESCO reports and advocacy documents, for example *Why and How Africa Should Invest in African languages and Multilingual Education* (Ouane & Glanz, 2010; see also Ouane & Glanz, 2011). Agencies, such as the SIL, as discussed earlier, with an interest in developing African languages in education for evangelical purposes, paid close attention to this development and adjusted the theoretical framing of their early transitional programmes in Africa. Together, UNESCO, through its channels and SIL, through its linguists who work assiduously in poor, linguistically diverse countries in many parts of the world, appear to have collaborated to increase the visibility of the term *MTB-MLE* beyond the contexts in which it was first developed or in which it was first intended for use.

Cabral and Martin-Jones are correct to pose questions of how MTB-MLE has come to be inserted into debates and practice in East Timor. At the very least, the Anglophone use of 'mother tongue' is not an exact equivalent of the Portuguese term *língua materna*, which may have been more suited to the linguistic ecology of East Timor. The circumstances in which MTB-MLE came to be used were themselves vexed even in South Africa. A concern here is where vocabulary and terminology take on particular historical and political circumstances in one context, these do not and should not translate to other contexts. For this reason, as Chimbutane as well as Cabral and Martin-Jones suggest, there is reason to be cautious of both terminology and associated programmes when these are transplanted from one setting to another. There are many risks; one of these is closing off local voice and agency.

Conclusions

Together the four chapters offer multi-perspectival insights into the dynamics of multi-scaled multilingualisms in four southern countries. They also illustrate that it may not be possible to form a universalized view of multilingualism(s). Rather, multilingualisms differ from context to context, certainly in southern settings, and most likely also in northern ones. An implication is that northern debates on languages and multilingualisms that seek terminological definitions with universal applicability or relevance are unlikely to engage with or capture local voice or the nuance of southern experiences. Equally, southern concepts and educational responses to linguistic diversity may not translate across southern contexts in ways that serve local agency and participatory citizenship. We note that there are questions in relation to how MTB-MLE has been appropriated by agencies that seek to empower marginal communities, yet they may do so with programmes that have evolved in external contexts rather than in ones that evolve from the ground upwards in domestic contexts.

These cautionary observations apply equally to ideological discourses of language rights as they do to semantic and ideological interpretations of mother tongue, bilingualism, multilingualism and education (in whatever form). It has been all too easy for linguists and other stakeholders trained in northern ideological frames to carry these frames to southern settings with good intent, only to find that, without local participation and decision-making, external frames do not bring equity or deliverance from marginality in the global south (Stroud & Heugh, 2004, 2011).

The mapping of educational approaches in one setting onto another, even if couched in international discourses of language rights and equity, runs the risk of layering new hegemony upon old. Another hegemony or ill-fitting orthodoxy is likely to exacerbate marginality and obscure voice, agency and participatory citizenship. It is for this reason that critical sociolinguists need to tread carefully as ethnographers. We need also to tread carefully as agents whose interests may lie within current orthodoxies of the academy, development agencies and NGOs. These are interests that are unlikely to synchronize with those of individuals and communities in the peripheries and borderlands. Linguistic citizenship offers us a useful lens to see through the limitations of emancipatory and language rights-based enterprises on the one hand, and also to see beyond the limitations of northern claims to the semantic interpretations of terminology used in southern contexts.

Notes

(1) Linguistic citizenship in this volume and in earlier discussions authored or co-authored by Stroud is not used in connection with the use of language tests for citizenship status, as has been misunderstood by some scholars (e.g. Ramanathan, 2013: 1).

(2) I use *Tetum* here, following Cabral and Martin-Jones. Elsewhere, authors use the term *Tetun* and refer to the regional varieties of Tetun, some of which may not be not mutually understood (Taylor-Leech, personal communication, 8 September 2016).

(3) I am able to indicate that the term originates from the research included in the volume *Multilingual Education for South Africa* (Heugh *et al.*, 1995), where it was discussed as 'bilingual education that is based on the home language'. The term was debated with several different variants over a decade within the Project for the Study of Alternative Education in South Africa based at the University of Cape Town, and with scholars from across Africa during a series of meetings, seminars, workshops and conferences between 1996 and 2005. Neville Alexander was to insist on using the term *MTB-MLE*, as an act of resistance and de-colonial re-appropriation of vocabulary and concepts colonized during apartheid. He was advised that this would not be understood as a de-colonial stance by colleagues whose research had informed its conceptualization.

References

Agnihotri, R.K. (2014) Multilinguality, education and harmony. *International Journal of Multilingualism* 11 (3), 364–379.

Alidou, H., Boly, A., Brock-Utne, B., Diallo Y.S., Heugh, K. and Wolff, H.E. (2006) *Optimizing Learning and Education in Africa – The Language Factor. A Stock-Taking Research on Mother Tongue and Bilingual Education in Sub-Saharan Africa.* Paris: UNESCO and Association for the Development of Education in Africa (ADEA).

Alidou, O.D. (2005) *Engaging Modernity: Muslim Women and the Politics of Agency in Postcolonial Niger.* University of Wisconsin Press.

Anchimbe, E.A. (2013) *Language Policy and Identity Construction: The Dynamics of Cameroon's Multilingualism.* Amsterdam/Philadelphia: John Benjamins.

Ansaldo, U. (2010) Identity alignment and language creation in multilingual communities. *Language Sciences* 32 (6), 615–623.

Bamgbose, A. (1987) When is language planning not planning. *Journal of West African Languages* 17 (1), 6–14.

Bamgbose, A. (2014) The language factor in development goals. *Journal of Multilingual and Multicultural Development* 35 (7), 646–657.

Cerutti, P.O., Tacconi, L., Lescuyer, G. and Nasi, R. (2013) Cameroon's hidden harvest: Commercial chainsaw logging, corruption, and livelihoods. *Society and Natural Resources* 26 (5), 539–553.

Chiatoh, B.A. (2014) Community language promotion in remote contexts: Case study on Cameroon. *International Journal of Multilingualism* 11 (3), 320–333.

Chimbutane, F. and Benson, C. (2012) Expanded spaces for Mozambican languages in primary education. Where bottom-up meets top-down. *International Multilingual Research Journal* 6 (1), 1–14.

Chumbow, B.S. (1987) Towards a language planning model for Africa. *Journal of West African Languages* 17 (1), 15–22.

Chumbow, B.S. (2013) Mother tongue-based multilingual education: Empirical foundations, implementation strategies and recommendations for new nations. In *Multilingual Education in Africa: Lessons From the Juba Language-in-Education Conference* (pp. 37–56).

García, O. (2009) *Bilingual Education in the 21st Century.* Oxford: Wiley-Blackwell.

Heller, M. (2007) Bilingualism as ideology and practice. In *Bilingualism: A Social Approach* (pp. 1–22). Basingstoke: Palgrave Macmillan UK.

Heugh, K. (1995) Disabling and enabling: Implications of language policy trends in South Africa. In R. Mesthrie (ed.) *Language and Social History: Studies in South African Sociolinguistics* (pp. 329–350). Cape Town: David Philip.

Heugh, K. (1999) Languages, development and reconstructing education in South Africa. *International Journal of Educational Development* 19, 301–313.

Heugh, K. (2006) Theory and practice – Language education models in Africa: Research, design, decision-making, and outcomes. In H. Alidou, A. Boly, B. Brock-Utne, Y.S. Diallo, K. Heughand and H.E. Wolff (eds) *Optimizing Learning and Education in Africa – The Language Factor. A Stock-Taking Research on Mother Tongue and Bilingual Education in Sub-Saharan Africa* (pp. 56–84). Paris: UNESCO and Association for the Development of Education in Africa (ADEA).

Heugh, K. (2011) Discourses from without, discourses from within: Women, feminism and voice in Africa. *Current Issues in Language Planning* 12 (1), 89–104.

Heugh, K. (2014) Shades, voice and mobility: Remote communities resist and reclaim linguistic and educational practices in Ethiopia. In M. Prinsloo and C. Stroud (eds) *Educating for Language and Literacy Diversity. Mobile Selves* (pp. 116–134). Houndsmills, Basingstoke: Palgrave Macmillan.

Heugh, K. (2015) Epistemologies in multilingual education: Translanguaging and genre-companions in conversation with policy and practice. *Language and Education* 29 (3), 280–285.

Heugh, K. (2017). Re-placing and re-centring southern multilingualisms: A de-colonial project. In C. Kerfoot and K. Hyltenstam (eds) *Entangled Discourses: South–North Orders of Visibility* (pp. 209–229). New York: Routledge.

Heugh, K., Siegrühn, A. and Plüddemann, P. (eds) (1995) *Multilingual Education for South Africa* (pp. 83–88). Johannesburg: Heinemann Publishers.

Kerfoot, C. and Hyltenstam, K. (eds) (2017) *Entangled Discourses: South–North Orders of Visibility*. New York: Routledge.

Kusch, R. ([1970] 2010) *Indigenous and Popular Thinking in América*. Durham, NC: Duke University Press.

Lewis, M.P., Simons, G.F. and Fennig, C.D. (eds) (2016) *Ethnologue: Languages of the World* (19th edn). Dallas, Texas: SIL International. Online version: http://www.ethnologue.com (accessed 15 November 2016)

Makoni, S. (2003) From misinvention to disinvention of language: Multilingualism and the South African Constitution. In S. Makoni, G. Smitherman, A. Ball and A.K. Spears (eds) *Black Linguistics: Language, Society and Politics in Africa and the Americas* (pp. 132–153). New York, NY: Routledge.

Makoni, S. and Pennycook, A. (eds) (2007) *Disinventing and Reconstituting Languages*. Clevedon: Multilingual Matters.

Maseko, P. (2016) The hidden voice: Recovering a century of the silenced voice of amaXhosa of the Eastern Cape, 1840s–1940s. Paper presented at the Sociolinguistics Symposium 22, 16 June 2016. Murcia, Spain.

Ouane, A. and Glanz, C. (2010) *Why and How Africa Should Invest in African Languages and Multilingual Education: An Evidence-and Practice-Based Policy Advocacy Brief*. Hamburg, Germany: UNESCO Institute for Lifelong Learning.

Ouane, A. and Glanz, C. (2011) *Optimising Learning, Education and Publishing in Africa: The Language Factor – A Review and Analysis of Theory and Practice in Mother-Tongue and Bilingual Education in Sub-Saharan Africa*. Hamburg, Germany: UNESCO Institute for Lifelong Learning.

Ramanathan, V. (ed.) (2013) *Language Policies and (Dis)Citizenship: Rights, Access, Pedagogies*. Bristol: Multilingual Matters.

Ruiz, R. (1984) Orientations in language planning. *NABE Journal* 8 (2), 15–34.

Sentumbwe, G. and Heugh, K. (2014) Local languages and primary education in Northern Uganda: Post-conflict community and local partnerships. In H. McIlwraith (ed.) *Language Rich Africa. Policy Dialogue. The Cape Town Language and Development Conference: Looking beyond 2015* (pp. 132–135). London: British Council.

Stroud, C. (2001) African mother tongue programs and the politics of language: Linguistic citizenship versus linguistic human rights. *Journal of Multilingual and Multicultural Development* 22, 339–355. Reprinted 2009 in J.E. Joseph (ed.) *Language and Politics. Major themes in English Studies Vol. IV*. London and New York: Routledge.

Stroud, C. and Heugh, K. (2004) Language rights and linguistic citizenship. In J. Freeland and D. Patrick (eds) *Language Rights and Language Survival: Sociolinguistic and Sociocultural Perspectives* (pp. 191–218). Manchester: St. Jerome Publishing.

Stroud, C. and Heugh, K. (2011) Language education. In R. Mestrhrie (ed.) *Cambridge Handbook of Sociolinguistics* (pp. 413–429). Cambridge: Cambridge University Press.

Ufomata, T. (1998) *Voices from the Marketplace: Short Stories*. Kraft Books Limited.

UNESCO (1953) *The Use of Vernacular Languages in Education*. Paris: UNESCO.

Watson, I. (2014) Re-centring first nations knowledge and places in a terra nullius space. *AlterNative* 10 (4), 508–520.

Part 3

Linguistic Citizenship in Resistance and Participation

9 Citizenship Theory and Fieldwork Practice in Sri Lanka Malay Communities

Umberto Ansaldo and Lisa Lim
The University of Hong Kong

Introduction

In current reflections on multilingual citizens and the politics of language that surround them, a central theme is the question of how to accommodate linguistic diversity in society and politics in ways that may facilitate the empowerment of minority language speakers as agents of their own social transformation. Our thoughts on the subject have developed on the basis of our involvement, in the past few years, in the documentation of Sri Lanka Malay (SLM)[1], whose circumstances are interesting in a discussion of minority language rights and empowerment.

All that most outsiders know of Sri Lanka in modern history – civil war, Tamil Tigers, etc. – have to do with language policy, specifically the rights afforded a particular ethnic group in the country, namely the Tamils, who are the largest minority group in Sri Lanka, and the consequences of the ensuing struggle for them. The Malays are a minority within minorities in Sri Lanka, classified as 'Muslims' in the current political system, together with other ethnic groups of Muslim faith. Historically of Malay/Indonesian descent, they arrived in Sri Lanka during Dutch and British colonial rule, where they developed as a multilingual community characterized by a restructured vernacular, SLM.

In recent decades, as a consequence of the Sinhala Only policy, their SLM language has become endangered. The community, in very recent years, has made a choice of 'revitalizing' their linguistic situation, but doing so with a different variety that they view as providing them with greater empowerment.

We present the situation in this chapter along the following lines:

(i)   a sketch of the SLM communities with a comparison of two different ecologies, one metropolitan and central, the other rural and peripheral;

(ii) a theorization of the SLM situation in terms of linguistic human rights (LHRs) and linguistic citizenship (LC); and

(iii) a contrastive analysis of the two communities and the differential diagnosis offered within a LC framework.

A Minority Community in Multilingual Context

Origins[2]

How the community of Malays came to be in Sri Lanka was through one of the central practices of Western colonialism, namely, the displacement of subjects from one colonized region to another. In this way, sizeable communities of people from Indonesia (the Dutch East Indies) and Malaya were settled on the island through various waves of deportation. It is possible that the community based in the Slave Island district in Colombo may have been there during Portuguese rule (until 1656), but the bulk of the SLMs trace their ancestry to the communities brought over during Dutch rule (1656–1796) and during British rule (1796–1948) (Hussainmiya, 1986).

While referred to homogeneously as 'Sri Lanka Malays', their origins are in fact very heterogeneous, covering an area from Northern Malaysia to the easternmost provinces of Indonesia (Hussainmiya, 1987, 1990). Naturally, their ethnic and linguistic backgrounds are similarly extremely diverse. Under the Dutch, political exiles, as well as convicts, were deported to Ceylon from different corners of the Indonesian archipelago and beyond, including Java, Borneo, the Moluku and Goa, among other places. The largest group of people attributed a 'Malay' origin came as soldiers also from disparate places such as Bali, Java, Riau, Ambon and peninsular Malaysia, such that 'almost all the major ethnic groups from the region of the Eastern archipelago were represented' (Hussainmiya, 1987: 48). In an earlier era, in fact, these peoples were known as *Ja Minissu* by the Sinhalese and *Java Manusar* by the Tamils: 'people from Java' (Saldin, 2003: 3). It was the British who, upon finding a community who spoke 'Malay', attached the corresponding ethnic label to the group, and it is this designation 'Malay' that has persisted.

As already suggested above, it is generally recognized that at least three different communities could be distinguished. First, there was a rather sophisticated diaspora of noblemen – nobility exiled during Dutch occupation of the East Indies – who typically would be deported together with their families. As mentioned above, political dissenters were also deported. Second was the large group of soldiers imported first by the Dutch to form a 'Malay' garrison, which would become the Ceylon Rifle Regiment under the British who continued the same practice (compare Ricklefs, 1974). The soldiers too could also be accompanied by their wives, a practice encouraged during Dutch and British rule (Ansaldo, 2008, 2009; Sourjah, 2003). A third group comprising convicts, slaves and indentured labourers was surely present from as early as Portuguese occupation, and such importation continued through both Dutch and British rule; this group would also have been rather heterogeneous ethnically and linguistically, but historical records do not provide us with any detail about size, specific provenance, etc. (Ansaldo, 2008, 2009; Hussainmiya, 1990). Contacts between the groups were indeed quite frequent, owing among other reasons to the practice of employing noblemen as officers of the troops, master–servant relations and a common, Islamic faith (Ansaldo, 2008, 2009; Hussainmiya, 1987, 1990). Overall, it can be seen that the community of Malays in Sri Lanka was one that constituted not just single individuals, but also included family, retinue and network ties, which settled in the community.

Vitality

Census data show that, from the late 1800s to the present time, the Malays have consistently comprised approximately 0.33% of the population, and are still today a numerical minority in Sri Lanka, with the majority Sinhalese comprising two-thirds to three-quarters of the population, and a significant minority of Tamils comprising a quarter of the population.[3] They can also, and perhaps more markedly, be seen to constitute a minority in name: they were grouped together in the Ceylon Citizenship Act of 1948 together with the Sri Lankan Moors (Tamil-speaking people tracing their ancestry to Arab traders who arrived in Sri Lanka between the 8th and 15th centuries) and Indian Moors (from India) as 'Moors' or 'Muslims' (Official Website of the Government of Sri Lanka (Presidential Secretariat of the Government of Sri Lanka, 2007) and Sri Lanka Government Web Portal (Government of Sri Lanka, 2007), both in the early 2000s), or, more recently, are grouped under 'All Other', a category which includes Burgher, Malay, Sri Lankan Chetty, Bharatha and other ethnic groups (Department of Census and Statistics, 2012; though in other pages the minority ethnic groups are sometimes separated), or as

'Moors, Malays, Burghers (of Portuguese and Dutch descent) and others' (Government of Sri Lanka, 2015)[4] – in short, they are not represented with a distinct identity as 'Malays' at this official level. A distinct SLM identity is however clearly perceived at the inter- and intra-communal level (more on this later). They may thus be seen to possess low symbolic capital within their own country, and the level of ethnolinguistic vitality from the objective criterion of institutional support (Giles *et al.*, 1977) can be assessed as low.

Their status within the country, nonetheless, can be seen to have always been quite high. As outlined in the previous section, a majority of the ancestors of the Colombo, Kandy and Hambantota communities would have been Javanese nobility exiled during the wars of succession in Java during Dutch rule. Official documents of 1792, for example, list 176 individuals belonging to 23 families of royalty and nobility exiled together with their families from Java, Batavia and Sumatra to Ceylon (Burah, 2006: 44). The older Javanese, because of their proficiency in Dutch, were appointed *Hoofd de Maha Badda* (Sinhala *maha badda* 'great trade', referring to the cinnamon industry first established by the Sinhala king in the 1500s for Portuguese trade) or *Hoofd de Cinnamon*, namely, the 'captain' supervising the cinnamon gardens, the spice being one of the most precious commodities during Dutch rule (Burah, 2006: 39–42f.); with increased production of cinnamon, these superior officers would be rewarded with more power, promotions and privileges (Burah, 2006: 59). Most of the exiles became enlisted in the military, and were later retained under the British as members of the Malay Regiment (as well as in the Police and the Fire Brigade; Conference of Sri Lanka Malays, 2002), where, although they dropped their royal titles, they did nonetheless maintain their status as was the practice of the time (Burah, 2006: 46–47). After the disbandment of the regiment in 1873, many of these joined the tea estates and functioned as intermediaries between the English superintendents and the Indian labour force (Saldin, 2003: 10). The Malays' contribution to sports has also been significant, with the Colombo Malay Cricket Club, founded in 1872, being the oldest cricket club in the country, producing numerous cricketers and hockey players who have represented Sri Lanka (Conference of Sri Lanka Malays, 2002). In short, although officially symbolic, recognition would appear to be low, the Malays have held a status among the communities that has been high, in no small part owing to their origins and their linguistic abilities (the latter elaborated on in the following section).

It is consequently not surprising that – in spite of their lack of identity in the Ceylon Citizenship Act – the SLMs' own identity has always been extremely vibrant. The Malays are found in various communities located around the island, who vary in their socioeconomic and educational status, and their linguistic repertoire and communicative practices, and whose SLM varieties show some variation, as summarized in Table 9.1 (Lim & Ansaldo, 2006a, 2007, adapted from Ansaldo, 2008).[5] While there is a strong sense of identity and separateness for each of the different communities (SLM community, personal communications, 2003–2006), they nonetheless all identify themselves as Sri Lankan Malays. This has surely been the case since colonial rule, where this 'Malay' diaspora is testified to being a close-knit community, in which contacts between the different Malay/Indonesian ethnicities as well as the different social extractions were maintained through the ranks of the army as well as through common religious practice (Ricklefs, 1974). There is also much awareness and expression of their culture and ancestry (e.g. Burah, 2006; Saldin, 2003), and there are a large number of social and cultural groups, including, for example, the Sri Lanka Malay Confederation (SLAMAC) (the umbrella organization), the Sri Lanka Malay Rupee Fund, the Conference of Sri Lanka Malays and Malay Associations of the communities located around the island, which are all extremely active in the organization of regular social, cultural,

Table 9.1 SLM communities (Lim & Ansaldo, 2006a, 2007, adapted from Ansaldo, 2008)

Community	Characteristics
1. Colombo	Middle–upper class community in capital city; restricted usage of SLM in old–middle generations; common Sinhala (and some Tamil) competence; English fairly fluent to native speaker competence; standardizing in Malay; no SLM in younger generation
2. Slave Island	Lower class community in a poor district of Colombo; strong Tamil influences; no English
3. Kandy and other Upcountry	Middle-lower/rural class communities in the central hill country area; SLM in old–middle generations, and in some younger generation; Sinhala competence; some English proficiency, especially in younger generation
4. Hambantota	Community on the south coast, traditionally heavy Sinhalese-speaking area; SLM in old–middle generations; often trilingual with Sinhala and Tamil; limited English
5. Kirinda	Fishing community on southeast coast; SLM dominant in all generations; fully trilingual with Sinhala and Tamil, especially in middle–younger generations; English limited to a few individuals

commemorative and fund-raising activities and initiatives (Ansaldo & Lim, fieldnotes, 2003–2007). Given their dense and multiplex networks, it is not surprising that SLM has been widely spoken as a home language for generations (Hussainmiya, 1986), that is, until recently, as will be shown in the next sections.

One particular point needs to be underlined here with regard to the various Malay communities on the island, and that is the distinction between the more urban and the more rural communities. Crucial to the arguments in this chapter is that the degree of centralness as opposed to periphery has an impact on issues, such as the degree of endangerment faced as well as the implications for the application of rights discourse or citizenship participation, as will be elaborated upon in the sections that follow. In this chapter, we focus on what may be considered two poles in the SLM communities, those of Colombo and Kirinda, with the former considered most central and urban, the latter most peripheral.

Cultural and linguistic reconstruction

As a small minority in Ceylon, it is not surprising that, over the centuries, various aspects of the Malay/Indonesian community underwent reconstruction to become 'Sri Lanka Malay'. While their religious practices were maintained in the Muslim tradition, other aspects of culture have converged to either or both of the other two dominant ethnic groups. For instance, until only very recently, the women have worn the South Asian sari as their traditional dress, rather than baju kurong or sarong kebaya as in Malaysia and Indonesia (Saldin, 2003: 1), and weddings involve payment of a dowry as in Hindu practice, whereas Islamic tradition only involves the groom's payment of mahar to the bride's father (Saldin, 2003: 67).

Owing to the religious affinity with Muslim Tamils, there have been historical and linguistic speculations suggesting that SLM communities descended from Tamil–Malay intermarriages. This is however a mistaken view based on wrongful interpretation of historical sources and not supported by recent historical and linguistic evidence (Ansaldo, 2008). The early Malays would have been speakers of the Malay lingua franca that existed since the 1st millennium AD in the monsoon Asia region, most often referred to as Bazaar Malay (Adelaar & Prentice, 1996). This Malay variety would have been in contact with two adstrates: colloquial Sinhala, the dominant language of the population of Sri Lanka and Lankan Tamil, spoken by, among others, traders and plantation workers. Mixed together these evolved to a unique restructured variety now known as SLM,[6] a mixed language of trilingual base, with lexical items predominantly from

Bazaar Malay and grammatical features from Sinhala and Tamil (Ansaldo, 2005, 2008, 2009, see also Aboh & Ansaldo, 2007, Ansaldo & Nordhoff, 2009).[7] However, the mistaken interpretation of SLM communities as Tamil–Malay 'hybrid', has led to the infelicitous classification of SLM as a 'creole': it is referred to as a creole in an early account by a historian (Hussainmiya, 1986), by linguists (see e.g. Smith *et al.*, 2004), and it is listed as Sri Lankan Creole Malay in *Ethnologue* (Gordon, 2005). As noted in Garrett (2006: 180f.), and as will be shown in the case of SLM (also elaborated on in Ansaldo & Lim, 2006a; Lim & Ansaldo, 2006a, 2007), such a classification, besides being defective on historical as well as theoretical grounds (Aboh & Ansaldo, 2007; Ansaldo & Matthews, 2007), in fact has a significant impact on the type of shift that may occur as well as its speed. The awareness of speaking a 'corrupt' or 'broken' variety, as is often implied in the current definition of creole languages, may lead to a perception of their linguistic variety as not being 'good' enough to maintain, and further strengthens a community's desire to move away to a more standard variety. Indeed, it has been argued that contact languages are particularly endangered, given their marginalization among languages in general and endangered languages in particular (Garrett, 2006: 178).[8]

What is often forgotten is that, in addition to their restructured variety SLM, another crucial feature of the linguistic repertoire of the Malays in Sri Lanka that is particularly significant is their multilingualism (Lim & Ansaldo, 2007): the Malay community has always been perhaps the most multilingual of all the co-existing Sri Lankan communities – Sinhalese, Tamils, Burghers – having in their repertoire the main languages spoken on the island, namely Sinhala and Tamil, alongside SLM (Ansaldo, 2008; SLM community, personal communication, 2003–2006), and in some strata, also that of their last colonizers, English. In both Dutch and British Ceylon, many SLMs were in positions in which they functioned as intermediaries between colonizers and locals, and were proficient in all the languages needed to interact with all parties concerned. A more contemporary small-scale survey of the Malays (Lim & Ansaldo, 2006b)[9] shows that they are still clearly multilingual – 66% speak at least four languages: SLM, English, Sinhala and Tamil; and the remaining 34% merely have Tamil absent from this multilingual repertoire.

Language and Politics in Sri Lanka

Before going on to assess the situation of the SLMs where language shift and rights are concerned, an appreciation is in order of the multilingual society in which they are situated, that of Sri Lanka, and the politics of language that are prevalent there. The tensions that are currently at the forefront of this nation's troubles are really a consequence of a heritage of the politics of language, a culmination of political decisions made at various points of the island's modern history, beginning primarily during British colonialism and continuing through the nation's independence and postcolonial challenges (also see Lim, 2013, for an overview).

The source of troubles can probably be traced to one of its legacies of the British Empire in all her colonies, namely the English language. While English education was introduced to the British subjects of Ceylon during British rule, as in all the other colonies, English was available only for a small and unbalanced proportion of the population. The Colebrooke-Cameron Report estimated that in 1828 less than 2% of the population were in school, and for those 250,000 under the age of puberty, only 800 were taught in the English language. Significantly, most of those who received English education were those in American mission schools in the Tamil north (Colebrooke, 1831, in Bailey, 1998: 210f.). At independence, there were more missionary-built schools in the Tamil-dominated north (Jaffna) than in the rest of the island. With this resource of English, Ceylon Tamils, although only 12.4% of the population in 1946 (and distinct from Indian Tamils, agricultural workers who were regarded as stateless persons but constituted another 10.4% of the population), were conversely well represented in government service, as well as in medicine and law, far more than their share of the population (Bailey, 1998: 216). Such a pattern continued through early post-independence Sri Lanka, and it is perhaps not surprising that, as a result, the dominating sentiment was of Tamil favouritism under colonial rule.

In the years leading to independence, from 1931, the discourse dominating policy involved language and rights it afforded the various ethnic groups in the nation. Already in 1943, Jayewardene introduced the sweeping resolution to declare Sinhalese the official language of the country. Even though this was later passed with the amendment to attach the words 'and Tamil' to each mention of Sinhalese, all other minorities felt threatened and would rather have had any other foreign language than Sinhalese as the official language (Bailey, 1998: 217; Russell, 1978: 61). Needless to say, the Tamils had the most to lose. Once the People's United Front Party did indeed take power, the Sinhala Only Act was introduced in 1956, making Sinhala the sole official language. The obvious consequence of this move was that it restricted many government jobs to Sinhala speakers and changed university admissions policies, which reduced the number of Tamils getting higher education. Subsequent legislative provisions did little to pacify the other groups (Bailey, 1998: 218). While the Burghers did 'burgher off to Australia' (as Bandaranaike allegedly endorsed; Roberts *et al.*, 1989: 170–171), the Tamils who remained in the country became increasingly territorial and separatist.

The Act was subsequently amended through various provisions and constitutions through to 1988. In the current constitution, both Sinhala and Tamil are national and official languages, languages of administration, legislation and the courts. English is officially the link language and remains the *de facto* language of rule (the business of government continues to be carried out in English, with the drafting of legislation being in English, although the law states that the Sinhala version should take preference). It is seen as an important key to advancement in technical and professional careers. Where education is concerned, either of the two national languages serves as medium of education. Though English was once the medium of instruction in schools, in particular the mission schools, this is no longer the case, not since 1972.

Language and Rights of the Malays

Response to politics

As the (stigmatized) language of a minority group, it goes without saying then that SLM has never been a language for public discourse in the country, and certainly not in modern history. Further, the fact that the Malays comprise a community that has seen displacement at some point in their history has been taken to suggest that the community by definition faces a lack of territorial rights (Errington, 2003). Given the social turmoil and economic decline witnessed in the country owing to the Tamil situation, where the Tamils do make claims on territorial rights in the country, at the outset, it can be simply said that there is not only no public, official space available in Sri Lanka's political climate for any kind of debate on SLM rights, but certainly no conducive conditions for any kind of rights solutions to be broached or to work (Ansaldo & Lim, 2007a). The SLM situation is surely not comparable with that of the Tamils in Tamil Eelam in Sri Lanka, where the policy of mother tongue revival, it is said (Canagarajah, 2005: 433–438), 'enables mobility', where the (monolingualist) policy of Tamil-only in official contexts 'helps the previously underprivileged groups to move up the class ladder'. As also noted (Ansaldo & Lim, 2007a), the empowerment of Tamil as a minority language can be seen to be successful only in the Liberation Tigers of Tamil Eelam (LTTE)-controlled state; moreover the status of

Tamil and Tamils has been achieved through immense and long-drawn out political struggle, with much bloodshed.

The implications of language policy naturally go further than this. Largely as a consequence of the more recent language and educational policies mentioned here, a decrease in linguistic vitality in the SLM home domain has been noted in recent decades (Ansaldo & Lim, 2006a; Lim & Ansaldo, 2006a, 2007). In the urban Colombo community, where the level of education is high, SLM parents and grandparents with the resources make the conscious decision to speak to their children in English in the home domain (Salma Suhood Peiris, personal communication, February 2003, January 2006; T.K. Azoor, personal communication, January 2006; also attested in Lim & Ansaldo, 2006a, 2007; Saldin, 2001: 26, 2003: 76–77), in order to provide them a resource recognized as requisite for communication and advancement internationally – 'the key to a good job and a comfortable life' (Saldin, 2003: 76). The general pattern displayed is a clear shift to English from SLM in the home domain. As a result, the community typically shows strong linguistic vitality in SLM in the oldest to middle generations and rapidly decreasing linguistic competence to nil in the vernacular in the young generation (Ansaldo & Lim, fieldnotes, 2003–2006; Lim & Ansaldo, 2006a, 2007). SLM is seen now to have a mere fifth position in the community, after Sinhala, Tamil, English and Arabic (the last in the religious domain) (T.K. Azoor, personal communication, January 2006). SLM in this community is no longer a home language for the younger generation of Sri Lankan Malays.

We can see the explanation for this choice in terms of the capital the various languages possess in the country. In the local linguistic market – of school, profession, politics – Sinhala is recognized as necessary capital and accepted without battle; it has in any case always been in the SLM's repertoire. Similarly, English has been an important variety in their linguistic repertoire; it was a language that allowed the SLM many privileges as colonial subjects. Although possessing less capital in postcolonial Sri Lanka, a multilingualism including English is recognized as crucial to the Malays. In consequence, SLM that has low capital in the local linguistic market is thus forfeited, and thus becomes not only minority and marginalized, but also endangered.

Here is where we see the first of the implications for the urban as opposed to the rural community. Such a shift from SLM to English has been taking place largely within the more (English-)educated well-to-do Colombo community (and to a lesser extent in very recent years in the other large urban centres, such as Kandy; Sebastian Nordhoff, personal communication, 2007). In sharp contrast to the central community of

Colombo are the more peripheral communities, such as that found in Kirinda, which is relatively isolated as a small fishing village on the southeast coast. A total of 90% of the village are Malay, and they comprise some 4% of the 46,000 SLM population. With a dense and multiplex social network, limited educational and employment opportunities, they exhibit strong maintenance of the vernacular.[10] The children of Kirinda (ca. 200) were said to be the only children to be native monolingual speakers of a variety of SLM (T.M.M. Hamin, personal communication, December 2003). There is thus no endangerment of the language here; on the contrary, it is still extremely vital, the dominant language of all generations of the community, spoken in all domains, even as the working language in the Tamil-medium *madrasah* (school). Kirinda is often said to be the only fully vital community of SLMs in which a young generation of speakers of a SLM variety as first language can be found.[11] We will return to further discussion of the Kirinda community in the next section.

Response to 'endangerment'

That SLM is an endangered linguistic variety has in fact not gone unnoticed by the community in recent years, and as a response to this, there are current thrusts within the SLM community in language revitalization.[12] As already pointed out, there is no place in the official spheres for addressing and politicking for minority rights. Instead, civil society organizations – outside of state structures – have stepped in and initiated discourse on the issues of their language being a minority and being endangered – with interesting consequences. The subaltern publics, that is, sites formed around social and civil movements, are the SLM groups already mentioned, as well as individuals in the SLM community, in particular in the Colombo community, who can be seen to be more linguistically aware, as well as to have the inclination and resources. The first of these may be seen to be the publication of an article in a local newspaper *The Daily News* on 'The Sri Lankan Malay Language and its future' (23 July 1987) followed by a public lecture on the same theme at the Sri Lanka Malay Association (9 October 1987), both by B.D.K. Saldin (Saldin, 2003: 94). Members of the community have on their own steam published books on their identity and language (e.g. Saldin, 2001, 2003), as well as books comparing SLM with Standard Malay (Saldin, 2000, 2001; Thaliph, 2003) and Malay primers (Emran Deen, 2001). What is significant is that this 'revitalization' taking place is not however of SLM itself, owing to a combination of two general phenomena.

First, as mentioned earlier, owing to previous publications on SLM, classifying it as a creole, the community's perception of their own language is less positive, viewing it as a creole, which is interpreted as an 'imperfect' code, and/or an ungrammatical dialect of Malay (e.g. Thaliph, 2003; Colombo SLM community, personal communication, August 2006).[13] Second, in contrast with the status the community has in their own country, greater recognition is attained instead from Malaysia (and also Indonesia), in at least two significant and related thrusts, both clearly seen as arising from scholarly and transnational contexts which have associated symbolic and material markets.

(a)   One of the objectives of Malaysia's Institute of Malay Language and Culture is 'to get in touch with Malays in different parts of the world and teach them the real Malay' (T.K. Azoor, personal communication, January 2006). One of the realizations of this has been the organization of language classes in the Standard Malay of Malaysia (Bahasa Melayu).

(b)   The Malaysian High Commission in Sri Lanka has in recent years demonstrated interest in, and strong support for, the SLM community, and provides aid in terms of student scholarships for undergraduate and postgraduate studies in Malaysia, as well as in job market openings; one of the requirements of the latter is competence in basic Malay. Before the setting up of (a), the previous First Secretary's wife also ran two classes in Standard Malay (Conference of Sri Lanka Malays, 2005).

With these two initiatives working together, it is not surprising then that it is with Malaysia that the SLM community align themselves, both in terms of language and identity. This also resonates with the suggestion that a community that has seen displacement at some point in their history tends to make some identification with a more remote community perceived as from their origins, and has a less coherent and robust identity (Errington, 2003; Le Page & Tabouret-Keller, 1985). The choice in the revitalization process is consequently not for SLM, which has so far been seen as an embarrassing, 'bad' or corrupt code and therefore unworthy of any effort of preservation, but for Malaysia's prestigious Standard Malay. After the two pioneering courses in Standard Malay in 2002, eight of the best students underwent a teacher's training course in Malaysia, and started conducting regular classes in Standard Malay for the community. One of the results of this is that encounters between Standard Malay-speaking Colombo Malays and other SLM speakers ensued in a lack of mutual intelligibility. In the annual *Hari Bahasa Melayu* (Malay Language

Day) organized by the community in Colombo in August 2006 and 2007, activities such as essay writing and oratory contests were conducted for both SLM and Standard Malay (Ansaldo & Lim, fieldnotes, 2006–2007; Lim & Ansaldo, 2007).

What is also significant to note is the implications that the discourse on language, centring in Colombo, has for other SLM communities, and here is the second point where we see a disjunction between centre and periphery. In Kirinda, the 'revitalization' efforts taking place in Colombo have trickled down in a different form. Obviously, there is no need for the Kirinda community to be concerned about their language being endangered, vital as it is; thus, there is in fact no need for any kind of revitalization. However, the increased prominence of Standard Malay of Malaysia in the SLM discourse has led to the Kirinda community becoming even more explicitly aware of the more prestigious variety and the possibilities it holds for them. In January 2006, plans were underway for Standard Malay to be taught in the village school as a subject, to children who in fact are native speakers of SLM, as well as to be used as a default language of discourse, for example, in the signs (e.g. 'no shouting'; 'show respect') displayed around the school (Ansaldo & Lim, 2006a; Lim & Ansaldo, 2006a).

The rationale is not difficult to understand, of course; it repeats itself every day in every minority community that wishes to join the global world. The belief is that the transition from an unworthy 'creole' to a national language, such as Standard Malay, will not only provide cultural capital, such as available written material for education, but, more importantly, increased economic and political capital, to plug into the global economy and direct their trajectory in social space upwards (after Bourdieu, 1984). As the president of the Conference of Sri Lanka Malays explains, 'Our educational upliftment is very very important. Because at the end of the day, the economy is what matters [...] If you are economically in a strong position, well, everything else looks after itself' (T.K. Azoor, personal communication, January 2006).

Rights and Citizenship; Urban and Periphery

Philosophies of choice

Approached from an LHR reading, the language choices made by the SLMs described would count the loss of SLM as a loss in terms of linguistic diversity, and the community would be seen to be sacrificing their right to the use of their own linguistic variety, when they should be trying to find empowerment of their minority language.[14] The choice of Standard

Malay in the Colombo community as the language for revitalization will mean new generations gaining a competence in a Malay variety, which is in fact not their 'own' SLM variety.[15] In the Kirinda community, the choice of Standard Malay as a school subject – where the school is an important domain for primary socialization in the village – can have a significant impact on the use of, and attitudes towards, SLM.[16] There was also the implicit suggestion that Standard Malay could eventually be used as a language of instruction. In such an event, such subtractive bilingualism (see e.g. Lambert, 1978), namely the use of a language as a medium of education that is not the vernacular of the children, can have a negative effect on the learning of the additional language and on other skills, as has been shown in many studies (see e.g. Cummins, 1979). Clearly such choices would be counter to the LHR concern of an 'instrumental interest in language as means of communication, aiming to ensure that language is not an obstacle to the effective enjoyment of rights with a linguistic dimension, to the meaningful participation in public institutions and democratic process, and to the enjoyment of social and economic opportunities that require linguistic skills' (Rubio-Marín, 2003: 56), not to mention proposals, such as UNESCO's stance on the use of the mother tongue in education (UNESCO, 1995–2009).

The other of LHR's main concerns lies in the 'expressive interest in language as a marker of identity, aiming at ensuring a person's capacity to enjoy a secure linguistic environment in their mother tongue, and linguistic group's fair chance of cultural reproduction' (Rubio-Marín, 2003: 56). By this token, the choice made by the SLMs for Standard Malay would be seen as the forsaking of their unique identity. Indeed, in one of our earliest reflections on the situation, we suggested that the choice of the Malays could be seen ironically as the product of the striving for an identity in a group of migrants displaced by economic rationales of the 18th to 20th centuries, in which, as globalization sweeps the world threatening diversity, in the hope of saving that same identity, the SLM communities may have to sacrifice what most defines them (Lim & Ansaldo, 2006c).

The LHR paradigm has, however, been critically evaluated in recent decades. Among other things, the LHR paradigm has been said, for example, by Stroud and Heugh (2004: 197), to endorse an ethno-linguistic stereotyping in the form of monolingual and uniform identities, and force a group of speakers to work actively to differentiate themselves from others, by claiming unique linkages of language and identity so as to gain political leverage in the competition for scarce resources – this however exacerbates problems of linguicism (Phillipson & Skutnabb-Kangas, 1986) that motivated the rights paradigm in the first place, they point out. The LHR paradigm also works on a very local perception of relevant language delimited by national territorial borders (Stroud & Heugh, 2004: 202).

If instead we take the view of language not as a discrete construct that can be owned or lost by a community, but rather the view of language articulated in terms of LC (Stroud, 2000; Stroud & Heugh, 2004), where language is all at the same time a semiotic resource for the (re)construction of agency and self-representation, an economic resource and site of political and economic struggle, a global resource to address local–global concerns, and an intimate resource as the foundation of respect for difference on a global level, then the ensuing response is different. In the LC paradigm, the community is served by its linguistic resources – which comprise pluralist alternatives reflecting the reality of the linguistic market, and, consequently, negotiable multiple, diverse and shifting identities – and is not restrained by its language. Individuals and speech communities choose to empower themselves in what they see as the best possible way with regard to existing power relationships.

The conscious 'shift' in the SLM community from SLM to Standard Malay – the latter a variety in which cultural and economic functions of language come together – is thus one that is made in appropriate circumstances, and which aids the acquisition of a resource on the semiotic, economic and global fronts. This outcome may thus be seen as a resource, rather than a threat, that enables a minority group to gain access to better education and enhanced political self-representation (Ansaldo & Lim, 2006a; Lim & Ansaldo, 2006a). In other words, the Malay communities of Sri Lanka can be seen to be achieving two ends:

(i)   They not only gain a useful economic tool, but
(ii) Also manage to preserve and represent their position through identity alignment (Ansaldo, 2009; Lim & Ansaldo, 2007), which involves:[17]
    (a) not contesting their *imposed* identity, which is not negotiable, of 'Muslim' in the context of the local nation-state, and
    (b) still maintaining their *presumed* ethnic identity as 'SLMs', and
    (c) aligning themselves with an *assumed* global 'Malay' identity, that is, one that is accepted and not negotiated.

Choices in practice

We have indeed presented this relatively positive evaluation of the SLM situation in previous reflections on the matter (Ansaldo & Lim, 2006a; Lim & Ansaldo, 2006a, 2007), but have also suggested that not all communities are equal (Ansaldo & Lim, 2006a, 2007a; Lim &

Ansaldo, 2008), and it is to this issue that we now turn. The reality is, as we have been hinting throughout this chapter, more complex than the picture painted so far, and hinges, as we have pre-empted, on the centre/ periphery divide.

The upper-class urban SLM communities, already in an advantageous position, stand to reap the potential benefits outlined more immediately and greatly from the acquisition of one more language in their repertoire, in particular the shift to a more global variety. Members of the community in urban contexts already have access to higher education, technology, as well as political representation and social networks within the SLM, Sri Lankan and global communities. Where the instrumental purpose (in LHR terms) or an economic resource and site of political and economic struggle (in LC terms) of a linguistic resource are concerned, they certainly are empowered by their acquisition of Standard Malay in the global linguistic market. We may also point out that, for many members of this community, there is 'little to lose' in the sense that they are no longer speakers of SLM anyway. Where the issue of identity is concerned, where language is a semiotic resource for the (re)construction of agency and self-representation, Standard Malay plays a positive role too. Identity options offered to individuals at a given moment in history are said to be subject to shifting language ideologies that legitimize and value particular identities more than others (Pavlenko & Blackledge, 2004). In these present global times, where formerly displaced communities do indeed have the option and the capacity to reconnect with their pre-colonial origins, the acquisition of Standard Malay and the inclusion in the larger Malay world that affords global economic opportunities is certainly a choice that is legitimized and valued (Lim & Ansaldo, 2007). And with the expansion of one's world – one's linguistic market – the link between a single language and a singular identity becomes tenuous: the lack of a need to rigidly associate SLM identity with the SLM language is markedly observed in a recent survey where, as a response to the statement 'Speaking SLM is crucial to my identity as SLM', the younger respondents in the urban sample chose the answer 'strongly disagree' (Lim & Ansaldo, 2006b).

On the other hand, it is unclear how this translates at the grassroots level. The periphery still struggles with basic problems of limited educational infrastructure and lack of higher education, limited economic resources and mobility, and lack of political representation within the SLM community itself (Ansaldo & Lim, fieldnotes, 2003–2006). Moving from a household where SLM is the dominant language to a school system where education is predominantly in Tamil, young Kirinda Malays already face the challenge of non-'mother tongue'-based education.

However, it may at least be argued that the structural proximity between SLM and Tamil allows for a relatively smooth transition from the home to the school domain. Substituting SLM with Standard Malay, or adding the latter to the curriculum, is unlikely to improve the situation, and quite likely to deteriorate it. It will certainly not automatically open doors to the larger Malay world for them; the fundamental hurdles of acquiring basic education, garnering economic resources (simply to venture to a neighbouring town for secondary or pre-university education, for example, before any possibility for education or work in Malaysia can be considered) and so on must still first be crossed. Conversely, and just as significantly, the periphery is situated within a local context for a day-to-day existence, and is in fact dependent on more local – namely Sinhala and/or Tamil – networks for economic survival. Their SLM language – which is typologically closer to the Lankan languages (Ansaldo, 2005, 2008, 2009), and which their Sinhala and Tamil neighbours can in fact also understand and even speak (Kirinda community, personal communication, 2003–2006) – is the resource that would appear to be more crucial for them, but it is a resource for local integration and Lankan rather than (global) Malay identity. In other words, in the linguistic market that is most essential to them, namely their local context (village, region, nation), it is not Standard Malay that holds high capital, whether cultural, social, symbolic or economic, but rather Sinhala and Tamil, which are their cultural, social and economic resources, and SLM. The addition of another linguistic variety – especially a 'global' one that has no relevance to their context – does not necessarily address these more fundamental problems.

Obviously different communities are the product of different sociohistorical circumstances and thus different linguistic ecologies; for a successful understanding of different contexts, it is of paramount importance that we consider the differential factors involved in their evolution so as to arrive to differential diagnosis. We propose that the SLM periphery requires a different conceptualization towards recognition of their dominant 'mother tongue', as well as of the immediate linguistic ecology that defines it. In fact, the Kirinda school, while *de facto* following the Tamil curriculum, is characterized by a widespread use of SLM in the classroom in the early years, an implicit recognition of the role of the 'minority' language in education. By implementing the use of SLM in the early school years, instead of Tamil and/or Sinhala, the Kirinda Malays may increase their performance in school and raise the levels of education, thus offering future possibility of higher education and increase the mobility of Kirinda's population. This in itself constitutes an implementation of LC (Stroud, 2001). It is thus essential to highlight that, rather than burdening the curriculum with a language like Standard Malay, it may be more advisable to focus on more urgent means of empowerment, in particular (a) access to Sinhala education, and (b) exposure to English, which appear to us as much more immediate concerns than issues of global positioning in a Malay world. It is crucial to stress that we are not here moving back to an LHR-like view of mother-tongue-based education, but rather, in line with LC thinking, pursuing differential analyses of local ecologies and recognizing that each human group is a unique mosaic of complex cultural, economic and political necessities that can and should be addressed, among other things, through language choice.

Final Remarks

The central theme we have been exploring in this chapter, using the SLM situation as a case in point, has been the question of how to accommodate linguistic diversity in society and politics in ways that may facilitate the empowerment of minority language speakers as agents of their own social transformation. Our final remarks in this concluding section are of two kinds. The first, as in the resolution of our discussion above, involves the recognition of what entails empowerment in more central and more peripheral communities. The second is meant simply to acknowledge the role of the linguist as soon as one is involved in research on minority language communities.

The discussion on LHR that emerges from the concept of LC provides the field of language policy and planning with a useful springboard for an essential realization: that the notion of 'language = identity' is not appropriate for all linguistic ecologies and needs to be revised. In particular, we have argued here and elsewhere (Lim & Ansaldo, 2007) that, in such multilingual communities, identity is realized in multilingualism itself and cannot be reduced to one single code. This is certainly the case of the SLM who are defined by being trilingual in an ancestral variety of Malay and the languages of Sri Lanka, Sinhala and Tamil. We also maintain that minority groups such as these, in their linguistic negotiations, align themselves with different codes at different times as responses to the shifting ecologies in which they live.

In this respect, we also point out that a contrast between the centre and the periphery needs to be recognized. There is differentiated empowerment from increased multilingualism in a 'global' language, with the centre standing to gain the most. The possible 'shift' to Standard Malay described for the urban community may be viewed as a case of this identity alignment that finds a positive rationalization within the LC framework in language as a tool for empowerment. The diagnosis of the peripheral community yields a different verdict, since empowerment there lies in maintenance of the SLM vernacular, culturally and socially more advantageous than the standard variety. In other words, while the Standard Malay 'shift' may be seen as a positive alignment in Colombo, the same shift may be a negative alignment in Kirinda, because of the fundamentally different nature of the empowerment that each group needs to achieve. Significantly, a view of LC contrasted on two similar yet distinct ecologies as the ones presented here shows clearly that shifts and choices are never really intrinsically good or bad, but must make sense within the targets that a group of speakers has in terms of social, political and cultural positioning.

Finally, we would like to suggest that linguists should take responsibility by actively engaging in a mutual sharing of knowledge and not simply in detached, 'objective' analyses, because linguistic classification too, as any other kind of linguistic activity, impacts on the community it investigates. As we have argued previously (Ansaldo & Lim, 2006a, 2007a; Lim & Ansaldo, 2006a), we believe that the role of the linguist cannot be innocent anthropologist, economic empowerer nor passive observer. Rather, we would argue that, in addition to our academic and scientific brief as linguists, we also bear a social brief, one that is more pro-active than Matras's (2005) and one more akin to Tsunoda's (2005: 225f.), where one needs to shoulder the role of disinterested educator: where the burden of responsibility must also be to provide the community in question with as much objectiveness and clarity as there can be in the issues pertaining to linguistic variation, multilingualism, acquisition, standards, imperialism, shift, etc, and their real-life implications, so as to avoid the kind of misunderstanding of linguistic issues and consequences as described earlier in this chapter. This is not a paternalistic take on our part, but a position in line with the paradigm of LC presented here: for a community to really be empowered agents of their own social transformation, they have to be *informed* agents, in order to make as enlightened a decision as possible about their language choices.[18]

Retrospective: December 2016

Since the Multilingual Citizen workshop in 2007 and the original writing of this chapter, Sri Lanka saw its most significant event in decades: the military defeat of the LTTE in 2009. In the wake of this, the then President Mahindra Rajapakse proclaimed to have erased the word *minorities* from the country's collective vocabulary: 'No longer are there Tamils, Muslims, Burghers, Malays and any other minorities. There are only two peoples in this country. One is the people that love this country.

The other comprises the small groups that have no love for the land of their birth. Those who do not love the country are now the lesser group'. In spite of this rhetoric of erasure, we can identify several developments that hold significant implications for social practices and voice for the SLM community.

Within-community voices

While the citizenship practices in the Sri Lankan Malay community have, as demonstrated in this chapter, always been initiated from within the community, the majority of academic input and output has been by researchers of the Global North. Such research practice has however undergone transformation. In no small part as a consequence of all the academic attention that the Sri Lankan Malay community and their vernacular were attracting in the 2000s, a young community member, who was at the time pursuing her doctoral research originally in another area, made the decision to work instead on SLM – this has meant an academic voice from within the community, which is significant not only symbolically, but also, and more importantly, for the sustainability of research on the community and their language(s).

Some of her work has represented the voice of the urban middle-class youth segment of the SLM community, who, crucially – in contrast with older Malays who lived through a change in language policy (as outlined earlier in this chapter) and who felt increasingly marginalized in the country – have grown up with an identification of Sri Lanka as home (Rassool, 2013: 137). Rassool suggests that the present generation of Lankan youth, influenced by such political rhetoric superficially promoting social cohesion and inclusiveness, are renegotiating their ethnic and linguistic identities in relation to their national identity, and their wish to align themselves with the Lankan form of Malay is a reflection of this evolution (Rassool, 2013: 138). We see this expression also on social media platforms (see following).

Heterogeneous voices

The attention that SLM received, as outlined in this chapter, has further strengthened the renewed prestige of a Sri Lankan Malay identity centred in, though – and this is crucial – not exclusively limited to, its ancestral language. Here again we see how a notion of identity alignment (Ansaldo, 2009; Lim & Ansaldo, 2007) is negotiated and renegotiated in social practice. While English is still the dominant language of the urban

Sri Lankan Malay community in Colombo, members now do make a point of holding their meetings at least partly in SLM (Ansaldo & Lim, fieldnotes, 2010–2015), and a weekly prayer in SLM continues to be offered at the Slave Island mosque (Ansaldo, 2014: 390). Through a revaluation of their linguistic capital, the SLM community is now turning back to symbolic maintenance and revitalization of their ancestral language – at least alongside the continued investment, in certain urban quarters, in the more global Standard Malay variety.

Such a situation has been analysed by Lim (2016) using the notion of postvernacularity (Shandler, 2006) – namely situations where a language serves the purpose of identity-building within a community even after it has ceased to be used as a vernacular for daily communication, used, for instance, in a number of cultural practices, such as amateur theatre, music and folklore, translation, attempts to learn the language in evening classes, and in its primarily symbolic value and the tendency to preserve only the language's most colourful or evocative elements. Lim (2016) goes further to argue that the Sri Lankan Malay context (as well as that of the Peranakans in Singapore) would appear to go beyond such postvernacularity – because the linguistic and cultural vitality the community is experiencing is embodied through their various, diverse language practices, that is, not only in SLM, but also in the other Lankan varieties in their repertoire, Sinhala and Tamil, as well as their emergent variety of Sri Lankan English, often manifested in a mixed code or plurilingual or translingual practice. We see this very evidently in the linguistic practices on social media, as the next section illustrates.

Virtual voices

The current era of digitality affords – to a greater extent and with increased ease than before – opportunities for diverse voices to be represented, transgressive and transformative. In what is Web 2.0 de rigeur, numerous websites and Facebook pages are in existence, created by and for the SLM community and/or language, such as the Sri Lanka Malay Association (SLMA), Sri Lanka Malay Youth Association (SLMYA), Save SL Melayu, and SL Malay Memes, to name just a few. The SLMYA write – in English – that they 'are here for many reasons', including bringing unity among the Malay youth around the island, fostering and building a sense of Malay culture among its members, and propagating and encouraging the use of the Malay language. SLMA posts are primarily in English, though comments may be in Malay or Sinhala, with cultural items and symbolic uses of SLM. SL Malay Memes has posts in the various Lankan languages, though posts with more global content, for example, Eid festival or new year wishes, are produced in a more Standard Malay. Significantly, one of its regular formulae is to have a post ask readers 'How to say X in Sri Lankan Malay? Please comment your answer'. Such a post, asking about the word *dates*, posted on 21 June 2017, drew 22 responses, while another asking about the word *fish*, posted 10 November 2016, drew 34 responses (as at 9 July 2017).

It is perhaps in the language practices on such social media platforms that the agency entailed in citizenship is best demonstrated – in the heteroglossic practices involved in the negotiations and renegotiations of the language/s and identity/ies of the virtual, transnational, reimagined SLM community.

Notes

(1) Research (August 2004–2008) was funded by the Volkswagen Stiftung's initiative for the Documentation of Endangered Languages (DoBeS) for the project 'The documentation of Sri Lanka Malay: Linguistic and cultural creolization endangered' (II/80 155) (Project director and principal investigator: Umberto Ansaldo; Co-investigator and project manager: Lisa Lim; Collaborators: Walter Bisang and Thiru Kandiah; PhD researcher: Sebastian Nordhoff). Fieldwork undertaken in February and December 2003 and January 2004 was partially supported by a National University of Singapore Academic Research Grant [R-103-000-020-112] for the project 'Contact languages of Southeast Asia: The role of Malay' (Principal investigator: Umberto Ansaldo, 05/2001–12/2003). We express our gratitude to all the SLM communities who have been warm and welcoming, and open to and immensely supportive of our research. We thank Christopher Stroud not only for the invitation to participate in *The Multilingual Citizen* workshop in Cape Town in February 2007 (as well as colleagues there for their reactions), but also for his discussions and support, particularly in our early forays into linguistic human rights/ linguistic citizenship (LHR/LC) issues.

(2) This section of the origins of the Malays in Sri Lanka is necessarily distilled; for a lengthier account, see Ansaldo (2008, 2009).

(3) Population census provides the following data (selected): in 1881: Sinhalese 66.7%, Tamil 25%; in 1953: Sinhalese 70%, Tamil 23%; in 2001: Sinhalese 80%, Tamil 9% (but this excludes Liberation Tigers of Tamil Eelam (LTTE) areas); in all census, Malays are a constant 0.33%.

(4) The Malays comprise about 5% of the 'Muslim group', which forms 7% of the Sri Lanka population (Library of Congress, 1988).

(5) In earlier scholarship, the Colombo dialect, meant to represent SLM as a whole, is the one usually described, though variation between the different communities is briefly acknowledged (Saldin, 2001); the issue of variation is addressed in more current analysis (see e.g. Ansaldo *et al.*, 2006). The high degree of variation in a speech community such as SLM, which in fact comprises a number of smaller communities in different geographical areas, can be accounted for by at least two factors: (a) the relation with network type; and (b) diffusion and linguistic openness (Foley, 2005).

(6)   Apart from an unpublished MA thesis by Bichsel-Stettler (1989), SLM until very recently had been only very briefly described, by Adelaar (1991), Hussainmiya (1986) and Saldin (2001), the former two based on small-scale studies, and the latter on personal knowledge. For more recent work, see for example Ansaldo (2008, 2009), Nordhoff (2009, 2013), Slomanson (2006), Smith *et al.* (2004), Smith and Paauw (2006).

(7)   Unlike its better-known Caribbean 'creole' counterparts, SLM – together with a very few other varieties of the region (e.g. Baba Malay, Cocos Malay) – is typologically in a unique position of providing us with an environment in which no Standard Average European acrolectal variety is involved in the dynamics of contact. Furthermore, with Sinhala and Tamil as its adstrates, the languages involved in the formation of SLM varieties come from three distinct language families: Austronesian, Dravidian and Indo-European. As such it can shed light on issues of universality and specificity in contact-induced language change (Ansaldo, 2008, 2009). The relationship between the three language groups involved in its evolution was similarly of an altogether different type than the better-known scenarios of exploitation/slavery/intermarriage, etc., and thus provides contrastive material for our understanding of typologies of language contact. From the linguistic point of view, SLM is a precious variety for studies of language contact, language evolution, as well as cultural creolization.

(8)   In spite of this, this present project documenting SLM was, in 2004, the first DoBeS project documenting a 'creole'.

(9)   The sample comprises a majority of Colombo Malays (i.e. more urban, English-educated, higher class), and middle and older generations.

(10) In initial investigations (Ansaldo, 2005; Ansaldo & Lim, 2005), the variety of Kirinda has been found to be structurally distinct from other SLM varieties: Ansaldo (2008) describes its nominal case system, a striking feature considering the rarity of complex morphological marking in contact languages in which a rare case of split is occurring, developing a new coding for object marking from a morpheme originally used for dative-like functions. Lexically and grammatically, there seems to be a stronger influence of Sinhala and Tamil, and trilingualism in SLM, Sinhala and Tamil is very common in all generations (Ansaldo, 2008).

(11) The Upcountry communities are reported to show similar vitality (Sebastian Nordhoff, personal communication, January 2006), though this is probably still less so than in Kirinda.

(12) The awareness and 'revitalization' activities described in this section pre-date this project's commencement in the community.

(13) It has also become clear to us in discussions and discourse that in many cases the community does not make a very clear distinction between SLM and Standard Malay. One of the local publications already mentioned, a textbook presented in Standard Malay with Sinhala, Tamil and English, is intended to 'help Sri Lankan Malays to study their mother tongue in its internationally recognized form' (Emran Deen, 2001: foreword).

(14) This would be similar to the negative knee-jerk reaction of the linguist involved in endangered languages, as pointed out previously (Ansaldo & Lim, 2006a; Lim & Ansaldo, 2006a).

(15) The perception that Standard Malay exposure may help in slowing down the attrition of SLM is quite strong in the community. This perception, albeit a commonly observed one, is unfortunately a mistaken one, and the sensitive relationship

between standard and local varieties within the contexts of endangered minorities needs to be paid attention to.

(16)   We see a parallel with the successful annual Speak Mandarin Campaign in Singapore, first launched in 1979 and meant to support the bilingual education policy: this led swiftly to a shift in most domains, in particular the home, from the other Chinese languages to Mandarin, and subsequently to a generation of children not being able to understand their grandparents.

(17)   For more on types of identity and ethnic identity, see Pavlenko and Blackledge (2004) and Edwards (1985), respectively. Their assumed identity is one that is recognizable through an empowered linguistic identity, and recognized by the Malay 'homeland'; we also see in this the identification of displaced communities with a more remote community.

(18)   In our attempt to fulfil such a role, our own contribution has been in the form of seminars and articles for the community itself (Ansaldo, 2006; Ansaldo & Lim, 2006d, 2007b), which are not just for circulation within the academic community, which aim to provide clarity in (i) linguistic issues, and (ii) the fact that the choices to be made lie with the community itself. As a consequence of this, it would appear that there is some (positive) impact: at a recent meeting of SLAMAC (the Confederation of 22 Malay organizations), the sentiment expressed was that they 'should also arrange to teach SLM and arrest the rot of SLM becoming an endangered language' (T.M.M. Hamin, personal communication, 20 December 2006), and discussions have begun within the SLM community and with us on a proposal for a literacy programme as part of the revitalization (in the urban communities) or maintenance (in the peripheral communities) of SLM, alongside the teaching of Standard Malay (T.M.M. Hamin and T.K. Azoor, personal communication, June 2007).

References

Aboh, E.O. and Ansaldo, U. (2007) The role of typology in language creation: A descriptive take. In U. Ansaldo, S. Matthews and L. Lim (eds) *Deconstructing Creole*. Typological Studies in Language 73 (pp. 39–66). Amsterdam/Philadelphia: John Benjamins.

Adelaar, K.A. (1991) Some notes on the origin of Sri Lankan Malay. In H. Steinhauer (ed.) *Papers in Austronesian Linguistics No. 1*. Pacific Linguistics A-81 (pp. 23–37). Canberra: The Australian National University.

Adelaar, K.A. and Prentice, D.J. (1996) Malay: Its history, role and spread. In S.A. Wurm, P. Mühlhäusler and D.T. Tryon (eds) *Atlas of Languages of Intercultural Communication in the Pacific, Asia and the Americas* (pp. 673–693). Berlin: Mouton de Gruyter.

Ansaldo, U. (2005) Typological admixture in Sri Lanka Malay. The case of Kirinda Java. Manuscript, University of Amsterdam. See http://home.medewerker.uva.nl/u.ansaldo/page2.html (accessed July 2009).

Ansaldo, U. (2006) Language documentation and description: Sri Lanka Malay. *The Ceylon Observer* August 2006.

Ansaldo, U. (2008) Revisiting Sri Lanka Malay. In A. Dwyer, D. Harrison and D. Rood (eds) *A World of Many Voices: Lessons from Documented Endangered Languages*. Studies in Language. Amsterdam/Philadelphia: John Benjamins.

Ansaldo, U. (2009) *Contact Languages: Ecology and Evolution in Asia*. Cambridge: Cambridge University Press.

Ansaldo, U. (2014) SLM is dead; long live Sri Lanka Malay. A review article of Nordhoff 2013. *Journal of Language Contact* 7, 381–391.

Ansaldo, U. and Lim, L. (2005) The KirJa collection: A corpus of Kirinda Java, a vital variety of Sri Lanka Malay. Manuscript, University of Amsterdam.

Ansaldo, U. and Lim, L. (2006a) Globalisation, empowerment and the periphery: The Malays of Sri Lanka. In R. Elangaiyan, R. McKenna Brown, N.D.M. Ostler and M.K. Verma (eds) *Vital Voices: Endangered Languages and Multilingualism. Proceedings of the FEL X Conference* (pp. 39–46). Bath: Foundation for Endangered Languages; Mysore: Central Institute of Indian Languages.

Ansaldo, U. and Lim, L. (2006b) Sri Lanka Malay: Between endangerment and empowerment. Language in Action seminar series, Department of Linguistics, University of the Western Cape, 24 April 2006. Cape Town, South Africa.

Ansaldo, U. and Lim, L. (2006c) Endangerment, empowerment and documentation: Dilemmas of Sri Lanka Malay. 19th European Conference on Modern South Asian Studies (ECMSAS), 27–30 June 2006. Leiden, The Netherlands: International Institute for Asian Studies (IIAS).

Ansaldo, U. and Lim, L. (2006d) Language documentation and description: Sri Lanka Malay. Lecture given to the Sri Lanka Malay community, 16 July 2006. Colombo, Sri Lanka.

Ansaldo, U. and Lim, L. (2007a) Out of reach: The Sri Lanka Malay periphery beyond rights and citizenship. Invited paper. Workshop on the multilingual citizen: Towards a politics of language for agency and change, 23–24 February 2007. Department of Linguistics, University of the Western Cape, Cape Town.

Ansaldo, U. and Lim, L. (2007b) Maintaining and revitalising Sri Lanka Malay. Hari Bahasa Melayu (Malay Language Day) 2007. Lecture given to the Sri Lanka Malay community, 26 August 2007. Colombo, Sri Lanka.

Ansaldo, U. and Matthews, S. (2007) Deconstructing creole: The rationale. In U. Ansaldo, S. Matthews and L. Lim (eds) *Deconstructing Creole*. Typological Studies in Language 73 (pp. 1–18). Amsterdam/Philadelphia: John Benjamins.

Ansaldo, U. and Nordhoff, S. (2009) Complexity and the age of languages. In E.O. Aboh and N. Smith (eds) *Complex Processes in New Languages*. Creole Language Library 35. Amsterdam/Philadelphia: John Benjamins.

Ansaldo, U., Lim, L. and Nordhoff, S. (2006) Variation and shift in Sri Lanka Malay: Preliminary reflections. DoBeS (Documentation of Endangered Languages) Workshop 2006, 15–16 June 2006. The Netherlands: MPI Nijmegen.

Bailey, R.W. (1998) Majority language, minority misery. In D.A. Kibbee (ed.) *Language Legislation and Linguistic Rights*. Impact: Studies in Language and Society 2 (pp. 206–224). Amsterdam/Philadelphia: John Benjamins.

Bichsel-Stettler, A. (1989) Aspects of the Sri Lanka Malay Community and its Language. M.A. dissertation, Bern University, Switzerland.

Bourdieu, P. (1984) *Distinction: A Social Critique of the Judgement of Taste*. London: Routledge & Kegan Paul.

Burah, T.A. (2006) *Saga of the Exiled Royal Javanese Unearthed*. Dehiwala, Sri Lanka.

Canagarajah, S. (2005) Dilemmas in planning English/vernacular relations in post-colonial communities. *Journal of Sociolinguistics* 9 (3), 418–447.

Conference of Sri Lanka Malays (2002) The Malay dilemma. *The Malay Dilemma*. (Issued on the occasion of the 42nd anniversary of the death of Dr T.B. Jayah.) Colombo, Sri Lanka.

Conference of Sri Lanka Malays (2005) *Majulah* 6: 1. (Newsletter of the Conference of Sri Lanka Malays.) Colombo, Sri Lanka.

Cummins, J. (1979) Linguistic interdependence and the educational development of bilingual children. *Review of Educational Research* 49, 221–251.

Department of Census and Statistics (2012) *Population Atlas of Sri Lanka 2012*. Ministry of Finance and Planning, Sri Lanka. See http://www.statistics.gov.lk/PopHouSat/PopulationAtla_2012/01_CoverPrefaceAndContents/Pages%20from%20001-DCS_Population_Atlas_of_Sri_Lanka-2012_CD_Version_Final.pdf (accessed July 2013).

Emran Deen, M.H.N. (2001) *Bahasa Melayu: Malay-Sinhala-Tamil-English. Book 1*. Mulleriyawa New Town, Sri Lanka.

Edwards, J. (1985) *Language, Society and Identity*. Oxford: Blackwell.

Errington, J. (2003) Getting language rights: The rhetorics of language endangerment and loss. *American Anthropologist* 105 (4), 723–732.

Foley, W.A. (2005) Personhood and linguistic identity, purism and variation. In P.K. Austin (ed.) *Language Documentation and Description* 3 (pp. 157–180). London: School of Oriental and African Studies.

Garrett, P.B. (2006) Contact languages as 'endangered' languages: What is there to lose? *Journal of Pidgin and Creole Languages* 21 (1), 175–190.

Giles, H., Bourhis, R.Y. and Taylor, D.M. (1977) Towards a theory of language in ethnic group relations. In H. Giles (ed.) *Language, Ethnicity and Intergroup Relations* (pp. 307–348). London: Academic Press.

Gordon, R.G. Jr (ed.) (2005) *Ethnologue: Languages of the World* (15th edn). Dallas, TX: SIL International. See http://ethnologue.com (accessed 11 March 2007).

Government of Sri Lanka (2007) Sri Lanka Facts. *Sri Lanka Government Web Portal*. See http://www.gov.lk/info/index.asp?mi=19&xp=0&xi=52&xl=3&o=0&t (accessed 14 March 2007).

Government of Sri Lanka (2015) Country overview. *Official Web Portal of Government of Sri Lanka*. See https://www.gov.lk/index.php (accessed July 2015).

Hussainmiya, B.A. (1986) Melayu Bahasa: Some preliminary observations on the Malay creole of Sri Lanka. *Sari* 4 (1), 19–30.

Hussainmiya, B.A. (1987) *Lost Cousins: The Malays of Sri Lanka*. Kuala Lumpur: Universiti Kebangsan Malaysia.

Hussainmiya, B.A. (1990) *Orang Rejimen: The Malays of the Ceylon Rifle Regiment*. Kuala Lumpur: Universiti Kebangsan Malaysia.

Lambert, W. (1978) Some cognitive and sociocultural consequences of being bilingual. In J.C. Alatis (ed.) *Georgetown Round Table on Languages and Linguistics 1978* (pp. 214–229). Washington DC: Georgetown University Press.

Le Page, R.B. and Tabouret-Keller, A. (1985) *Acts of Identity: Creole-based Approaches to Language and Ethnicity*. Cambridge: Cambridge University Press.

Library of Congress, Federal Research Division (1988) October. *A Country Study: Sri Lanka*. See http://lcweb2.loc.gov/frd/cs/lktoc.html (accessed 13 February 2007).

Lim, L. (2013) The politics of English (and Sinhala and Tamil) in Sri Lanka: *Kaduva* of privileged power, tool of rural empowerment? In L. Wee, R. Goh and L. Lim (eds) *The Politics of English in Asia: Language Policy and Cultural Expression in South and Southeast Asia and the Asia Pacific*. Studies in World Language Problems 4 (pp. 61–80). Amsterdam/Philadelphia: John Benjamins.

Lim, L. (2016) The art of losing: From *java* and *patois* to post-vernacular vitality – Repositioning the periphery in global Asian ecologies. In L. Filipović and M. Pütz (eds) *Endangered Languages and Languages in Danger: Issues of Ecology, Policy and*

Documentation (pp. 283–312). (IMPACT Studies in Language and Society.) Amsterdam/Philadelphia: John Benjamins.

Lim, L. and Ansaldo, U. (2006a) Keeping Kirinda vital: The endangerment-empowerment dilemma in the documentation of Sri Lanka Malay. In E.O. Aboh and M. van Staden (eds) *Amsterdam Centre for Language & Communication Working Papers* 1, 51–66. Also at: http://aclc.uva.nd/binaries/content/assets/subsites/amsterdam-center-for-language-and-communication/general-aclc/volume-2006-issue-1.pdf?1160677383000 (accessed 10 December 2017).

Lim, L. and Ansaldo, U. (2006b) Preliminary findings of a sociolinguistic survey of the Sri Lanka Malays. Manuscript, University of Amsterdam.

Lim, L. and Ansaldo, U. (2006c) Beyond identity: Sri Lanka Malay from trade language to language trade. First international conference on Language Contact in Times of Globalisation, 28–30 September 2006. University of Groningen. Groningen, The Netherlands.

Lim, L. and Ansaldo, U. (2007) Identity alignment in the multilingual space: The Malays of Sri Lanka. In E. Anchimbe (ed.) *Linguistic Identity in Multilingual Postcolonial Spaces*. Cambridge Scholars Publishing.

Lim, L. and Ansaldo, U. (2008) Micro or macro connections? Language choice and identity alignment in the Sri Lanka Malay community. Sociolinguistics Symposium 17: Micro and Macro Connections, 3–5 April 2008. Amsterdam, The Netherlands.

Matras, Y. (2005) Language contact, language endangerment and the role of the salvation linguist. In P.K. Austin (ed.) *Language Documentation and Description* 3. London: SOAS.

Nordhoff, S. (2009) *A Grammar of Upcountry Sri Lanka Malay*. PhD dissertation, Utrecht: LOT.

Nordhoff, S. (ed.) (2013) *The Genesis of Sri Lanka Malay: A Case of Extreme Language Contact*. Leiden/Boston: Brill.

Pavlenko, A. and Blackledge, A. (2004) Introduction: New theoretical approaches to the study of negotiation of identities in multilingual contexts. In A. Pavlenko and A. Blackledge (eds) *Negotiation of Identities in Multilingual Contexts* (pp. 1–33). Clevedon: Multilingual Matters.

Phillipson, R. and Skutnabb-Kangas, T. (1986) *Linguicism Rules in Education*. Roskilde: Institute VI, Roskilde University Centre.

Presidential Secretariat of the Government of Sri Lanka (2007) Policy Research & Information Unit (PRIU). Sri Lanka in brief. Official Website of the Government of Sri Lanka. See http://www.priu.gov.lk/TourCountry/Indextc.html (accessed 14 March 2007).

Rassool, R. (2013) Issues of power and privilege in the maintenance of Sri Lanka Malay: A sociolinguistic analysis. In S. Nordhoff (ed.) *The Genesis of Sri Lanka Malay: A Case of Extreme Language Contact* (pp. 121–145). Leiden/Boston: Brill.

Ricklefs, M.C. (1974) *Jogjakarta under Sultan Mangkubumi, 1749–179. A History of the Division of Java*. London/New York: Oxford University Press.

Roberts, M., Raheem, I. and Colin-Thomé, P. (1989) *People in Between: The Burghers and the Middle Class in the Transformations within Sri Lanka, 1790–1960s*. Ratmalana: Sarvodaya Book Publishing Services.

Rubio-Marín, R. (2003) Language rights: Exploring the competing rationales. In W. Kymlicka and A. Patten (eds) *Language Rights and Political Theory* (pp. 52–79). Oxford: Oxford University Press.

Russell, J. (1978) Language, education and nationalism – The language debate of 1944. *Ceylon Journal of Historical and Social Studies* 8, 38–64.

Saldin, B.D.K. (2000) *A Guide to Malay*. Kurunegala, Sri Lanka.

Saldin, B.D.K. (2001) *The Sri Lankan Malays and their Language* (2nd edn) Kurunegala, Sri Lanka.

Saldin, B.D.K. (2003) *Portrait of a Sri Lankan Malay*. Kurunegala, Sri Lanka.

Shandler, J. (2006) *Adventures in Yiddishland: Postvernacular Language and Culture*. University of California Press.

Slomanson, P. (2006) Sri Lankan Malay morphosyntax: Lankan or Malay? In A. Deumert and S. Durrleman (eds) *Structure and Variation in Language Contact* (pp. 135–158). Amsterdam/Philadelphia: John Benjamins.

Smith, I. and Paauw, S. (2006) Sri Lanka Malay: Creole or convert? In A. Deumert and S. Durrleman (eds) *Structure and Variation in Language Contact* (pp. 159–181). Amsterdam/Philadelphia: John Benjamins.

Smith, I., Pauuw, S. and Hussainmiya, B.A. (2004) Sri Lanka Malay: The state of the art. In R. Singh (ed.) *Yearbook of South Asian languages 2004* (pp. 197–215). Berlin/New York: Mouton de Gruyter.

Sourjah, M.A. (2003) Malays in Sri Lanka: Came with their women-folk. *WWW Virtual Library – Sri Lanka*. See http://www.lankalibrary.com/cul/malays.htm (accessed 8 January 2004).

Stroud, C. (2000) Language and democracy: The notion of linguistic citizenship and mother tongue programmes. In K. Legère and S. Fitchet (eds) *Talking Freedom: Language and Democratization in the SADC Region* (pp. 67–74). Windhoek: Macmillan.

Stroud, C. (2001) African mother-tongue programmes and the politics of language: Linguistic Citizenship versus Linguistic Human Rights. *Journal of Multilingual and Multicultural Development* 22 (4), 339–355.

Stroud, C. and Heugh, K. (2004) Language rights and linguistic citizenship. In J. Freeland and D. Patrick (eds) *Language Rights and Language Survival: A Sociolinguistic Exploration*. Manchester: St Jerome Publishing.

Thaliph, M.F. (2003) *Book on Malay Grammar (Nahu): A Guide to Write and Speak Grammatical Malay*. Wattala, Sri Lanka.

Tsunoda, T. (2005) *Language Endangerment and Language Revitalisation*. Berlin/NY: Mouton.

UNESCO (1995–2009) Education. UNESCO. See http://www.unesco.org/education/en/sector (accessed January 2010).

10 Linguistic Citizenship in Sweden: (De)Constructing Languages in a Context of Linguistic Human Rights

Tommaso M. Milani* and Rickard Jonsson**
*University of Gothenburg and University of the
Witwatersrand, Johannesburg; **Stockholm University

From Linguistic Human Rights to Linguistic Citizenship

During the last 20 years or so, linguistic human rights (LHR) has become a well-established ideological framework that informs language policy and planning (LPP) decisions in several socio-political contexts. In an influential overview of LPP research, Thomas Ricento (2000) posits LHR as the 'strategic factor', that is, 'the explicit or implicit reasons for which researchers undertake particular kinds of research', which has arisen in conjunction with the so-called post-modern turn in LPP scholarship in the 1990s. Needless to say, any attempt *a posteriori* to find patterns and regularities in academic scholarship results in an oversimplification of a more complex reality. In this regard, Ricento's (2000) account is no exception, because it inadvertently erases the extremely broad diversity of the theoretical approaches that characterize LPP research pursued within post-modern epistemologies (see however, Ricento, 2006a, 2006b; Pennycook, 2006, for more nuanced representations). But, if we leave aside this critique for a moment, what is more pressing to ask is whether LHR is at all compatible with post-modernism.

This is an important question that has been raised recently by Christopher Stroud and his associates in a number of workshops and publications (see Kerfoot, 2009; Stroud, 2001, 2003, 2010; Stroud & Heugh, 2004; Williams & Stroud, 2015). The main argument advanced by Stroud is that LHR is badly attuned to post-modernism because it rests on (1) structuralist, bounded notions of language and ethnic identity, and (2) on an *essentialist* relationship between these two, so that one language is assumed to univocally mirror one, and only one, ethnic identity. If we agree that the most basic characteristic of any post-modern enterprise is 'finding questions where others had located answers' (Dean, 1994: 4), it appears clear then that LHR is destined to fail to meet this condition, not least because it takes 'ethnic identity' – whatever this may mean – as a given, and as the point of departure of language minority advocacy.

One could respond that it is because of the essentialist premises of the relationship between language and ethnic identity that LHR has gained terrain as a paradigm for the acknowledgement and promotion of minority languages. This framework has not only been mobilized by linguistic minorities in their struggle for recognition, but has also been embraced by many national and supra-national institutions in their wish to accommodate ethno-linguistic diversity (see Skutnabb-Kangas, 2006, for an overview). Mary Bucholtz (2003) reminds us that essentialism should not necessarily be viewed in a negative light, as it can be a necessary *strategic means* through which to achieve particular political purposes (see also Spivak, 1988). Minority politics, whether it pertains to issues of race, ethnicity, or sexuality, has typically been buttressed by some kind of strategic essentialism. 'Gay Liberation' in the 1980s is one of the most telling examples (see Cameron & Kulick, 2003; Stroud, 2001). However, it is also true that, if applied to the case of linguistic minorities, strategic essentialism can prove to be detrimental to certain speakers, however useful it may be to others. This is because too rigid a link between language and ethnicity fails to acknowledge the fluidity and hybridity of linguistic practices and identities in multilingual settings (Stroud, 2001; see also Pavlenko & Blackledge, 2004).

Taking Southern African contexts as a case in point, Stroud (2001, 2003) has put forward *linguistic citizenship* as a conceptual alternative that, without simplifying the complexity of sociolinguistic arrangements in multilingual environments, should enhance 'minority language speaker participation in governance' (Stroud & Heugh, 2004: 23). In this sense, linguistic citizenship shares with LHR 'the desire to combat linguistic discrimination' (Wee, 2007: 325). Unlike LHR, however, it does not set out to do so by proposing an 'affirmative strategy' (Stroud, 2001: 345; see also Fraser, 1995) through which linguistic minorities are given certain benefits by virtue of their speaking a particular language variety and belonging to a particular ethnic group. Rather, linguistic citizenship is perhaps the most lucid endeavour, *pace* Makoni and Pennycook (2007), to 'disinvent' languages as static and bounded entities, and 'reconstitute' them as inherently messy and dynamic *practices*. Hence, the scope of an approach informed by linguistic citizenship is to engage in a deeper 'transformative' project (Fraser, 1995; Stroud, 2001: 344), according to which 'sociopolitical rights and obligations should in fact follow from, and be defined by, *the representations, practices and ideologies* of language and society that circumscribe communities of speakers in their everyday associational networks' (Stroud, 2001: 350). It is our contention that this politically charged project of sociolinguistic disinvention and reconstitution should not be limited to South Africa, but that it is also highly pertinent to a 'Western' context, such as Sweden.

In the literature on multiculturalism, Sweden is often praised as a typical example of 'multicultural pluralist citizenship' (Koopmans & Statham, 1999: 661), namely a political context in which 'the state not only offers easy access to full social and political rights, but actually sponsors ethnic difference by recognizing immigrant groups as "ethnic minorities" with their own cultural rights and privileges' (Koopmans & Statham, 1999: 661). Such a formulation fails to take into account the *practical implementation* of Swedish policies with regard to immigration, which have not always been as consistent and successful as Ruud Koopmans and Paul Statham seem to suggest (see in particular Hyltenstam & Milani, 2005, 2012; Municio, 1987). Nonetheless, multiculturalism/linguistic diversity [*mångkultur/mångfald*] has been the *ideological scaffolding* framing the Swedish political agenda and rhetoric since the end of the 1960s.

To cite a few important political decisions in this regard, a milestone in the acknowledgement of multilingualism in Sweden was the ratification in 1968 of the UNESCO Convention against Discrimination in Education, which led to the endorsement on the part of the state of immigrants' *rights* to maintain and develop their home languages (*hemspråk*). In practice, such a 'pluralist turn' (Milani, 2008) had its most palpable outcome in the introduction of state-financed mother-tongue instruction in 1977. Also moved by a wish to respect and promote ethno-linguistic diversity was the signature (1995) and later ratification (2000) of the Council of Europe's Framework Convention for the Protection of National Minorities as well as the European Charter for Regional or Minority Languages. The endorsement of these conventions resulted in the proclamation of five 'national minority languages' – Finnish, Meänkieli, Romani, Saami and Yiddish – (SOU, 1997a, 1997b). This meant that the speakers of these languages were accorded more comprehensive (language) rights than other ethno-linguistic minorities (see Huss, 2008; Hyltenstam, 1999, for a detailed overview).

That a *rights rhetoric* informs Swedish political discourse about multi-lingualism can also be witnessed more recently in the debate surrounding the proposal to legislate Swedish as the 'main language' [*huvudspråk*] in Sweden. Unlike in similar public discussions where the arguments in support of a state language can assume openly chauvinistic and discriminatory overtones (see for example the English-only movement in the United States), the promotion of Swedish went hand in glove with the acknowledgement of the importance of multilingualism (see Milani, 2007a; Milani & Johnson, 2008). This is particularly clear in the proposal that a language law should enshrine 'everyone's right to language: Swedish, mother tongue, and foreign languages' [*allas rätt till språk: svenska, modersmål och främmande språk*] (SOU, 2002). Unsurprisingly, the final version of the language law, which was passed by the Swedish parliament in 2009, states that:

(1)

14 § Var och en som är bosatt i Sverige ska ges möjlighet att lära sig, utveckla och använda svenska. Därutöver ska

1. den som tillhör en nationell minoritet ges möjlighet att lära sig, utveckla och använda minoritetsspråket, och

2. den som är döv eller hörselskadad och den som av andra skäl har behov av teckenspråk ges möjlighet att lära sig, utveckla och använda det svenska teckenspråket.

Den som har ett annat modersmål än de språk som anges i första stycket ska ges möjlighet att utveckla och använda sitt modersmål.

15 § Det allmänna ansvarar för att den enskilde ges tillgång till språk enligt 14 §.

§ 14 Everyone residing in Sweden must be given the opportunity to learn, develop and use Swedish. In addition,

1. every person belonging to a national minority must be given the opportunity to learn, develop and use their minority language, and

2. every person who is deaf, hearing-impaired or who needs sign language for any other reason must be given the opportunity to learn, develop and use Swedish sign language.

Every person who has a mother tongue other than the languages referred to in item one above must be given the opportunity to develop and use their mother tongue.

§ 15 The state is responsible for providing the individual with access to language according to § 14. (Språklag, 2009: 600)[1]

In light of this contextual backdrop, Sweden might sound like a text-book example of a *good state*, that is, a political entity that 'controls its demonic proclivities by cleansing itself with, and internalising human rights' (Mutua, 2002: 10; see also Wee, 2007: 326), including LHR. The 'right to multilingualism' is enshrined in the language law, and the state is made responsible for 'providing the individual with access to language'. Provocatively, however, we would argue that this piece of legislation only works under the proviso that there is such a thing as a set of discrete, internally homogenous entities that linguists call 'languages'. Several socio-linguists have repeatedly objected to such a view because it is an idealiza-tion that has more to do with historical processes of standardization and unification than with 'real' communicative practices (see in particular Makoni & Pennycook, 2007). Reasoning along similar lines, we do not dispute that an idealized concept of language might be a suitable or even necessary pre-condition for conducting formal linguistic analysis. However, once such a construct becomes embedded in the law, it is not without political implications. If one believes that a language is a fairly homogenous code, and if the right to language is only accorded to those who can prove that their linguistic practices 'count' as a language in the first place, then there are many linguistic phenomena that will fall outside the remit of the law. The key point that we want to make here is that the lack of fit between the construct of language enshrined in Swedish politi-cal discourse and actual communicative performances *intrinsically* disen-franchises speakers of those 'hybrid' forms that cannot be easily pigeon-holed in rigid schemata of linguistic categorization.

Rinkebysvenska (Rinkeby Swedish)[2] is the most well-known example of such linguistic practices. Resulting from language contact among ado-lescents in Swedish metropolitan spaces, rinkebysvenska has become something of a Foucauldian conundrum: a problem to be scrutinized, a category to be defined, and a disorder to be regulated. In particular, recent studies have demonstrated (Jonsson & Milani, 2009; Milani, 2010; Stroud, 2004) that there is a dominant discourse that has held sway in the Swedish media landscape over the last 30 years or so that portrays rinke-bysvenska in highly negative tones as an inherently non-Swedish phenom-enon, the cause of social trouble and educational underachievement, as well the manifestation of male 'immigrants' sexist and homophobic tendencies.

In line with these studies, our concern in the present chapter is not to offer a typological or sociolinguistic account of rinkebysvenska in terms of its lexical, morphological, and syntactic features, or contexts of usage, nor do we intend to determine whether rinkebysvenska is a linguistic variety in its own right, rather, we want to concentrate on what different social actors say or write *about* rinkebysvenska. Unlike existing scholarship, however, we want to show that linguistic disenfranchisement from political discourse as well as a dominant negative representation in the media is not necessarily tantamount to lack of agency. To paraphrase one of Foucault's (1978: 95) most cited formulations, where there is power, there is linguistic citizenship. It is such forms of linguistic agency that we analyse in this chapter; we focus in particular on two examples of the ways in which some speakers seek to *take control over* rinkebysvenska, and hence contest dominant discourses.

'It's Our Language': Linguistic Citizenship in a Site of Mediation

In an article on public pronouncements about rinkesbysvenska, Stroud (2004) has illustrated how metalinguistic discourses play an important identity function in Sweden. Negatively laden representations of rinkebysvenska 'are not about language alone' (Woolard, 1998: 3), but constitute the outer manifestation of broader processes of social categorization in a society like Sweden where 'explicitly racist discourse which describes particular groups of people in negative terms is no longer permitted' (Blackledge, 2005: i). The overt devaluing of rinkebysvenska in public discourse, together with its concomitant counterpart – the valorization of (standard) Swedish – are the only culturally acceptable discursive strategies through which the Swedish 'Self' can distinguish itself and assert its superiority *vis-à-vis* the ethnic 'Other'. Put simply, it might be taboo in contemporary Sweden to openly say that We (Swedes) are better than Them (immigrants/non-Swedes), but it is fully acceptable to claim that Their language is worse than Ours. In a typically Bourdieuan (Bourdieu, 1991) fashion, Stroud offers us a convincing example of the ways in which discourses about language can be a safe haven for the '*reproduction* of dispossession among immigrant groups' (Stroud, 2004: 195), which brings with it the 'reproduction of hierarchical and unequal societies' (Stroud, 2004: 210).

What is missing from this rather dismal picture, however, is resistance and opposition. Indeed, an overview of media discourses about rinkebysvenska reveals that voices of dissent were quite rare between 1980 and 2000. That being said, it is important to highlight that this discursive regime underwent a substantial change at the beginning of the 21st century. The year 2001 saw the publication of the first literary text that is written with linguistic features typically associated with rinkebysvenska, the collection of short-stories *Till vår ära* (To our honour) by Alejandro

Leiva-Wenger. Using similar linguistic features, Jonas Hassem Kemiri's novel *Ett öga rött* (One eye red) appeared in 2003, and soon became a national best-seller (see also Lacatus, 2007).[3] In 2004, rinkebysvenska acquired even stronger public visibility in the print-media landscape thanks to the newly founded magazine, *Gringo*. Circulated as a monthly supplement to the free daily newspaper, *Metro*, the magazine soon gained considerable momentum not simply as a result of the rather bald choice of a non-standard Swedish register as its code of expression, but also because of the no less astute decision of its editorial staff to style themselves as representatives of the voices of the multicultural Swedish suburbs.[4] Quite predictably, this position of 'authorized speaker' (Bourdieu, 1991) did not remain uncontested. Alejandro Leiva-Wenger objected that 'by offering the expectation of a mandate from the "suburbs" and giving themselves the "task" of spreading suburban slang, they [Gringo] continue to build up their brand image' [*genom att förespegla ett representationsmandat från 'förorten' och ge sig själv 'uppgiften' att sprida förortsslangen bygger man vidare på sitt varumärke*] (Leiva-Wenger, 2006). Taking a different standpoint, the writer Kurdo Baksi feared that *Gringo* was promoting and circulating discourses that actually reinforced rather than destabilized ethnic boundaries between 'they' (Swedes) and 'us' (non-Swedes). In contrast, the anthropologist Corina Lacatus suggested that *Gringo* should be read as a continuation of Leiva-Wenger's and Hassem Kemiri's 'ideological agenda of problematizing the dichotomy us/them' (Lacatus, 2007: 87). Whichever stance one takes, what should not be underestimated is the proactive role of the editorial staff of *Gringo* in working for the valorization of the language spoken in the multicultural suburbs. Such an attempt of linguistic valorization manifested *inter alia* in the proposal to replace the name rinkebysvenska with miljonsvenska (lit. 'million Swedish'), and to claim for it the status of a dialect.

This endeavour of sociolinguistic re-branding and re-signification is most clearly rationalized in the extract below, which is taken from a heated discussion that unfolded in April–May 2006 in the columns of one of Sweden's most read quality newspapers, *Dagens Nyheter*. We have already analysed several facets of this debate elsewhere (Jonsson, 2007; Jonsson & Milani, 2009; Milani, 2010). Therefore, we will not delve into all its details here. For the sake of contextualization, however, it should be mentioned that the debate was initiated by a prominent Swedish academic, Ebba Witt-Brattström, who was at that time Professor of Literature at Södertörn University College. Witt-Brattström feared that enhanced state support for mother-tongue instruction/bilingual education *instead of* Swedish language instruction would result in the development of what she termed *blattesvenska* ('immigrant Swedish'). In her view, this linguistic phenomenon would relegate its speakers to 'selling bananas' in a suburban market, and, hence, prevent them from career opportunities and socio-economic enablement. Crucially, what started as a disagreement about the presumed or perceived social effects of mother-tongue instruction/bilingual education soon developed into a conflict about the definition of the linguistic practices in suburban Sweden. Witt-Brattström denied that such practices constituted a distinct linguistic variety. As she forcefully put it, 'The truth is that there cannot be a "blattesvenska" that is shared by Sweden's 12.2 % immigrants [...] For the majority of these, it can hardly feel natural to speak *Gringo*'s "miljondialekt" [lit. "million dialect"]' (Witt-Brattström, 2006). In response, the editorial staff of *Gringo* explained that:

(2)

Vi kallar det andra benämnt som Rinkebysvenska eller invandarsvenska för "miljonsvenska". Det är inget vedertaget begrepp i miljonprogrammen utan något vi har hittat på. Som så mycket annat i Gringo vill vi ta tillbaka makten att definiera orden som benämner människorna och kulturen i miljonprogrammen.

Vi valde miljonsvenska för att dialekten mer än något annat är geografiskt kopplad. Den pratas inte bara i Rinkeby och heller inte bara av "invandrare". Människorna som bott i de uppradade betonghusen har med åren utvecklat en dynamisk kultur med allt ifrån konst, litteratur, musik och film.

[...]

Själva använder vi miljonsvenskan för att det är vårt språk, det vi växt upp med och tycker om att uttrycka oss med efter att vi bara för några år sen tvingades tvätta bort den ur våra munnar för att få en plats. Vi vill inte pracka på någon den, vi visar inte den som ett ideal alla borde ta till sig. Det som är viktigt för oss är att den får en värdig status så att den som vill kan använda den både i tal och skrift som vilken annan dialekt som helst utan att få knasiga blickar på sig

[...]

Miljonsvenskan i sig är det perfekta exemplet på något vackert som skapas när olika människor från världens alla hörn möts och skapar ihop. De kommande åren kommer miljonprogrammens frukter regna över oss och lära oss något om oss själva. Gringo försöker bli katalysator för en naturlig samhällsrörelse som kommer hjälpa oss att förenas i en större svenskhet än den som normalt ryms på DN Kulturs sidor.

What others have called Rinkeby Swedish or immigrant Swedish we call 'Million Swedish'. This is not an established term from the Million Programme but rather something we have created. Like so much else in *Gringo*, we want to reclaim the power to define the words that designate the peoples and cultures of the Million Programme.

We chose miljonsvenska because a dialect is more geographically-bound than anything else. It's not only spoken in Rinkeby nor indeed only by 'immigrants'. Over the years, the people who've been living in the rows of concrete houses have developed a dynamic culture running the gamut of art, literature, music and film.

[…]

We use miljonsvenska because it is our language – what we have been brought up and like to express ourselves with, but only a few years ago we were obliged to wash it away from our lips in order to have a place. We don't want to impose it on anyone, we do not hold it up as an ideal that everyone should aim towards. What's important to us is that miljonsvenska gains a respectable status so that those who wish to can use it both in speech and writing just like any other dialect, preferably without getting funny looks.

[…]

Miljonsvenska is the perfect example of how something beautiful can come into being when different people from every corner of the Earth meet and create things together. The coming years will bear the fruit of the Million Programme and teach us something about ourselves. *Gringo* aims to become a catalyst for a natural social movement that will help us unite in a greater Swedishness than that which normally fits on the pages of *DN Kultur*. (Gringoredaktionen, 2006)

In order to appreciate fully the meaning of the label *miljonsvenska*, it should be clarified that *miljon* (lit. 'million') alludes to a social and architectural project that took place in Sweden in the mid-1960s – the so-called *Miljonprogrammet* (lit. 'Million Programme'). Pressed by the needs of a growing population, the Social Democratic government of the time set out to construct one million dwellings within a period of 10 years (1965–1974), with the aim of providing good housing conditions at reasonable prices. Rising immigration rates, together with particular housing allocation policies and practices, led to an increasingly high concentration of migrants living in the high-rise buildings of the Million Programme.[5]

In the light of this, it is possible to understand how, through the label miljonvenska, the editors of *Gringo* are trying to dissociate a set of linguistic practices from an actual *space*, the Stockholm neighbourhood of

Rinkeby (compare Stroud, 2004), and, instead, discursively construct a sense of *place* (compare Feld & Basso, 1996). In other words, they are seeking to imbue a larger section of the urban landscape 'with [...] social, cultural, epistemic, and affective attributes' (Blommaert, 2005: 222). Such a meaning-making enterprise is realized through the creation of a link between a linguistic phenomenon and specific living conditions. As is suggestively presented at the end of the extract, miljonsvenska is the linguistic epitome or *icon* (Irvine & Gal, 2000) that mirrors the multiethnic and multicultural encounters in the suburbs. What is interesting to note is how the editors of *Gringo* imbue their arguments with authority by positioning themselves as authentic speakers of *miljonsvenska* ('it's our language') (for a discussion of authority of authenticity see Gal & Woolard, 2001).

As sociolinguists and linguistic anthropologists, we might be tempted to dismiss both Witt-Brattström's and *Gringo*'s arguments as 'lay' and 'unfounded,' because they do not rest on sound research evidence. However, Sally Johnson (2001: 594) provocatively calls for a 'suspension of judgment' when analysing public understandings of language. In other words, whether miljonsvenska is 'really' a dialect or not is beside the point. But it is only from a vantage point of 'respect' (Johnson, 2001: 594) for both positions that we can appreciate better the discursive struggle embodied in the debate on blattesvenska/miljonsvenska. On the one hand, Witt-Brattström's arguments encapsulate the long-lasting discourse according to which linguistic practices in the suburbs are 'non-Swedish', 'bad', and 'socially disempowering' (see Stroud, 2004). On the other hand, the editors of *Gringo* forge a counter-discourse in which miljonsvenska is portrayed as a broad and positive phenomenon transcending neat dichotomies of ethnicity, space, and class. Despite this typically late-modern example of linguistic citizenship through which the editors of *Gringo* seek to blur clear-cut boundaries, they employ nonetheless a modernist language construct – the notion of dialect. This is, in our view, one of the clearest instances of deadlock in which linguistic citizenship finds itself caught up, in a context like Sweden, dominated by linguistic (human) rights. In fact, the editors of *Gringo* are trying to destabilize and move away from a linguistic construct strongly rooted in conceptions of a bounded ethnic community and geographical locale. Paradoxically, however, they mobilize a static and spatially bound notion of 'dialect' in order to characterize miljonsvenska. But, if one considers that the 'right to language' in Sweden is accorded only to those who can prove that their linguistic practices count as a bounded linguistic variety in the first place, invoking 'dialect' is not an unmotivated discursive move. Rather, it is possibly the most available strategy through which the editors of *Gringo* can claim for miljonsvenska the status of a linguistic variety in its own right, and thus justify their demand of public recognition for it.

'What's Wrong with Rinkeby?' Linguistic Citizenship in an Educational Context

While the example in the previous section was taken from media discourse, the following interaction was tape-recorded during an ethnographic study conducted by the second author of the chapter in a school in a multicultural suburb of Stockholm between September 2007 and February 2008. Participant observation in five of the school's classes was complemented with semi-structured group interviews with 18 pupils. The suburb in question lies on the same underground line as the more well-known Rinkeby, and can be described as socio-economically disadvantaged as well as ethnically segregated. Most notably, the school stands out because a large proportion of its pupils are described by teachers as young people 'with immigrant background' [med invandrarbakgrund], that is, youth whose parents have immigrated to Sweden, or who have themselves immigrated. The relationship between Rinkeby and ethnicity emerged many times in various discussions among the pupils during the time the project unfolded. Some of the young people in the study could identify themselves as 'immigrants' in relation to other peers whom they saw as more 'typically Swedish'. However, they considered themselves 'more Swedish' in relation to those who studied in Rinkeby. Furthermore, when asked about future plans, many replied that they could *not* think of living in Rinkeby when they were adults, even though some of them do live there, and enjoy living there now. The main reason given for this attitude was that Rinkeby is not Swedish, and to continue living there would mean a career failure. Some of the pupils also stated that they could not think of letting their own children grow up in Rinkeby. In these answers, it is striking that the dominant media representations of Rinkeby are reproduced by young people who live in the area or nearby. While these ideas are by far prevailing in the interviews, there are also a few instances of *resistance*, as example (3) below illustrates.

Berivan and Jasmine were born in Sweden, but their parents are from Lebanon and Kurdistan, respectively. They are very good students; they have high marks, and want to study to become doctors. They are very close friends, and they explain that the way in which they talk to each other is an important part of their friendship. For example, they say that they teach each other words from their own languages. They also think that it is fun to speak slang, which they call rinkebysvenska. But this language usage is often met with disapproval by the school staff. In the extract below, they report a situation in which one of their teachers scolded them during a break for their non-standard language usage.

(3)

Berivan: *Hon [deras lärare] kom till oss och vi får inte bryta (.) vi <u>får inte</u> bryta*

Jasmine: *Hon kommer till oss bara (.) ni bor inte i Rinkeby (.) skärp er!*

Rickard: *Vem?*

Berivan: *[En lärare] (.) hon bara (.) ni bor inte i Rinkeby ni får inte bryta som rinkebysvenska*

Jasmine: *Alltså <u>jag</u> lyssna (.) <u>jag</u> (.) jag pratar svenska i skolan och jag pratar arabiska hemma*

Rickard: *ja*

Jasmine: *Det är så jag är uppväxt (.) och jag pratar inte (.) alltså inte att jag inte <u>får</u> prata svenska hemma (.) det är klart jag pratar svenska ibland hemma (.) men jag <u>försöker</u> prata arabiska (.) jag vill inte glömma bort min arabiska (.) det är en del av mig (.) min kultur och mitt ursprung (.) det är en del av mig (.) eller hur (.) jag vill inte glömma bort det (.) och när hon säger sådära (.) jag vet inte*

Rickard: *När brukar hon säga det då (.) när ni pratar?*

Jasmine: *I utvecklingssamtal eller när hon ser oss ibland (.) ibland vi driver med varandra*

Berivan: *Vi skojar skitmycket med varandra*

Jasmine: *Vi skojar skitmycket (.) och vi har såna*

Berivan: *Vi slangar (.) vi slangar väldigt mycket sådära (.) 'oh bre (.) va göru' [hej kompis (.) vad gör du?] sådär vet du*

Jasmine: *Och vi har samma ord ibland på (.) våra språk är nästan likadana (.) så <u>vi förstår</u> varandra ibland (.) så vi pratar och hon lär mig lite grand*

[---]

Jasmine: *och när hon säger så där till oss (.) alltså att vi inte får bryta (.) jag tycker inte det där är att bryta!*

Rickard: *Nä*

Jasmine: *Men på lektionerna jag bryter aldrig (.) <u>aldrig</u> har jag brutit på en lektion!*

Berivan: *Och så säger hon att vi bryter! Hon bara (.) men ni får prata efter skolan*

Jasmine: *Men jag bryter (.) alltså (.) inte att jag går fram till en lärare och säger 'ey bre va göru?' (.) Det är såklart inte! Men om jag står och pratar med Berivan och hon bara går förbi (.) vad ska jag göra? Och inte ser henne [läraren] ens (.) och hon går fram 'bryt inte för i helvete' jag vet inte vad (.) vad ska jag*

[---]

Rickard: *Vad säger ni när hon säger så då?*
Berivan: *Det känns konstigt för först så*
Jasmine: *Det känns som hon försöker göra oss (.) svenskar!*
Rickard: *Ja*
(2.0)
Berivan: *Och inte bara det (.) hon säger rinkebysvenska (.) ja vad är det för fel på Rinkeby?*
Jasmine: *Vad är det för fel på Rinkeby?*
Berivan: *Det är mångkulturellt (.) alltså det finns hur många språk som helst där (.) bara för det alltså (.) och det går ju jättemånga här som är från Rinkeby sådär*
Jasmine: *Okay alla vet (.) Rinkeby det bor många invandrare där (.) och hon kan ändå inte säga sådär.*

Berivan: She [their teacher] came up to us and said we mustn't speak broken Swedish (.) we mustn't speak broken Swedish.
Jasmine: She just came over to us (.) 'you don't live in Rinkeby (.) pull yourselves together!'
Rickard: Who?
Berivan: [A teacher] (.) she just said you don't live in Rinkeby (.) you mustn't speak broken Swedish like Rinkeby Swedish
Jasmine: So me (.) listen me (.) I speak Swedish in school and I speak Arabic at home
Rickard: I see
Jasmine: That's how I grew up and I don't speak it's not that I'm not allowed to speak Swedish at home (.) of course I speak Swedish at home at times but I try to speak Arabic (.) I don't want to forget my Arabic (.) it's a part of me (.) my culture and my origin (.) it's a part of me(.) don't you see? I don't want to forget it and when she talks like that (.) I don't know
Rickard: When does she say that when you're talking?
Jasmine: In teacher student talks or when she sees us sometimes (.) sometimes we make fun of each other
Berivan: We pull each other's legs a lot
Jasmine: We pull each other's legs a lot and we have such
Berivan: We talk slang (.) we talk slang a lot you know 'oh bre (.) va göru' [hi guys (.) what's doing mate] like that you know
Jasmine: And sometimes we have the same words (.) our languages are quite alike so we understand each other sometimes (.) so we chat and she teaches me a bit
[---].
Jasmine: And when she tells us that (.) that we must not use broken language (.) I don't think we do use a broken language!
Rickard: No

Jasmine: 'Cos at the lessons (.) I never (.) I have <u>never</u> used broken language in the classroom!

Berivan: And then she tells us we speak broken language! She like 'you may talk like that after school'

Jasmine: But my broken (.) I mean I would never walk up to a teacher and say 'ey bre va göru?' [hi guys (.) what's doing mate] (.) Of course not! But if I am standing with Berivan having a chat (.) and she just walks by what can I do? And I don't even notice her [the teacher] (.) and she goes 'don't use broken language for fucks sake' I don't know what (.) what shall I

[---]

Rickard: What do you two say when she talks like that?

Berivan: It feels strange 'cos first

Jasmine: It feels like she's trying to make us (.) Swedish!

Rickard: I see (2.0)

Berivan: And it's not just that (.) she says Rinkeby Swedish (.) well what's wrong with Rinkeby?

Jasmine: What's wrong with Rinkeby?

Berivan: It's multicultural (.) there are all sorts of languages there (.) just that's enough (.) and like lots and lots of people from Rinkeby go here

Jasmine: Okay (.) everyone knows loads of immigrants live there (.) but she still can't say so

It is important to underscore that this extract encompasses the girls' own recollection of an event that occurred during a school break. We do not know how the conversation to which they refer actually unfolded. Nor can we assess whether their report is a fair account of what the teacher actually said. However, what is most interesting for our purposes here is how the girls *relate to* an adult's perception – whether real or invented – of non-standard linguistic practices.

To begin with, one should consider the word choice used to label non-standard linguistic behaviour. The terms rinkebysvenska and slang are present, but what is repeated most often in the interaction above is the verb '*bryta*'. According to the definition provided by the Swedish Academy, one of the meanings of *bryta* is 'to speak in a manner that reveals the influence of or that reminds of (a foreign language or a specific dialect or the like); esp: to speak with a foreign or dialectical pronunciation or inflection or the like; sometimes of works and the like: to show an influence from (a foreign language or the like)' [*tala på ett sätt som förråder inflytande l. reminiscenser från (ett främmando språk l. en viss dialekt o. d.); i sht: tala med främmande l. dialektiskt uttal l. tonfall o. d.; ngn gg om skriftalster o. d.: visa inflytande från (ett främmande språk o. d.).*] (SAOB online, retrieved on 22 June 2010). Obviously, this definition presupposes that some people 'speak with an accent', while those who speak 'standard language' do not. But, as Rosina Lippi-Green (1997) has powerfully argued, 'non-accent' is just a myth, a shared societal narrative that is 'used to justify social order, and to encourage or coerce consensual participation in that order' (Lippi-Green, 1997: 41). Ultimately, everyone has an accent. Interestingly, however, the accent of some speakers becomes over time *undetectable* because of historical processes of normalization that make that specific accent the benchmark against which all other pronunciations are judged (compare Blommaert *et al.*, 2006; Coupland, 2007). Obviously, these observations can be applied to any sociolinguistic case of normalization of spoken language. But what is particularly interesting in Swedish is that the verb *bryta* also encodes the meaning 'to break', and 'regarding speech sounds, words, verbal expressions and the like: to alter, distort, twist' [*med afs. på språkljud, ord, språkligt uttr. o. d.: förändra, förvanska, förvrida*] (SAOB online, retrieved on 22 June 2010). So *bryta* can only make sense provided that one views standard Swedish metaphorically as a bounded and somewhat fragile physical entity, something that can be broken, corrupted, and twisted.

Against this backdrop, it is perhaps unsurprising that the teacher, in the girls' account, forcefully ordered Jasmine and Berivan: 'you mustn't speak broken Swedish like rinkebysvenska'. In this context, the conflation between rinkebysvenska and speaking with an accent can be justified by a view of both linguistic phenomena as bad and deviant, a rupture from what counts as Swedish. The teacher's comment is a fleeting but nonetheless powerful reminder that rinkebysvenska is something irresponsible, a problem to be dealt with, and a form of sloppiness that has to be stopped. In this sense, the reprimand is an expression of well-meant preoccupation with regard to the pupils' language, which is not dissimilar from Witt-Brattström's concerns voiced in the media debate in 2006 (see above). Crucially, the teacher's order is rationalized on the basis of a static and univocal link between linguistic practices and space. Unlike the editors of *Gringo* who attempted to uncouple miljonsvenska from a particular suburb, the teacher employs the following chains of arguments: rinkebysvenska is spoken in Rinkeby; Jasmine and Berivan do not live in Rinkeby; therefore, they should not speak rinkebysvenska. However, this argumentation does not remain unchallenged by the two girls. In their account, Jasmine and Berivan clearly spell out that they do not use broken Swedish all the time: it is rather an identity resource on which they rely during school breaks; certainly, as Jasmine asserts emphatically, it is not a linguistic code that is suitable in the classroom. In saying 'I don't go up to a teacher and say Hi mate, what's doing? Of course not!', Jasmine shows to be highly aware of what are considered appropriate language practices in the school, practices that in turn are tied to particular social positions: that of a 'good friend' or a 'good student'. In sum, as much as Jasmine underscores the importance of slang/broken Swedish/rinkebysvenska in cementing her friendship with Berivan, she knows that such a linguistic practice in class would jeopardize the opportunity to occupy the position of a good student and be awarded top marks.

The gist of this metalinguistic discourse is not dissimilar to the many pronouncements in the media arguing that proficiency in standard Swedish is a pre-requisite to success. The difference, however, lies in Berivan's and Jasmine's realization that slang/broken Swedish/rinkebysvenska and standard Swedish do not necessarily exclude one another, but can very well occur in parallel. This also means that young speakers of rinkebysvenska do not necessarily lack proficiency in standard Swedish, as was assumed by Witt-Brattström in the article that opened the debate in *Dagens Nyheter*.

Finally, we saw in the introduction that multilingualism and multiculturalism have become something of a mantra in Swedish political discourse. This, however, does not prevent people from viewing multilingual and multicultural schools and suburbs as *less* desirable places, and making subtle, negative comments about them (Bunar, 2001; Jonsson, 2007). The devaluing of diversity is perhaps most patent in the subtle ways in which its counterpart – the promotion of assimilation – is expressed (Milani, 2007b, 2008). It is precisely assimilation that Jasmine sees as underpinning the teacher's hostility to slang/broken Swedish/rinkebysvenska. In her view, the teacher's attempt to stop them from speaking broken Swedish/rinkebysvenska is synonymous with trying to 'make them Swedish', thus failing to acknowledge the complexity of Berivan's and Jasmine's social positions in Swedish society. The paradox between the promotion of multilingualism/multiculturalism in political discourse and its lack of actual recognition in daily reality emerges even more clearly when Berivan and Jasmine ask themselves: 'What's wrong with Rinkeby? Many immigrants live there but all the same she mustn't say so'. Note in particular how the adverb 'all the same' does important ideological work in this context. On the one hand, the sentence 'Many immigrants live there' is a way of explaining why adults (including the teacher) speak about multicultural suburbs in derogatory terms – it is a form of 'double voicing' (Bakhtin, 1984) through which the speaker appropriates someone else's words; it is a way of looking at the situation for a moment from an adversary's point of view (compare Blackledge, 2005: 15). On the other hand, the girls quickly add that it is *nonetheless* unacceptable to speak deprecatorily about Rinkeby. In this way, Jasmine and Berivan show that they are highly aware of the existence of a negatively laden discourse on immigration and multiculturalism; they relate to this discourse, use its logic, but simultaneously *dissociate from* it.

Where are We Heading?

Stroud (2001) explains that linguistic citizenship denotes 'the situation where speakers themselves exercise control over their language, deciding *what* languages are, and what they may *mean*, and where language issues [...] are discursively tied to a range of social issues – policy issues and questions of equity' (Stroud, 2001: 353, italics in original). As an example, he offers the case of northern isiNdebele, which, unlike southern isiNdebele, was not recognized as one of the official languages of post-apartheid South Africa. The speakers of northern isiNdebele constitute a clear manifestation of linguistic citizenship in the sense that they 'found themselves in the position of having to argue that Northern siNdebele was a language, which meant a grassroots investment in developing orthography, grammar and glossaries for school' (Stroud, 2001: 349). Furthermore, they 'developed grassroots strategies to demand the use of siNdebele as a medium of instruction in primary education, such as lobbying provincial and national departments of education with evidence of number of pupils and teachers who speak the language, and schools where this language could be justifiably used' (Stroud, 2001: 349).

In comparison, the examples provided in this chapter may appear to be of a more trivial nature. Admittedly, the editors of *Gringo* published their pronouncements in one of the most read Swedish quality newspapers. However, they never proposed to standardize rinkebysvenska; nor did they ever call for its recognition as a medium of instruction. By the same token, Berivan and Jasmine's resistance took place in a more or less private interview with a researcher. That said, feminism has taught us that the private is no less political than the public, and the boundary between the two is itself a social construction (Gal, 2002). In a similar vein, we would like to highlight that linguistic citizenship should not be restricted to describing events of political mobilization, but that it can be usefully employed in order to capture the many ephemeral and apparently 'banal' (Billig, 1995) occurrences of agency *on grounds of language* that unfold in daily interactions (see also Williams & Stroud, 2015). After all, politics, in the sense of the dynamic interplay between power and agency, 'happens when one may be led to least expect it – in the nooks and crannies of everyday life, outside of institutionalized contexts that one ordinarily associates with politics' (Besnier, 2009: 11).

One might wonder though to what extent 'local practice [can] challenge the hegemony of national and global policy' (Blackledge & Creese, 2010: 6). Put simply, how can a linguistic citizenship approach, with its focus on localized, arguably mundane, but no less important forms of agency, inform state-driven language policies? A suggestion would be for linguistic citizenship researchers to engage in a long-term conversation with key sociolinguistic gate-keepers at the grassroots, in particular teachers, journalists, and politicians. Such a proposal resonates well with Joan Pujolar's argument that:

> The challenge for sociolinguistics in the twenty-first century is precisely to find the ways to disseminate its findings and its critique so that they permeate the multiple social spaces and practices where the modern ideology of language is still hegemonic, and particularly wherever linguistic ideologies are mobilized in ways that intentionally or unintentionally produce exclusion and reproduce relationships of domination. (Pujolar, 2007: 91)

The risk, however, would be for linguistic citizenship as an academic pursuit to be incorporated into a normative framework of language policy, which ultimately ropes everyone into a rights discourse. So perhaps the question is whether a linguistic citizenship approach *should* inform state language policies at all. For linguistic citizenship to retain a radical edge, it might need to remain within the realm of oppositional discourses, destabilizing the *status quo* from the margins, overtly refusing to seek acceptance from political centres.

Post-script: A Self-Reflexive Gaze on the Politics of Voice and its Hazards[6]

The analysis presented in this chapter follows a post-structuralist tradition that treats language(s) not as pre-existing entities but as ideological constructs produced in interactions among a variety of social actors (see also Quist & Svendsen, 2010). From such an analytical perspective, what needs understanding is how rinkebysvenska is *talked about* in several discursive arenas, for example, the media, the school, etc., which values are attached to it, and what communicative and symbolic functions are realized by the deployment of linguistic features 'ideologized' (Androutsopoulous, 2010) as rinkebysvenska in specific interactions.

While our focus here is on both media representations in a national daily and school practices among two female pupils, we studied in other publications (Milani & Jonsson, 2011, 2012) male adolescents in other

Swedish educational contexts. Similar to what we said about Jasmine and Berivan in the interaction above, we illustrated how, in the schools in question, speaking standard Swedish is an index of being a good student, whereas youth language is synonymous with unruly behaviour. And, while pupils often subscribe to such dichotomy, the usage of standard Swedish is not always serious but may be mocking in daily interactions. This led us to conclude that the adolescents in our study are staging a Bakhtinian carnival that is 'both critical of social order and complicit with it' (Wolfreys, 2004: 27). On the one hand, these adolescents skilfully mobilize the dichotomy between standard Swedish and youth language, together with the associations related to them. The parodic keying of the interaction subtly disturbs this order, however, not least because parody is never sheer imitation of an original but 'simultaneously change[s] the original through recontextualization' (Pennycook, 2007: 587).

Our analyses, and those of several other scholars (see e.g. Haglund, 2005), are intended to be well-meant attempts to counter wide-spread societal perceptions that paint linguistic practices in Swedish suburbs with highly dark hues as inherently non-Swedish phenomena, the causes of social trouble and educational underachievement, as well as the outer manifestations of young men's inner sexist and homophobic tendencies. For example, we argued elsewhere that 'heteronormativity and homophobia do not "naturally" flow from the young men's ethnicity, but are part of the school as a whole, as well as key components in the teaching strategy of a Swedish teacher' (Milani & Jonsson, 2011: 265). Such scholarly work is also a genuine academic effort to question a conception of languages as monolithic bounded entities that can be easily demarcated. In this respect, we showed how multilingual youth in Swedish suburbs are sophisticated language users that can skilfully activate a plethora of voices in order to comment on, resist, and resignify those media discourses that view Swedish urban multilingualism as a social malaise.

In a sense, it could be argued that this research is undergirded by a *transformative* agenda that seeks to question and ultimately transcend too easy dichotomies of Swedish/non-Swedish, male/female speakers, and educational success/failure; it is also an academic attempt to help speakers of non-normative linguistic phenomena in their search for recognition of their linguistic practices. Such an emancipatory agenda is not realized through a linguistic human rights logic that says: these individuals form a linguistic community that speaks a specific language; hence they should be recognized as a linguistic minority. Rather, following a linguistic citizenship approach, recognition should follow from the documentations of 'the situation[s] where speakers themselves exercise control over their language, deciding *what* languages are, and what they may *mean*, and where language issues [...] are discursively tied to a range of social issues – policy issues and questions of equity' (Stroud, 2001: 353, italics in original). Whether researchers – including ourselves – succeeded in such a transformative project is more questionable.

When we first started working on representations of rinkebysvenska in the media and then moved on to analyze linguistic practices in Swedish schools, we were moved by a thrust to 'do good', to show the complexity of the life of language in daily interaction, something that was consistently erased in the debates taking place in the Swedish media. Good intentions aside, we might nonetheless have been complicit in reinforcing a view of rinkebysvenska as an exotic aberrance. We might have turned rinkeby-svenska into a margin in the Swedish sociolinguistic soundscape. This is mostly the result of two interrelated factors: (1) the choice of speakers on which we focused; and (2) the vocabulary that we employed to describe the interactions among those speakers.

Our analyses are based nearly exclusively on those adolescents that have been singled out by the media or their peers as immigrant youth (*invandrarungdom*) despite the fact that the greatest majority of them was actually born and raised in Sweden. One could argue that such choice was ethnographically motivated. It stemmed from the researcher's insights in the school in which he spent several months observing everyday life there. One of us – Rickard Jonsson – was moved towards a particular group of male pupils because they were constantly talked about by teachers and peers; they were at the same time feared and hated, desired and despised. It is their position as Other (see also Jaworski, 2007) that justified the researcher choosing them as object/subject of sociolinguistic investigation. But that very choice was not unproblematic. Why not consider those adolescents who are perceived as 'ethnically Swedish' but nonetheless employ rinkebysvenska in the school? These are the wannabes, as they are called by the 'immigrant youth'. Empirically, the answer is simple. In the schools studied by us, the wannabes were less interesting; they were never at the centre of attention; their interactions both with their peers and the researcher were more banal, less dramatic than the highly stylized performances (Coupland, 2007) of the 'immigrant youth', who were constantly playing with language and ethnic boundaries, at the same time reproducing and contesting such divisions. However, by failing to fully investigate the wannabes, we might have contributed to reproducing a link between rinkebysvenska and non-Swedishness.

Put differently, we cast a stage light on the 'immigrant youth'; we wanted to put them at the centre of academic attention with a view to

telling a different story, a more complex and nuanced narrative of these
adolescents, their lives, and their aspirations, showing why they employed
certain linguistic strategies in order to accomplish particular identity purposes. Yet, the very act of singling them out might have backfired in re-
inscribing their Otherness as marginal. Such a process of academic
othering was most likely reinforced through the vocabulary we employed,
a set of metalinguistic labels influenced by post-colonial theories of
hybridity and third space. To take an example, we argued that it is a:

> duality of positions that constitutes the shared experience among many
> adolescents in the schools under investigation. It is perhaps the most tan-
> gible manifestation of what Homi Bhabha calls 'the third space': a locus
> where static forms of affiliation are no longer tenable. These adolescents
> are neither 'foreign' to Sweden [...] nor 'indigenous'. Instead they find
> themselves caught up in the very interstices between these two opposite
> positions, juggling creatively with available linguistic resources in order to
> express this experience of in-betweeness. (Milani & Jonsson, 2012: 59)

Also following Bhabha, we described this 'creative juggling' in terms of
linguistic hybridity. Our intentions were indeed celebratory; but 'the celebration of happy hybridity', as Otsuji and Pennycook (2010: 244) call it,
is not entirely innocuous. As Bailey notes, hybridity 'is only meaningful
against a backdrop of essentialism that analysts claim to have rejected
[...]' (Bailey, 2007: 207). This is because, it 'carries with it connotations of
pure and coherent anterior systems', from which it is supposed to stem.
From this, it follows that '"hybridity" [....] pay lip service to certain types
of social difference, whiles implicitly reinforcing the political and economic boundaries that constitute those groups as different and unequal'
(Bailey, 2007: 207).

This is not to say that an analysis informed by linguistic hybridity
should be discarded completely. Rather, linguistic hybridity is an important concept as long as it is specified that there is no anterior purity from
which it originates. Or to put it differently, linguistic hybridity is not the
debris formed from the cross-fertilization of pure elements. As long as it
is not essentialized as the dirty trait of the margins, linguistic hybridity
can be a powerful concept through which to dislocate the alleged homo-
geneity and purity of the centre, namely standard languages.

Despite our transformative intentions, we might have ended up affirming and valorizing the hybridity of rinkebysvenska and urban multilingual
speakers as peculiar. A more radical, academic act of linguistic citizenship
from the margin then should highlight that rinkebysvenska is not an
exception, nor are urban multilingual speakers peculiar. Rather they are

powerful reminders that all languages are ultimately pidgins, creoles, or hybrids (see also Mufwene, 2001), and the difference between those linguistic practices that have taken on the label 'language' and those that have not has ultimately to do with power, and everything that comes with it, for example, codification, standardization, etc. A focus on multilingual speakers in Swedish suburbs should also be the entry point for foregrounding that speakers are differentially heteroglossic (Bakhtin, 1984): we have different registers/voices/styles available to us, owing to differing life experiences, levels of exposure, and license/authority to speak. What appears to be an exceptional case of language practice – rinkebysvenska – actually makes palpable the often-forgotten nature of all linguistic phenomena and their speakers, namely the ideologically laden power struggles that undergird linguistic life.

Notes

(1)   All translations from Swedish texts are our own.
(2)   *Rinkeby* is the name of a neighbourhood of Stockholm where this linguistic practice allegedly originated. In Swedish media and popular discourse *Rinkeby* has become the icon of 'immigrantness' and social problems.
(3)   We are aware that it is an oversimplification to use the term *rinkebysvenska* to define the literary register deployed by Leiva-Wenger and Hassem Kemiri. As Peter Leonard points out, these authors' 'language is [...] anything but uniform' (2005: 22). In this respect, Hassem Kemiri prefers the terms 'innovative Swedish' or 'Halim Swedish' after the name of the main character of his novel, but strongly objects to *rinkebysvenska* because 'that's such a simple box to close the language into' (*Autodidakt*, 2003, cited and translated by Leonard, 2005: 24).
(4)   We employ 'suburb' as a synonym of 'neighbourhood outside the city centre'. In the Swedish context, 'suburb' (*förort*) does not carry the same middle-class connotations as in other socio-political contexts.
(5)   The space of the Million Programme is not limited to the neighbourhood of Rinkeby in Stockholm, but includes several other Swedish metropolitan areas.
(6)   This post-script is a revised version of a section of an article written by the first author of this chapter (Milani, 2014).

References

Androutsopoulos, J. (2010) Ideologizing ethnolectal German. In S. Johnson and T.M. Milani, (eds) *Language Ideologies and Media Discourse: Texts, Practices, Politics* (pp. 182–202). London: Continuum.
Bailey, B. (2007) Heteroglossia and boundaries. In M. Heller (ed.) *Bilingualism: A Social Approach* (pp. 257–274). Basingstoke: Palgrave Macmillan.
Bakhtin, M. (1984) *Problems of Dostoevsky's Poetics*. Minneapolis: University of Minnesota Press.
Besnier, N. (2009) *Gossip and the Everyday Production of Politics*. Hawai'i: University of Hawai'i Press.

Billig, M. (1995) *Banal Nationalism*. London: SAGE Publishing.

Blackledge, A. (2005) *Discourse and Power in a Multilingual World*. Amsterdam: John Benjamins.

Blackledge, A. and Creese, A. (2010) *Multilingualism: A Critical Perspective*. London: Continuum.

Blommaert, J. (2005) *Discourse: A Critical Introduction*. Cambridge: Cambridge University Press.

Blommaert, J., Creve, L. and Willaert, E. (2006) On being declared illiterate: Language-ideological disqualification in Dutch classes for immigrants in Belgium. *Language & Communication* 26 (1), 34–54.

Bourdieu, P. (1991) *Language and Symbolic Power*. Cambridge, MA: Harvard University Press.

Bucholtz, M. (2003) Sociolinguistic nostalgia and the authentication of identity. *Journal of Sociolinguistics* 7 (3), 393–416.

Bunar, N. (2001) *Skolan mitt i förorten. Fyra studies om skola, segregation, integration och multikulturalism*. Eslöv: Symposium.

Cameron, D. and Kulick, D. (2003) *Language and Sexuality*. Cambridge: Cambridge University Press.

Coupland, N. (2007) *Style: Language Variation and Identity*. Cambridge: Cambridge University Press.

Dean, M. (1994) *Critical and Effective Histories: Foucault's Methods and Historical Sociology*. London: Routledge.

Feld, S. and Basso, K.H. (1996) Introduction. In S. Feld and K.H. Basso (eds) *Senses of Place* (pp. 3–12). Santa Fe, NM: School of American Research Press.

Foucault, M. (1978) *The Will to Knowledge. The History of Sexuality: Volume 1*. Harmondsworth, UK: Penguin.

Fraser, N. (1995) From redistribution to recognition? Dilemmas of justice in a 'post-socialist' age. *New Left Review* 212, 68–91.

Gal, S. (2002) A semiotics of the public/private distinction. *differences: A Journal of Feminist Cultural Studies* 13 (1), 77–95.

Gal, S. and Woolard, K.A. (2001) Constructing languages and publics: Authority and representation. In S. Gal and K.A. Woolard (eds) *Languages and Publics: The Making of Authority* (pp. 1–12). Manchester: St. Jerome.

Gringoredaktionen (2006) 'Miljonsvenska' är språkglädje. *Dagens Nyheter* 2 May 2006.

Haglund, C. (2005) Social interaction and identification among adolescents in multilingual suburban Sweden: A study of institutional order and sociocultural change. PhD dissertation, Stockholm University, Stockholm.

Huss, L. (2008) Scandinavian minority language policies in transition: The impact of the European charter for regional or minority languages in Norway and Sweden. In K.A. King, N. Schilling-Estes, L. Fogle, J.J. Lou and B. Soukoup (eds) *Sustaining Linguistic Diversity: Endangered Minority Languages and Language Varieties* (pp. 129–144). Washington, DC: Georgetown University Press.

Hyltenstam, K. (ed.) (1999) *Sveriges sju inhemska språk – ett minoritetsspråksperspektiv*. Lund: Studentlitteratur.

Hyltenstam, K. and Milani, T.M. (2005) Nationella minoriteter och minoritetsspråk. Uppföljning av Sveriges efterlevnad av Europarådets konventioner på nationell nivå: ett minoritetsspråksperspektiv. In Konstitutionsutskottet (ed.) *Nationella minoriteter och minoritetsspråk*. Rapporter från riksdagen 2004/05:RFR3 (pp. 23–74). Stockholm: Sveriges riksdag.

Hyltenstam, K. and Milani, T.M. (2012) Flerspråkighetens sociopolitiska och sociokulturella ramar. [The sociopolitical and sociocultural framing of multilingualism.] In K. Hyltenstam, M. Axelsson and I. Lindberg (eds) *Flerspråkighet: En forskningsöversikt* (pp. 17–152). Vetenskapsrådets rapportserie, 5–2012. Stockholm: Vetenskapsrådet.

Irvine, J.T. and Gal, S. (2000) Language ideology and linguistic differentiation. In P.V. Kroskrity (ed.) *Regimes of Language: Ideologies, Polities, and Identities* (pp. 35–83). Santa Fe, NM: School of American Research Press.

Jaworski, A. (2007) Commentary – Language in the media: Authenticity and othering. In S. Johnson and A. Ensslin (eds) *Language in the Media: Representations, Identities, Ideologies* (pp. 271–280). London: Continuum.

Johnson, S. (2001) Who's misunderstanding whom? Sociolinguistics, public debate and the media. *Journal of Sociolinguistics* 5 (4), 591–610.

Jonsson, R. (2007) *Blatte betyder kompis: Om maskulinitet och språk i en högstadieskola.* Stockholm: Ordfront.

Jonsson, R. and Milani, T.M. (2009) Här är alla lika! Jämlikhetsideologi och konstruktionen av den 'Andre' i media och skola. *Utbildning & Demokrati* 18 (2), 67–86.

Kerfoot, C. (2009) Changing conceptions of literacies, language and development. PhD thesis in Bilingualism Nr. 18., Stockholm University, Stockholm.

Khemiri, J. H. (2003) *Ett öga rött.* Stockholm: Bonnier.

Koopmans, R. and Statham, P. (1999) Challenging the liberal nation-state? Postnationalism, multiculturalism and the collective claims making of migrants and ethnic minorities in Britain and Germany. *American Journal of Sociology* 105 (3), 652–96.

Lacatus, C. (2007) What is a *blatte*? Migration and ethnic identity in contemporary Sweden. *Journal of Arab & Muslim Media Research* 1 (1), 79–92.

Leiva-Wenger, A. (2003) *Till vår ära.* Stockholm: Modernista.

Leiva-Wenger, A. (2006) Förortsslangen står för språkglädje. *Dagens Nyheter* 27 April.

Leonard, P. (2005) Imagining themselves: Voice, text, and reception in Anyuru, Khemiri and Wenger. MA thesis, University of Washington, Seattle. See http://students. washington.edu/pl212/ma-thesis.pdf (accessed 5 August 2010).

Lippi-Green, R. (1997) *English with an Accent: Language, Ideology, and Discrimination in the United States.* London: Routledge.

Makoni, S. and Pennycook, A. (eds) (2007) *Disinventing and Reconstituting Languages.* Clevedon: Multilingual Matters.

Milani, T.M. (2007a) Voices of endangerment: A language ideological debate on the Swedish language. In A. Duchêne and M. Heller (eds) *Discourses of Endangerment: Ideology and Interest in the Defence of Languages* (pp. 169–196). London: Continuum.

Milani, T.M. (2007b) Voices of authority in conflict: The making of the expert in a language debate in Sweden. *Linguistics and Education* 18 (2), 99–120.

Milani, T.M. (2008) Language testing and citizenship: A language ideological debate in Sweden. *Language in Society* 37 (1), 27–59.

Milani, T.M. (2010) What's in a name? Language ideology and social differentiation in a Swedish print-mediated debate. *Journal of Sociolinguistics* 14 (1), 116–142.

Milani, T.M. (2014) Marginally speaking. *Multilingual Margins* 1 (1), 9–20.

Milani, T.M. and Johnson, S. (2008) Language politics and legitimation crisis in Sweden: A Habermasian approach. *Language Problems & Language Planning* 32 (1), 1–22.

Milani, T.M. and Jonsson, R. (2011) Incomprehensible language? Language, ethnicity and heterosexual masculinity in a Swedish school. *Gender & Language* 5 (2), 241–269.

Milani, T.M. and Jonsson, R. (2012) Who's afraid of Rinkeby Swedish? Stylization, complicity, resistance. *Journal of Linguistic Anthropology* 22 (1), 44–63.

Municio, I. (1987) Från lag till bruk. Hemspråksreformens genomförande. Stockholm Studies in Politics Nr 31. Stockholm: Stockholm University.

Mutua, M. (2002) *Human Rights: A Political and Cultural Critique*. Philadelphia: University of Pennsylvania Press.

Mufwene, S. (2001) *The Ecology of Language Revolution*. Cambridge: Cambridge University Press.

Otsuji, A. and Pennycook, A. (2010) Metrolingualism: Fixity, fluidity and language in flux. *International Journal of Multilingualism* 7 (3), 240–254.

Pavlenko, A. and Blackledge, A. (eds) (2004) *Negotiations of Identities in Multilingual Contexts*. Clevedon: Multilingual Matters.

Pennycook, A. (2006) Postmodernism in language policy. In T. Ricento (ed.) *An Introduction to Language Policy: Theory and Method* (pp. 60–76). Malden, MA: Blackwell.

Pennycook, A. (2007) 'The rotation gets thick. The constraints get thin': Creativity, recontextualization, and difference. *Applied Linguistics* 28 (4), 579–596.

Pujolar, J. (2007) Bilingualism and the nation-state in the post-national era. In M. Heller (ed.) *Bilingualism: A Social Approach* (pp. 71–110). Basingstoke: Palgrave Macmillan.

Quist, P. and Svendsen, B.A. (eds) (2010) *Multilingual Urban Scandinavia: New Linguistic Practices*. Bristol: Multilingual Matters.

Ricento, T. (2000) Historical and theoretical perspectives in language policy and planning. *Journal of Sociolinguistics* 4 (2), 196–213.

Ricento, T. (2006a) Theoretical perspectives in language policy: An overview. In T. Ricento (ed.) *An Introduction to Language Policy: Theory and Method* (pp. 3–9). Malden, MA: Blackwell.

Ricento, T. (2006b) Language policy: Theory and practice. In T. Ricento (ed.) *An Introduction to Language Policy: Theory and Method* (pp. 10–23). Malden, MA: Blackwell.

SAOB. *Svenska Akademiens ordbok*. https://www.saob.se

Skutnabb-Kangas, T. (2006) Language policy and linguistic human rights. In T. Ricento (ed.) *An Introduction to Language Policy: Theory and Method* (pp. 273–291). Malden, MA: Blackwell.

SOU (1997a) Statens offentliga utredningar 1997: 192 *Steg mot en minoritetspolitik. Europarådets konvention om historiska minoritetsspråk*. Stockholm: Fritzes.

SOU (1997b) Statens offentliga utredningar 1997: 193 *Steg mot en minoritetspolitik. Europarådets convention för skydd av nationella minoriteter*. Stockholm: Fritzes.

SOU (2002) Statens offentliga utredningar 2002: 27 *Mål i Mun. Förslag till handlinsprogram för svenska språket*. Stockholm: Fritze.

Spivak, G.C. (1988) Subaltern studies: Deconstructing historiography. In R. Guha and G.C. Spivak (eds) *Selected Subaltern Studies* (pp. 3–34). Oxford: Oxford University Press.

Språklag. (2009) Språklag 2009: 600. Svensk författningssamling. https://www.riksdagen.se/sv/dokument-lagar/dokument/svensk-forfattningssamling/spraklag-2009600_sfs-2009-600.

Stroud, C. (2001) African mother tongue programs and the politics of language: Linguistic citizenship versus linguistic human rights. *Journal of Multilingual and Multicultural Development* 22 (4), 339–355.

Stroud, C. (2003) Postmodernist perspectives on local languages: African mother tongue education in times of globalization. *International Journal of Bilingual Education and Bilingualism* 6 (1), 17–36.

Stroud, C. (2004) Rinkeby Swedish and semilingualism in language ideological debates: A Bourdieuean perspective. *Journal of Sociolinguistics* 8 (2), 163–230.

Stroud, C. (2010) Towards a postliberal theory of citizenship. In J.E. Petrovic (ed.) *International Perspectives on Bilingual Education: Policy, Practice and Controversy* (pp. 191–218). New York: Information Age Publishing.

Stroud, C. and Heugh, K. (2004) Linguistic human rights and linguistic citizenship. In D. Patrick and J. Freeland (eds) *Language Rights and Language Survival: A Sociolinguistic Exploration* (pp. 191–218). Manchester: St. Jerome.

Wee, L. (2007) Linguistic human rights and mobility. *Journal of Multilingual and Multicultural Development* 28 (4), 325–338.

Williams, Q.E. and Stroud, C. (2015) Linguistic citizenship: Language and politics in postnatonal modernities. *Journal of Language and Politics* 14 (3), 406–430.

Witt-Brattström, E. (2006) Vem äger svenskan? *Dagens Nyheter* 19 April.

Wolfreys, J. (2004) *Critical Keywords in Literary and Cultural Theory*. Basingstoke: Palgrave Macmillan.

Woolard, K.A. (1998) Introduction: Language ideology as a field of inquiry. In B.B. Schieffelin, K.A. Woolard and P.V. Kroskrity (eds) *Language Ideologies: Practice and Theory* (pp. 1–47). Oxford: Oxford University Press.

11 Linguistic Citizenship in Post-Banda Malawi: A Focus on the Public Radio and Primary Education

Gregory Kamwendo
University of Zululand

Introduction and Background

This chapter takes linguistic citizenship (Kerfoot, 2011; Stroud, 2001, 2002, 2003, 2009; Stroud & Heugh, 2004) as its theoretical backbone. The central argument in the cited literature is that the notion of linguistic citizenship is better placed to illuminate issues regarding language development and promotion than the linguistic human rights (LHR) paradigm. Stroud (2001: 353) defines linguistic citizenship as 'the situation where speakers themselves exercise control over their language, deciding what languages are, what they may imply and where language issues (especially in educational sites) are discursively tied to a range of social issues, policy issues and questions of equity'. The key point is that it is the language speakers themselves who should take action on and about their languages. However, this does not and should not imply the dismissal of the contribution of the state towards language development and language promotion matters. There is no doubt that the state has a critical role to play. For instance, under the LHR paradigm, the state is expected to promote and protect language rights. But, from the linguistic citizenship perspective, the role of the state is not to be taken for granted since the state may fail to deliver in some areas. That is why the language speakers themselves must seize spaces and opportunities created by the state in order to promote or develop their own languages. In this chapter, I explore the extent to which linguistic citizenship can be linked to language development and promotion in Malawi since 1994 in two public domains, namely the radio and primary schools. But the key questions are: To what extent do speakers of indigenous languages seize opportunities to practice participatory democracy through exercising agency towards the promotion and development of their language(s)? Or do citizens or language speakers leave it up to the state to do the job of language development and promotion? These are the two key questions at the heart of the chapter. It is important to point out that the year 1994 was a year of change in Malawian politics. It is the year when Malawi changed into a multi-party and democratic state after 30 years of one-party rule under president Dr Hastings Kamuzu Banda and his Malawi Congress Party (hereafter, MCP). The Kamuzu Banda era was characterized by the policy of one nation, one language, which led to linguistic assimilation through which Chichewa (the national language) was developed and promoted at the expense of other indigenous languages (Kamwendo, 2005a; Kayambazinthu, 1998).

As mentioned earlier, the focus of the chapter is on two public domains, namely national radio, and the primary school sector. These two publicly funded domains were chosen for the following reasons. First, these two domains were the first to benefit from LHR paradigm efforts in the early phases of the post-Banda era. The radio is the most widely used medium of information dissemination in Malawi and other contexts that are characterized by low literacy levels and an infant culture of accessing information through the written word. Second, in most countries in Africa, language-in-education policies tend to attract the most attention given the high affinity for the previously colonial languages (e.g. French, English, etc.), which are often used and preferred at the expense of indigenous languages. Language-in-education policy is, therefore, the most hotly contested terrain in Africa, and Malawi is no exception. It is against this background that it has been remarked that 'the history of language in education planning in Malawi is characterized by the dilemma of when to use the vernacular language and when to introduce English' (Kayambazinthu, 1998: 388–389). It is therefore worthwhile to examine the extent to which examples of linguistic citizenship are at work in this hotly contested domain. This chapter proceeds as follows. In the next section, I provide a brief sociolinguistic and political background of Malawi. After this, I briefly introduce the rise of language association in Malawi, a development that is closely linked to what is called politics of recognition. In the section that follows, I lay out theoretical perspectives for the chapter, that is, linguistic citizenship and LHR. The following section covers information sources. In the next section, I apply the notion of linguistic citizenship to the public radio and the public primary education sector. The chapter ends with a summary and conclusion.

Malawi: A Brief Sociolinguistic and Political Background

Malawi is a small landlocked country that is located in Southern Africa. Then known as Nyasaland during the colonial era, the country attained independence from Britain in 1964. Malawi is multilingual and multicultural. The exact number of languages is not easy to establish against a background of a problematic boundary that lies between language and dialect. In view of the fuzziness of the boundary between language and dialect, there is reference to between 13 and 15 languages in Malawi. Chichewa is the most widely used language of household communication. Other languages of household communication are Yao, Tumbuka, Sena, Lomwe, and Tonga. Though the Northern Region has Tumbuka as its dominant language, the region does have minority languages such as Tonga, Lambya, Sukwa, and Ngonde. English is the official language. This status of English was inherited from British colonial rule. To this end, English is the main language of education, government, the judiciary, the legislature, and mass media. Malawi is therefore classified as an Anglophone African country, but this label applies to the state and not to the citizens, since their use of English as a language of household communication is very low. The citizens' languages of household communication are predominantly indigenous languages (Kayambazinthu, 1998).

When Malawi attained independence from Britain in 1964, the country had to address the delicate challenge of building and strengthening nationhood out of competing modes of belonging and identities. National unity and cohesion were perceived to be under serious threat owing to the country's linguistic and cultural diversity. To this end, linguistic assimilation was identified and advanced as one of the tools for nation building. As a result, Malawi pursued the policy of one nation, one language – a policy that made the state develop and promote Chichewa at the expense of other indigenous languages. Consequently, indigenous languages other than Chichewa did not enjoy any official recognition. Furthermore, the general climate in Malawi at that time was one of a dictatorship state in which various freedoms and rights were muzzled. In 1993, Malawi held a national referendum in which two-thirds voted in favour of a change in the political system from a single party state to a multi-party state. In 1994, multi-party general elections took place, and the then president and dictator, Dr Hastings Kamuzu Banda, and his MCP lost.

In the post-Banda political dispensation, there have been moves by the state to recognize linguistic diversity through official recognition of more than one indigenous language. This is in sharp contrast to the Pre-1994 era when only one indigenous language (Chichewa) enjoyed official recognition and support under the umbrella of nation building. The post-Banda constitution grants various freedoms and rights. For example, with reference to language and culture, the constitution stipulates that 'every person shall have the right to use the language and to participate in the cultural life of his or her choice' (Republic of Malawi, 1995: 18). The constitution also provides for the establishment of institutions that promote and protect human rights in one way or the other. Such institutions include the Human Rights Commission and the Law Commission. Through the freedom of speech granted by the post-Banda Constitution, people could now openly debate language issues – something they could not dare to do during the Banda dictatorship. In addition, one also sees the establishment of language–culture association as being a direct product of the freedom of association. Some scholars (e.g. Kamwendo, 2005b; Makoni et al., 2008) have described the work of language associations as language planning from below. Later in the chapter, I will explore the link between language planning from below and linguistic citizenship.

Language Associations

The freedom of association offered by the post-Banda constitution in Malawi (Republic of Malawi, 1995) has given birth to a politics of recognition. Ethnic groups whose languages and cultures had been marginalized by the linguistic and cultural assimilation of the Kamuzu Banda administration now seek recognition. As a result, a number of language and/or culture associations came into existence. These include the Abenguni Revival Association (see Kamwendo, 2005a, 2005b; Kishindo, 2002), the Chitumbuka Culture, and Language Association (see Kamwendo, 2005a, 2005b), and Mulhako Wa Alhomwe. Though the Chewa did not undergo marginalization of their language and culture (Kamwendo, 2005a; Kayambazinthu, 1998), they have also formed an association. The most recent and highly talked about association is the Mulhako Wa Alhomwe (for the Lomwe), launched by the late president Bingu Wa Mutharika on 25 October 2008 – with the aim of preserving Lomwe customs, beliefs, and language.

In line with the description of the work on language–culture associations as language planning from below (Kamwendo, 2005b; Makoni et al., 2008), I argue in this chapter that language associations operate from a self-help perspective. That is, if the state cannot do it, then citizens will do it since it is them who need it. At this stage, I would like to connect the notion of self-help to linguistic citizenship. In my view, language planning becomes a kind of self-help when communities take initiatives to develop and promote their languages. It is interesting to note that during the era of the Banda dictatorship, the leadership of the day encouraged Malawians to engage in self-help projects. These were projects that were initiated by communities in response to their needs. A community would, for example, mobilize financial and other resources and proceed to build a bridge or a classroom or a clinic. The state would, where resources permitted, come in with a top-up of resources. The understanding behind self-help projects was that the state alone could not provide all the needs of the communities. This spirit made a lot of sense and it strengthened peoples' participation in the development of their own communities. But what is interesting to note is that when it came to language matters, the one-party state did not give room to communities to engage in self-help projects. In other words, communities could not embark on projects aimed at developing their own languages. The state had the complete monopoly over this domain. The fear was that the development and promotion of more than one indigenous language would threaten national unity. In concluding this section, I take language associations, by virtue of their self-help spirit, to be possible avenues where linguistic citizenship can be exercised.

Theoretical Perspectives

Some language scholars (e.g. Rubagumya *et al.*, 2011; Stroud, 2001, 2002, 2003, 2009; Stroud & Heugh, 2004; Trudell, 2008) have extended the notion of citizenship to language matters 'in an attempt to broaden and diversify the meaning of citizenship to language issues' (Stroud, 2001: 346). Stroud argues that linguistic citizenship 'provides a more theoretically grounded and adequate conceptualization of the problems confronting a politics of languages than does the notion of linguistic human rights' (Stroud, 2001: 346). Linguistic citizenship puts emphasis on the participation of members of linguistic communities in the transformation of their own linguistic landscape(s). Instead of solely relying on legal instruments as enabling tools for language development and promotion, linguistic communities themselves take up the challenge of doing the job. The task of language development and promotion should not be left to the state alone, especially when the state is either unwilling or has inadequate resources to perform the job. It is against this background that local agency becomes one of the central pillars of linguistic citizenship. That is, the ability of people to act and bring about change to their own lives (see Kerfoot, 2011; Orman, 2012; Pluddemann, 2007; Rubagumya *et al.*, 2011; Stroud, 2001–2003, 2009; Stroud & Heugh, 2004; Trudell, 2008; Williams & Stroud, 2013).

On the other hand, the LHR perspective stresses the role of the state in ensuring that language rights are safeguarded. The role of the state can be addressed from two perspectives, namely language rights tolerance and language rights promotion (Chen, 1998; Kymlicka & Patten, 2003). Let us begin with the language rights tolerance perspective. This refers to language rights that require the state to abstain from interfering with their observance and protection. With respect to the language promotion perspective, the state has the obligation to take positive and practical actions (including the use of financial and other resources) to ensure that language rights are realized (Chen, 1998; Kymlicka & Patten, 2003). It should be recalled that it is this role of the state that linguistic citizenship advocates do not take for granted, as they argue that agency is critical given that the state may fail to deliver. The LHR paradigm is backed by various instruments, such as charters, covenants, and clauses in constitutions. Sometimes instruments that are supposed to pressurize states into taking positive action on language rights are so vaguely phrased that escape routes are created. As a result, the state can run away from its responsibility through such escape routes (Skutnabb-Kangas & Phillipson, 2001).

Sources of Information

Information on the two domains, namely radio and primary school, which has been used for the construction of the current chapter, was gathered through a number of sources. Some of the information was gathered through archival sources. I have also made use of published literature on the language situation in Malawi to extract relevant activities that fit into the linguistic citizenship domain. Third, I have made use of information that I gained through interactions with various language groups in Malawi during the period 1996 and 2002. The interactions took various forms – both formal and informal meetings and data gathering encounters during research.

The Public Radio

During the Kamuzu Banda political reign (1964 to 1994), the airwaves were heavily controlled by the state, and as such, private or commercial radio stations did not exist. The dictatorial state severely curtailed freedom of expression as well as access to information. To this end, the public radio, the Malawi Broadcasting Corporation (MBC), served as a mouthpiece of the Kamuzu Banda dictatorship. The radio was a praise singer of the Banda regime. Like other state-run institutions, MBC implemented the politically correct philosophy of the day, that being the promotion of Chichewa (as national language) and English (as the official language and the language for linking up with international community). This meant that minority languages (meaning languages other than English and Chichewa) did not have space on the national radio. Speakers of these minority languages could not enjoy access to information through their mother tongues.

In view of the fact the Kamuzu Banda era broadcasting policy did not reflect and respect the reality of Malawi's sociolinguistic diversity, the post-Banda political atmosphere, backed by a constitution that espoused democracy and human rights, necessitated transformation of the language policy. As a result, the radio's language changed from a bilingual policy (English and Chichewa) to a seven-language policy (English plus five minority indigenous languages, namely Tumbuka, Yao, Sena, Tonga and Lomwe). The language policy change was largely an outcome of state directives, with only one case being associated with linguistic citizenship. The first act of transformation of the broadcasting policy touched on Tumbuka. On 25 June 1994, President Bakili Muluzi issued a directive that reinstated Tumbuka on the national radio station. The language had been removed from the airwaves following the 1968 declaration of Chichewa as the national language.

Following the reinstatement of Tumbuka on the national radio, the Chitumbuka Language and Culture Association (CLACA) decided 'to monitor Chitumbuka spoken on the radio and make comments' (Minutes of CLACA meeting, 14 April 2000). This decision can be described as the gaining of voice by Tumbuka speakers. Their voice on the use of Tumbuka on the national radio could now be made known to the state, but as Lin (2010) would ask: did the top (the state) listen to the voice from below? The answer is no. CLACA went further to call on the MBC to introduce programmes that would reflect traditional culture as it obtains in the rural areas. The language association took a hard stance against urban speakers and banned them from taking part in such cultural programmes 'since their Chitumbuka is not as good' (Minutes of CLACA meeting, 14 April 2000). But the state, through its radio, did not implement this proposal. By rejecting urban varieties of Tumbuka, CLACA demonstrated its failure to appreciate that the notion of homogenous speech community is a myth since 'any speech community will comprise various groups distinguished along parameters such as age, urbanity-rurality, modern-traditional and social economic status' (Stroud, 2009: 196).

Another language policy directive targeting the MBC came on 13 September 1997, when President Bakili Muluzi directed that Tonga should become one of the languages of newscasts on the national radio. This directive came as a response to a Tonga-speaking chief who had asked the President to consider directing the MBC to offer newscasts in Tonga. A traditional chief represents the views of his/her community, and therefore acts as the mouthpiece of the grassroots. The chief seized the opportunity presented by the presence of the state president, and pressed for the recognition and installation of his language (Tonga) on the national radio. As a public broadcaster, MBC has the triple mission of informing, educating, and entertaining the Malawian public, and the request for the inclusion of Tonga meant that speakers of the language would now enjoy the triple mission in their own mother tongue, to some extent (given that the radio still remains dominated by Chichewa).

Looking at the post-Banda era, one notices that the public radio underwent language policy transformation through which five indigenous languages were added on the list of media of newscasts. This inclusion spoke directly to LHR. In the case of four languages (Tumbuka, Yao, Sena and Lomwe), their entry into the languages of newscast list was a direct result of a government directive. One can argue that the government was aware of the need to unblock linguistic barriers to access to information. The state, in line with LHR tradition, had fulfilled its obligation. But when the speakers of Tonga found that their language had not been included, they exercised linguistic citizenship, and used the state president's political rally as an occasion for addressing their demand for linguistic inclusion. A language policy directive issued by government is what Lin (2010) would call voice from above; and when speakers of a language (for example, speakers of Tonga) demand linguistic inclusion, that act represents Lin's (2010) voice from below. Government obliged, thus listened to the voice from below. If the voice from below had not been spoken, or if the voice had been spoken but the state had turned a deaf ear to that voice, Tonga would not have been one of the languages used in newscasts on the public radio.

Public Primary Education

The education domain was touched by the LHR influence in the post-Banda era. On 28 March 1996, the Ministry of Education issued a policy directive that from then onward, Standards (Grades) 1 to 4 should be taught through mother tongues. English would serve as the medium of instruction beginning in Standard 5. English and Chichewa would, however, continue to be offered as examinable subjects in the primary curricula (Kamwendo, 2008). This new policy provided official recognition and space to minority languages. The policy clearly echoed the LHR position that mother tongue education is a human right. From a LHR point of view, mother tongue speakers of non-dominant languages would now have the opportunity to enjoy one of their language rights in the education sector. This was also a move towards creating a decentralized language-in-education policy in that primary schools would select a catchment area's most dominant language as the medium of instruction during the first four years.

The policy directive received mixed reactions. While some people were excited with the granting of mother tongue education to primary education, others were uncomfortable with how the directive came into being. It was argued the policy had come in a top-down fashion that came without input from the constituents who were supposed to implement the policy. In addition, the usual arguments that have been levelled against mother tongue education elsewhere in Africa were raised. We can only summarize such arguments as being: the fear that the policy would strengthen ethnic loyalties at the expense of national unity; the lack of local research backing; the restriction of teacher movement since teachers would end up teaching only in the areas where their own mother tongues are spoken; the lack of learning and teaching materials; and the lack of mother tongue teachers (see Kamwendo, 2008). The state went silent on the policy, leading to non-implementation, and this amounted to what Bamgbose (1991) calls policy declaration without implementation. This is also exactly what Rubagumya et al. (2011: 79) say about rights-based thinking in education: 'it can successfully create an enabling political framework within which languages can claim their place, but says very little about implementation. Governments may commit themselves to equity between languages, for example as media of instruction but fail to enact this in concrete terms within the education system'.

While proponents of LHR would have been happy that the right to mother tongue education had been granted, CLACA (a non-state actor) felt that more still needed to be done. The site of struggle was the production of learning and teaching materials for Tumbuka. The Teachers Union of Malawi (TUM) was of the view that subject content textbooks that were in Chichewa would be translated into Tumbuka and other local languages. The idea was to make the same content available in different languages across the country. CLACA vehemently rejected this proposal. CLACA argued that the existing textbooks were dominated by Chewa culture, and that, as such, it would not be acceptable to have Chewa culture in textbooks that were meant for Tumbuka-speaking learners: 'All Tumbuka books should not be reprinted at random but after the approval of the Association for Tumbuka Language and Culture. We want the orthography which is generally acceptable to appear in the readers today. These should not be literal translations of Chichewa teaching materials' (CLACA's letter to the Ministry of Education, 24 October 1996). CLACA went further to advise the Ministry of Education: 'We know the Ministry has a big task of finding proper and relevant books that would not contradict with the Tumbuka culture and it is in this regard that we want to recommend the types of books to be used' (CLACA's letter to the Ministry of Education, 24 October 1996).

The work of CLACA (Kamwendo, 2005a, 2005b) can be located in the domain of linguistic citizenship. First, Tumbuka speakers were in favour of the 1996 policy directive on mother tongue education as they saw it as a way of restoring the glory of their language that had been removed from the curriculum by the Kamuzu Banda regime in 1968. One can say that the loudest voice in support of mother tongue education directive came from Tumbuka speakers. Speakers of other indigenous languages remained unmoved by the mother tongue directly, partly because of the erroneous belief that policy would deny learners from acquiring English and that education standards would go down (see Kamwendo, 2008). But Tumbuka speakers, through CLACA, made attempts to revise Tumbuka orthography and also assembled some old textbooks that had been in use previously. Though the orthography revision was not professionally done, given that CLACA members lacked the skills and expertise of trained linguists, one can say that there was a strong and positive desire to engage in corpus planning in support of the mother tongue education directive. Unfortunately, owing to lack of resources on the part of CLACA, and also lack of support from the state itself, Tumbuka speakers were unable to see their language go back into the curriculum. The state dragged its feet (Kamwendo, 2008), and the mother tongue directive became what Bamgbose (1991) would call declaration without implementation. The 1996 mother tongue directive has since been replaced by a policy that has English serving as the medium of instruction straightaway from Grade 1. The new policy was announced in 2014.

Summary and Conclusion

The chapter is a contribution to the on-going debates on linguistic citizenship. The chapter focuses on the post-Banda era in Malawi (1994 to the present time), and responds to two questions, namely: To what extent do speakers of various indigenous languages seize the opportunity to exercise participatory democracy through exercising agency towards the promotion and development of their language(s)? Or do citizens (language speakers) leave it up to the state to do the job? With reference to the radio, I have cited the case of Tonga, which was elevated to being one of the languages of newscasts following a direct request from a Tonga-speaking chief. Apart from this, no other minority language group has voiced its demand for inclusion on the radio. With regard to the language-in-education policy, the state proclaimed a mother tongue education policy in 1996, but it is only Tumbuka speakers (through their language association) that took special interest. Other language groups remained silent, probably engulfed and dwarfed by the multitude of myths and misconceptions about what mother tongue instruction can do to English language acquisition and standards of education. The state itself dragged its feet, and finally the mother tongue instruction policy was abandoned in 2014. One can say that acts of linguistic citizenship are still in their infancy in the post-Banda era in Malawi. The state drives the language agenda, and not enough voices from below are being sent to the top (state) regarding the development and promotion of indigenous languages. In addition, the voices from below are not being accompanied by visible action by the indigenous language speakers themselves.

Retrospective: A Reversal of Language-in-Education Policy in Malawi, August 2015

Introduction

In this retrospective account, I focus on Malawi's language-in-education policy. I started writing the chapter with the 1996 language policy directive in mind. The directive had stipulated that a mother tongue or a widely used language in the school catchment area would serve as the medium of instruction in the first four classes of primary school. This policy was in full conformity with UNESCO (1953, 2003) as well as empirical evidence provided in the literature (see, for example, Babaci-Wilhite, 2014; Brock-Utne & Skattum, 2009; Brock-Utne et al., 2010; Williams, 2006). In March 2014, 18 years after the declaration of the 1996 language policy directive, Malawi announced a reversal of the language policy. The Education Act of 2012, which had replaced the 1962 Act, supplied the new language policy. Section 78 (1) of the Act states that 'the medium of instruction in schools and colleges shall be English'. In Section 78 (2), it is stipulated that 'without prejudice to the generality of subsection (1), the Minister may, by notice published in the *Gazette* prescribe the language of instruction in schools' (Republic of Malawi, 2012).

Luscious Kanyumba, the then Minister of Education, justified the new language policy by arguing that 'English speaking has been a problem to our pupils even to those who completed secondary school education. It is the wish of government to see most of the pupils write and speak good English while at primary school' (Masina, 2014). The Minister's argument was flawed. He had missed the point that there is a clear distinction between English as medium of instruction versus English as a subject of study (Simango, 2015). While the state was right in having the desire to improve proficiency in English, the strategy adopted (namely, early use of English as medium of instruction) was flawed and out of touch with the principles of language learning. Proficiency in any language cannot be improved through using the target language as the medium of instruction. Rather, what Malawi needs to do is to improve the teaching of English as a subject. This requires a significant upgrade of the resources that are used in the teaching of English in Malawian schools. Currently, Malawi has one of the most poorly resourced primary education systems in the world (Williams, 2006; World Bank, 2010). Such a teaching and learning environment cannot either effectively support an early use of English as medium of instruction or contribute to improvement in learners' proficiency in English.

Reactions to the new policy: Any traces of linguistic citizenship?

So, how have citizens or speakers of various languages responded to the new language policy? Can we detect any trace(s) of linguistic citizenship in response to the new language policy? In response to the new language policy, two voices have emerged: the voice of acceptance versus the voice of rejection. The voice of acceptance salutes the state for doing the right thing by putting in place a policy, which in their view, will enable learners to improve proficiency in English. These supporters of the new policy proceed to argue that the use of Chichewa as a medium of instruction is to blame for the deteriorating standards of education in Malawi. In addition, within the voice of acceptance is the erroneous equation: English = quality education.

The voice of rejection is articulated by academics and researchers, some non-government organizations (NGOs), university students, and some members of the general public. While they agree that the state has to put in place mechanisms that will improve proficiency in the English language, they are of the view that the noble goal cannot be attained through early deployment of English as medium of instruction. The voice of rejection of the new language policy draws its confidence and authority from UNESCO (1953, 2003) and scholarly research evidence (e.g. Babaci-Wilhite, 2014; Brock-Utne & Skattum, 2009; Brock-Utne et al., 2010; Williams, 2006). Featuring in this camp are some Malawian academics (e.g. Kamwendo, 2015; Kishindo, 2015; Simango, 2015), University of Malawi students (see Kishindo, 2015), international scholars such as Miti (2015b), and some members of the British Association of Applied Linguistics. Locally in Malawi, students from Chancellor College, a constituent college of the University of Malawi delivered a petition to the state through the Zomba district commissioner. The students also engaged in a debate with the public on a local radio, Radio Maria on 19 March and 12 April 2014 (see Kishindo, 2015). Another site where opposition to the new language policy was voiced was the national language-in-education policy held in Mangochi on 24 July 2014, which tried unsuccessfully to persuade the state to withdraw the new language policy (see Miti, 2015a). I was approached by the British Association of Applied Linguistics to assist in the drafting of a petition to be delivered to the state through the Malawi embassy in London in the United Kingdom. As I write the chapter, Malawians and non-Malawians are signing the petition online. The petition asks the state to withdraw the straight for English policy with regard to medium of instruction.

It is clear from the public debates in newspapers, radios, and other spaces that Malawians are divided over the new language policy – acceptance versus rejection. These competing voices can be classified as acts of linguistic citizenship. Language use in education is the site for people's struggle for quality education. The interest is not on language per se, but rather with what people think certain languages can bring about. For example, the voices accepting the new language policy think that English as a medium of instruction will improve the quality of education. They also believe that it is Chichewa (as medium of instruction) that is to blame for the country's deteriorating standards of education. On the other hand, other Malawians are waging a verbal struggle to retain Chichewa (and/or other indigenous languages) as media of instruction in the first four classes of primary and also calling on the state to improve the teaching of English as a subject. Malawians taking competing positions on the new language policy via media debates (compare the case of Afrikaans in Milani & Shaikjee, 2013) and University of Malawi students marching to the Zomba district commissioner to deliver a petition against the new language policy, and other Malawians joining international scholars in signing an online petition are all acts of linguistic citizenship. Citizens are trying to influence the state on a very important socio-economic and political issue – language. The case of university students is quite interesting given that in the then apartheid South Africa, the 1976 Soweto riots were ignited by students' dislike of the imposition of Afrikaans as a medium of instruction.

References

Babaci-Wilhite, Z. (ed.) (2014) *Giving Space to African Voices: Rights in Local Languages and Local Curriculum*. Boston: Sense Publishers.

Bamgbose, A. (1991) *Language and the Nation: The Language Question in Sub-Saharan Africa*. Edinburgh: Edinburgh University Press.

Brock-Utne, B. and Skattum, I. (eds) (2009) *Languages and Education in Africa: A Comparative and Transdiciplinary Analysis*. Oxford: Symposium Books.

Brock-Utne, B., Desai, Z. and Pitman, A. (2010) *Language of Instruction in Tanzania and South Africa – Highlights from a Project*. Rotterdam: Sense Publishers.

Chen, A.H.Y. (1998) The philosophy of language rights. *Language Sciences* 20 (1), 45–54.

Kamwendo, G. (2005a) Language, identity, and the politics of recognition in the post-Banda Northern Malawi. *Ufahamu* 31 (1–2), 40–69.

Kamwendo, G. (2005b) Language planning from below: An example from Northern Malawi. *Language Policy* 4 (2), 143–165.

Kamwendo, G. (2015) The straight for English policy in Malawi: The road not to be taken. In L.M. Miti (ed.) *The Language of Instruction Question in Malawi* (pp. 29–39). Cape Town: Centre for Advanced Studies of African Society.

Kamwendo, G.H. (2008) The bumpy road to mother tongue instruction in Malawi. *Journal of Multilingual and Multicultural Development* 29 (5), 353–363.

Kayambazinthu, E. (1998) The language situation in Malawi. *Journal of Multilingual and Multicultural Development* 29 (5), 353–363.

Kerfoot, C. (2011) Making and shaping of participatory spaces: Resemiotization and citizenship agency in South Africa. *International Multilingual Research Journal* 5 (2), 87–102.

Kishindo, P.J. (2002) 'Flogging a dead cow?': The revival of Malawian Chingoni. *Nordic Journal of African Studies* 11 (2), 206–223.

Kishindo, P.J. (2015) The bird that was not allowed to fly: The case of the mother tongue language-in-education policy in Malawi. In L.M. Miti (ed.) *The Language of Instruction Question in Malawi* (pp. 9–28). Cape Town: Centre for Advanced Studies of African Society.

Kymlicka, W. and Patten, A. (2003) Language rights and political theory. *Annual Review of Applied Linguistics* 23, 3–21.

Lin, A.R. (2010) Voices from above – voices from below. Who is talking and who is listening in Norwegian language politics? *Current Issues in Language Planning* 11 (2), 114–129.

Makoni, S., Makoni, B. and Nyika, N. (2008) Language planning from below: The case of the Tonga in Zimbabwe. *Current Issues in Language Planning* 9 (4), 413–439.

Masina, L. (2014) Malawi schools to teach in English. See www.aljazeera.com/news/africa/2014/08/malawi (accessed 5 March2015).

Milani, T. and Shaikjee, M. (2013) Afrikaans is bobaas: Linguistic citizenship on the BBC voices website. In C. Upton and B.L. Davies (eds) *Analysing Twenty-First Century British English* (pp. 71–90). London: Routledge.

Miti, L.M. (ed.) (2015a) *The Language of Instruction Question in Malawi*. Cape Town: Centre for Advanced Studies of African Society.

Miti, L.M. (2015b) Language policies and the development of African languages. In L.M. Miti (ed.) *The Language of Instruction Question in Malawi* (pp. 61–88). Cape Town: Centre for Advanced Studies of African Society.

Orman, J. (2012) Language and 'new' African migration to South Africa: An overview and some reflections on theoretical implications for policy and planning. *Language Policy* 11, 301–322.

Pluddemann, P. (2007) Linguistic rights for multilingual citizens. *LEAP News* 13, 14–15.

Republic of Malawi. (1995) *Constitution of the Republic of Malawi*. Zomba: Government Printer.

Republic of Malawi. (2012) Education Act of 2012.

Rubagumya, C.M., Afitska, O., Clegg, J. and Kiliku, P. (2011) A three-tier citizenship: Can the state in Tanzania guarantee linguistic human rights? *International Journal of Educational Development* 31, 78–85.

Simango, R. (2015) Learning English or learning in English: Some thoughts on the language question in the Malawian classroom. In L.M. Miti (ed.) *The Language of Instruction Question in Malawi* (pp. 41–60). Cape Town: Centre for Advanced Studies of African Society.

Skutnabb-Kangas, T. and Phillipson, R. (2001) Discrimination and minority languages. In R. Mesthrie (ed.) *Concise Encyclopedia of Sociolinguistics* (pp. 545–550). Amsterdam: Elsevier.

Stroud, C. (2001) African mother tongue programmes and the politics of language: Linguistic citizenship versus linguistic human rights. *Journal of Multilingual and Multicultural Development* 22 (4), 339–355.

Stroud, C. (2002) Language and democracy: The notion of linguistic citizenship and mother tongue programmes. In K. Legere and S. Fitchat (eds) *Talking Freedom: Language and Democratisation in the SADC Region* (pp. 77–94). Windhoek: Gamsberg Macmillan.

Stroud, C. (2003) Postmodernist perspectives on local languages: African mother-tongue education in times of globalisation. *International Journal of Bilingual Education and Bilingualism* 6 (1), 17–36.

Stroud, C. (2009) A postliberal critique of language rights: Toward a politics of language for linguistics contact. In J. Petrovic (ed.) *International Perspectives on Bilingual Education: Policy, Practice and Controversy* (pp. 191–218). New York: Information Age Publishing.

Stroud, C. and Heugh, K. (2004) Language rights and linguistic citizenship. In D. Patrick and J. Freeland (eds) *Language Rights and Language Survival: A Sociolinguistic Exploration* (pp. 191–218). Manchester: St Jerome.

Trudell, B. (2008) Practice in search of a paradigm: Language rights, linguistic citizenship and minority language communities in Senegal. *Current Issues in Language Planning* 9 (4), 395–410.

UNESCO (1953) *The Use of Vernacular Languages in Education*. Paris: UNESCO.

UNESCO (2003) *Education in a Multilingual World*. Paris: UNESCO.

Williams, E. (2006) *Bridges and Barriers: Language in African Education and Development*. Manchester: St Jerome Publishing.
Williams, Q.E. and Stroud, C. (2013) Multilingualism in transformative spaces: Contact and conviviality. *Language Policy* 12, 289–311.
World Bank. (2010) The Education System in Malawi: Working Paper 182. Washington, DC: World Bank.

Archival Materials Cited

CLACA letter to the Ministry of Education, 24 October 1996.
Minutes of CLACA meeting of 14 April 2000.

12 Making and Shaping Participatory Spaces: Resemiotization and Citizenship Agency in South Africa

Caroline Kerfoot

Centre for Research on Bilingualism, Stockholm University

> *We have spoken in all these languages, Tswana, Zulu, Afrikaans,*
> *English, but no one listens. Please will someone just listen*
> (Male community leader, service delivery protests, Northwest
> province
> South African radio news, SAfm, 17 November 2005)

> *For us, Black Economic Empowerment means the right to a life*
> *without hopelessness ... not the empowerment of an elite*
> (Zwelinzima Vavi, COSATU General Secretary, Workers' Day
> television interview
> South African Broadcasting Corporation, SABC 2, 1 May 2006)

These quotes encapsulate key challenges of democratic consolidation in present-day South Africa. Celebration of South Africa's progressive constitution and Bill of Rights has, after 18 years, given way to a more sober appraisal of the extent to which democracy has been able to redress severe social and economic disparities. Persistent structural inequalities, the uneven and unpredictable impacts of globalization, and a neoliberal macroeconomic policy have given rise to 'a lopsided structure – two nations disguised as one, a hybrid social formation consisting of increasingly deracialized insiders and persistently black outsiders' (Bundy, 1999: 11). For these outsiders, a disproportionate number of whom are women, political and civil rights have limited meaning unless socio-economic rights are made tangible (Liebenberg, 1999; McEwan, 2005; Tørres *et al.*, 2000).

In this chapter, I argue that the realization of socio-economic and other rights can be promoted through a rethinking of the public sphere (compare Fraser, 1991, 2007, 2010). Key to this reshaping of the public sphere is the recognition of a range of languages, language varieties, and modes of representation as legitimate for political participation. Such a perspective would take *voice* rather than *language* as the point of departure (Bailey, 2007; Stroud, 2009), reconstituting 'the grammar of justice' and enabling the subaltern to 'speak *in authoritative terms* (original emphasis)' (Fraser, 2008: 422). Promoting epistemic and linguistic authority in this way constitutes a form of 'linguistic citizenship' (Stroud, 2001, 2009, this volume; Stroud & Heugh, 2003), which can further the goals of equal participation and collective agency.

The primary point of contact for accessing citizenship rights is local government, which continues to be shackled by severe lack of capacity, centralized decision-making processes, inadequate funding, and high levels of corruption (Atkinson, 2007; Hemson *et al.*, 2008; Makgetla, 2007). However, this is only part of the equation: democratic consolidation involves not only building a new state, but also new interfaces between state and society (Beall *et al.*, 2005: 681). The delivery of services, such as cash grants or free water rations, that require relatively 'anonymous brief direct contact between state and citizen' has partly succeeded; however, efforts to build or transfer assets, such as land reform and housing, which require 'ongoing and substantial contact between public service providers and the citizenry' (Beall *et al.*, 2005: 697) have met with less success. Yet the creation or transfer of assets is an essential ingredient of a pro-poor growth policy: without them, poorer citizens are limited to small-scale strategies and extremely vulnerable to risk (Bruthiaux, 2002; May, 2000). For asset-building programmes to succeed, the 'demand side' of public service delivery, the civil society groupings that can engage the state, must be created or strengthened (Beall *et al.*, 2005).

Part of this challenge involves the development of the capabilities for participatory development and governance: the kind of skills required under the new dispensation are substantially different from those needed for pre-1994 mobilization and resistance. Effective participation in a democracy requires facilitation, advocacy, and management abilities: 'the mundane but critical practices of engaging accountable authorities' (Marais, 2001: 284) as well as familiarity with the norms of deliberation (Young, 1996). Thus, while many citizens strongly desire to participate in the development of their communities, they are not often sure how to go about it (McEwan, 2005), and are consequently unable to pressure the state to realize socio-economic rights.

Popular protests, the visibility of social movements, and rights-based court challenges have increased significantly in the last decade. Nevertheless, those protesting conditions of extreme deprivation have received little response. The right to speak and be heard in a language of one's choice may give those formerly excluded from power a 'voice' – daily newscasts are packed with live voice recordings of citizen speakers, such as the one quoted at the beginning of this chapter – yet as this speaker makes plain, voice is not enough. The problem is not lack of access to the languages and literacies of power, it is the lack of what Bakhtin (1986) calls a 'responsive understanding' from the state. Blommaert (2005: 72) has pointed out that the value, meaning, and function of utterances are a matter of 'uptake' and must be granted by the addressee.

The question, then, is how citizens living in poverty can engage the state and influence the wider decision-making processes that affect their lives. In South Africa, as in other nations undergoing revolutionary change, adult basic education and the provision of literacy was seen as one way of promoting participatory development, and of beginning to reverse some of the asymmetries of citizenship. Language and literacy were resources to be used in exercising citizenship rights, building livelihoods, and working towards social change. Nearly 20 years on, connections between these ideals and the nature of provision in the state adult learning centres remain tenuous. Moreover, persistent ideologies of languages as bounded and inextricably tied to monolithic and unchanging ethnic or cultural identities ensure that the regimented linguistic practices of apartheid education continue. Nevertheless, initiatives, such as the one discussed in this chapter, shed light on the potential of both formal and non-formal adult education for catalysing and supporting citizen involvement and for moving 'rights' from the symbolic to the material realm.

This chapter explores the practices of a group of adult educators working in impoverished communities and traces the ways in which they recontextualized a set of participatory development discourses acquired during a tertiary level education programme. I use the concept of resemiotization (Iedema 1999, 2001) to investigate the ways in which meaning-making unfolded in the different spaces they created and 'transmogrif[ied] as (part of larger) dynamic processes' (Iedema, 2003: 31). I analyse which meanings were mobilized through which modes and for what purposes and examine the purposeful shifts that participants made among languages, language varieties, or registers. Overlaying the two perspectives, mode and code, illuminates the specific ways in which multilingual discursive practices mediated participation and planning for citizenship action.

Researching Meaning-Making In and Across Participatory Spaces

My approach in investigating participants' practices is interdisciplinary: located at the intersection of development studies, sociolinguistic ethnography, and critical discourse analysis. (1) From the study of citizenship and governance within development studies, I take the notion of participatory spaces as neither neutral nor separable from other spaces of association whether domestic, spiritual, or occupational (Cornwall, 2002: 8). Such a perspective necessitates an awareness of flows of power across and within spaces and raises questions, such as who participates, on what basis, and with what resources. (2) From sociolinguistic ethnography, I take the concept 'regimes of language' (Kroskrity, 2000) which offers a lens on space as constitutive of patterns of multilingualism, which either encourage or discourage participation by particular groups or individuals (Blommaert et al., 2005). Studies of literacy as a social and political practice within the New Literacy Studies (Martin-Jones & Jones, 2000; Street 1993, 1995) similarly point to the potential for spaces to impose normative regimes of literacy in one or more languages. Studies within sociolinguistics and literacy studies have inevitably privileged verbal and written modes of communication. However, as Kress and Van Leeuwen (1996: 37) suggest, 'transcoding between a range of semiotic modes, represents [...] a better, a more adequate understanding of representation and communication'. The study of multimodality thus allows a broadening of the focus from verbal or written texts, to all modes of meaning-making and their interrelationships. (3) Finally, therefore, from the study of multimodality and its intersections with critical discourse analysis (CDA), I take the understanding that the language and other semiotic resources that people use at a local level inserts them into discursive patternings associated with wider social institutions (Fairclough, 1995, 2003; Maybin, 2000). Looking at multimodality from within CDA calls for attention not only to 'the multimodal nature of the semiotic construct itself' (Van Leeuwen, 2000, as cited in Iedema, 2003: 49), but also to its place in a sequence of discursive events and the ways in which meanings in this sequence mutually transform one another (Iedema, 2003). Such a perspective leads to a concern with how 'meaning-making shifts from context to context, from practice to practice, or from one stage of a practice to the next' defined by Iedema as *resemiotization* (Iedema, 2003: 41). He cites as an example

Mehan's (1993) study of the progressive institutional construction of a child as a 'special education' student: an initial interaction between teacher and child (talk) became a referral form (written text), which resulted in a battery of tests, the results of which (written formal report) were then discussed at a meeting (formal talk), the outcome of which was noted in a file. For Iedema (2003: 41), the study of resemiotization complements that of multimodality by illuminating the 'issues of concern to the meaning maker, e.g. the choice of material relations of meaning [and] the social dynamics that shape our multimodal meanings as they emerge'.

This more dynamic view of semiosis lends itself well to the study of participatory development contexts. There have, however, been few studies of resemiotization in such contexts. Kell (2006), for example, focuses on the movement of one text across contexts and the resultant 're-orderings of textualized meanings' (Silverstein & Urban, 1996, as cited in Blommaert, 2008: 12), but does not address the other forms of semiosis that accompanied these re-orderings. This chapter addresses the potential of different semiotic modes and codes to enable or constrain interaction in multilingual participatory spaces, and the material consequences of these interactions.

Background: The CACE Programme for Educators of Adults

Immediately after liberation in 1994, previously separated groups were called upon to work together in developing their communities. New policies in local government and social services opened the potential for participation in decision-making by previously excluded citizens. The negotiations and contestations involved in such processes required new contextual understandings, new ways of interacting and, in particular from the perspective of this study, the deployment of formerly unrecognized multilingual repertoires.

In the Northern Cape, the new provincial government saw Adult Basic Education as a crucial component of development and entered into a capacity-building partnership with the Centre for Adult and Continuing Education (CACE) at the University of the Western Cape, 1000 km away. As part of this partnership, a tertiary level Certificate for Educators of Adults was offered to members of previously disadvantaged communities. Its aims were to enable educators to plan and implement Adult Basic Education and Training (ABET) programmes with development potential and to act as agents of participatory development more broadly. The programme was run twice, part-time, between 1996–1999. Altogether 221 people took part, with a completion rate of 67%.

Participants reflected the multiracial, multilingual profile of the province: seven language groups were represented, including minority languages such as Nama. A total of 43.5% of participants were 'coloured' and 56.5% black African.[1] The majority had reasonable proficiency in English, which had been the language of communication for the liberation struggle, while proficiency in Afrikaans, which had formerly been the language of bureaucracy and state control, was greater among 'coloured' participants. Participants came from small, widely dispersed and predominantly rural towns and settlements. Most had completed their secondary schooling, while a few had only Grade 10 or 11. In the first intake a large percentage (57%) were unemployed, but this dropped to 14% in the second when many students were employed in the Public Adult Learning Centres. Other participants were employed in churches, resource centres, non-government organizations (NGOs), pre-primary centres, schools, parastatals (as trainers), local government, and development organizations. In the second intake, a small percentage (9%) held positions in state departments, such as Social Services, Health, and Correctional Services (Kerfoot *et al.*, 2001). Both sides of the civil society/state interface were thus represented.

Socio-economic indicators at the time showed this province to have the highest proportion of children living in income poverty in the country (63%) (Statistics South Africa, 2005), persistent disparities in income by race, gender, class, and location, and an unemployment rate for the poorest fifth of the population of 53% (May, 2000: 53).[2] Education that could assist citizens to realize socio-economic rights and access resources was thus a high priority. CACE staff sought to achieve this aim through a 'pedagogy of possibility' (Simon, 1987), which invited participants to become change agents in learning centres and in society.

This pedagogy, underpinned by humanistic and radical theories of adult learning, was carried through five modules: *Contextual Studies, Facilitating Adult Learning, Organising Skills, Research Methods, and ABET for Development*, which contained components on *Linking ABET to development* and *Mother Tongue Literacy*. A further component *Training Small Business Developers* was added in 1998 in an attempt to meet the need for sustainable livelihoods. Together, this set of modules inducted participants into the discourses of participatory development where discourses are understood in the sense defined by Gee (1996: 127) as socially and culturally formed, but historically changing 'saying (writing)-doing-being-valuing-believing combinations, [...] ways of being in the world [...] which integrate words, acts, values, attitudes, and social identities as well as gestures, glances, body positions, and clothes'. Such ways of being include 'distinctive ways of using various symbols, images, objects, artefacts, tools, technologies, times, places and spaces' (Gee, 2005: 308).

An earlier study (Kerfoot *et al.*, 2001) found that participants were able to recontextualize these discourses in a surprising range of contexts: overall 84% of the interview sample were involved in community projects, which they linked directly to the Certificate course. These projects spanned a wide range of rights-building initiatives on the state-society interface, from those concerned with social rights, such as access to housing, water and sanitation, health care, policing, and environmental protection, to economic rights, such as training for unemployed citizens, various social grants, and start-up funds for small businesses. Five participants went on to become local councillors as a result of their effectiveness on such projects. The high visibility of their work led the head of another international funding agency to remark: 'If any development has taken place in the province, it's because of those students' (W. Leumer, Institute for International Cooperation of the German Adult Education Association, personal communication, 14 November 2000).

The focus of this chapter is on the nature of the processes and practices that enabled this level of agency. The next section describes in detail two community-based workshops undertaken as part of a final assessment for the *Facilitating Adult Learning* module.

Creating Participatory Spaces

For their final assessment, programme participants were required to research an issue of importance to their local community, then plan and organize a workshop using the principles of adult learning acquired on the module. The purpose of the workshops was to engage community members in collective analysis of the structural causes of the problem and to formulate an action plan; in other words, to catalyse participatory citizenship. In this task, participants would have been able to draw on knowledge and skills gained in two other modules, for example, critical contextual analysis and 'organizing skills' that included drafting agendas, chairing meetings, negotiating, listening, and conflict resolution.

The accounts that follow are drawn from interviews with the lecturers who travelled thousands of miles from site to site to observe participants' workshops as well as from photographs. They also draw on participant reports and interviews with participants themselves and with others who attended the workshops or participated in later stages of the processes set in motion by these workshops (compare Kerfoot *et al.*, 2001). Fieldwork for the original study took place over six months from July 2000 to January

2001: while literacy and language practices were not the focus of the research, evidence of patterns of use was embedded in interviews recorded in three languages, in photographs, and in field notes. After an initial analysis of these sources of information, I re-interviewed two lecturers to probe their very vivid memories of these events and to request critical engagement with the accuracy and validity of the analyses presented here. I was not present at these workshops; I have met and personally interviewed only three of the six student participants who facilitated the workshops described. Here I follow Blommaert (2008: 13, original emphasis) in understanding ethnography as 'a *theoretical perspective* on human behaviour' and not simply a collection of methods and techniques. Such a position assumes, among other things, that human actions are always situated and that macro-structures can be explored through micro-details (Blommaert, 2008: 13).

In the original report, I made extensive use of participants' voices in an attempt to present a range of different, situated perspectives. These voices were presented as speaking for themselves. Yet as the team leader and the only person to have an overview of all the data collected, I had to weave these different voices into a coherent, linear text and to choose whose voices to include and how. In this way, I exercised 'archontic power': the power to create an archive and to decide what should be included in it and what not (Derrida, 1996, as cited in Blommaert, 2008: 86). Equally, with regard to the various accounts of workshops, I was in a position to see similarities and differences, identify emerging patterns, and in the process, decide what was significant and what not. As Blommaert (2008: 86) points out, such power runs the risk of creating a regime of Truth, especially in conditions of systemic inequality and linguistic difference where participants rely on researchers to represent their positions and practices to those with economic or political power. During the fieldwork stage, this risk was mitigated somewhat by report-back and analysis sessions with the multilingual, multiracial research team, and with different groups of participants. As a further means of reducing this danger, Blommaert (2008: 89, following Fabian, 1974; Bourdieu, 1990) suggests that researchers make their interpretive procedures explicit and show their subjectivity in these procedures. This I have attempted to do.

Sites for workshops ranged from tiny isolated settlements with largely homogeneous profiles to crowded townships in the regional capital where several languages or language varieties were represented. The examples chosen below reflect different ends of the spectrum within this range of contexts.

Mediating Generational Cultures

The first workshop was organized by a female participant in her thirties working in Steinkopf, an isolated rural village in an arid, sparsely populated area that contains one of the last remaining Nama-speaking communities. Nama is spoken by about 6000 people and is part of the Khoekhoe linguistic tradition that used to stretch from the Cape to Namibia (Crawhall, 1997, as cited in Traill, 2002: 28). The settlement itself was home to a Rhenisch mission station founded in 1818, which converted most of the Nama to Christianity. Most community members today are bilingual in Nama and Afrikaans. However, compulsory school education in Afrikaans may have led to a shift in loyalty among the youth towards this language (Traill, 2002: 28). There are few opportunities for income generation other than communal stock farming and few material resources, correspondingly little political voice, but strong social networks, particularly religious ones.

After a period of research or 'listening' (Freire, 1970) in this settlement, the CACE student/facilitator identified the issue of alcohol abuse as one that community members felt deeply about. For the workshop, she drew together a range of community members and high school students. Her aim was to engage the youth, but also to 'bridge in' existing capacity in the community. She also invited her mother, an octogenarian with extensive counselling experience, from a church-based organization.

On the day of the workshop, as participants entered the school hall, they stepped through a tableau staged by the CACE facilitator: a scene of chaos, broken glass bottles, clothing, smashed furniture, and other objects strewn around the entrance. Thereafter they watched a series of role plays depicting different experiences of the consequences of alcohol abuse. They then worked in small groups to define these problems in greater detail and analyse some of the social causes. These ideas were reported back to the whole group, supported by mindmaps drawn on newsprint. Before participants broke into groups once more to plan for action, the input of the elderly counsellor was sought – she spoke from a religious perspective about the power of love as the only way to bring about change in those who abuse alcohol. Participants then moved into groups again to brainstorm strategies for action: bulleted points on newsprint sheets mapped out what could be done, with plans ranging from support groups to meetings with the Departments of Health, Social Services and Labour in order to leverage social grants, small business grants, and training of various kinds. For the lecturer/observer, at the end of the workshop there was a strong sense of social cohesion and possibility. The workshop could thus be seen as the beginning of a problem-posing process or popular education cycle that moved from 'codifying' (Freire, 1970) or defining the problem, to relating it to participants' own experiences, to analysing the deeper structural causes, and finally discussing alternatives for action and planning the way forward, with specialist input or information where necessary. The process continued outside this space, with the facilitator's reflective report to CACE and with further steps taken to implement some of the solutions proposed.

I now turn to an analysis of the array of semiotic resources through which this process was realized. Here I have used Kress and Van Leeuwen's (2001: 4) four strata or domains of practice in which meaning-making takes place: discourse, design, production, distribution. Designing an act of meaning-making involves simultaneously '(1) a formulation of a discourse or combination of discourses, (2) a particular (inter)action, in which the discourse is embedded, and (3) a particular way of combining semiotic **modes**' (Kress & Van Leeuwen, 2001: 21, original emphasis). This design is then produced in one or more material forms, which in turn add meaning to the design. The design of the workshop as detailed in Table 12.1 embeds a series of (inter)actions within the discourses of participatory development, using various combinations of semiotic modes realized in a range of media.

Table 12.1 Designing participation

Stage of problem-posing practice	(Inter)actions	Semiotic modes	Production
Code or trigger to represent an issue in participants' experience	Tableau [display]	Spatial, visual	Objects and the relations between them
Compare with own experiences	Role-plays/drama	Speech, gesture	Voice (tone, language variety), gesture, movement
Analyse deeper causes	Group discussion	Speech, writing, spatial	Voice Mindmaps on newsprint
Get input	Speaker	Speech, gesture	Voice, gesture
Plan for action	Group discussion then plenary	Speech, writing, spatial	Voice Bulleted points on newsprint

Resemiotizing moves

Meaning-making processes were driven by the sequential logic of the popular education cycle: codifying experiences, dialogue, critical analysis, planning for collective action (and later, reflection on this action) detailed. Successive layers of meaning were created from the tableau to the final set of bulleted points, deepening understanding of the causes, consequences, and possible means of addressing alcoholism in this context. This conceptual logic was realized through the shift in semiotic modes that accompanied each stage of the cycle.

In the first phase, participants were drawn into the heart of the tableau by walking through it but were still observers/interpreters; in the role-play phase some were performers and others emotionally engaged spectators; in the third phase, through the use of group discussions, all became responsible for critical analysis; in the input phase they were listeners; in the final planning stage, participants took collective responsibility for decision-making. Each 'resemiotizing move' (Iedema, 2003: 43) thus brought about a progressive shifting of responsibility for analytical work and decision-making towards the participants, signalling a shift in 'footing' (Goffman, 1975, 1981) when roles and expectations were redefined and communicative organization re-ordered.

These shifts in roles and responsibilities were realized by forms of organization and semiotic events that de-emphasized the facilitator, made connections with participants' experiences, and engaged their emotions and analytical abilities. A closer look at the articulation of modes used at each stage illuminates a tension between what Kress (2003: 45) terms 'time-based modes', such as speech, dance, gesture, action, or music, and 'space-based modes', such as image, sculpture, and 3D forms like layout or architectural models. As Kress points out, the logics of the two types of modes differ: the logic of space 'leads to spatial distribution of simultaneously present significant elements; both the elements and their relations are resources for meaning' while in the logic of time 'the elements and their place in a sequence constitute a resource for meaning' (Kress, 2003: 45). Some modes are mixed in that they 'participate in both logics: gesture is in the logic of space and time, writing to some extent also has begun to make use of spatial resources e.g. indents, bullet points' (Kress, 2003: 46).

What stands out when analysing the different stages of the workshop from this perspective is the predominance of space-based and mixed logics. The initial tableau fell almost entirely within the spatial realm: meanings were created by objects and their inter-relationships, but also to some extent narratively as each person made his/her way through the 'landscape': physical movement through the space decreased the traditional distance between image and onlooker. At two other key moments, analysis and planning, there was time-based discussion and noting of points, but this was balanced by the use of newsprint and thick marker pens to afford more spatial representations of ideas. At the moments of greatest analytical depth, therefore, the lack of hierarchy implicit in mind-maps and bullets constructed participants as equals capable of collectively addressing social issues. The use of spatial logics in writing changed both the 'force' and the 'feel' of the text (Kress, 2003: 16), crystallizing key moments of synthesis while representing in material form the restructured roles and relationships of the facilitator and the other participants. At the same time, it provided a durable, accessible, and legitimate record of discussions and decisions for future engagement with the state.

Recoding moves

A second dimension of meaning-making was its encoding in one or more registers. The elderly counsellor spoke 'high' Afrikaans, a very formal register associated with the 'church' Afrikaans of the former mission settlement, while the youth and other participants used a more colloquial register (possibly the local Orange River Afrikaans variety).[3] This intergenerational gap was mediated by the facilitator who restated whatever the elderly counsellor said in this latter register. The bulleted points from the group discussions were written in colloquial Afrikaans.

These recoding moves functioned in the same way as the resemiotizations: to promote inter-group dialogue and to reshape existing distinctions between formal and informal speech along with the power relations bound up in them. In this way, these moves helped to bridge divisions of generation, socio-economic status, educational background, and linguistic repertoire, and to overcome entrenched obstacles to fair engagement.

This ability to recode meanings to promote participation became increasingly important in more multilingual sites where participants spoke a wide variety of languages and language varieties.

Mediating Participation in More Multilingual Spaces

Workshops in other sites followed the same broad format while adjusting topic and content to local contexts. The second example discussed is a workshop held by three young men in the township of Galeshewe in Kimberley, the provincial capital. All three spoke Xhosa, Tswana, Afrikaans, and English. Participants in the workshop were Xhosa or

Tswana-speaking, each group able to understand the other language to some extent as well as Afrikaans, which serves as a lingua franca in Kimberley.

The topic chosen for the workshop was health and hygiene. It is estimated that nearly 100,000 children under five years of age die each year in South Africa with a combination of diarrhoea, malnutrition, and respiratory tract infections accounting for 20.3% of these (Solarsh & Goga, 2004). Galeshewe is one of the oldest 'black' townships in South Africa, established in the 1870s for workers on the diamond mines. In 2000 many residents were without running water in their homes and still used the bucket system for sanitation. The aim of the workshop was thus to raise awareness about the causes of diarrhoea in young children and to strategize interventions.

Participants were invited by word of mouth through community meetings and church groups. As in the Steinkopf workshop, they were a mix of unemployed youth and older community members with varying levels of formal schooling. Each of the three facilitators was responsible for a section of the workshop.

After introducing the CACE lecturer, whose first language was Xhosa, in English, there was a prayer in Xhosa and in Tswana followed by an icebreaker (singing, again in both languages). The topic of the workshop was introduced in Xhosa by the first CACE student facilitator who then asked in Tswana if everyone could understand him. Tswana-speaking participants said they could and told him to go ahead. He then presented a series of pictures, for example, on food and flies, as a trigger for discussion. Interestingly, these pictures had captions in English. The facilitator gave a verbal explanation of the pictures in Afrikaans, as a language common to all and one, which had been a medium of instruction for those who attended high school – concepts would be more familiar in this language than in another used more for communicative purposes. Participants then broke into small groups to discuss the causes of diarrhoea and what to do. Groups were organized by language, both because it was felt that it would take a long time to do translations in the groups and that participants needed to be speaking their own language 'if you want their real, real views' (CACE lecturer, F., Xhosa speaking, 13 October 2008). Points were written on newsprint in the language of the discussion, often by the younger participants. The newsprints were brought back to a plenary session and read through by the facilitator who at the same time translated them into English. The CACE lecturer present notes that this was for her benefit as the natural language to use at this point would have been Afrikaans as a lingua franca, but her Afrikaans was not strong. Plans for

Table 12.2 Designing participation in multilingual spaces

Stage of problem-posing practice	(Inter)actions	Semiotic modes	Production	Language
Ice-breaker	Introduce observer Prayer Song	Speech Speech Music, song	Voice Voice	English Xhosa, Tswana Xhosa, Tswana
Introduction of topic		Speech	Voice	Xhosa with check for understanding by Tswana speakers
Code or trigger	Images with verbal explanations	Spatial, visual + speech	Objects and the relations between them Voice	Afrikaans
Analyse deeper causes and plan for action	Group discussion	Speech, writing, spatial	Voice Bulleted points on newsprint	Language-based groups: Xhosa, Tswana
Reportback	Plenary	Speech, writing, spatial	Voice Bulleted points on newsprint	Xhosa, Tswana with translation into English

the way forward ranged from raising awareness about the importance of hand washing, to engaging with local government over infrastructure development for sanitation (Table 12.2).[4]

Resemiotizing and Recoding Moves

The use of participants' first language was encouraged in those stages of the workshop that required critical analysis, in order to promote deep engagement and unconstrained involvement. Drawing people together was done through common languages: a different one at different stages. The Xhosa-speaking observer was introduced in English as a courtesy to her as she might not have understood Tswana or Afrikaans; the topic was introduced in Xhosa with a check that Tswana speakers could follow. This had the effect of deformalizing proceedings and altering perceptions of roles and status relations. The choice of Afrikaans for the subsequent description and explanation of the picture 'codes' could be seen as emphasizing participants' common experience of such health concerns. In the reportback stage after the group discussions, ideas were reported using English rather than the more natural Afrikaans translations as explained above. Nevertheless, this was a common language, used in this synthesizing stage in order to promote unity and gain consensus on the way forward.

The resemiotizing logics used here were thus similar to that of the Steinkopf workshop discussed above with non-hierarchical communicative organization mirrored in semiotic materialization. These materializations were however entwined with shifts in and among languages, language varieties, or registers for the purposes of mutual understanding and inclusion. These multiple shifts served to legitimize speakers – to reorganize and restructure the linguistic hierarchies historically associated with public forums and to constitute all participants as equals.

There are a number of ways in which one could take issue with these workshops in relation to power and representation: it is possible that lack of experience in running such workshops meant that facilitators did not engage sufficiently with local inequalities and networks of power relations, particularly in relation to gender. Power remnants from other sites surfaced linguistically, for example, in the use of 'very heavy Setswana or deep Xhosa' (CACE lecturer, 13 October 2008) for the purposes of excluding other language groups at certain times, such as when very sensitive points were raised. They also surfaced semiotically, for example, in the fact that some participants preferred not to write up their ideas on the newsprint but to hand them to the facilitator on tiny scraps of paper. This latter strategy may have resulted from participants' lack of confidence in their ideas and/or their literacy skills. Time pressures prevented such issues from being worked through at that point. Yet observers at both workshops came away with a strong sense of possibility.

Constructing Spaces: Creating Linguistic and Epistemic Authority

This chapter so far has offered an account of resemiotization in new participatory spaces. In both the Steinkopf and Kimberley workshops outlined above, the creation of these spaces was enabled by the discourses of participatory development that participants carried with them from the CACE programme. These discourses were given mobility and legitimacy by broader social and political processes (see Kerfoot, 2008). However, it was participants' ability to recontextualize these discourses in different sites and shape them to different interactants and local conditions that was a major factor in their success.

In each of the two detailed studies above, meaning-making processes were driven by a social action imperative: the choice of modes and languages in each stage was driven by the desire to construct participants as valued, equal, and active citizens. As Kress has argued, 'representation is always "engaged", it is never neutral: that which is represented in the sign, or sign complex, realizes the interests, the perspectives, the position and values, of those who make signs' (Kress, 2003: 44). The need to configure power relations within each space, to re-order expected patterns of communicative organization and redefine roles, led to the choice of sign complexes that legitimized language varieties, re-organized language hierarchies, and de-emphasized written text as the semiotics of power. Where written text was used, its material form and shape indexed commonality, inclusion, and joint decision-making as opposed to silence and exclusion, and thus helped to avoid the 'ideological and technical constraints that characterize schooled, normative literacy' (Blommaert, 2008: 9). At the same time, it created an accessible but durable 'official' record of decisions or demands that could be used as the basis for engagement with the state.

Where successful, this ability to choose combinations of languages and other semiotic modes – to resemiotize meanings in different moments of a practice – could be said to have succeeded in validating what Chandoke (2003: 186) calls the 'linguistic and epistemic authority' of subaltern actors and in mobilizing collective agency.

The process was not always successful, however. Where less successful, it appeared that facilitators were unable to suppress or reconfigure the traces of social relations and counter-discourses from other sites; as Cornwall and Coelho (2007: xv) point out, initiatives that are designed as potential 'spaces for change' may 'interact with different histories, cultures and forms of power to produce radically different outcomes across various settings'. The more stratified the participant profile, it would seem, the more necessary the 'third language' of participatory discourses that eases and deformalizes the use of language (CACE lecturer, 22 May 2008) and brings into play a range of other modes of semiosis. The potential of these other modes to open up different modalities of human experience (Iedema, 2003) appears to help change pre-existing ways of relating within and across groups.

As described above in each of these case studies, a similar set of interconnected practices or intersemiotic shifts emerges. These shifts were not always realized in the same mode or in the same language variety, or brought about in the same order, but are nevertheless recognizable and distinct. This set of practices was broadly representative of those of many other participants interviewed or observed. As such, they could be seen as an emerging reconfiguration of the 'genres of governance', those which figure in 'governing the way things are done' (Fairclough, 2003: 32). As

Fairclough argues, changes in genre chains can be significant indicators of social change. This particular genre chain can be seen as emerging alongside the processes of democratization throughout the country, which created a need for 'less prescriptive and systematic semiotic principles' (Kress & Van Leeuwen, 2001: 10). It began in a small way to create new social rules and the confidence to begin a process of engaging with the state.

Towards Linguistic Citizenship

The acquisition of the discourses of participatory development on the Certificate course enabled facilitators to enter new spaces with 'pretextually marked resources and capabilities' (Blommaert, 2005: 77). Their ability to insert these discourses into new spaces in different modes and languages can be seen as enacting a form of 'linguistic citizenship' (Stroud, 2001), which includes the use of informal multilingual networks to link 'linguistic practices to resource distribution of a [...] material and economic kind' (Stroud & Heugh, 2003: 10).

The dynamic mixes in which facilitators chose to encode their meanings served to draw out and legitimate previously silenced voices and to include in decision-making those without access to 'normative' literacy practices. In particular, the incorporation of modes characterized by non-hierarchical spatial logics helped to validate workshop participants as active and analytical citizens. Here, for example, the layout of textual forms, such as mindmaps and bulleted points, functioned to change both social arrangements and knowledge structures, altering the channels along which ideas flowed. Heightened awareness of language and new ways of interacting that involve the moment-by-moment negotiation of language have long been recognized as a feature of contexts of socio-political change (Heller, 1982: 109). This study illustrates how this awareness can also be extended to other forms of semiosis. What is important about these insights is what they reveal about the nature of literacy and language within processes of participatory development and governance: most significantly, that they are one of many semiotic resources on which people can draw and that written or spoken 'texts' may be produced in two or more language varieties within the same discourse 'event'.

The challenge for those concerned with creating spaces for participatory citizenship and development is to investigate how particular literacies, languages, and other semiotic and technological resources might be used productively to shape agency within local and wider structures of power. Resemiotization as a conceptual tool allows an analysis of this kind of 'semiotic mobility' (Blommaert, 2005), in which participants become the transformers of the representational resources available to them, in this case, with the purpose of engaging in participatory citizenship.

Conclusion

In studying processes of resemiotization in this chapter, I have thus attempted to illuminate a series of local semiotic practices forged in relation to larger social dynamics of rapid democratization, new formations of discourse, and an economy in transition. My purpose in addressing readers who have an interest in participatory development and governance has been to show how research on participatory spaces can be deepened through detailed analyses of sociolinguistic and semiotic complexity. Through a focus on the 'social unfolding of the processes and logics of representing' (Iedema, 2003: 50), I attempt to show the potential of different configurations of modes and codes to enable participation in multilingual contexts. My purpose in addressing readers interested in literacy and multilingualism has been to draw attention to the need to consider the full range of semiotic resources in play in any particular context and the dynamics that govern their material forms. This in turn has made possible a richer picture of the ways in which meanings were transformed linguistically and materially from one stage of a practice to the next. It has also highlighted the written, visual, and other forms that succeeded in mediating engagement in deliberation and action planning. My purpose in addressing readers interested in discourse analysis has been, following Iedema (2003: 50), to displace 'analytical attention from discourse as structured meaning towards practice as material affordance'. In this way, an analytical shift from the multimodal complexity of the interactions themselves to the facilitators' choices of material realizations has illuminated some of the dynamics in the construction of new spaces of possibility. These three perspectives together have enabled an analysis of how, why, and which meanings become recontextualized (Bernstein, 1990) and the tracing of new paths of meaning-making in this rapidly transforming context.

As argued at the beginning of this chapter, nurturing voice and capabilities is not enough to ensure transformation in the absence of resources and structural change. Heller (2001: 158) has argued that what is required for sustained transformative projects is an 'ecology of agents', which blends 'the institutional capacities of the state and the associational resources of civil society'. Writing in 2001, he claimed that South Africa had a relatively high degree of central state capacity, a fairly well-developed civil society and an organized political force, 'specifically non-Leninist left-of-centre political parties that have strong social movement characteristics' (Heller, 2001: 138–139). As such, he maintained that it was one of the few countries of the South well-placed to expand democratic spaces and promote democratic governance. Developments since 2001 have shown the fragility of such spaces, reminded us of the hegemonizing potential of even liberatory discourses, and highlighted the need for substantial capacity-building at local and regional government levels.

Expanding citizen participation in public decision-making means both incorporating previously marginalized groups into public politics and bringing a wider range of socio-economic issues into the domain of politics (Heller, 2001; Hickey & Mohan, 2004). As indicated in this chapter, it also means breaking down the formal/informal political divide and adding complexity to the range of languages, language varieties, and modes of representation considered legitimate for political participation. As Stroud (2009: 204) has pointed out, later versions of deliberative democracy have stressed the need to de-emphasize a sovereign and privileged Habermasian public sphere in favour of 'multiple, hierarchically layered, and contested public spheres'. The processes of participatory citizenship presented in this chapter and the altered social arrangements and knowledge structures constructed through them offer one example of such a reconfigured public sphere: they illustrate one route to developing new languages of engagement with state power, legitimating new norms of deliberation, and enabling the subaltern to speak in authoritative terms (Fraser, 2008).

Promoting this form of linguistic citizenship appears to have a greater chance of catalysing and supporting locally rooted participatory development, promoting access to socio-economic rights and holding government to account. Whether any of these outcomes materialize, however, depends on complex combinations of factors, which are little understood (Houtzager & Moore, 2003). This chapter has offered an account of why a particular set of semiotics were mobilized to do certain things at certain times: to construct spaces in which power relations were reconfigured, language hierarchies re-organized, and political identities asserted and legitimized. It has shown the potential of such spaces to provide opportunities for citizenship agency and avenues for strengthening the 'demand side' for participatory governance.

Retrospective: From a Politics of Anticipation to a Politics of Impatience, May 2016

The year 2015 brought with it a spectacular rise in service delivery protests, from an average of 1058 a year during the period 2009 to 2012[5], to a staggering 14,740 in 2014, of which 12,451 were peaceful and 2289 turned violent (*The Citizen*, 2015). These protests by the poorest of the poor in small towns and informal urban settlements were quickly over-shadowed by the student-led movement #RhodesMustFall, which had at its core the decolonization of the mind (Ngugi, 1986), of knowledge, and of the academy. This explosion of intellectual discontent was closely fol-lowed by #FeesMustFall, triggered by a 10% rise in student fees. Both drew attention to a lack of transformation: in epistemic traditions and in economic restructuring.

Mbembe (2015) recognizes a Fanonian element in this moment, that is, the rise of a predatory new black elite, progressive institutional col-lapse, a de-moralizing economy (Ferguson, 2006), and a new generation of 'born-frees' impatient to gain the rights and resources that have thus far proved elusive and which seem to be slipping ever further from their reach. This 'politics of impatience' brings with it a re-interrogation of the extent of decolonization and restorative justice, yet, as in Fanon's time, sees no contradiction in excluding, often violently, Africans from the rest of the continent.

At the same time, Mbembe points out that South Africa is unlike other postcolonies in that even the black middle class feels that not enough meaningful change has taken place to secure its future, that an over-whelming percentage of the economy remains in white hands[6] and at the same time that the economy is strong enough to transform living condi-tions for the majority of citizens if directed appropriately.

It is nevertheless significant that the student protests began in elite, formerly white universities attended by largely middle-class black students and only later spread to historically black universities attended by the far larger proportion of working class students. The initial classed and urban nature of these movements can be attributed in part to the more visible persistence of white privilege, manifested in staffing, curriculum, and eco-nomic disparities among students.

Notable in all the student protests was the lack of any language but English on posters and in (reported) speeches, thus indicating a savvy eye to the international media or superaddressee (Bakhtin, 1986: 126) – an appeal to 'an invisible third party, the court of social justice, or simple humanity', which presumably would bring greater pressure on the state to respond, as had the prominence of spectacle, 'highly dramatic and highly performative' (Ndebele, 1986: 143), under apartheid. Spectacle then was a necessary public representation of defiance and hope for change, which however, masked myriad small deliberative engagements taking place in factories, farms, homes, and organizational spaces. Since 1994, a signifi-cant decline in non-governmental and community-based organizations, along with a progressive weakening of trade unions, suggests a narrowing of deliberative spaces open to those who as yet have 'no part in anything' (Rancière, 2004), leaving public protest as the only viable option in the face of a continued lack of responsive engagement from the state. These protests still act within a frame of 'common sense', of existing relations; they do not constitute a dispute over 'the frame within which we see something as given' (Rancière, 2010: 69), but rather a hardening of the frame as a basis for action and counter-action.

While local government aspires in principle to a policy of Integrated Development Planning, which involves the municipality and citizens working together to achieve sustainable long-term development (Ministry for Provincial Affairs and Constitutional Development, 1998), the implementation of the policy has been sporadic at best (Marais, 2011). Moreover, when consultation has taken place, this has been within rigid and conservative processes that tend to reduce citizens to the status of objects and seldom challenge the status, often perpetuating gender, class, ethnicity, and other lines of exclusion (Everatt *et al.*, 2010; Sithole *et al.*, 2007).

As Marais (2011: 394) argues, the 'dented legitimacy' of the state, especially at local level, calls for attention to features that distinguish successful democratic variants of the developmental state in the South (Kerala, India and Porto Alegre, Brazil). These features include a strong emphasis on inclusiveness and accountability, 'institutional arrangements to enable widespread public participation', and initiatives to build capacity for both citizens and state officials. As such, the workshops described in the chapter still offer a vision of the possibilities for emancipatory change in local processes: for overcoming some of the obstacles to fair engagement and reshaping social arrangements.

However, before such processes can bear fruit, it is clear that what is needed is a series of social seismologies (Ross, 1991) such as those of 2015 to dislodge the myth of participatory parity and reconstitute the 'grammar of justice' (Fraser, 2008). A transformative politics needs to hold in tension the necessity of new and as yet unauthorized modes of disagreement and disorder, an ethics of fair engagement, and the need for alternate ways of knowing and being: a 'becoming-with-others', which extends beyond race, ethnicity, gender, class, or nation (Mbembe, 2015; Ngugi, 1986). The politics of language are a constitutive part of this aspiration: enlarging the knowledges, practices and agents considered essential to a deepened democracy requires both a recognition and an investigation of the languages, language varieties, and modes of representation that are drawn upon in processes of planning, deliberation, and mobilization, largely out of the public eye where English holds sway. Such practices of linguistic citizenship can illuminate both the obstacles and the potentials of linguistic diversity in reframing the conditions of possibility.

Acknowledgements

This work was supported by Grant No. 62314 of the National Research Foundation of South Africa and by the UK Department of International Development in Southern Africa, DFIDSA. An earlier version of this chapter was published in the *International Multilingualism Research Journal* (2011), 5 (2), 87–102, and is reworked here with permission. I would like to thank Christopher Stroud, Lucy Alexander, Elsa Auerbach, Zannie Bock, and Nomvuyo Dayile for insightful comments on an earlier draft.

Notes

(1) In South Africa the terms 'black', 'African' and 'coloured' are used variously and never without contestation. For statistical purposes, the present government retains the former apartheid 'race' categories in order to be able to assess development needs and implement policies designed to ensure redress and equity.

(2) More recent figures indicate that these challenges have worsened over the past decade (Statistics South Africa/United Nations Development Programme, 2010; University of Cape Town Children's Institute/UNICEF, 2010).

(3) Despite some evidence of a recent emergence of pride in Nama identity (anthropologist E. Boonzaier, as cited in Traill, 2002: 34), the language used in the workshop was Afrikaans.

(4) This later became an anchor project in the Galeshewe Urban Renewal programme (address by Deputy Minister Botha at the opening of this programme, 2 February 2002).

(5) Minister of Police, 19 March 2012, cited in Alexander (2012).

(6) A study by the Johannesburg stock exchange in October 2011 suggests that about 83% of the country's listed shares are owned by white South Africans and foreign investors (Ntingi & Gqubule, 2012). In 2012 land ownership was as follows: 67% largely white commercial agricultural land, 15% mostly state-owned black communal areas, 10% other state land, 8% other, including urban areas (Walker & Dubb, 2014).

References

Alexander, P. (2012) A massive rebellion of the poor. *Mail & Guardian*, 13 April 2012. See http://mg.co.za/article/2012-04-13-a-massive-rebellion-of-the-poor (accessed 14 April 2012).

Atkinson, D. (2007) Taking to the streets: Has developmental local government failed in South Africa? In S. Buhlungu, J. Daniel, R. Southall and J. Lutchman (eds) *State of the Nation: South Africa 2007* (pp. 53–77). Cape Town: HSRC Press.

Bailey, B. (2007) Heteroglossia and boundaries. In M. Heller (ed.) *Bilingualism: A Social Approach* (pp. 257–276). London & New York: Palgrave Macmillan.

Bakhtin, M.M. (1986) *Speech Genres and Other Late Essays* (V.W. McGee, Trans.). Austin: University of Texas Press.

Beall, J., Gelb, S. and Hassim, S. (2005) Fragile stability: State and society in democratic South Africa. *Journal of Southern African Studies* 31 (4), 681–700.

Bernstein, B. (1990) *The Structuring of Pedagogic Discourse: Class, Codes and Control, Vol. IV.* London: Routledge.

Blommaert, J. (2005) *Discourse: A Critical Introduction.* Cambridge: Cambridge University Press.

Blommaert, J. (2008) *Grassroots Literacy: Writing, Identity and Voice in Central Africa.* London: Routledge.

Blommaert J., Collins, J. and Slembrouck, S. (2005) Spaces of multilingualism. *Language and Communication* 25, 197–216.

Bourdieu, P. (1990) *The Logic of Practice.* Cambridge: Polity.

Bruthiaux, P. (2002) Hold your courses: Language education, language choice, and economic development. *TESOL Quarterly* 36 (3), 275–297.

Bundy, C. (1999) Truth or reconciliation. *Southern Africa Report.* Toronto: Toronto Committee for Links between Southern Africa and Canada (TCLSAC), August 1999.

Chandoke, N. (2003) *The Conceits of Civil Society.* Delhi/Oxford: Oxford University Press.

Cornwall, A. (2002) Making spaces, changing places: Situating participation in development. IDS Working Paper 170. Brighton: Institute for Development Studies.

Cornwall, A. and Coelho, V.S.P. (2007) Spaces for change? The politics of participation in new democratic arenas. In A. Cornwall and V.S.P. Coelho (eds) *Spaces for Change? The Politics of Citizen Participation in New Democratic Arenas* (pp. 1–29). London: Zed Books.

Everatt, D., Marais, H. and Dube, N. (2010) Participation … for what purpose? Analysing the depth and quality of public participation in the Integrated Development Planning process in Gauteng. *Politikon* 37 (2–3), 223–249.

Fabian, J. (1974/1991) Genres in an emerging tradition. Chapter 3. In *Time and the Work of Anthropology.* Chur: Harwood.

Fairclough, N. (1995) *Critical Discourse Analysis.* London: Longman.

Fairclough, N. (2003) *Analysing Discourse: Textual Analysis for Social Research.* London: Routledge.

Ferguson, J. (2006) *Global Shadows: Africa in the Neoliberal World Order.* Durham/London: Duke University Press.

Fraser, N. (1991) Rethinking the public sphere: A contribution to the critique of actually existing democracy. In C. Calhoun (ed.) *Habermas and the Public Sphere* (pp. 109–142). Cambridge, MA: MIT Press.

Fraser, N. (2007) Transnationalizing the Public Sphere on the legitimacy and efficacy of public opinion in a post-Westphalian world. *Theory, Culture & Society* 24 (4), 7–30.

Fraser, N. (2008) Abnormal justice. *Critical Inquiry* 34 (3), 393–422.

Fraser, N. (2010) *Scales of Justice: Reimagining Political Space in a Globalizing World.* New York: Columbia University Press.

Freire, P. (1970) *Pedagogy of the Oppressed.* New York: Continuum.

Gee, J. (1996) *Social Linguistics and Literacies: Ideology in Discourses.* London: Taylor Francis.

Gee, J. (2005) Critical Discourse Analysis. In R. Beach, J. Green, M. Kamil and T. Skanahan (eds) *Multidisciplinary Perspectives on Literacy Research* (2nd edn) (pp. 293–318). Cresskill, NJ: Hampton Press.

Goffman, E. (1975) *Frame Analysis*. New York: Harper and Row.

Goffman, E. (1981) *Forms of Talk*. Philadelphia: University of Pennsylvania Press.

Heller, M. (1982) Negotiations of language choice in Montreal. In J. Gumperz (ed.) *Language and Social Identity* (pp. 108–118). Cambridge: Cambridge University Press.

Heller, P. (2001) Moving the State: The politics of democratic decentralization in Kerala, South Africa, and Porto Alegre. *Politics and Society* 29 (1), 1–28.

Hemson, D., Carter, J. and Karuri-Sebina, G. (2008) Service delivery as a measure of change: State capacity and development. In P. Kagwanja and K. Kondlo (eds) *State of the Nation: South Africa 2008* (pp. 151–177). Cape Town: HSRC Press.

Hickey, S. and Mohan, G. (eds) (2004) *Participation – from Tyranny to Transformation? Exploring New Approaches to Participation in Development*. London: Zed Books.

Houtzager, P. and Moore, M. (eds) (2003) *Changing Paths: International Development and the New Politics of Inclusion*. Ann Arbor: Michigan University Press.

Iedema, R. (1999) The formalization of meaning. *Discourse and Society* 10 (1), 49–65.

Iedema, R. (2001) Resemiotization. *Semiotica* 137 (1/4), 23–39.

Iedema, R. (2003) Multimodality, resemiotization: Extending the analysis of discourse as multi-semiotic practice. *Visual Communication* 2 (1), 29–57.

Kell, C. (2006) Crossing the margins: Literacy, semiotics and the recontextualization of meanings. In K. Pahl and J. Rowsell (eds) *Travel Notes from the New Literacy Studies: Instances of Practice* (pp. 147–169). Clevedon: Multilingual Matters.

Kerfoot, C. (2008) Transforming identities and enacting agency: The discourses of participatory development in training South African adult educators. *Journal of Education* 45, 95–128.

Kerfoot, C., Geidt, J., Alexander, L., Cornelius, R., Egan, J., Jack, X., Hendricks, N., Marais, A., Matholengwe, T., Mjekula, B., Qutsu, P., Rabie, J. and Steyn, A. (2001) *ABET and Development in the Northern Cape Province: Assessing Impacts of CACE Courses (1996–1999)*. Bellville, South Africa: DFIDSA (UK Department for International Development in Southern Africa) and the Centre for Adult and Continuing Education (CACE), University of the Western Cape, ED 473176.

Kress, G. (2003) *Literacy in the New Media Age*. London: Routledge.

Kress, G. and Van Leeuwen, T. (1996) *Reading Images: The Grammar of Visual Design*. London: Routledge.

Kress, G. and Van Leeuwen, T. (2001) *Multimodal Discourse: The Modes and Media of Contemporary Communication*. London: Arnold.

Kroskrity, V. (2000) Regimenting languages: Language ideological perspectives. In V. Kroskrity (ed.) *Regimes of Language: Ideologies, Polities, and Identities* (pp. 1–34). Santa Fe, New Mexico: School of American Research Press.

Liebenberg, S. (1999) Social citizenship – a precondition for meaningful democracy. *Agenda* 24, 27–36.

Makgetla, N. (2007) Local government budgets and development: A tale of two towns. In S. Buhlungu, J. Daniel, R. Southall and J. Lutchman (eds) *State of the Nation: South Africa 2007* (pp. 146–167). HSRC Press, Cape Town.

Marais, H. (2001) *South Africa Limits to Change: The Political Economy of Transition*. Cape Town: UCT Press and London: Zed Books.

Marais, H. (2011) *South Africa Pushed to the Limit: The Political Economy of Change*. London: Zed Books.

Martin-Jones, M. and Jones, K. (eds) (2000) *Multilingual Literacies: Comparative Perspectives on Research and Practice*. Amsterdam: John Benjamins.

May, J. (ed.) (2000) *Poverty and Inequality in South Africa: Meeting the Challenge*. Cape Town: David Philip.

Maybin, J. (2000) The new literacy studies: Context, intertextuality and discourse. In D. Barton, M. Hamilton and R. Ivaniç (eds) *Situated Literacies: Reading and Writing in Context* (pp. 197–209). London: Routledge.

Mbembe, A. (2015) Decolonizing knowledge and the question of the archive. Blog post, 4 May 2015. See http://readingfanon.blogspot.se/2015/05/decolonizing-knowledge-and-question-of.html (accessed 3 January 2016).

McEwan, C. (2005) Gendered citizenship in South Africa: Rights and beyond. In A. Gouws (ed.) *(Un-)thinking Citizenship: Feminist Debates in Contemporary South Africa* (pp. 177–198). Cape Town: UCT Press/Ashgate Publishing.

Mehan, H. (1993) Beneath the skin and between the ears: A case study in the politics of representation. In S. Chaiklin and J. Lave (eds) *Understanding Practice: Perspectives on Activity and Context* (pp. 241–268). Cambridge: Cambridge University Press.

Ministry for Provincial Affairs and Constitutional Development (1998) White Paper on Local Government. Pretoria: Government Press. See http://mfma.treasury.gov.za/MFMA/Guidelines/whitepaper.pdf (accessed 14 May 2015).

Ndebele, N.S. (1986) Rediscovery of the ordinary: Some new writings in South Africa. *Journal of Southern African Studies* 12 (2), 143–157.

Ngugi, wa T. (1986 [1981]) *Decolonising the Mind: The Politics of Language in African Literature*. Portsmouth, NH: Heinemann Educational Books.

Ntingi, A. and Gqubule, T. (2012) SA's black wealth accumulation crisis. *Fin24*, 29 April 2012. See http://www.fin24.com/Economy/SAs-black-wealth-accumulation-crisis-20120429 (accessed 4 April 2016).

Rancière, J. (2004) The order of the city. *Critical Inquiry* 30 (2), 267–291.

Rancière, J. (2010) *Dissensus: On Politics and Aesthetics*. London, New York: Bloomsbury Academic.

Ross, K. (1991) Translator's introduction. In J. Rancière (ed.) *The Ignorant Schoolmaster. Five Lessons in Intellectual eEmancipation*. Stanford, CA: Stanford University Press.

Simon, R.I. (1987) Empowerment as a pedagogy of possibility. *Language Arts* 64, 370–383.

Sithole, P., Todes, A. and Williamson, A. (2007) Gender and women's participation in municipality-driven development: IDP and project-level participation in Msinga, eThekwini and Hibiscus Coast. *Critical Dialogue* 3 (1), 31–37.

Solarsh, G. and Goga, A. (2004) Child health. In P. Ijumba, C. Day and A. Ntuli (eds) *South African Health Review* (pp. 101–128). Durban, South Africa: Health Systems Trust.

Statistics South Africa (2005) General household survey 2004. Pretoria.

Statistics South Africa/United Nations Development Programme (2010) *Millenium Development Goals Country Report 2001–2010: South Africa*. Pretoria: United Nations Development Programme.

Street, B. (1993) *Cross-Cultural Approaches to Literacy*. Cambridge: Cambridge University Press.

Street, B. (1995) *Social Literacies: Critical Approaches to Literacy in Development, Ethnography and Education*. New York/London: Longman.

Stroud, C. (2001) African mother-tongue programmes and the politics of language: Linguistic citizenship versus linguistic human rights. *Journal of Multilingual and Multicultural Development* 22 (4), 339–355.

Stroud, C. (2009) A postliberal critique of language rights: Toward a politics of language for a linguistics of contact. In J.E. Petrovic (ed.) *International Perspectives on Bilingual Education: Policy, Practice, and Controversy* (pp. 191–217). Charlotte, NC: Information Age Publishing.

Stroud, C. and Heugh, K. (2003) Language rights and linguistic citizenship. In D. Patrick and J. Freeland (eds) *Language Rights and Language Survival: A Sociolinguistic Exploration* (pp. 191–218). Manchester: St Jerome.

The Citizen (2015) 14,740 service delivery protests recorded in SA. *The Citizen*. 15 May 2015. See http://citizen.co.za/382924/14-740-service-delivery-protests-recorded-in-sa/ (accessed 2 February 2016).

Tørres, L., Bhorat, H., Leibrandt, M. and Cassim, F. (2000) Poverty and the labour market. In J. May (ed.) *Poverty and Inequality in South Africa: Meeting the Challenge* (pp. 73–96). Cape Town: David Philip.

Traill, A. (2002) The Khoesan languages. In R. Mesthrie (ed.) *Language in South Africa* (pp. 27–49). Cambridge: Cambridge University Press.

University of Cape Town Children's Institute/UNICEF. (2010) *The Impact of the International Financial Crisis on Child Poverty in South Africa*. Pretoria: UNICEF South Africa and the Financial and Fiscal Commission of South Africa. See http://www.unicef.org/southafrica/SAF_resources_childpoverty.pdf (accessed 22 February 2012).

Walker, C. and Dubb, A. (2014) *The Distribution of Land in South Africa: An Overview*. Cape Town: Institute for Poverty, Land and Agrarian Studies (PLAAS).

Young, I.M. (1996) Communication and the other: Beyond deliberative democracy. In S. Benhabib (ed.) *Democracy and Difference: Contesting the Boundaries of the Political* (pp. 120–135). Princeton: Princeton University Press.

13 Commentary – On Participation and Resistance

Ana Deumert
University of Cape Town

Linguistic Citizenship: Agency, Structure and History–Present–Future

The notion of *linguistic citizenship* is concerned with what Christopher Stroud (2001: 345) calls 'political subjects', and the ways in which they engage with language and linguistic forms in everyday life. It reflects the so-called 'agentive turn' in the social sciences; a theoretical 'turn' that was shaped by developments taking place during the second half of the 20th century in society and politics. Thus, from the 1960s onwards, social movements across the world have 'reconfigured the relationship between state and society', and within the academy, poststructuralist critiques 'have called into question impersonal master narratives that leave no room for tensions, contradictions, and oppositional actions on the part of individuals and collectivities' (Ahearn, 2001: 110). Once we move away from these master narratives – from the grand histories of languages to diverse practices of speaking/writing – we are able look at what people 'do' with linguistic resources in their everyday lives. Adopting a practice-perspective allows us to focus on *languaging* (rather than speaking/writing '*a* language'), and this locates linguistic citizenship within longstanding philosophical traditions of performance and performativity, of language-as-a-mode-of-action. In this intellectual tradition, emphasis is placed on the ways in which language is embedded in practical activities, meaning is not given but situated and co-constructed, and language can bring about a change in the world.

Although agency is often seen as transformative, reflecting our ability 'to make a difference' and to bring about change, it can also reproduce and stabilize existing social relations and structures. The ways in which we shape society while, simultaneously, being shaped by it, is reflected in

Karl Marx's much-cited words in Chapter One of *The Eighteenth Brumaire of Louis Bonaparte* (1852):

> People make their own history, but they do not make it just as they please in circumstances they choose by themselves; rather they make it in present circumstances, given and inherited. The tradition from all the dead generations weighs like a nightmare on the brain of the living. (Translation slightly adjusted from the original; Cowling & Martin, 2002: 19; translation by T. Carver)

Marx's words bring to mind not only the ways in which agency interacts with existing structures, but also with history and temporality. In much of his writing he reflects on the 'ghosts of the past', the spectres that inevitably haunt the present: we are compelled, but also restricted, by the past, its imagination, its symbols and its practices (Derrida, 1994). Paying due attention to history – to the practices, ideologies and inequalities that we have been socialized into, that we have inherited – is, as I have argued elsewhere, key if our aim is to understand the complexities, and indeed turbulences, of human agency and its consequences (Deumert fc; on turbulence see Stroud, 2016). At the same time, Marx reminds us about the importance of utopian visions of the future: the ways in which the revolution can break free and is able to take 'its poetry from the future not the past' (Marx 1852, in Cowling & Martin, 2002: 22). Poetry in this context refers to Greek *poesis* – rather than to rhymes and stanzas – describing the act of making, of creating and changing the world (Puchner, 2006: 1). Thus, when discussing agency and transformation we need to keep past–present–future simultaneously in focus: the actions people engage in might occur in the present, but are shaped by the ghosts of the past (German *Gespenst*) and oriented towards a future whose spirit (*Geist*) is being imagined. In other words, history and time are not linear; past–present–future do not follow upon one another, but are entangled and intertwined (see also Stroud & Guissemo, 2015). Language plays an important role in Marx's thinking: social transformation, change and indeed revolution, is similar to learning, and thus creating, a new language for oneself and others.

In the discussion below, I take a closer look at the themes of participation and resistance. In the second section I reflect on forms of participation and the public sphere; and in the third section I return to the question of agency: Who performs acts of linguistic citizenship? I conclude with a brief discussion on writing: If our aim is to understand the agency of people, how could we write about people without reducing the messiness, complexity and temporality of their agency?

On Participation – Deliberation and Disobedience

Caroline Kerfoot's contribution considers participation and the public sphere in post-apartheid South Africa. She looks at 'the capabilities for participatory development and governance' and argues that '[e]ffective participation in a democracy requires facilitation, advocacy and management abilities ... as well as familiarity with the norms of deliberation'. Her chapter reports on a university-run programme that, between 1994 to 1999, provided teaching in precisely these areas. The aim was to train facilitators who would be able to 'formulate an action plan' and to 'catalyse participatory citizenship' in their communities. Implicit in the programme description is the character of the 'good citizen', a common, and indeed normative, persona in citizenship discourse. The local interventions, conducted by those who went through the programme, reflect this political-pedagogical intention and aspiration: the students, now trained as facilitators, created orderly public dialogues that conformed to the ideals of 'deliberative' or 'discursive' democracy. For example, one of the students organized an inter-generational workshop in an isolated rural village in the Northern Cape. The workshop programme started with an installation that was meant to raise awareness about alcohol abuse in the community; this was followed by role play, small group work, report-back sessions, mindmaps and the development of a plan for action. Participants used a variety of languages and ways of speaking; a diversity of semiotic resources was present. This diversity notwithstanding, the process of participation appears exceedingly orderly and well-structured in the description. I wondered at this order, at the calm that was conveyed: living with alcoholism – whether in the family or in the community – is far from orderly and predictable; it is messy, it can be violent, hopeless and destructive; it is emotionally traumatic and damaging. How can we provide a space for the expression of *these* experiences, a space that allows for forms of expression that might be upsetting the order that has been so carefully taught and crafted?

In her retrospective, Caroline Kerfoot reminds the reader that South Africa has changed significantly since the 1990s: the second decade of the 2000s has seen what she calls a 'politics of impatience' (drawing on Achille Mbembe's work).[1] This, in her analysis, has resulted in a 'narrowing of deliberative spaces' and a rise in 'public protest'. How can, and should we – as citizens and scholars – deal with the tension that has arisen between such 'new modes of disagreement and disorder' and an 'ethics of fair engagement'? As I am writing this commentary, university students are protesting across South Africa for free, decolonial, decommodified education. This is citizenship in action. However, it is also a form of citizenship, a form of activism, that has been criticized heavily by those in power, who have framed it as an undesirable 'disruption' of the 'normal' business of the university. William Smith (2013) notes in *Civil Disobedience and Deliberative Democracy* that such assessments of protest action are increasingly common at the global level, where diverse forms of direct (non-violent) action (such as roadblocks and occupations) are framed as 'violent', and 'disruption' is thus put *en par* with 'destruction'. Such acts of disobedience are frequently contrasted to the idea of the 'public sphere'. In his seminal work on 18th century publics, Jürgen Habermas (1962) described the public sphere (*Öffentlichkeit*) as a space where all citizens can come together and deliberate freely on a variety of issues. While feminist scholars, such as Nancy Fraser (1992), have long argued against the idea of a unified public sphere and for the recognition of subaltern publics, these publics are nevertheless assumed to be based on forms of rational deliberation. What happens when we move away from the idea of deliberation, away from rationally designed 'action plans' and consider the possibility of a wild and unruly public sphere – not as a problematic and temporary aberration, but as a space of possibility? The idea of *wild publics* was developed by the feminist scholar Iris Young in the 1980s. Like Jürgen Habermas, Young (1985) looks back at the 18th century, but paints a very different picture: the public life she describes was 'wild, playful and sexy' (1985: 387), not rational and measured. She argues that it was European political philosophy that tried to order the popular and linguistic heterogeneity of publics, and to control the necessarily transgressive elements of social and political disobedience. She links the re-awakening of 'wild' and 'playful' publics to the civil rights politics of the 1960s, demonstrations, sit-ins, bed-ins and other forms of disobedience.

I have suggested elsewhere (Deumert, 2015) that another way of re-thinking publics as spaces of transgression might be through exploring the idea of 'noise'. In everyday discourse, a distinction is commonly made between *language* and *noise* – the latter is seen as meaningless, uncontrollable, usually unwanted, bad and disturbing; it is the sonic equivalent to filth, foul smells and dirty matter. A collocation analysis based on the vast Google books corpus (accessed via Google Ngram Viewer, https://books.google.com/ngrams) shows that 'noisy' collocates – not surprisingly – with adjectives such as 'troublesome', 'restless', 'violent', 'riotous' and 'turbulent'. And indeed a particular type of noise accompanied the student protests: the sound of the fire alarm was used to disrupt lectures, to interrupt the sense of normalcy at institutions that are deeply entangled in the oppressive and, indeed, catastrophic legacy of colonialism (Maldonaldo-Torres, 2016). And it is no coincidence that the student movement started with the material equivalent of noise: faeces were thrown at the statue of the arch-colonialist Cecil John Rhodes at the University of Cape Town by student activist Chumani Maxwele.

Noise, like disobedience and disruption, is not welcome in the Habermasian public sphere, which is further based on a particular philosophy of language. Language is seen as a neutral, stable and normative system that allows for the clear and unambiguous expression of thought and mutual understanding (Habermas, 1990). Consequently, Habermas sees noise and its equivalents – what he calls 'systematically distorted communication' – not only as 'abnormal', but as a form of 'violence', a source of social discord and overt conflict (Ashenden, 2014; Habermas, 1970). In *Philosophy in a Time of Terror* (Borradori, 2003: 35) he notes programmatically: 'The spiral of violence begins with a distortion in communication'. Yet, as poststructuralism has taught us, language is not determinate, well-defined and transparent. And while noise might be outside of language – at least in the way linguists think about language – it is certainly not outside of communication. Screaming and shouting, inarticulate anger, speaking gibberish or maybe just another language, as well as silence, are forms of communication and acts of linguistic citizenship – it is not just about a politics of recognition and dialogue, but also about non-recognition and monologue, of signifying difference without, necessarily, making it readable and transparent, thus resisting control (Deleuze, 1995). Work on wild and noisy publics challenges how we think about citizenship and participation, and how we assess, and judge the 'politics of impatience' – the term itself filled with negative loading. Impatience, like anger, is something we are told, moralistically, to control, to work against – yet it is there, it is present, it is experienced, it might even consume us. Political 'grammars of engagement', and thus acts of linguistic citizenship, include deliberation *and* disobedience, and it is vital that our theoretical apparatus can speak to both (see also Stroud, 2015, on what he calls 'insurgent citizenship').

On Resistance – Whose Agency?

The linguistic human rights (henceforth LHR) paradigm is heavily invested in the state as an actor. In contrast, linguistic citizenship assumes a 'weak' state, that is a state with limited power, legitimacy or willingness to intervene. Although political theory in the global south continues to engage with the idea of a 'developmental state', neoliberal ideologies and the presence of, especially, global financial networks make it difficult for any state to become more than a 'partial' developmental state (Evans, 2014). The situation is not much different in the global north where neo-liberal policies have largely eroded the 'welfare' state of the 1970s. The case of Sweden – discussed by Tommaso Milani and Rickard Jonsson – provides an interesting counter-point. While the other three chapters in this section look at countries in the global south (Malawi, South Africa, Sri Lanka), Milani and Jonsson discuss language policy and language ideologies in a country that still has a – comparatively – 'strong' and inter-ventionist state. Indeed, Milani and Jonsson note that 'Sweden might sound like a textbook example of a *good state*' (emphasis in the original). A strong reliance on legislative frameworks is characteristic of such a 'good state'. Like most language legislation, Sweden's *Language Law* (2009) relies on the idea that languages are bounded and well-defined entities, and as such – good intentions notwithstanding – struggles to come to terms with the reality of actual linguistic practices: there is a 'lack of fit between the construct of language as enshrined in Swedish political discourse and actual communicative performances'.

While the state is a central actor within the LHR paradigm, other actors also appear in the chapters, both collective actors and individu-als. The role of language associations – as discussed by Gregory Kamwendo in the context of post-Banda Malawi – seems ambiguous: is this linguistic citizenship or a form of institutionalized agency that draws directly on the LHR framework established by national legisla-tion (in this case radio broadcasting and medium of instruction)? While language associations can certainly be spaces for resistance against state policies, they are often conservative and hegemonic spaces, which, like states, rely on the idea of bounded, well-defined languages, value certain varieties over others and thus re-inscribe linguistic hierarchies and hegemonies. The *Chitumbuka Language and Culture Association* (CLACA), for example, 'took a hard stance against urban speakers' and wanted to ban their voices from radio broadcasting; a proposal that was rejected by the state broadcasting agency. In this case it was the lan-guage association that seemed blind to 'actual communicative perfor-mances', and not the state. This suggests that we are not looking at a simple dichotomy: state versus 'the people' (often glossed as 'grass-roots'), but rather that non-state actors are inherently diverse, with some 'seeing like a state'; that is, interpellating, through their discourses and actions, collectives – including language communities – that are legible and, thus, governable (Scott, 1998). The agency of both state actors and collectives frequently serves to support elite interests, and to establish authoritative discourses that legitimize their actions. Authoritative discourses of a different kind are also articulated by academics and researchers, who are equally ambiguous actors within the theoretical framework of citizenship. For example, the rejection of English-medium schooling (in Malawi) is largely based on expert-discourses (which tend to be positioned as superior to lay-discourses), and is implicated in global networks – and hierarchies – of knowledge production, such as when Gregory Kamwendo explains how he was approached by the *British Association of Applied Linguistics* 'in assisting in the drafting of a petition' against this policy.

Writing about Sri Lankan Malay, Umberto Ansaldo and Lisa Lim suggest that it is imperative to develop an approach that 'facilitate[s] the empowerment of minority language speakers as agents of their own social transformation', and they comment on the Sri Lankan Malay 'community', which has 'made a choice of "revitalizing" their linguistic situation'. Similar to the language associations discussed by Kamwendo, 'communities' are collective phenomena, and they too raise the question of 'who acts?'. The very idea of 'community' is an old sociolinguistic, and sociological, conundrum. Raymond Williams ([1976] 1983: 76) describes 'community' as a 'warmly persuasive word', an emic, rather than academic, that 'never seems to be used unfavourably'. Unlike the language associations described by Kamwendo, communities are not organized collectives – with statutes and appointed or elected leaders – but emergent formations that are not easily legible, or controllable; they are not uniform actors, but might pull in different directions simultaneously, showing complex constellations of insiders and outsiders. Yet, several times in the discussion 'the community' emerges as a uniform actor and even as an information source: '(SLM community, personal communication, 2003–2006)'. Linguistic citizenship, however, reminds us that we need to go beyond ideas of community and should ask: whose voice spoke this '*personal communication*'?

In the Sri Lankan case we further see an intertwining of community (however defined and delineated) and the state; in this case not the Sri Lankan state, but Malaysia, which has demonstrated – via its High Commission in Sri Lanka – 'strong support for the SLM community, and provides aid in terms of student scholarships for undergraduate and post-graduate studies in Malaysia'. However, this transnational support focuses on Standard Malay, rather than on the local variety which is 'seen as an embarrassing, "bad" or corrupt code'. For those who have embraced Standard Malay, the Sri Lankan Malay identity is re-imagined as being part of a larger and more comprehensive Malay identity. Ansaldo and Lim work with the notion of 'choice' and see language as a *'semiotic resource* for the (re)construction of agency and self-presentation, an *economic resource* and a site of political and economic struggle, a *global resource* to address global-local concerns, and an *intimate resource* as the foundation of respect for difference' (my emphases). However, as a resource, language functions differently in different localities. Thus, it might be an economic resource in some, a liability in others; it might enable voice in some contexts, and remain unheard and unnoticed in others, and so forth. There is a dichotomy at play in the argument made: between centre (urban) and periphery (rural). It is in the context of the former that choices – which could be read as resistance to the local meanings of Sri Lankan Malay as 'bad' – are made and Standard Malay is embraced as a global resource and marker of identity. In rural contexts, however, Sri Lankan Malay remains, at this stage, an unmarked, everyday medium of interaction, an intimate resource (with Tamil being the core economic resource). Yet, diverse localities and their orders of discourse are entangled, and Standard Malay appeared in 2006 on linguistic signage at the rural school. Ten years later, I wonder, are the children of Kirinda now studying Standard Malay at school? What shape has their agency taken? Resistance or conformity? And to what?

The theme of resistance is perhaps most clearly visible in the case of Rinkeby Swedish, an ethnolect that emerged in urban contexts. Milani and Jonsson show that the use of Rinkeby Swedish as an expressive resource, rather than a marker of lack of education, was closely linked to creative writing, and thus the agency of artists and cultural activists. Literature and journalistic writings shaped discourses about Rinkeby Swedish in the early 2000s, resulting in what Milani and Jonsson call 'sociolinguistic re-branding and re-signification'. This, I believe, is not incidental: literary language is a powerful tool, and writers can be important actors within processes of language activism. The situation is similar to Germany, where *Kanaksprak* ('the language of foreigners/racial others [derogatory]') rose to prominence in the mid-1990s, following the publication of the novel *Kanaksprak* by the German–Turkish author Feridun Zaimoğlu. And in a recent article on linguistic citizenship, Christopher Stroud (2015) discusses the South Africa hip-hop opera *Afrikaaps* as an example of precisely such citizenship: it is through the creative-artistic act that a shift of agency and voice becomes possible.

In their post-script, Milani and Jonsson reflect critically on the fact that much work on Rinkeby Swedish focuses on the agency of certain speakers. They note that research on migrant youth has often focused on specific groups of male adolescents who were 'at the same time feared and hated, desired and despised'. Their language was positioned as creative, performative and performed, as more 'interesting' than that of other, more ordinary, speakers (women, older migrants, Swedish youth who also make use of Rinkeby Swedish). Male migrant youth were thus exoticized as the embodiment of difference, of danger and desire – and it is this 'proliferation of Otherness' that links current sociolinguistic work to colonial discourses that thrived in the creation of 'difference and division' (Stroud, 2015: 20). Yet, Raymond Williams (1958) never tired of reminding us: 'culture is ordinary'. How can we learn to notice – and thus study – the unremarkable, the unmarked, the ground and not the figure? For example, much linguistic citizenship research focuses on multilingualism and diversity – yet what about monolingualism? What might, for example, the linguistic citizenship practice of a monolingual British office worker look like? What about those young people who accept the hegemony of the standard, and do not challenge or transgress its norms? To rephrase Williams: *linguistic citizenship is ordinary – this is the first fact.*

Writing About People and Agency: Final Reflections

The focus on participation and agency is integral to the notion of linguistic citizenship: 'speakers themselves exercise control over their language, deciding what languages are, and what they may *mean*, and where language issues ... are discursively tied to a range of social issues' (Stroud, 2001: 353; emphasis in the original). Practical knowledge, informal processes and linguistic choices by speakers in the context of uncertainty and unpredictability shape acts of citizenship in the 21st century.

But who are these speaker/writer-actors who speak and act, and how can we speak/write about them? Many years ago, my doctoral supervisor Roger Lass, warned me about paying too much attention to speakers/ writers: he described them as 'messy, complicated things', and suggested that linguists might be better off subscribing to a minimalist ontology, which does not put much emphasis on speakers as people, and keeps language – or situated linguistic practice – as its object of analysis (Lass, 1997). I always disagreed; yet, at the same time I realize that it is not easy to write about people. Too often do speakers and hearers, especially in theoretical work, appear as idealized, cardboard-like characters – as members of communities and collectives – not as living, breathing human beings; as individuals with feelings, desires, ideas, beliefs and hopes. Whether engaged in deliberation or in disobedience, actors quickly become prototypes. In the discussions of the student movement previously mentioned, we might read about 'protesters', 'student activists' or, in the pejorative language of some, 'marauding thugs'. Yet, each student is part of the collective and a person too – motivated by complex sets of circumstances, some collective, some individual, some rational, some emotional, some about the present, others about past or future. Maybe, to write about this, we need to turn to poetry and art, not just as the act of making, but as a different mode of writing. And we also need to guard against appropriation, and respect the other's fundamental opacity: their right to opacity, their right not to be studied and analysed. As Édouard Glissant reminds us:

> If we examine the process of 'understanding' people and ideas from the perspective of Western thought, we discover that its basis is this require-ment for transparency. In order to understand and thus accept you, I have to measure your solidity with the ideal scale providing me with grounds to make comparisons and, perhaps, judgements. I have to reduce ... But maybe we need to bring an end to the very notion of a scale. Displace all reduction. Agree not merely on the right to difference but, carrying this further, to the right to opacity that is not enclosure within an impenetra-ble autarchy but subsistence within an irreducible singularity. (Glissant, 1997: 189–190)

And finally, when writing about agency in 2016, we also need to pay atten-tion to post-humanist debates: what about the agentive capacities of non-humans? Of animals, spirits, machines and signs? How can they be incorporated into the ways in which we speak about linguistic citizenship? (See, for example, Stroud, 2016, on the agency of signs, bodies and spaces; also Williams & Stroud, 2013).

Note

(1) http://africasacountry.com/2015/09/achille-mbembe-on-the-state-of-south-african-politics/.

References

Ahearn, L.M. (2001) Language and agency. *Annual Review of Anthropology* 30, 109–137.
Ashenden, S. (2014) On violence in Habermas's philosophy of language. *European Journal of Political Theory* 13, 427–452.
Borradori, G. (2003) *Philosophy in a Time of Terror. Dialogues with Jürgen Habermas and Jacques Derrida*. Chicago: University of Chicago Press.

Cowling, M. and Martin, J. (eds) (2002) *Marx's Eighteenth Brumaire. (Post)modern Interpretations*. London: Pluto.

Deleuze, G. (1995) *Negotiations 1972–1990*. New York: Columbia University Press.

Derrida, J. (1994) *Spectres of Marx. The State of the Debt, the Work of Mourning, and the New International*. London: Routledge.

Deumert, A. fc. The multivocality of heritage: Moments and encounters. In A. Blackledge et al. (eds) *Handbook of Superdiversity*. London: Routledge.

Deumert, A. (2015) Wild publics: Twitter as the continuation of politics by other means. 6th International Language and the Media Conference. Hamburg, Germany.

Evans, P. (2014) The developmental state: Divergent responses to modern economic theory and the twenty-first century economy. In M. Williams (ed.) *The End of the Developmental State?* (pp. 220–240). Pietermaritzburg: UKZN Press.

Fraser, N. (1992) Rethinking the public sphere: A contribution to the critique of actually existing democracy. In C. Calhoun (ed.) *Habermas and the Public Sphere* (pp. 108–142). Cambridge: MIT Press.

Glissant, É. (1997) *Poetics of Relation*. Ann Arbor: University of Michigan Press.

Habermas, J. (1962) *Strukturwandel der Öffentlichkeit: Untersuchungen zu einer Kategorie der bürgerlichen Gesellschaft*. Neuwied: Luchterhand.

Habermas, J. (1970) On systematically distorted communication. *Inquiry* 13, 205–218.

Habermas, J. (1990) *Moral Consciousness and Communicative Action*. Massachusetts: MIT Press.

Lass, R. (1997) *Historical Linguistics and Language Change*. Cambridge: Cambridge University Press.

Maldonaldo-Torres, N. (2016) *Ten Theses on Coloniality and Decoloniality*. Lecture delivered at the University of Cape Town, South Africa.

Puchner, M. (2006) *Poetry of the Revolution. Marx, Manifestos and Avant-Gardes*. Princeton: Princeton University Press.

Scott, J.C. (1998) *Seeing Like a State. How Certain Schemes to Improve the Human Condition Have Failed*. New Haven: Yale University Press.

Smith, W. (2013) *Civil Disobedience and Deliberative Democracy*. London: Routledge.

Stroud, C. (2001) African mother-tongue programmes and the politics of language: Linguistic citizenship versus linguistic human rights. *Journal of Multilingual and Multicultural Development* 22 (4), 339–355.

Stroud, C. (2015) Linguistic citizenship as utopia. *Multilingual Margins* 2, 20–37.

Stroud, C. (2016) Turbulent linguistic landscapes and the semiotics of citizenship. In R. Blackwood, E. Lanza and H. Woldemariam (eds) *Negotiating and Contesting Identities in Linguistic Landscapes* (pp. 3–18). London: Bloomsbury.

Stroud, C. and Guissemo, M. (2015) Linguistic Messianism. *Multilingual Margins* 2, 6–19.

Williams, R. ([1958] 2002) Culture is ordinary. In B. Highmore (ed.) *The Everyday Life Reader* (pp. 91–100). London: Routledge.

Williams, R. ([1976] 1983) *Keywords* (2nd edn). Oxford: Oxford University Press.

Williams, Q. and Stroud, C. (2013) Multilingualism in transformative spaces: Contact and conviviality. *Language Policy* 12, 289–311.

Young, I. (1985) Impartiality and the civic public: Some implications of feminist critiques of moral and political theory. *PRAXIS International* 4, 381–401.

Index

Note: n refers to notes.

Multiple voices, 27–28
Multivocality, 26, 27, 36
Music, 24, 28, 33, 152, 213, 229, 273
Muslim, 193, 195, 198, 207, 211, 214n4
Myths, 235, 253, 257, 283

National belonging, 76
National language policy, 128, 162, 168, 169, 171
National referendum, 249
Nationalism, 67, 103, 150, 151–152, 165
Network, 5, 9, 56, 85, 112, 135, 156, 198, 223, 277, 279, 294, 295
Non-implementation (of language policy), 255
Non-official mother tongues, 75

Optimality in language planning, 42, 77, 90
Orthography, 10, 51, 126–127, 154, 156–157, 163, 169, 237, 256

Parents, 79, 111–112, 138, 158–159, 163, 179, 202, 231
Past, 23, 29, 35, 36, 42, 89, 94, 104, 105, 111, 168, 284n2
Performance, 18, 22–26, 29, 30, 35, 225, 240, 289
Periphery, 198, 205–210, 296
Plurilingual, 213
Political consciousness, 103
Political independence, 8, 99, 103, 104–107, 120, 121, 124, 125, 129, 200, 249
Political participation, 102, 113, 116, 264, 281
Political resistance, 123, 124, 237, 293–297
Politics, 3, 4, 5, 10–11, 19, 22, 27, 36, 41, 48, 59, 67, 86, 95, 98, 99–114, 124, 175, 193, 199–203, 238–242, 248, 250–251, 281–284, 293
Portuguese, 7, 10, 17, 24, 36, 98, 99–107, 109, 113–116, 120, 121, 123–125, 126–127, 128–130, 132,

138, 140–142, 145n1, 145n8, 178, 180, 184, 185, 194, 196
Postvernacularity, 213
Poverty, 66, 265, 268
Public sphere, 168, 264, 281, 290–293

Rationality, 53, 205, 206, 292, 298
Reconciliation, 68, 161, 162, 168
Reductionism, 68, 182, 298
Reductionist, 68, 182
Regimes of language, 27, 36, 183, 266
Remote areas, 180, 182
Resemiotization, 263–280
Revitalization, 17, 84–85, 87, 153–156, 158, 164, 167, 169, 203–206, 213, 215n12, 216n18
Rights discourse, 4, 9, 11, 41, 42–43, 44–47, 51–60, 60n5, 136, 198, 238
Rights, citizenship, 85, 264, 265
Rinkeby Swedish, 225, 229, 296–297
Rinkebysvenska, 225–228, 231–242, 242n3
Rural, 5, 9, 93, 111, 113, 180, 182–183, 198, 202, 254, 268, 291, 296

Self-reflexive gaze, 238–242
Shift, 7, 10, 21, 24, 34, 55, 59–60, 79, 88, 99, 108–110, 128, 139, 150, 156, 164, 199, 202, 207–208, 210–211, 266, 271, 273, 277, 280
Singapore, 2, 40, 44, 51, 213, 214n1, 216n16
Sinhala, 48, 52, 53, 68, 193, 196–202, 209–210, 213, 215n7
Social media, 212–214
South Africa, 1, 2, 4, 19, 22, 24–27, 29, 35, 44, 50–51, 109, 124, 176, 182, 260, 263, 265, 291, 294, 296
Southern scholar/ scholarship, 181
Spaces, participatory, 263–284
Sri Lanka Malay, 193–214
Sri Lanka, 44, 48, 52, 53, 67–68, 193, 195, 198, 200, 208, 295
Stakeholders, 7, 19, 131, 139, 143, 144, 156, 161, 163, 167, 177, 186